CARRIER STRIKE

Books by Eric Hammel

76 Hours: *The invasion of Tarawa*

Chosin: *Heroic Ordeal of the Korean War*

The Root: *The Marines in Beirut*

Ace!: *A Marine Night-Fighter Pilot in World War II (with R. Bruce Porter)*

Duel for the Golan *(with Jerry Asher)*

Guadalcanal: *Starvation Island*

Guadalcanal: *The Carrier Battles*

Guadalcanal: *Decision at Sea*

Munda Trail: *The New Georgia Campaign*

The Jolly Rogers *(with Tom Blackburn)*

Khe Sanh: *Siege in the Clouds*

First Across the Rhine: *(with David E. Pergrin)*

Lima 6: *A Marine Company Commander in Vietnam (with Richard D. Camp)*

Ambush Valley

Fire in the Streets: *The Battle for Hue*

Six Days in June

Aces Against Japan

Aces Against Japan II

Aces Against Germany

Air war Europa: *Chronology*

Carrier Clash

Aces at War

Air War Pacific: *Chronology*

Aces in Combat

Bloody Tarawa

Marines at War

Carrier Strike

CARRIER STRIKE

THE BATTLE OF THE SANTA CRUZ ISLANDS OCTOBER 1942

ERIC HAMMEL

ZENITH PRESS

Published by arrangement with Pacifica Military History.

This edition published in 2004 by Zenith Press, an imprint of MBI Publishing Company, Galtier Plaza, Suite 200, 380 Jackson Street, St. Paul, MN, 55101-3885 USA.

Zenith Press titles are also available at discounts in bulk quantity for industrial or sales-promotional use. For details write to Special Sales Manager at Motorbooks International Wholesalers & Distributors, Galtier Plaza, Suite 200, 380 Jackson Street, St. Paul, MN 55101-3885 USA.

Cover design by Tom Heffron

ISBN: 0-7603-2128-0

Printed in the United States of America

For Mom

Glossary and Guide to Abbreviations

A6M IJN Mitsubishi "Zero" fighter
A6M2-N IJN Nakajima "Rufe" floatplane fighter
ACRM Aviation chief radioman
ACTG Advanced carrier training group
Adm Admiral
Airacobra USAAF Bell P-39 fighter
AirSoPac Aircraft, South Pacific Force
AM1 Aviation metalsmith 1st class
AMM3 Aviation machinist's mate 3d class
Angels Altitude expressed in thousands of feet
AOM2 Aviation ordnanceman 2d class
AP1 Aviation pilot 1st class
ARM2 Aviation radioman 2d class
AvCad Naval aviation cadet
Avenger USN Grumman TBF light/torpedo bomber
B-17 USAAF Boeing "Flying Fortress" four-engine heavy bomber
B-25 North American "Mitchell" twin-engine medium bomber
B5N IJN Nakajima "Kate" attack/torpedo bomber
BB Battleship

Betty IJN Mitsubishi G4M twin-engine attack bomber
Bf-109 German Messerschmitt fighter
BM1 Boatswain's mate 1st class
BriGen Brigadier General
Buntaicho IJN unit leader
Buster Radio code for "immediate"
Butai Unit
CA Heavy cruiser
Cactus Code name for Guadalcanal
CAP Combat Air Patrol
Capt Captain
Carp Warrant Carpenter
Catalina USN Consolidated PBY twin-engine amphibian patrol bomber
Cdr Commander
CEM Chief electrician's mate
ChElec Chief warrant electrician
ChMach Chief warrant machinist
Chutai IJN flight, usually six to nine planes
CinC Commander in chief
CL Light cruiser
CLAA Light antiaircraft cruiser
CMM Chief machinist's mate
CO Commanding officer
Col Colonel
ComAirSoPac Commander, Aircraft, South Pacific
ComSoPac Commander, South Pacific Area and South Pacific Force
Cox Coxswain
Cpl Corporal
CQM Chief quartermaster
CSF Chief ship fitter
CTF Commander, Task Force
CV Fleet aircraft carrier
CVE Escort aircraft carrier
CVL Light aircraft carrier
CWT Chief watertender

BORDERS®

BORDERS
BOOKS AND MUSIC
4575 ROSEWOOD DR
PLEASANTON CA 94588
(925) 227-1412

STORE: 0117 REG: 02/99 TRAN#: 8868
SALE 06/26/2008 EMP: 00021

GIFT RECEIPT

PERIODICAL
074470647652 06 PR T BJMM
CALIFORNIA 8.75%TAX

06/26/2008 02:51PM

For returns within 30 days of purchase accompanied by a Borders Gift Receipt the purchase price (after applicable discounts) will be refunded via a gift card.

CXAM RCA experimental air-search radar
CY Chief yeoman
D3A IJN Aichi "Val" dive-bomber
D4Y IJN Kugisho single-engine carrier reconnaissance plane
Dauntless USN/USMC Douglas SBD dive-bomber
DD Destroyer
Dinah IJA Mitsubishi Ki-46 twin-engine reconnaissance plane
E13A IJN Aichi "Jake" reconnaissance floatplane
EM3 Electrician's mate 3d class
Emily IJN Kawanishi H8K four-engine amphibian patrol bomber
Ens Ensign
Exec Executive officer
(F) Flagship
(FF) Fleet flagship
F1M IJN Mitsubishi "Pete" reconnaissance float biplane
F3 Fireman 3d class
F4F USN/USMC Grumman "Wildcat" fighter
FC3 Fire controlman 3d class
FDO Fighter direction officer
Fish Radio slang for enemy torpedo or torpedo bomber
1stLt First lieutenant
1stSgt First sergeant
Fulmite Chemical fire retardant
G4M IJN Mitsubishi "Betty" twin-engine attack bomber
Gen General
GI Government Issue; refers to U.S. Army soldier
GM2 Gunner's mate 2d class
Gun Warrant gunner
GySgt Gunnery sergeant
H6K IJN Kawanishi "Mavis" four-engine amphibian patrol bomber
H8K IJN Kawanishi "Emily" four-engine amphibian patrol bomber
Hawk Radio slang for enemy dive-bomber
Hey Rube Radio slang for "Return to base if no enemy planes found."
HIJMS His Imperial Japanese Majesty's Ship
Hikokitai IJN carrier air group

Hikotaicho IJN air group leader
IFF Identification, Friend or Foe
IJN Imperial Japanese Navy
Jake IJN Aichi E13A reconnaissance floatplane
(jg) Junior grade
Kate IJN Nakajima B5N attack/torpedo bomber
Ki-46 IJA Mitsubishi "Dinah" twin-engine reconnaissance plane
LCdr Lieutenant commander
LSO Landing signal officer
Lt Lieutenant
Lt(jg) Lieutenant junior grade
LtCol Lieutenant colonel
LtGen Lieutenant general
Mach Warrant machinist
Maj Major
MajGen Major general
Maru Japanese transport or cargo ship
Mavis IJN Kawanishi H6K four-engine amphibian patrol bomber
MG Warrant marine gunner
MGySgt Master gunnery sergeant
mm Millimeter
MM1 Machinist's mate 1st class
MoMM2 Motor machinist's mate 2d class
NAP Naval aviation (enlisted) pilot
OS2U USN Vought "Kingfisher" observation scout floatplane
P-400 USAAF Bell Airacobra fighter (export model)
Pancake Radio code for "land immediately"
PB Patrol boat
PBY USN Consolidated "Catalina" twin-engine amphibian patrol bomber
Pete IJN Mitsubishi F1M reconnaissance float biplane
Pfc Private first class
PhM1 Pharmacist's mate 1st class
PhoM3 Photographer's mate 3d class
PlSgt Platoon sergeant
PO1 Petty officer 1st class

PT-boat Patrol-torpedo boat
Pvt Private
RAdm Rear admiral
RAN Royal Australian Navy
RBA Rescue breathing apparatus
RE Warrant radio electrician
Rikusentai IJN special naval landing unit
RM3 Radioman 3d class
RN Royal Navy
Rufe IJN Nakajima A6M2-N floatplane fighter
S1 Seaman 1st class
SBD USN/USMC Douglas "Dauntless" dive-bomber
SC-1 USN gunnery radar
2dLt Second lieutenant
Sgt Sergeant
SgtMaj Sergeant Major
Shotai IJN fighter/bomber element, usually three planes
SM2 Signalman 2d class
SOC USN Curtiss observation scout floatplane
SoPac South Pacific Area/Force
Sub-Lt Sub-Lieutenant (as in Royal Australian Navy)
TBD USN Douglas "Devastator" light/torpedo bomber
TBF USN Grumman "Avenger" light/torpedo bomber
TBS "Talk Between Ships" voice radio
TSgt Technical sergeant
USS United States Ship
VAdm Vice admiral
Val IJN Aichi D3A dive-bomber
VB USN bombing squadron
VF USN fighting squadron
VMF USMC fighting squadron
VMO USMC observation squadron
VMSB USMC scout-bomber squadron
VP USN patrol squadron
VS USN scouting squadron

VT USN torpedo squadron
Wildcat USN/USMC Grumman F4F fighter
WO Warrant officer
WT1 Watertender 1st class
Y2 Yeoman 2d class
YE/ZB U.S. radio homing system
Zero IJN Mitsubishi A6M fighter

# Acknowledgements

The original version of this battle narrative appeared as half of my book *Guadalcanal: The Carrier Battles*, which was published in 1987. I could not have written the human side of the story without help from nearly a hundred participants, many of whom appear as players in this text. A large number of these heroes have passed away since 1987, and I have lost touch with most of the others. Nevertheless, my gratitude for their help remains, and will remain, profound.

I also wish to single out my friend and colleague, the naval aviation historian John B. Lundstrom, for a special acknowledgement. In the years after my first effort to write the Santa Cruz battle history, John was able to secure records giving the Japanese side of the story. Through meticulous research and brilliant analysis, John was able to piece together a better, more complete account of Japanese air operations during the Guadalcanal Campaign than was remotely possible earlier. The result of John's labors is his superb book *The First Team and the Guadalcanal Campaign*. To complete this volume, and with deep gratitude, I have drawn heavily upon John's book, and upon his expertise, which he willingly shared. It must be said of John Lundstrom that he always comes through.

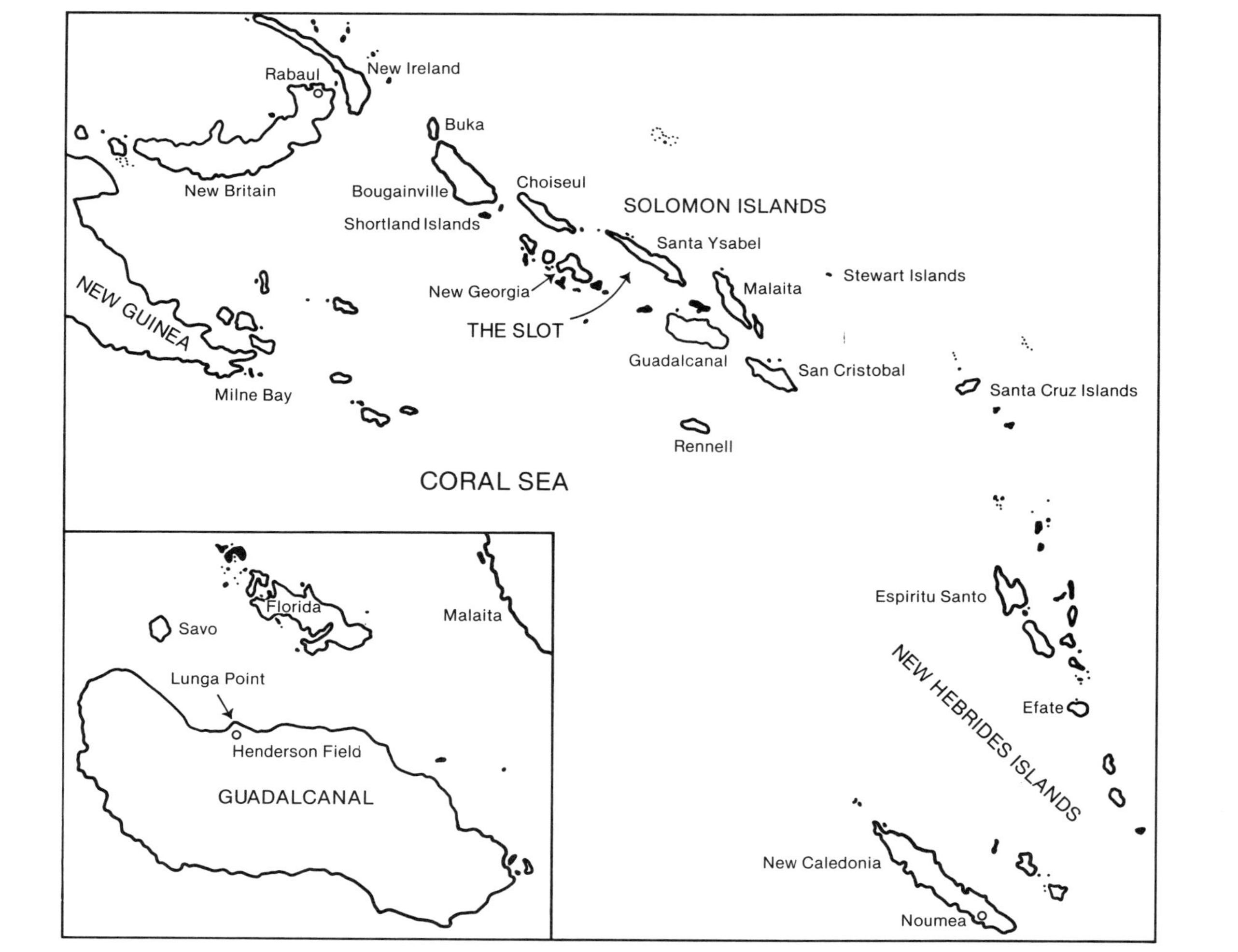
Rabaul
New Ireland
Buka
New Britain
Bougainville
Shortland Islands
Choiseul
SOLOMON ISLANDS
Santa Ysabel
Stewart Islands
New Georgia
Malaita
NEW GUINEA
THE SLOT
Guadalcanal
San Cristobal
Milne Bay
Santa Cruz Islands
Rennell
CORAL SEA
Espiritu Santo
Florida
Savo
Malaita
Lunga Point
Henderson Field
GUADALCANAL
NEW HEBRIDES ISLANDS
Efate
New Caledonia
Noumea

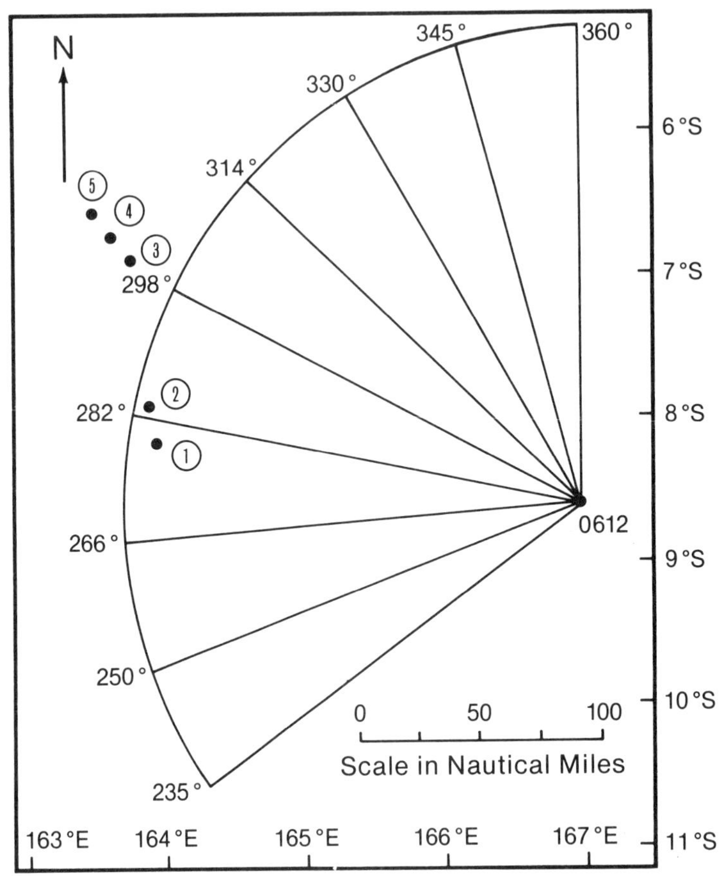

BATTLE OF THE SANTA CRUZ ISLANDS
Air Group 10 Search
October 26, 1942

Sector	Pilots
235-250	Wakeham Stevens
250-266	Buell Wakeham
266-282	Welch McGraw
282-298	Burnett Miller
298-314	Lee Johnson
314-330	Ward Carmody
330-345	Strong Irvine
345-360	Ramsay Bloch

CONTACTS WITH JAPANESE SHIPS
by Air Group 10 Searchers

1. Welch and McGraw find Abe's surface force, 0717
2. Burnett and Miller find Abe's surface force 1740
3. Lee and Johnson find Nagumo's carriers, 0750
4. Ward and Carmody find Nagumo's carriers, 0820
5. Strong and Irvine find Nagumo's carriers, 0830

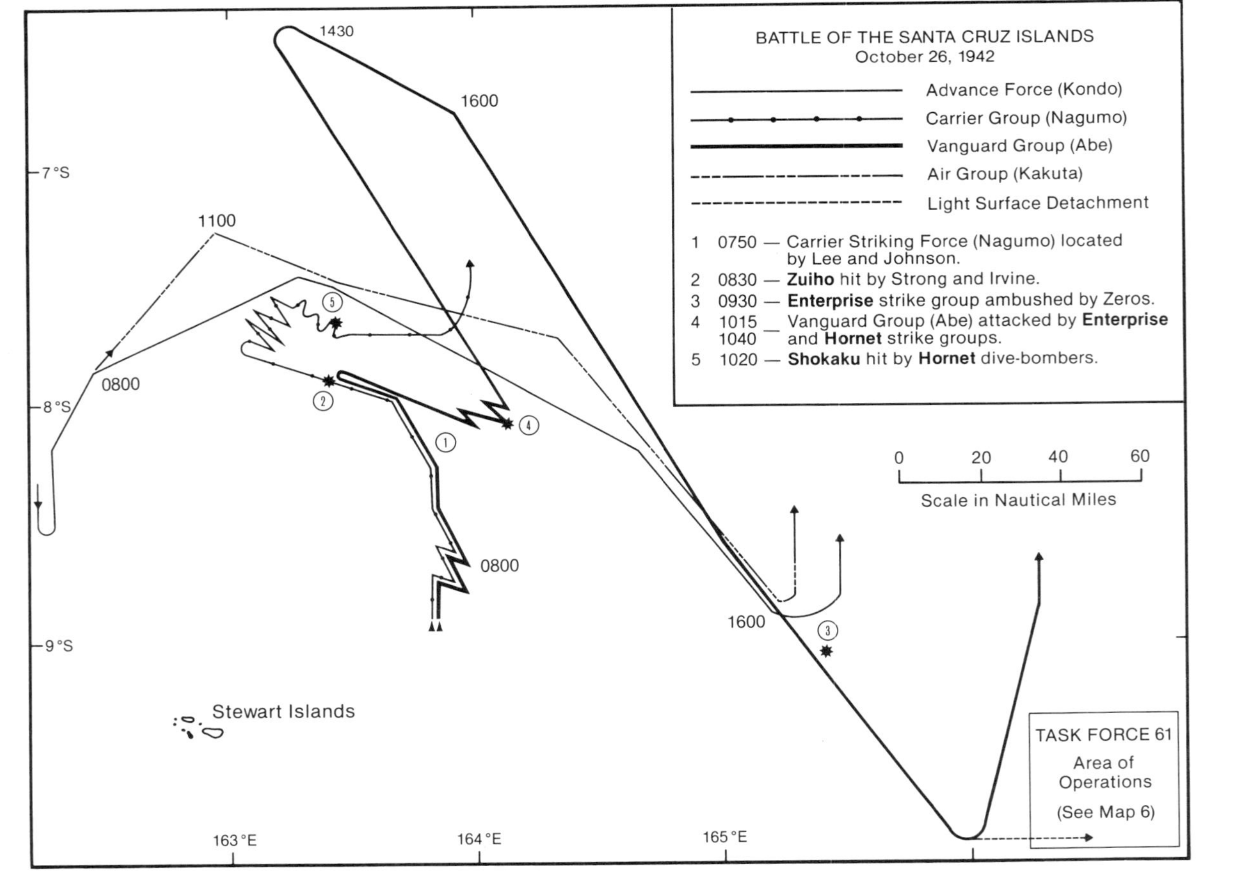

BATTLE OF THE SANTA CRUZ ISLANDS
October 26, 1942
Advance Force (Kondo)
Carrier Group (Nagumo)
Vanguard Group (Abe)
Air Group (Kakuta)
Light Surface Detachment
1 0750 — Carrier Striking Force (Nagumo) located by Lee and Johnson.
2 0830 — **Zuiho** hit by Strong and Irvine.
3 0930 — **Enterprise** strike group ambushed by Zeros.
4 1015 — 1040 Vanguard Group (Abe) attacked by **Enterprise** and **Hornet** strike groups.
5 1020 — **Shokaku** hit by **Hornet** dive-bombers.
0 20 40 60
Scale in Nautical Miles
TASK FORCE 61
Area of Operations
(See Map 6)
1430
1600
1100
0800
0800
1600
7°S
8°S
9°S
163°E
164°E
165°E
Stewart Islands

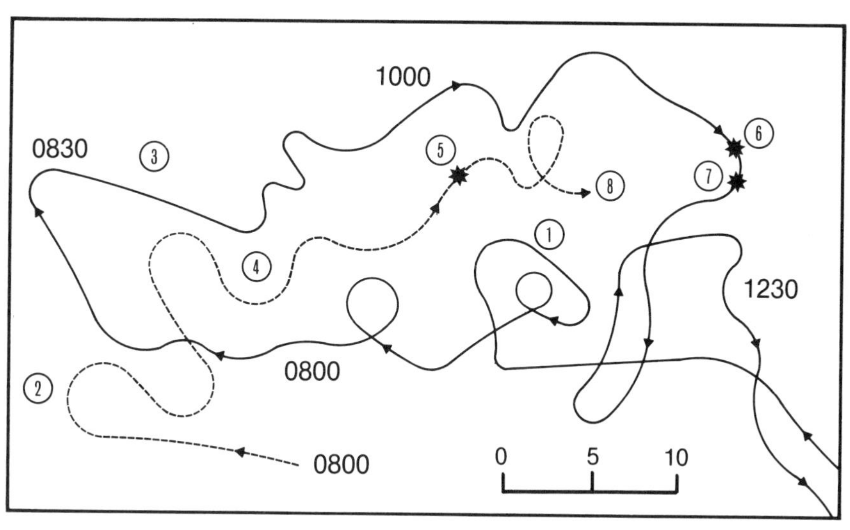

TASK FORCE 61
October 26, 1942

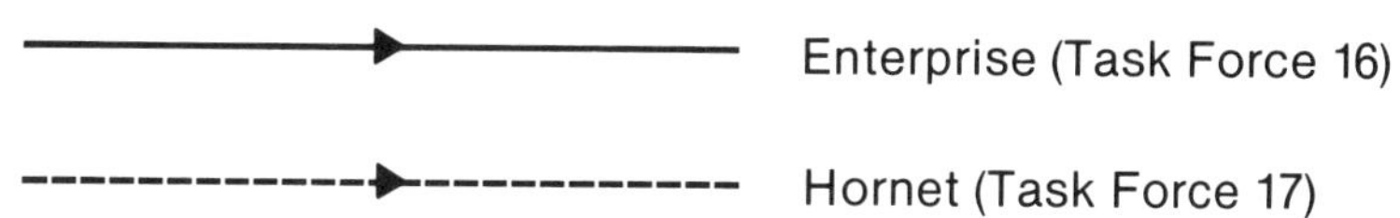

1 0612 — **Enterprise** launches search planes
2 0832 — **Hornet** launches first strike
3 0902 — **Enterprise** launches strike
4 0910 — **Hornet** launches second strike
5 1015 — **Hornet** crippled
6 1100 — **Porter** torpedoed
7 1115 — **Enterprise** bombed
8 2140 — **Mustin** and **Anderson** leave **Hornet**

BOW
Port Bow
Starboard Bow
Port Beam
Starboard Beam
Port Quarter
Starboard Quarter
STERN

Part I

Torpedo Junction

Chapter 1

It was the morning of August 25, 1942, the day after History's third carrier clash—the Battle of the Eastern Solomons. The destroyer USS *Grayson* was steaming alone, far behind Task Force 61, the U.S. Navy carrier task force that had taken part in the previous day's battle. The *Grayson*, originally part of Task Force 16 (a sub-unit of Task Force 61 built around the fleet carrier USS *Enterprise*), was looking for survivors from missing carrier airplanes that might have been shot down or ditched for lack of fuel in the wide, open sea to the west of the retiring carrier force.

At 0330, the *Grayson's* lookouts spotted Task Force 18 (a part of Task Force 61 around the small fleet carrier USS *Wasp*). Caught out of position while refueling, Task Force 18 and the *Wasp* Air Group had missed taking part in the Battle of the Eastern Solomons; they were now were arriving on station to perform the critical duty of guarding the withdrawal of the battle-damaged USS *Enterprise* and the refueling of Task Force 11, the portion of Task Force 61 built around the fleet carrier USS *Saratoga*.

The *Grayson* sighted Task Force 18 at a distance of six miles shortly after 0330, August 25, and exchanged light and radio recognition signals.

She then proceeded southward past the *Wasp* and her escorts and, at 0625, encountered the *Saratoga's* Task Force 11, which was by then beginning refueling operations. The destroyer joined the *Saratoga* force, which happened to be heading in a southerly direction, toward the retiring and diminished *Enterprise* task group. In time, since the *Enterprise* was sailing from the scene of any possible action, the *Grayson* was officially reassigned to Task Force 11, and she assumed station with the Task Force 11 screen.

At 1143, the *Grayson's* lookouts sighted what appeared to be a carrier's island superstructure far to the west-southwest. The destroyer's captain, LCdr Frederick Bell, reported the sighting to RAdm Carleton Wright, the Task Force 11 screen commander, and was ordered to sail out alone to investigate the sighting. At that moment, the destroyer's lookouts reported seeing what appeared to be smoke rising beside the distant object.

Within two minutes of the original sighting, as the *Grayson* peeled out of the screen formation, the distant object resolved itself into the less-distant conning tower of a surfaced submarine, hull-down on the horizon an estimated twelve miles out. As the *Grayson* put on full power to give chase, the target—the Japanese long-range fleet submarine HIJMS *I-9*—disappeared.

The *Grayson* made her approach on the basis of the estimated distance, and, upon reaching the nine-mile mark at precisely noon, her sonar operators made a firm sound contact. The destroyer began her first depth-charge attack at 1223. As the *Grayson* completed her approach, the *I-9* increased speed and turned to starboard, which brought her inside the *Grayson's* own turning circle. The sonar contact was thus lost in the noise of the stalker's propellers.

Sonar contact was reestablished at 1244, and the *Grayson* dropped the first of her second string of depth charges at 1247, as the *I-9* went deep at a speed of 7 knots, about as fast as she could. The American sonar operators reported that the target remained on a steady course until just before the conclusion of the attack, when she turned to starboard.

At 1247, Lieutenant Commander Bell decided to shift tactics in order to conserve his limited supply of depth charges. His ship would launch dummy attacks in order to wear the Japanese down. The game of cat-and-mouse continued through 1310, when an SBD dive-bomber from the *Wasp*

Air Group arrived over the *Grayson*. At 1312, the destroyer made a normal approach at 12 knots upon the sound-originated target, which was making an estimated 8 knots. At the end of the destroyer's run, the *I-9* turned to port and was lost amidst the noise of the surface ship's screws.

Contact was reestablished at 1329, and the first drop of the third live attack was made. At this point, the sonarmen reported that the target was making only 4 knots and heading due west. The *Grayson*, which was on an intercepting course, dropped the remainder of her third string of depth charges just as the destroyer USS *Patterson* appeared on the horizon.

Sonar contact was lost until 1347, fully two hours after the first sighting. At 1351, the *Grayson* began her fourth attack. The *I-9* was fleeing to the west-northwest at nearly 7 knots, which seemed like an extraordinary feat to the destroyermen following a lengthy chase that had surely depleted the output of the submarine's electrical batteries, her only source of power while running submerged.

The destroyer USS *Patterson* joined the *Grayson* at 1402 in order to deliver the next attack, but the *Grayson* regained contact with the *I-9* and was directed to proceed with the attack. As the *I-9* turned away from south of west to almost due east at 4 knots, the *Grayson* opened her fifth attack from the southwest. The submarine turned away to port at the very last moment, but the depth charges appeared to detonate far closer than had any of the earlier spreads.

The *Grayson* stood clear at 1418 to allow the *Patterson* to deliver the next attack. The *Patterson's* sonarmen, however, were unable to establish sound contact on their ship's first pass, probably because the target had not yet sailed clear of the turbulence created by the *Grayson's* most recent attack.

The destroyer USS *Monssen* arrived on the scene at 1438, as the *Grayson* was maneuvering to reestablish sound contact. The sonarmen reported at 1440 that they had a target, and the word was passed to the *Patterson*, which moved to attack. At that point, the *Patterson* lookouts and the *Grayson's* bridge watch could clearly see the Japanese submarine as it hovered directly beneath the surface at precisely the spot at which the *Grayson* sonarmen had said it would be. Undoubtedly, the *Grayson's* latest attack had severely damaged the Japanese boat, forcing it to the surface.

The hovering SBD dropped a smoke marker just as the *Patterson* completed her attack, and then the *Monssen* launched her first attack. At that moment, the *Grayson*, which had expended all her depth charges and needed to refuel, was ordered to leave the area to find and rejoin the *Enterprise's* Task Force 16. (She arrived safely at 1537 and immediately refueled.)

Although the American destroyermen eventually claimed a kill following repeated depth-charge attacks, the *I-9* survived the afternoon ordeal, albeit with heavy damage.

That same day, another Japanese fleet submarine, the HIJMS *I-17*, was attacked by a carrier-based Dauntless dive-bomber, whose pilot claimed that day as a sure kill. In fact, the aerial bomb, which fell close aboard the *I-17*, merely damaged the boat, which was able to limp home for repairs.

Altogether, an even dozen Japanese submarines had participated in the Battle of the Eastern Solomons. Though American pilots claimed many as kills, none was sunk and only two—the *I-9* and the *I-17*—were sufficiently rattled by American bombs and depth charges to be withdrawn for repairs. When the carrier battle ended, the remaining ten Imperial Navy submarines spread out to interdict the Allied supply lines to Guadalcanal as well as to track the *Saratoga* and *Wasp* task forces.

The first post-battle contact came on August 28 in waters southeast of Guadalcanal, when a pair of Dauntlesses from the *Wasp's* Scouting Squadron 72 (Scouting-72) drove down a surfaced Japanese submarine within fifty miles of Task Force 18.

The first hard contact between a U.S. Navy warship and a Japanese submarine occurred at 0805, August 29, when lookouts aboard the destroyer-minelayer USS *Gamble* sighted the conning tower of the HIJMS *I-123* at a distance of about 9,000 yards. At that moment, the *Gamble*, a World War I–vintage four-stack destroyer that had been downgraded and converted for minelaying operations, was screening a supply convoy bound from the New Hebrides Islands to Guadalcanal. Fortunately, the *Gamble* had retained her depth-charge armament, and she prompty gave chase to the submarine, which hastily submerged. The first depth-charge attack was launched at 0844, and the *Gamble* made numerous additional attacks until 1147, when a large pool of oil and splintered decking floated to the surface. The *I-123* was no more.

That left nine Japanese submarines prowling the waters—near and far—off Guadalcanal.

Following the defeat of a U.S. Navy surface force by Imperial Navy cruisers off Savo island on August 8, the U.S. Navy had been hard-pressed to muster the will or the surface forces required to secure the adjacent to and approaching the vulnerable U.S. Marine perimeter at Lunga on Guadalcanal. Indeed, in the immediate aftermath of the epic night surface battle, numerically inferior Japanese surface forces ruled the waves. The American South Pacific Force's response to the Japanese carrier-borne challenge of August 23–24—the Battle of the Eastern Solomons—was a major attempt to mitigate the moral decline of U.S. naval power in the area. The Japanese had been held from their objectives on August 24, but the severe damage sustained by the *Enterprise* had put a hold on any designs VAdm Frank Jack Fletcher, the carrier force commander, might have had about seizing the initiative from the Imperial Navy.

In fact, Fletcher was kept on a tight leash by his superior, VAdm Robert Ghormley, the commander-in-chief of all U.S. and Allied air, ground, and naval forces in the South Pacific (SoPac) Area. Following the Eastern Solomons battle, Ghormley ordered Fletcher to patrol the area southeast of Guadalcanal but to remain south of the tenth parallel unless in pursuit of an enemy force. The effect of the order was to restrict Fletcher's two operational carriers—the *Saratoga* and the *Wasp*—to an area only 250 miles long by 60 miles wide east and southeast of San Cristobal Island. This placed the carrier air groups beyond supporting range of the Lunga Perimeter, where an inadequate air defense was being cobbled together against a powerful Imperial Navy bombing campaign based at Rabaul, the Japanese regional base 600 miles to the northwest of Guadalcanal. In essence, in order to save Fletcher's two carriers for a possible do-or-die battle with a large Japanese fleet bent upon recapturing Guadalcanal, Ghormley was unwilling to allow the two veteran carrier air groups to take part in a day-to-day battle of attrition over Guadalcanal itself.

What, on the face of it, the Japanese failed to accomplish while losing a great many of their best carrier bomber pilots on August 24—the landing of infantry reinforcements at Guadalcanal—was attempted at a far more modest and realistic level on August 28. On that date, four Imperial Navy troop-carrying destroyers operating under the command of RAdm Raizo Tanaka left the Shortland Islands anchorage with the first contingent of a crack infantry brigade whose mission it was to crush the Lunga Perimeter and recapture Henderson Field.

At 1700, August 28, a pair of Marine Scout-Bomber Squadron 232 (VMSB-232) SBD Dauntless dive-bombers based at Henderson Field and piloted by 1stLt Danny Iverson and 2dLt Hank Hise were tooling along on evening patrol over the Russell Islands at 130 knots when Hise spotted the four destroyers silhouetted against the setting sun only seventy miles off Cape Esperance, Guadalcanal's western extremity.

Because they both lacked working radios, Hise thought Iverson might have failed to see the targets. But Iverson had seen them; he just assumed they were Americans. To Hise's chagrin, the flight leader dropped down so his radioman-gunner could flash a recognition signal with his Aldis lantern. The Japanese blinked back with their antiaircraft batteries. Iverson pulled up, with Hise following, to 7,000 feet, where both SBDs topped a thin layer of clouds.

Next, without any warning whatsoever, Iverson pitched through a hole in the clouds. Startled, Hise armed his single 500-pound bomb and followed. The Japanese ships were by then maneuvering every which way. Hise selected a target running straight across his flight path and continued to bore in, frightened by the number of guns that were firing at him. He cut his bomb loose at 2,500 feet, certain he had missed by a good half-mile.

Unable to find Iverson upon recovering from his dive, Hise headed home, where he taxied straight up to the Pagoda—a distinctive Japanese-built building that housed the air operations center—to report his find. Soon, Iverson arrived safely home with his bomb still aboard to tell how he had been unable to get lined up on either of two dives.

Hise's report resulted in a late scramble by eleven Marine and Navy Dauntlesses. The Navy SBDs were from Lt Turner Caldwell's Flight 300, a squadron-size component of *Enterprise* Air Group SBDs that had been marooned on Guadalcanal on the night of August 24 and which, by this date, had become an important part of Guadalcanal's emerging ad hoc multi-service air command known as the Cactus Air Force (CACTUS was Guadalcanal's code name).

The eleven Navy and Marine SBDs bored through the failing light to score a direct hit on one destroyer. Ens Chris Fink, whose bomb had struck a fat Japanese transport during the Eastern Solomons battle, planted his 500-pound bomb directly amidships on the destroyer HIJMS *Asagiri*, which instantly exploded and sank. Another destroyer was damaged by near misses, and a Marine SBD and its two-man crew were lost while strafing this ship.

Only one of the four Japanese destroyer-transports emerged from the air strike without damage, and the two damaged vessels were incapable of proceeding. The landing was called off, and the three survivors headed back to the Shortlands.

Next day, August 29, five of Admiral Tanaka's troop-carrying destroyers safely landed 450 Imperial Army soldiers at Guadalcanal's Taivu Point, well to the east of the Lunga Perimeter.

On August 30, the destroyer HIJMS *Yudachi* left the Shortland Islands with still another group of fresh Japanese infantrymen, also bound for Taivu Point. At 1512, a Japanese diversionary air strike from Rabaul caught two U.S. Navy destroyers and an auxiliary cargo vessel in motion as they ran away from Lunga Point. The destroyer USS *Colhoun* was near-missed by the Japanese bombs, but she suffered so much damage that she sank within two minutes. A total of fifty-one American seamen went down with her.

As if the loss of the *Colhoun* were not sufficient to claim mastery of the waters off Guadalcanal, the Japanese infantry was landed by the *Yudachi* at Taivu Point without being discovered or challenged.

On the other hand, August 30 was also marked by the safe arrival at Henderson Field of two fresh Marine squadrons, VMF-224 and VMSB-231, flying Wildcat fighters and Dauntless dive-bombers.

As the rather weak—but vital—exchanges were taking place close in to Guadalcanal, Frank Jack Fletcher's two-carrier Task Force 61 remained tethered to its patrol sector southeast of San Cristobal. There had been no hostile sightings since August 27, when two *Wasp* patrol bombers drove off a Japanese submarine, but this is not to say that the Japanese submarines had not been at work shadowing and stalking the American carriers.

On August 29, Task Force 61 was joined by RAdm George Murray's Task Force 17, centered around the fleet carrier USS *Hornet*, which had not been in action since Midway and which had been held in reserve when the U.S. Navy's other three operational fleet carriers had been sent to support the Guadalcanal invasion. Murray's task force had been dispatched to the Solomons upon the withdrawal of the damaged *Enterprise* following the Eastern Solomons clash. With Task Force 17's arrival, Admiral Fletcher released the *Wasp's* Task Force 18 to revictual at the nearby Allied base, Noumea.

At 0330, August 31, radars aboard both the *Saratoga* and the battleship USS *North Carolina* made contacts with what appeared to be the same small surface target, but which could very well have been a squall. Immediately, the destroyer USS *Farragut* was sent to investigate, but she found no sign of an intruder after combing an ever-widening circle centered on the surface-radar contact.

Task Force 61 continued to sail northwestward.

Dawn general quarters was routinely sounded at 0600, and all hands went to their battle stations. At 0655, Admiral Fletcher ordered the course reversed to the southeast, initiated a standard zigzag sailing pattern, and brought his vessels up to a speed of 13 knots. All hands except those assigned to the routine morning watch were released from general quarters at 0706, and breakfast was served aboard the *Saratoga* and most of the other warships.

Until 0746, August 31 promised to be another dull day at sea. At that minute, however, the destroyer USS *MacDonough's* sonarmen made a hot contact dead ahead, lookouts saw a submarine periscope only thirty feet from the ship's bows, and the destroyer's hull scraped the submarine's conning tower.

Within that minute—0746—the *MacDonough* also hoisted submarine-warning signal flags and dropped a pair of depth charges with such haste that no one had time to activate the depth-setting device on either charge.

Also within that same minute, the submarine HIJMS *I-26* launched a spread of six torpedoes at the largest target in her periscope sights. One of the deadly cylinders porpoised just astern of the *MacDonough*, but the remaining five continued on.

Lt(jg) Ivan Swope and Lt(jg) Phil Rusk, both pilots with the *Hornet's* Scouting-8, had been idling away the morning in their ship's forecastle, watching a pair of dolphins keeping pace with the *Hornet* at what, to the pilots, was the incredible rate of 17 knots. Both pilots looked up at once to see the distant *Saratoga* veer off the track both carriers had been following. Swope commented aloud, "I wonder where Sara is going," for the *Hornet* had the air duty and should have been the first of the two aircraft carriers to turn into the wind if aircraft needed to be launched or recovered.

Quite simply, the *Saratoga's* Capt DeWitt Ramsey had seen the *MacDonough's* warning flags as they were being hoisted, and he had instantly ordered the helmsman at his elbow to swing the huge carrier's rudder hard right. Immediately upon execution of the precipitous turn, Ramsey ordered all engines to full speed.

Two interminable minutes passed as the five remaining Japanese torpedoes passed through the *Saratoga's* protective ring of surface warships and beat a foaming path toward the carrier's vast hull.

The two young aviators watching from the *Hornet's* forecastle had a clear view as a single huge plume of water and smoke erupted on the *Saratoga's* starboard beam right abreast the island. Throughout the great ship, hundreds and hundreds of sailors and officers were thrown off their feet.

This was the second time in 1942 that the *Saratoga* had been struck by a submarine-launched torpedo. The first incident had occurred almost within sight of the California coast, on the carrier's first wartime sally from home. She had spent months in port being repaired.

All hands braced for additional impacts, but none came.

As screening vessels surged away from their stations to fight off the attacker—and others, if there were any—electricians and engineers dashed toward the engine rooms to see how their ship's giant electric motors had fared. (An early and aborted experiment in electrical propulsion had been undertaken by the *Saratoga* and her dead sister, the USS *Lexington*.) As many had feared from the outset, the worst had happened. The detonation had jarred a high-tension cable, which momentarily closed an arc, which amounted to an explosion, which filled below-decks spaces with fumes, which caused automatic emergency devices to shut down the two main electrical power generators, which threw the largest part of the ship's power grid thoroughly out of kilter.

The *Saratoga's* power output fell to negligible levels. After hours of grueling labor, the engineers and electricians would be able to assure Captain Ramsey of, at best, 12 knots of speed.

Even before the *Saratoga* was struck her painful blow, the *MacDonough* was joined by the destroyer USS *Phelps*, and together they went after the *I-26* with a vengeance. Sonarmen achieved repeated contacts, and depth charges were repeatedly unleashed, but the *I-26* successfully evaded the two destroyers. At last, the destroyer *Monssen* was detached from the screen to merely hold down the intruder until nightfall, by which time it was hoped the *Saratoga* could be gotten clear of the ongoing danger—for there was no assurance that the *I-26* could not slip away from the destroyers and launch more torpedoes at the crippled carrier, nor that other submarines were not arriving on the scene to do the same.

The *Monssen* eventually lost contact and put in a claim for a kill, but the *I-26* had really slipped away.

When it became apparent that the *Saratoga* would have to be withdrawn from the battle arena to undergo repairs, the heavy cruiser USS *Minneapolis* passed up a towing cable and, with the aid of a stiff breeze, pulled the carrier along quickly enough for the Sara to be to able launch a total of twenty-one carrier bombers and nine Wildcat fighters, which all flew 347 miles to Espiritu Santo. (Between September 6 and September 13, these and other *Saratoga* Air Group veteran aircrews from Fighting-5, Torpedo-8, and the two SBD squadrons—amalgamated into Scouting-3—would all be committed to the Cactus Air Force. And they would, as much as anything, save Henderson Field.)

The *Saratoga* eventually reached Tongatabu without suffering any additional problems. Temporary repairs were made, and the Sara soon departed for a major refit that would keep her out of the war for three crucial months.

Only an even dozen Americans were hurt in the torpedo attack. Eleven of them were *Saratoga* crewmen, who were all treated and returned to duty. The twelfth casualty was the only one who was actually wounded. Though light, the wounds were sufficient to force VAdm Frank Jack Fletcher to stand aside as commander of Task Force 61. This satisfied many naval aviators in the Pacific Fleet, for Fletcher was a surface-warfare specialist whom the aviators felt was unsuited to command carriers. Be that as it may, at the moment of his departure, Fletcher was in fact the Navy's most experienced carrier commander, and not an unsuccessful one at that.

Command of the diminished carrier armada passed temporarily to the Task Force 17 commander, RAdm George Murray, a distinguished naval aviator who had recently been promoted to flag rank after commanding the *Enterprise* with great distinction at the start of the Pacific War. Unless a senior officer was dispatched from outside the region, Murray would turn Task Force 61 over to the Task Force 18 commander—RAdm Leigh Noyes—when the *Wasp* returned from her revictualing at Noumea.

That same night, at least seven Japanese troop-carrying destroyers landed fresh veteran Imperial Army infantrymen, engineers, and artillerymen at Guadalcanal's Taivu Point. The operation was not molested.

Chapter 2

By September 1, 1942, the American strategic offensive at Guadalcanal had pretty much bogged down. The Guadalcanal invasion's initial successes of August 7 and 8, in which all strategic and tactical objectives had been secured by the 1st Marine Division, had been replaced by the isolation of the Marines following the withdrawal of the invasion fleet on August 9 and a confusion and loss of purpose on the part of the region's naval staff.

Though things were looking up a bit by the end of August, it was evident that the Marines at Lunga were by no means capable of mounting large or sustained operations against Japanese ground forces on Guadalcanal. This was because the 1st Marine Division had not completed its combat training when it was assigned to undertake the invasion, and because of the horrendous logistical situation caused by the August 9 withdrawal of the transports and by the Imperial Navy's subsequent interdiction of the Marines' seaborne lines of supply. As it was, the 1st Marine Division literally had to learn on the job to fight as a fully integrated combat division, for Marines had not fought in even battalion strength since

1918. The lack of supplies and ammunition all but precluded any meaningfully sustained ground or air operations. The psychology of defeat imposed from a distance by the weak naval command in Noumea also played havoc with the institutionally combative spirit of this large body of U.S. Marines.

The fault lay squarely at the feet of VAdm Robert Lee Ghormley, the commander of the South Pacific Area and South Pacific Force. Ghormley and many of his close advisors were so devastated by the defeat at Savo—not to mention the long string of Allied setbacks through the first half of 1942—that they were unable to conceive of Guadalcanal as anything more than a defensive operation. Having suffered the loss of four first-line heavy cruisers on August 9, Ghormley was unwilling to commit his command's limited force of transports and surface warships to any sort of meaningful logistical support of the Marine enclave at Lunga. Land-based warplanes, admittedly in short supply, were likewise held back—in premature anticipation by Ghormley himself that they would be needed to defend rear bases once Guadalcanal had fallen, an eventuality he fervently believed would take place. By the same self-fulfilling logic, veteran carrier pilots and aircrewmen were held in sterile readiness aboard ships one step removed from the central arena.

Henderson Field was held by the Marines during the first month of the Guadalcanal Campaign for only two reasons: the Japanese were unable to mount a meaningful offensive on short notice, and, after August 20, a very thin line of American land-based fighters and dive-bombers achieved aerial dominance around Lunga during the day. By night, however, Japanese air and naval forces ruled the air space and sea lanes around Guadalcanal.

On the night of August 24, the ad hoc Cactus Air Force consisted of one Marine fighter squadron (VMF-223), one Marine dive-bomber squadron (VMSB-232), eleven *Enterprise* Air Group dive-bombers (Flight 300) marooned in the wake of the Eastern Solomons battle, and a handful of obsolescent Army Air Forces P-400 fighters from the New Hebrides–based 67th Fighter Squadron. As Task Force 61 withdrew to lick its wounds in the wake of the Eastern Solomons battle—the *Enterprise* had been severely damaged by three bombs—this tiny aerial force was all that stood between Henderson Field and oblivion. The fighters' job was to hold Rabaul-based bombers and strafers more or less at bay, and the SBDs were the eyes and flying artillery of the American outpost. Together, they would go a long way toward slowing the build-up of Japanese ground forces and their supplies on Guadalcanal, and toward softening the crippling naval bombardments that were to be sustained by the Lunga Perimeter.

The Eastern Solomons battle had been the second part of a multi-objective Japanese grand plan that had gone awry. In addition to losing a light carrier—the HIJMS *Ryujo*—and the battle itself on August 24, the Japanese were thwarted once again on August 25 when a small force of troop-laden transports was turned back by Cactus-based dive-bombers. The Imperial Army infantrymen aboard the transports were reinforcements for a similar force whose night attack on August 20–21 had been defeated by the Marines.

That so few Japanese soldiers were being committed at the time was the result of a serious misjudgement by the Japanese regarding the size and purpose of the Marine force occupying the Lunga Perimeter. The Japanese were unable to conceive at the time that the Americans even had a complete combat division on hand in the Pacific to undertake the invasion, and they were hopeful that the Marines were conducting a mere raid-in-force aimed at denying the Japanese use of the Lunga air base until stronger Allied forces could be brought in to bolster island bases and bastions to the rear.

So, based on a faulty appreciation of American strength on the ground at Guadalcanal, and a false premise as to American intentions, the Japanese sent too few ground troops (less than 2,000) to take back the Lunga airfield, and then directly supported the ground phase of the Eastern Solomons action with too few aircraft (little more than a dozen carrier bombers and no land-based bombers). Moreover, it turned out that the reinforcement and land phases of the grand strategy culminating in the Eastern Solomons battle were a sham. The real intent of the Japanese senior commander—Adm Isoroku Yamamoto, commander-in-chief of the Imperial Navy's operational arm, the Combined Fleet—was to draw out the American carriers and defeat them. This plan had also failed. Although not soundly defeated, the Japanese lost the battle. Hundreds of veteran Japanese soldiers were killed in the August 20–21 night battle, hundreds more perished when their transports were sunk or damaged by Cactus dive-bombers on August 25, and the light carrier HIJMS *Ryujo* was sunk by American carrier-based bombers on August 24.

It would take time for the Japanese to recover from their across-the-board defeat in the Eastern Solomons battle, but Adm Isoroku Yamamoto and his Combined Fleet would be back, carriers and all. In the meantime, except for naval combat air groups and a small surface force based at Rabaul, plus a changing roster of submarines prodding the American carriers and interdicting Lunga's lines of supply, the Imperial Navy all but withdrew from the Solomons arena.

It was a significant characteristic of the Japanese Pacific War effort that the Imperial Army and Imperial Navy failed to achieve operational unity except informally, between individual commanders, at very low operational levels.

At the beginning of the Allied South Pacific offensive, the Solomon Islands were the exclusive domain of the Imperial Navy. The first responses to the Allied invasion at Guadalcanal were by naval air and surface units, and the first infantry unit sent was one-half of a naval infantry battalion. Shortly, however, the scope of the Marine occupation—dimly perceived as it was—obliged the commitment of Imperial Army ground forces. This the Imperial Army had been able to achieve by simply rerouting an independent, self-contained, regiment-size infantry force on its way home to Japan—which is to say, without drawing resources away from any ongoing or contemplated operation on its Pacific agenda.

While Imperial Navy warships and land-based warplanes shelled and bombed Henderson Field at will for nearly two weeks after August 9, the Imperial Army force commander, Col Kiyano Ichiki, struck a personal deal with the Imperial Navy's regional transport specialist, RAdm Raizo Tanaka, to ship the first half of *Ichiki Butai* (Ichiki Force) to a spot east of the Lunga Perimeter, there to await the balance of the force and the onset of the naval offensive. When the presence of *Ichiki Butai* was prematurely and inadvertently disclosed by a Marine patrol, Colonel Ichiki precipitously assaulted the Marine defensive line on the night of August 20–21, and was utterly defeated. He and most of his soldiers were killed.

While the implementation of the naval grand strategy rolled forward days after Ichiki's death, the Imperial Army at last routed an independent infantry brigade—the crack, veteran 35th Infantry Brigade, commanded by MajGen Kiyotake Kawaguchi—from the Palau Islands, through Rabaul, to the Shortland Islands. There, General Kawaguchi struck a personal deal with Admiral Tanaka for the shipment of his brigade to Guadalcanal, partly by slow-moving landing barges and partly by swift destroyers. Kawaguchi and several groups of his infantrymen were landed from Tanaka's destroyers around Taivu Point beginning August 29, the night after the first group of four troop-carrying destroyers was defeated near the Russell Islands by Cactus dive-bombers.

By August 29, the Cactus Air Force consisted of two Marine fighter squadrons, two Marine dive-bomber squadrons, what amounted to one land-based Navy dive-bomber squadron, and part of one Army Air Forces fighter squadron. This tiny force was charged with preventing superior Japanese naval air and surface units from molesting Henderson Field or the Lunga Perimeter. Its total support was provided on occasion by Army Air Forces B-17 heavy bombers of the 11th Heavy Bombardment Group, based at Espiritu Santo, and pilots rotated forward from a Marine fighter squadron (VMF-212) and a Marine reconnaissance squadron (VMO-251), also based at Espiritu Santo. No Allied warships were committed to keeping the Japanese at bay; the only surface warships to reach Guadalcanal were older, ultimately expendable destroyer-transports, minesweepers, and minelayers assigned to guard infrequent and inadequate sallies by supply ships, which had to sneak into the area between Japanese air raids and be gone by sunset.

The mission was ludicrous for so insignificant an aerial force, but the Cactus pilots and aircrewmen halfway pulled it off. The Japanese were quickly put on notice that the Cactus Air Force ruled the skies and sea approaches to Guadalcanal during the day. The Marine and Navy pilots attempted to extend the hours of their hegemony into the night, but they had not the numbers, training, nor equipment to launch sustained or even successful night operations.

So, while Imperial Navy land-based fighters and bombers daily tested the mettle of the Cactus Air Force, Japanese warships and troop-carrying vessels pretty much conceded the day and opted for night landings and frequent night gunnery passes along the beaches around Lunga Point. The objective of the night naval bombardments—a stream of individual night bombers—was twofold: the destruction of vital facilities, particularly warplanes and airfield infrastructure; and the demoralization of Americans on the ground, including pilots and aircrewmen, whose rest was constantly disrupted. Daylight bombing raids by Rabaul-based bombers escorted by Zero fighters aimed to achieve similar results, along with the destruction of Cactus fighters in combat and the death of Cactus pilots.

The war at Guadalcanal in late August and early September 1942 was a war of attrition. Each side had precisely the same objectives: to maintain an active presence; to wear down the other side; and to build up ground, air, naval, and logistical assets for the ultimate battle each side knew was inevitable.

To those ends, both sides moved to commit far-flung forces of all types to the central struggle. The Imperial Army was more or less compelled by events to halt its Papua New Guinea offensive in order to redirect a fresh full-strength infantry division from that theater to the Solomons, and the United States command was forced to move up its schedule to replace a reinforced Marine regiment in American Samoa so that it could be landed at Lunga.

Crucial in making these commitments was the disparate attitudes of the men making the decisions.

The senior Japanese Army commander in the region, LtGen Harukichi Hyakutake, considered the commitment of a fresh infantry division necessary only insofar as it helped pull the Imperial Navy's chestnuts from the fire; his mind was firmly set on taking Papua New Guinea, and he would be slow to commit additional Imperial Army units if they were requested. Moreover, the Imperial Army would steadfastly refuse to commit even one warplane from its vast strategic reserve to the Solomons Campaign.

Most of the American Pacific War senior commanders outside of South Pacific Area headquarters *wanted* to commit everything they had to the vortex at Guadalcanal, but prudence dictated the schedule. For the time being, only small ground and air units guarding vital rear bases could be replaced, so only those small units could be committed.

Notwithstanding the prevailing attitudes at high Imperial Army levels, the task of committing fresh resources in the Solomons was easier for the Japanese than it was for the Allies, because the Japanese had standing units in or near the Pacific that could be withdrawn or redirected from ongoing and contemplated offensive operations. The U.S. Army, Navy, and Marine Corps forces then in the Pacific were thinly spread across a defensive barrier many considered to be the last line of defense. The small part of the Australian Army not engaged in fighting Axis forces in North Africa was fully committed to defending its homeland and mounting a land war in New Guinea. So, while the Japanese had ample resources and controlled their own offensive schedule, the Americans had inadequate resources that had to be tied down to far-flung island bases, because the Japanese had the initiative and the means for striking many of those bases while simultaneously mounting operations at Guadalcanal.

The Japanese commanders expected to win at Guadalcanal while the senior American regional commander—Ghormley—and many of his chief subordinates pretty much expected to lose at Guadalcanal. The respective psychologies, along with the respective availability of resources, would rule the second—tactical—phase of the Guadalcanal Campaign, on land, in the air, and at sea.

The two sides merely sparred during the first dozen days of September 1942. The Japanese naval air establishment based around Rabaul delivered regular air strikes at the extremity of the 600-mile operational range of their Zero fighters, and Cactus fighters continued to fend off such air strikes, taking and inflicting losses as they did. Indeed, the Japanese lost an average of about four aircraft and pilots each day they flew, while the Cactus Air Force averaged far fewer losses in airplanes and pilots.

Japanese warships continued to sail into Ironbottom Sound—as the channel fronting Guadalcanal's northern beaches came to be known—and Cactus dive-bombers and fighters continued to harass them for as long as there was sunlight. The Japanese vessels continued to land infantry and support units without great loss, and to bombard Henderson Field at night with virtual impunity.

The significant blows and counterblows of the period were minimal, though equally damaging. Cactus pilots discovered the whereabouts of General Kawaguchi's 35th Infantry Brigade's barge-borne element as it slowly chugged southward through the Solomons chain. This led to repeated strafing missions that sank many of the troop barges and killed as many as a thousand of the veteran soldiers. Cactus Air also discovered the 35th Infantry Brigade's main base camp at Taivu Point and launched daily bombing and strafing raids that killed or injured many Japanese soldiers, totally disrupted the brigade's schedule, and hurt its morale.

On the other hand, the destroyer-transports USS *Little* and USS *Gregory* were both sunk in Ironbottom Sound on the night of September 5 by marauding Japanese warships. This tragedy was just about the last straw for the American naval commanders in Noumea, who ordered all of their vessels of every type to stand clear of the deadly waters by sunset each day.

On September 8, the 1st Marine Raider Battalion, attached to the 1st Marine Division, struck at the 35th Infantry Brigade's base camp at Taivu Point. As it turned out, the main body of the brigade had already slipped off into the rain forest on its way to assault the Lunga Perimeter, so the battle was brief and anticlimactic. The Raiders hauled off what stores they could carry and destroyed the camp. Then they returned to Lunga to take up a new defensive position on a small patch of high ground overlooking the back way into Henderson Field and the Lunga Perimeter.

On the nights of September 12 and 13, the main body of the 35th Infantry Brigade struck the Raider battalion and the minuscule 1st Marine Parachute Battalion, which were holding the ridge overlooking Henderson Field. In the end, the 35th Infantry Brigade lost more than six hundred soldiers killed on or in front of the slopes of what would evermore be called Bloody Ridge. Hundreds of sick and wounded Japanese died along the trail as the defeated main body of the brigade retreated. Two rather desultory side attacks on the eastern and western flanks of the Lunga Perimeter were also turned back.

The *Hornet* and the *Wasp*—the United States Fleet's two remaining operational fleet carriers—had remained distantly active during the see-saw actions leading up to the Bloody Ridge battle at Guadalcanal. The period was not without incident for the sailors and pilots of Task Force 61, but the overall characteristic of the period was stultifying, boring routine. Frequent submarine sightings—or scares, at any rate—provided some excitement, but even they became routine as the memory of the *Saratoga's* crippling torpedo damage receded amidst feelings of good luck and narrow escapes. Until September 6.

The *Hornet's* captain was resting in his sea cabin during the noon hour, and, at 1247, the command duty officer was on the signal bridge watching the last of a series of routine launches to replace the antisubmarine and combat air patrols. Ens Earl Zook, a twenty-three-year-old who had graduated from the Naval Academy on December 19, 1941, with the Class of '42, had the conn. The ship's junior assistant navigator and junior officer-of-the-deck, Zook had been getting a lot of time at the helm despite his lowly status.

It was coming up on 1250 when Ensign Zook and others were alerted to unusual goings-on by the sudden detonation of at least one and possibly two depth charges aft of the *Hornet's* port beam.

Ens John Cresto, a green twenty-three-year-old TBF Avenger pilot serving with the *Hornet* Air Group's Torpedo-6, saw "something" heading right for his ship and made the only contribution he felt he reasonably could make on extremely short notice; he dropped a pair of depth charges.

When Ensign Zook heard the detonations, his years of training at Annapolis paid off all at once. Instantly, without any thought about his lowly rank, he coolly ordered his great ship to turn hard left. As the *Hornet* steadied on a course forty-five degrees left of the base course, hundreds of her crew, including Ensign Zook, saw torpedo wakes pass down either flank.

It is probable that Ensign Cresto's quick action detonated at least one of the torpedo warheads. And it is *certain* that Ensign Zook's quick action saved the carrier.

After Cresto landed, he was escorted to the cabin of the task force commander, RAdm George Murray, himself a pilot of wide experience. When Murray congratulated the youngster on his unparalleled detonation of the torpedo, all those present saw the pilot's expression dim. "I didn't know it was a torpedo," he half-complained, "I thought it was a submarine."

♦

The most significant contribution made by carrier air during the period was not administered by the carrier squadrons on duty with Task Force 61. On September 6, a part of LCdr Bullet Lou Kirn's Scouting-3 joined the Cactus Air Force as a vital addition to the weary force of Marine and *Enterprise* Flight 300 SBD dive-bombers charged with finding, tracking, and hitting Japanese warships and destroyer-transports en route to Guadalcanal. On September 11, LCdr Roy Simpler's Fighting-5—a *Saratoga* Air Group unit which by then mustered a large number of pilots transferred from the *Enterprise* Air Group's Fighting-6—flew into Henderson Field in twenty-four F4F-4 Wildcat fighters.

The commitment of a large part of the *Saratoga* Air Group to the Cactus Air Force immediately and significantly turned the tide against burgeoning Japanese air strikes leading up to the 35th Infantry Brigade's assault at Bloody Ridge. Moreover, on September 13, Marine fighter pilots who had been ferried aboard the *Wasp* and *Hornet* the day before flew eighteen Wildcats to Guadalcanal to make good some of the losses of the intense air fighting of the period. This brought to forty-two the number of new Wildcats arriving at Henderson Field in only three days, a vital addition of what turned out to be strategic proportions. Also on September 13, Lt Swede Larsen's Torpedo-8, which by then mustered a large number of pilots and aircrewmen transferred from the *Enterprise's* Torpedo-3, also flew into Henderson Field. It was the first TBF bomber squadron to join the Cactus Air Force.

The Japanese had again been soundly defeated on land, and the Cactus Air Force was growing. Things around Lunga were beginning to look up.

Chapter 3

On September 14, 1942, as victorious Marines around newly named Bloody Ridge were rooting out 35th Infantry Brigade stragglers south of Henderson Field, RAdm Kelly Turner, the South Pacific transport chief, sailed from Espiritu Santo with a group of six heavily escorted transports carrying the first large force of Marines to be committed to Guadalcanal in the aftermath of the Savo debacle. This was one of two reinforced Marine infantry regiments that had been sent to the Pacific early in the war to defend Samoa. Turner, a combative leader who had grudgingly ordered his transports away from Guadalcanal in the immediate aftermath of the Savo battle, was morally determined to make this delivery and thereby keep the faith with the all-but-castaway Marines holding the Lunga Perimeter and Henderson Field.

In addition to the cruisers and destroyers under his immediate command, Turner could count on support from Task Force 61, which at the time consisted of two fleet aircraft carriers, the *Wasp* and the *Hornet*. In addition, a fresh surface battle force built around the USS *Washington*, a new fast battleship, had just arrived for duty in the South Pacific Area. The *Washington* was the only sister ship of the USS *North Carolina*, which had been on duty with the carriers since the Guadalcanal invasion. If needed, the two fast battleships and a significant force of cruisers and destroyers could be dispatched to Turner's aid, as, of course, could the *Wasp* and *Hornet* air groups.

Despite the seeming boldness of Kelly Turner's reinforcement effort, the admiral and his colleagues were rightfully fearful that the Japanese would concentrate their strength and strike a major blow. Thus, the transports and screening warships took a long loop far from the usual routes between Espiritu Santo and Guadalcanal, well away from the Santa Cruz Islands, which were known to harbor Japanese tender-based amphibian warplanes and fast destroyers.

At 1105 on September 15, Turner's force was gathering for the final dash to Lunga when a large bogey lumbered into radar range of the *Wasp*, which was about 100 miles to the north of transports, interposed between Turner and a Japanese battle force the American carriers had been hoping to attack for two days.

As soon as the radar sighting was reported to the *Wasp's* fighter director, a division composed of four Fighting-71 Grumman F4F Wildcat fighters was dispatched see to the bogey, a Kawanishi H6K Mavis four-engine patrol bomber. The flying boat, now within thirty miles of the *Wasp*, attempted to evade the Wildcats with a diving left turn, but Lt(jg) John McBrayer attacked from above and behind to set fuel tanks in the parasol wing on fire.

The *Wasp* sailed by the grave of the downed Mavis at 1230 and then proceeded west with her screen. Task Force 18, including the *Hornet*, was on a parallel course five miles to the northwest. The *Wasp* Air Group was undertaking all of the day's routine antisubmarine and combat air patrols, and the *Hornet* Air Group was being held in readiness to launch strikes against Japanese carriers thought to be in the area. These were the veteran fleet carriers HIJMS *Shokaku* and HIJMS *Zuikaku*, and the new light carrier HIJMS *Zuiho*, which together constituted the Imperial Navy's Carrier Division 1. (There had been three Japanese carriers in the area. On

September 13, Task Force 61 had inadvertently sailed beyond strike range of the Japanese air groups, and on September 14, neither side was able to obtain enough of a fix to complete strikes. Late on the 14th, the Japanese battle force withdrew, but RAdm Leigh Noyes, the American carrier-force commander, did not know that, so he was obliged to hold one air group in readiness to launch a strike.)

At 1320, the *Wasp* turned northeast into the wind and launched the first of fourteen Scouting-71 SBDs that were to search for the Japanese carriers in seven two-plane elements to distances of about 200 miles out in the direction of Guadalcanal. Four Scouting-72 Dauntlesses were launched to beef up the Inner Air Patrol—a submarine watch—and eight Fighting-71 Wildcats were sent up to relieve the combat air patrol (CAP). Most of the strike aircraft remaining aboard the *Wasp* and all of those aboard the *Hornet* were ready or being readied to launch in the event Japanese warships were pinpointed by the carrier-based searchers or a number of land-based and tender-based search aircraft.

As soon as the patrol launches were completed, the *Wasp* recovered eight Fighting-71 Wildcats and three SBDs. In response to the task force commander's order, Capt Forrest Sherman ordered his ship to turn to the northwest. The screen vessels instantly responded, as did the entire *Hornet* task force, which was now less than two miles away to the northeast.

As soon as the *Wasp* came to her new heading, Captain Sherman ordered sixteen Wildcats to be respotted for takeoff and all dive-bombers struck below to the hangar deck. All aircraft were fully armed. Most of the *Wasp* Air Group's remaining Wildcats and Dauntlesses were fully fueled as well, but the ten torpedo-armed Torpedo-7 Grumman TBF Avengers aboard the smallish fleet carrier still had inert carbon dioxide in their fuel tanks. The dive-bombers and fighters that had just landed were being struck below to the hangar deck on the midships elevator to be refueled, and additional fighters were being brought up to the flight deck on the same elevator.

At 1342, as aircraft were being stowed or moved, the *Wasp* came to the task force's base course, 280 degrees, at a speed of 16 knots. It was a gorgeous day. The sky was breathtakingly clear, and visibility was unlimited. If there was a worry at all, it was over the condition of the sea.

A 20-knot trade wind blowing up from the southeast had covered the surface with whitecaps, which were perfect concealment for the relays of submarines that had been dogging the carriers nearly every day since the *Saratoga* had been struck by a torpedo two weeks earlier. But there was nothing that could be done about the threat beyond keeping search pilots, lookouts, and sonarmen at a high state of alert.

Unbeknown to the American commanders, Task Force 61 had just sailed into the center of a line of submarines the Japanese naval commanders had set out as scouts in anticipation of the carrier confrontation so narrowly missed on September 13 and 14. The Japanese carriers and a powerful surface force had withdrawn, but the submarines had not.

At 1344, Cdr Takaichi Kinashi, captain of the Imperial Navy fleet submarine HIJMS *I-19*, ordered six torpedoes to be fired. For nearly an hour, Kinashi had been tracking a sea full of fat targets and had finally fallen heir to a clear shot at one of the two American carriers that were crossing at right angles to his boat's approach track.

When the moment to fire came, Commander Kinashi adhered strictly to his tactical doctrine and fired a fan of six torpedoes along slightly diverging tracks at the nearest target, the *Wasp*. As soon as the torpedoes were away, the *I-19's* commander began the arduous task of slinking away as he waited to hear how well he had done. If he was lucky and if his skill was certain, he would hear from one to six detonations. Perhaps some of his torpedoes would overshoot the target, which had been moving rapidly across his line of sight when he fired. In that case, all or several errant torpedoes might strike any number of the screening cruisers and destroyers that from Kinashi's vantage point had seemed to march in a solid steel wall across the horizon.

At 1345, only a minute after the *I-19* fired the last torpedo, RAdm Leigh Noyes's attention was pulled from whatever it had been focused upon by a lookout's yell, "Torpedo wake!" From his vantage point on the *Wasp's* flag bridge, Noyes saw three torpedo wakes only 300 feet away. He heard a young ensign at his elbow say, "These have got us," but the admiral did not reply as he braced himself for the multiple detonations.

The ship's gunnery officer, LCdr George Knuepfer, was standing his routine afternoon watch in Sky Control, high up in the tripod mast over the bridge, when his assistant, who was standing well to starboard, blurted, "Torpedoes!" Knuepfer rushed to that side of the platform and was just in time to see two torpedoes closing to within fifty yards of the ship. He yelled down to the bridge, "Torpedoes! Hard left rudder!"

Capt Forrest Sherman also saw the approaching torpedoes, and he ordered the rudder changed from right-standard to right-full—about the only thing he could do on such short notice.

LCdr John Greenslade, the ship's navigator, heard, "Torpedoes on the starboard bow!" as he sat in the charthouse. He stood up, stepped to the hatchway leading to the starboard catwalk, and immediately saw two torpedoes arrow out of sight beneath the edge of the bridge decking just forward of the bridge and immediately beneath the forward 1.1-inch antiaircraft gun group. The starboard side of the ship was instantly enveloped in smoke and debris. Greenslade was forced to retreat back into the charthouse, which had become a shambles of broken fixtures.

Lt(jg) T. D. Wells, who was on duty in the forward 5-inch gun group, clearly heard the shouted warning from Lookout-1 and saw one of the gunners point to starboard. Wells had just enough time to order all hands to stand as far back as possible before the first torpedo struck just aft, beneath a 1.1-inch gun group.

LCdr George Knuepfer, in Sky Control, clearly saw the second torpedo slam into the ship forward of the first, directly beneath Lieutenant (jg) Wells's forward 5-inch gun group. The cumulative effect of the two blasts threw Knuepfer to his knees. Sky Control was whipsawed in several directions at once, and the foremast tripod on which it was perched seemed about to break up.

On the flag bridge, Admiral Noyes's knees were buckled, but he remained on his feet. Captain Sherman also remained standing. By and large, throughout the ship, anyone who was on his feet was knocked down by one or another of the quick succession of crippling body blows.

Cdr Mike Kernodle, the carrier's air officer, was in Air Plot at 1345. His talker, an enlisted communicator fitted out with sound-powered battle phones, whispered a message from Lookout-1 just loud enough for Kernodle to hear: "Torpedo wake on starboard bow." The words were barely spoken when the first detonation occurred. The second detonation was almost instantaneous. Air Plot, which was high up in the island, was severely whipped around by the force of the first two warheads detonating in quick succession. All the lightbulbs were blown out, fixtures were blasted loose, and a great volume of mixed glass, gear, and papers was thrown to the deck along with every man in the now-darkened compartment. Compartments throughout the ship suffered similar damage.

Cdr Fred Dickey, the carrier's executive officer, was sitting in a closed compartment when the three torpedoes struck the starboard side of the ship. He immediately headed for Battle-II, the secondary command and control center from which he would conn the ship in the event Captain Sherman was unable to do so from the primary control bridge. As Dickey passed an open hatchway leading out to the flight deck, he saw what looked to be damage from high-altitude bombs. Debris and spray were flying over the deck, and a pall of thick smoke was hanging over the forward part of the flight deck. In fact, he probably witnessed the secondary detonation of ready ammunition and powder among the starboard 1.1-inch guns.

All hands throughout the ship climbed to their feet—just in time to be felled again by yet another violent detonation. The third torpedo had breached in the waves but had plunged on to strike the side of the ship about sixty feet forward of the bridge and quite near the surface. Damage above the waterline, particularly to antiaircraft guns mounted along the starboard catwalks, was considerable.

When everyone in Air Plot had recovered from the triple shock, Mike Kernodle ordered battle lanterns to be lighted and all hands in Air Plot to remain at their stations. Officers, petty officers, and leading seamen throughout the ship did the same. Long months of training took hold; there seemed to be nothing to do but carry on.

No one in the forward starboard 5-inch gun gallery had been hurt when the second torpedo detonated almost directly beneath their feet, but several gunners were overcome by noxious fumes thrown off in the wake of the third torpedo detonation. The gun-group commander, T. D. Wells, ordered the gallery abandoned, and the sickened gunners were carried to the port forward 5-inch gun gallery, where all hands who were able helped dump ready ammunition and powder over the side. Meanwhile, Wells attempted to enter the berthing compartment where most of his gunners were quartered to try to locate members of the gun group who had been off duty. He was driven out by thick smoke.

At the moment the first torpedo struck, about sixty plane handlers, armorers, and mechanics were working on the hangar deck forward of Elevator-2, the midships elevator. Lt Raleigh Kirkpatrick was standing by beside the elevator, which had just gone up to the flight deck after an SBD had been rolled off on the hangar deck. Four refueled fighters were waiting to be rolled on for movement to the flight deck, and fueling of the recently recovered patrol bombers was under way.

The hangar deck was made an instant shambles by the sheer force of the first two torpedo detonations. The second blast was accompanied by a sheet of flames, which seemed to Lieutenant Kirkpatrick to engulf the entire starboard side of the forward half of the enclosed work area. A number of the sailors forward of Kirkpatrick's position had to jump overboard to escape the flames, and at least one aviation metalsmith was blown over the side. Thick, dark smoke instantly permeated the cavernous work area.

Many of the twelve F4Fs, ten SBDs, ten TBFs, and one observation plane on the hangar deck were lifted up and bounced down with such force as to shatter their landing gear. At least two of the four spare Wildcats lashed to the overhead were jarred loose from their bindings and fell on the planes on the deck. The result was an impenetrable mass of aircraft scrap and armaments that could not be moved from the soup of aviation gasoline leaking from the ruptured aircraft fuel tanks.

Lieutenant Kirkpatrick immediately grasped the extremity of the situation and yelled for the men on the hangar deck to trip all the sprinklers and water curtains. But there was no water pressure, and the two men who tried to start the sprinkler were trapped by the flames. (They saved themselves only by taking a circuitous and arduous path to the rear of the ship.) Kirkpatrick next found ChMach Elmo Runyan, who had just returned from the flight deck after doing all he could to secure the gasoline fuel lines. Kirkpatrick asked Runyan to go below to open the main sprinkler valve by hand, but Runyan was unable to get forward to the valve junction because of the spreading fire on the second deck. He did reach a set of valves on the port side of the second deck, but activating these brought forth no water.

LCdr J. T. Workman was on the flight deck beside Elevator-2 overseeing the respotting of the ready fighters when the first torpedo struck without warning. The flight deck in front of Workman buckled, and he saw flames shoot up from the starboard side. A second explosion followed within seconds; it was the second torpedo, though Workman thought it was an internal blast. The hatch over Elevator-1, the forward elevator, was blown open, and flames belched out of the elevator shaft. Elevator-2, which was caught at flight-deck level, was severely buckled.

Behind Workman, several of the Wildcats spotted on the flight deck were blown over the side. Others were damaged in place and subsequently jettisoned into the sea.

Even before the effects of the third detonation had dissipated, Captain Sherman ordered the *Wasp* slowed to 10 knots and the rudder put over hard to the left. Next, he backed the ship at full right rudder to get the wind to blow the flames and smoke away from the carrier's undamaged portion as well as to stand clear of the volatile fuel oil that had spilled into the sea from fuel tanks ruptured by the explosions. Though communications were marginal, the engineers responded without difficulty to all the captain's requests. The bulk of the ship's power plant was intact and available.

The ship's damage-control officer, Cdr John Hume, was in Air Plot when the first two torpedoes struck. As soon as he lifted himself from the deck, he was gone, headed for Central Station to orchestrate efforts to save the ship. Before Commander Hume could reach his objective, however, he was informed that it had had to be abandoned.

Eight sailors under Lt(jg) R. D. Taylor were on duty at Central Station at the time of the blasts. It took a few moments for all hands to get untangled and find battle lanterns clipped to the bulkheads, but they soon settled into the earnest workmanlike routine they had trained hard to achieve. Alarms were ringing, but the bank of indicator lights that would have told them where the damage was greatest was out. There was neither AC nor DC power, and a smooth shift to an emergency transformer yielded no results. Central Station was literally in the dark. Worse, the ship had rapidly taken on a 15-degree list, and the vital control center was beginning to take in water and fuel oil through a tear in the forward bulkhead and by way of the trunk leading up through the island.

Realizing that the station was not functioning and in danger of being swamped, Taylor decided to evacuate. He and three sailors made their way up the trunk to the third deck and eventually reached the flight deck, where Taylor reported to Commander Hume, the damage-control officer.

The fifth man to enter the escape trunk from Central Station was driven back by a powerful explosion directly over his head at the level of the third deck. He and the three sailors still remaining in Central Station dogged down all the hatches to adjacent spaces and reported by phone to the bridge. Instructed to leave at their discretion, they were soon forced to move when the compartment began to flood. By the time they left, however, the bubble level in Central Station showed that the ship's list had come back and that she was only 5 degrees down by the bows.

The loss of control from Central Station was not itself catastrophic—there were numerous back-up systems in place—but it would significanty hamper damage-control efforts.

Lt(jg) C. A. Rogers was in the starboard 1.1-inch clipping room when the torpedoes struck. All hands were thrown to the deck, but none was injured. Rogers ran straight to the gun mount through smoke billowing up from below. No one was manning the starboard 1.1-inch guns, so Rogers returned to the clipping room to help break out the nearest fire hose for combatting flames that were about to penetrate from the adjacent hangar deck. Neither the hose nor the clipping room's sprinkler system issued any water, so all hands began throwing ammunition over the side as fast as they could. They had barely gotten started when a huge explosion and ball of flame swept over the entire 1.1-inch mount. Everyone immediately abandoned the area by way of the 20mm catwalk and then struggled toward the stern of the ship, which seemed cooler and safer. Rogers was burned about the face and arms while negotiating the catwalk, and several of his gunners were also hurt, but they all reached the fantail.

Shortly after Rogers's gun crew left the area, LCdr George Knuepfer ordered all the starboard clipping rooms cleared and flooded. Nevertheless, the flooding system was inoperative, and the fire was moving in. All hands were ordered away before the 1.1-inch and 20mm ammunition stowed throughout the vicinity began cooking off.

A fire-induced explosion on the powder hoist for one of the starboard 5-inch guns blew the gun mount right up onto the flight deck and the splinter shield into the water. A sailor who failed to heed a last-instant warning before the blast was killed when a powder case he had cradled in his arms was set off by the blast. At least one other forward powder hoist laden with its explosive cargo was detonated by the encroaching fires.

Below decks, throughout the injured carrier's berthing and working spaces, officers and sailors took stock of the fearful events and resolutely made their way in the dark by the most direct route available to their battle stations or to safety, whichever made more sense. All hands had trained rigorously to get to safety from even the least accessible compartments. But so many of the regular passageways in the forward part of the ship were filled with smoke or blocked by damaged fixtures or fires that sheer luck and perseverance alone often spelled the difference between danger and safety, between life and death.

Officers' country, well forward, rapidly filled with smoke, and that resulted in the suffocation of a number of ship's officers and pilots in their staterooms or in darkened, smoke-filled passageways as they groped their way toward clear air and cool safety.

The forecastle was completely isolated from the rest of the ship by smoke and flame, and the failure of fire mains in the vicinity of the forward detonations made fire control a wishful endeavor. At least one gasoline-filled pipe against the starboard hull was actively spewing burning fuel. Sailors, particularly damage controlmen, in the isolated forecastle area did what they could to mitigate the effects of the blast and fire. Someone tripped the carbon-dioxide system in the volatile paint-storage locker, and all doors and hatchways were closed and dogged to fully compartmentalize that part of the ship (as, indeed, they were throughout the ship).

Lt(jg) J. L. Edwards and his roommate made their way from their stateroom on the third deck through dark, smoke-filled passageways to a ladder leading up to the second deck, which was also filled with smoke. A red glow could be seen up the passageway leading starboard and aft through officers' country. Overhead, Edwards could hear a fellow officer urging men crowded around the foot of the next ladder to safety: "Take it easy; you are all okay." Edwards also heard many voices crying for help, but he saw through the smoke that many of the pleaders were moving under their own power. It was impossible to move aft to the hangar deck, because the only passageway was filled with flames. Fortunately, the lower part of the ladder leading from the first deck up to the 01 Deck—a space located forward of the high hangar deck between the flight deck overhead and the level of the hangar deck—had been lowered from its usual secured position against the overhead. Thus, the passage to the 01 Deck was made with ease. Once on the 01 Deck, which was clear of smoke, Edwards found about 150 sailors milling about in confusion, for the flight deck overhead appeared to be on fire. There was really only one way to go, and that was forward, into the isolated forecastle. There, Edwards and other refugees from berthing spaces below were joined by numerous gunners who were forced to retreat in the face of spreading flames and exploding ammunition in the starboard gun galleries.

By then, fires were raging virtually out of control in many below-decks spaces along the starboard side of the ship. Many men were simply consumed in leapfrogging flash fires, while others succumbed to smoke and a variety of chemicals as they groped along escape routes that were often cut off by the effects of the torpedo detonations and numerous secondary blasts. For example, the four sailors who had been left behind in Central Station managed to escape through a fire-control tube to the forward mess compartment, but only one man from the post office, one deck up but otherwise adjacent to Central Station, survived the detonation of what was probably the third torpedo.

The torpedoes had struck the carrier while she was most vulnerable. Returning patrol planes were on the hangar deck being refueled. Thus, highly volatile aviation gasoline was flowing freely through a maze of pipes throughout the vicinity of all three torpedo hits. Nothing else could have been as catastrophic.

It appears that the first torpedo ruptured an important and quite large set of gasoline lines at the level of the second deck. The fuel thus leaked down to the third deck. The second torpedo, which struck forward of the first, caused at least one direct fire below the second deck, and this fire eventually spread to the leaking fuel. The third torpedo ruptured other fuel lines, possibly including an external fuel line running down the starboard side of the ship well above the waterline.

Nearly everyone who was working or resting below decks at the time of the torpedo hits reported smelling gasoline vapors. The detonation of these volatile vapors caused an extremely violent sympathetic explosion at about 1405, nearly twenty minutes after the third torpedo hit. This blast detonated fuel, torpedoes, and bombs on ready aircraft on the hangar deck, and those blasts certainly ruptured fuel lines passing by on the outside of the hull. The fuel in those lines was instantaneously ignited.

The sympathetic explosion was fatal to the ship.

Cdr John Hume, the damage-control officer, ruefully concluded his damage-control report as follows: "Had water pressure been available, the hangar deck fire might have been controlled, but it is extremely doubtful that the fire below, embracing the gasoline tank area, could have been extinguished."

The *Wasp* was thus doomed more by secondary gasoline fires than she was by the considerable direct structural damage caused by the torpedo detonations against her hull. That structural damage was vast: From Elevator-2 forward, the starboard side of the ship was pretty much open to the sea; the bulkheads between officers' country and the well of Elevator-2 were blown open; two forward auxiliary diesel generators were knocked from their foundations; and the entire forward part of the ship was without lights or power.

Within only a minute of the last torpedo blast, the entire forward end of the hangar deck was a raging inferno, and Lt Raleigh Kirkpatrick and the surviving hangar-deck crew had completely run out of ways to fight the fire. The danger was compounded by thousands of rounds of .30-caliber and .50-caliber machine-gun ammunition that were by then cooking off in the airplanes stowed forward of Elevator-2. Indeed, Kirkpatrick and others were repeatedly struck by tiny fragments of exploding machine-gun rounds, though no one was badly hurt.

Soon, ChMach Elmo Runyan found some active water mains in the after part of the hangar deck, and he oversaw the laying of hoses from the mains to the fire line. A mere dribble of water arrived through these hoses—about enough to help the deck crew keep the conflagration from spreading aft of Elevator-2.

Exploding bombs and airplane fuel tanks added to the carnage and constantly bowled over the hosemen. While Lieutenant Kirkpatrick oversaw the fire fighting, Chief Machinist Runyan saw to running more hoses forward. Spare airplane wings lashed to the overhead began falling, one by one, considerably adding to the danger.

Lt(jg) Joseph Bodell, a damage-control officer who had been stopped by flames on the hangar deck on his way to assess damage in the forward part of the ship, noticed that the paint on bulkheads and the overhead was adding a great deal of fuel to the fire. Surprisingly, the *Wasp* had not joined other ships of the fleet in extensively stripping paint, particularly from areas where volatile materials were stored or used. (The *Enterprise*, for example, undoubtedly had been spared enormous grief when struck by three bombs at Eastern Solomons because paint in such areas had been thoroughly stripped.) Lieutenant (jg) Bodell perceived that burning paint carried the flames into uptakes, where it certainly spread farther out of sight and beyond the reach of any fire-fighting tools. Perhaps fire spreading across painted surfaces and through painted air intakes and ventilators carried the flames to magazines and ammunition hoists, for these certainly could be heard detonating from Bodell's place on the hose line.

The sheer magnitude of the great sympathetic blast caused by the detonation of fuel vapors and leaking fuel felled nearly every fire fighter on the hangar deck. Lieutenant Kirkpatrick was blown through a fire curtain that had been run out to bifurcate the hangar space, and he came to rest fully fifty feet astern of his last position. Miraculously, no one in the area was burned or severely injured.

By then, the feeble hose pressure had been dropping off a little at a time, and the fires seemed to be gaining. About all Kirkpatrick could think of doing was to head for the aft end of the hangar deck to help push undamaged airplanes into the water so they would not add to the creeping inferno. Unfortunately, a great many of the surviving airplanes were entangled with two spare Wildcats that had been jarred from the overhead. The task seemed as impossible as holding back the fire.

LCdr John Shea, who had come down from his battle station at Primary Flight Control to help fight the fires on the hangar deck, was constantly at the closest point to advancing fires despite the continuous detonation of one ruptured aircraft fuel tank or bomb, depth charge, or torpedo after another. He was killed leading one such foray, one of the few fire fighters to succumb to the intense heat and smoke.

The bridge became untenable following the great 1405 secondary explosion, so Captain Sherman made his way aft to Battle-II. He arrived at about 1410, a few minutes ahead of Cdr Mike Kernodle, who had been inspecting the inferno on the hangar deck. Kernodle's report—which indicated that there was no water for fighting the fires on the hangar deck and elsewhere—was so depressing that Captain Sherman told his executive officer, Cdr Fred Dickey, that it was about time to abandon ship. Dickey reluctantly agreed with the pronouncement, and Sherman ordered all engines stopped as a preliminary move to get all the living men safely into the water. Commander Dickey noted at that moment that flames from the hangar deck had burned through the decking of the forward part of the flight deck.

Leaving the exec in charge for a few moments, Captain Sherman climbed to the flag bridge to apprise Admiral Noyes of his decision. The task force commander returned to Battle-II with Sherman, who ordered Dickey to pass "Abandon ship" to all hands.

It was then 1420.

The word quickly spread through the viable portions of the ship. As most of the officers and sailors continued to stand off the fires as best they could, individuals and work teams began staging life rafts or deploying lifelines over the side. The routine had been drilled into all hands during quieter times, so, despite the dislocations of large areas and escape routes closed off by fire or damage and debris, and the loss of a number of key players and control systems, the effort to get as many men as possible off the ship alive was smoothly run.

Lt Ben Semmes, the assistant gunnery officer, who had taken charge in the crowded and isolated forecastle, ordered volunteers to cut life rafts from the overhead and place them on the deck. No one had heard of an order from higher authority to abandon ship, but Semmes realized that he was on his own and would have to act on his own authority. As it happened, his decision to order everyone in the forecastle into the water neatly coincided with Captain Sherman's abandon-ship order. Mattresses were brought to the forecastle from nearby berthing spaces and thrown into the water to provide flotation for the many non-swimmers who had arrived without life belts.

Cdr Theo Ascherfeld, the carrier's engineering officer, was extremely surprised to receive the order to abandon ship. He knew that the *Wasp* was badly hurt, but he was at work deep in her bowels and could not see or hear any of the fire-fighting or damage-control action. Until Ascherfeld secured the engineering plant and made his way topside, he thought the order was a temporary one. He had no idea until then that his ship had suffered mortal injuries.

While Admiral Noyes and Captain Sherman remained at Battle-II to oversee the operation, Commander Dickey toured the ship to see that the matter was settled in the briefest possible time and with the lowest possible additional loss of life.

After delivering his sad damage assessment to the captain, Cdr Mike Kernodle returned to the hangar deck to help fight fires and oversee the movement of the wounded to the safer, cooler fantail. Among the first men Kernodle contacted was Lt Raleigh Kirkpatrick, who had lost all communication with the world outside of his focus on the hangar-deck fires. Kirkpatrick had already seen sailors and officers going over the side from the flight deck, but he had no idea that abandonment had been sanctioned until he heard the news from Kernodle. Kirkpatrick moved among his fire fighters, giving them the word, until he came upon a seaman with badly burned arms. He retrieved some tannic-acid jelly from a nearby compartment and rubbed it into the seaman's burns. Then he ordered the man over the side and followed a few moments later by way of a lifeline from the fantail. Many of the men who survived the ordeal credited Kirkpatrick's stand against the flames at Elevator-2 with preserving viable escape routes and with saving the ship from being consumed even more rapidly than it was.

As relays of fire fighters and volunteers held the flames at bay, large groups moved to the extremities of the ship and formed orderly lines to await the opportunity to go into the water. Not everyone left his station, however. LCdr Laurice Tatum, the ship's dentist, was too busy treating the wounded in the isolated forecastle to heed an order to go to safety. He breathed in too much smoke and passed out. Though Dr. Tatum was dragged to safety and eventually taken from the ship, he succumbed to smoke inhalation.

The ship's gunnery officer, LCdr George Knuepfer, reached the fantail from the flight deck and found quiet, orderly lines of sailors waiting their turn to go over the side. Nearly a dozen of them willingly answered Knuepfer's call for help in moving a pair of undamaged airplanes from the path of the fire. Then he oversaw the rigging of many lines over the side of the ship, for the abandonment was proceeding at far too slow a pace given the rate of the advancing flames. When an insufficiency of life jackets materialized, Knuepfer sent volunteers to the nearby Marine Detachment's living compartment to fetch mattresses and pillows, which were passed out or thrown overboard to swimmers.

Lt Dave McCampbell, a red-hot fighter pilot serving as the *Wasp's* senior landing signal officer, undertook his only approximation of flying during the entire cruise after he had coaxed upwards of 200 other men over the side by means of lifelines. McCampbell escaped from the ship nearly as he had always intended if it came to that; a former Annapolis diving champion, McCampbell had always thought he would show off his technique if this moment ever arrived. Rather, he climbed to the landing signal officer's platform, held his nose, gripped the family jewels, and stepped into space. He joined Raleigh Kirkpatrick and Elmo Runyan, of the hangar-deck fire fighters, as they clung to a plank bobbing in the swell beside the dying ship.

Capt Forrest Sherman saw to the evacuation of all flag and bridge personnel, then left Battle-II to begin a long walk through the viable areas of the ship. He arrived at the after extremity of the flight deck and paused to see the last of the men there and in the after gun galleries go over the side. Then he climbed to the fantail, where he again joined up with Admiral Noyes. Nearby, the ship's chaplain was helping a badly wounded sailor over the side. Cdr John Hume, the ship's first lieutenant, arrived to report that the hangar deck was clear of injured. As the admiral's party swung out onto the lifelines, Captain Sherman put off his departure to walk forward into the huge hangar bay. He found only one man there, Carp Joseph Machinsky, whose enduring contribution to the abandonment had been the orderly movement of buoyant lumber from stowage areas throughout the ship to the men in the water. Machinsky was still singlehandedly collecting lumber and mattresses when the captain arrived and ordered him to leave the ship. Only after Carpenter Machinsky left did Sherman concede the loss of his ship and leave by way of a lifeline from the fantail.

The exec, Cdr Fred Dickey, was the last man off the flight deck; he left the ship at 1556 by means of a lifeline affixed to the starboard catwalk. Mike Kernodle and George Knuepfer lowered themselves from the fantail at 1557, among the very last half-dozen officers and sailors to leave by that route.

Many of the men in the water were threatened—and some were killed—by burning fuel oil that was blazing forward of the island. The ship was drifting, and even the non-burning oil slick presented a number of navigational and health risks to the hundreds of tired and shocked survivors. Everyone who could pulled for the safety of clear seas and five nearby destroyers, which had lowered whaleboats to help pick up the swimmers and tow life rafts.

The work of war continued. Mike Kernodle and George Knuepfer both felt the concussion from a depth charge dropped by a destroyer only 500 yards from the swimmers. The underwater blast squeezed Kernodle's bladder dry and caused him a significant amount of abdominal pain. Knuepfer was merely discomforted. Any number of swimmers might have been severely injured; some no doubt were killed.

Cdr Fred Dickey, the doomed carrier's exec, eventually wound up aboard the destroyer USS *Lansdowne*, where he learned from the destroyer-division commander that orders had been received at 1555 to sink what remained of the *Wasp's* fire-gutted hulk with torpedoes. Dickey and other senior officers who had been brought aboard the *Lansdowne* watched with great emotion as the first torpedo was launched at the *Wasp* from 1,500 yards at 1808. It was set for thirty feet and apparently passed beneath the keel of the ship without detonating.

The second torpedo was set for twenty-five feet and launched at the carrier's starboard beam beside the island. It clearly struck the aiming point, but it did not appear to add to the *Wasp's* starboard list.

The third torpedo, set for twenty feet, was also launched at the starboard beam beside the island. It failed to detonate, leaving observers to speculate that it might have entered a hole in the hull and detonated unobserved.

The fourth torpedo, which was set for fifteen feet, struck true just aft of the island and caused a large explosion. The starboard list increased significantly, but not enough to carry the hulk under.

The *Lansdowne* had just one torpedo left. This was fired at the port beam at a depth of only ten feet. It exploded on the exposed bottom of the ship at about 1915.

By the time the last torpedo struck the *Wasp*, the carrier was engulfed in flames from forecastle to fantail. As the *Lansdowne* passed down the starboard side of the carrier, the hulk's list noticeably increased. Commander Dickey could plainly see that she was going down by the head.

At 2000, September 15, 1942, the USS *Wasp*, America's seventh fleet carrier, completed her long roll to starboard and disappeared beneath the Pacific's waves.

Of the *Wasp's* crew of 2,247 officers and men, 193 were killed outright or succumbed to their wounds. Nearly all of the 366 wounded officers and men were burn cases.

The *Wasp* was struck by only three of the six torpedoes fired by the *I-19*. Two other U.S. Navy warships were also struck by Japanese torpedoes within a matter of minutes. It appears likely certain they also fell victim to the *I-19*.

The first warning the *Hornet's* Task Force 17 had of the tragedy unfolding at the center of its sister task force was a partial voice-radio alarm raised within a minute of the first torpedo impact on the *Wasp*. The destroyer *Lansdowne*, which was then on station several thousand yards off the *Wasp's* starboard quarter, warned in a garbled and barely audible message: "Torpedo headed for [your] formation, course zero-eight-zero."

The *Hornet* was just then routinely coming around to the task force's base course, 280 degrees, when a second partial message reached her from a then-unidentified source: "Torpedo just passed astern of me. Headed for you!" At almost the same moment, the source of the warning, the destroyer USS *Mustin*, a member of the *Hornet* screen, raised emergency flags to her yardarm.

If a torpedo had passed astern of the *Mustin's* position in the screen, it was probably heading for the heart of the *Hornet* formation, which was the *Hornet* herself. As all eyes topside on every ship in Task Force 17 went to the water to try to find telltale torpedo wakes, the *Hornet's* officer-of-the-deck ordered "Hard right rudder!" The great carrier heeled over to starboard.

As the *Hornet* swung through her emergency turn, the battleship *North Carolina's* captain ordered his great warship to follow suit. Emergency power was laid on, and the modern battleship vibrated from stem to stern as her huge propellers bit deeper into the waves. But it looked to be a little too late. As the battleship began to lean into her hard turn, everyone who could see, and everyone who could not, instinctively tensed as the unseen torpedoes bore down on them.

FC3 Larry Resen had been aft on the boat deck when he heard someone shout, "The *Wasp* is on fire!" After the briefest of looks, Resen had instinctively started for his battle station, Sky Control, at a dead run. The quickest way was up the port side, and he was passing the aft dual-5-inch antiaircraft mount when he saw an enormous explosion several thousand yards off the port beam. There was so much smoke at the point of detonation that Resen could not see what had exploded.

The second U.S. warship to be struck by a torpedo was the destroyer USS *O'Brien*, which was holding station on the *Hornet* through the carrier's precipitous turn. At 1352, the *O'Brien's* turn carried her right into the path of one of the three *I-19* torpedoes that had passed the *Wasp*. The destroyer's bows were utterly blown away in the blast. At the same moment, someone saw a second torpedo pass close astern of the *O'Brien*. Given the destroyer's position relative to the *Wasp*, these were probably the two rightmost torpedoes fired by the *I-19*, then traveling at the extremity of their range.

Less than a minute later—the chronometers still showed 1352—FC3 Larry Resen was still heading for his battle station at Sky Control when the last remaining *I-19* torpedo detonated at the extremity of its range right on the battleship's thickly armored port bow just beneath the forward 16-inch turret. Given the *North Carolina's* position relative to the *Wasp*, this must have been the leftmost of the six torpedoes the *I-19* had fired in a standard fanlike spread. If so, it is clear that the battleship unfortunately and inadvertently ran into it while she was following the *Hornet's* precipitous evasion maneuver.

A great column of water and fuel oil boiled up over the main deck and rained down upon the passing superstructure. Dense smoke halted Larry Resen in his path; it was too dark for him to see the side of the ship a foot or two away. The smoke briefly engulfed the control bridge and reached as high as gunnery-control and lookout stations high up in the main mast. Many tons of seawater fell back upon the superstructure and main deck, and one sailor was washed away.

The *North Carolina* completed her turn—and two more in quick succession—matching those of the *Hornet* and the smaller escorts. Indeed, she got up 25 knots of speed and kept station on the U.S. Navy's last fully operational fleet carrier.

The *Hornet* sent off fifteen of her ready SBDs to the base at Espiritu Santo to make room for the twenty-six *Wasp* search and patrol planes aloft at the time of the torpedoing. Ten SBDs reached the island base, but five overshot the mark in hazy weather and ditched at sea, from which all the pilots and radioman-gunners were eventually rescued. One Scouting-71 SBD returning from a patrol ran out of fuel and ditched beside the rescue destroyers attending the *Wasp;* the pilot was severely injured, but he and his gunner were rescued. All the other *Wasp* Air Group aircraft aloft when their ship was torpedoed safely landed aboard the *Hornet.* When noses were counted, it was seen that Scouting-71 was a nearly intact squadron; for practical purposes, it was all that remained of the *Wasp* Air Group, which lost forty-five first-line fighters and light bombers aboard the *Wasp*—a stupendous loss of aircraft in view of the Cactus Air Force's urgent needs.

Next day, eight surviving Fighting-71 F4Fs and seventeen surviving Scouting-71 and Scouting-72 SBDs were launched from the *Hornet* to fly to Espiritu Santo. There the *Wasp* Air Group survivors joined castaways from the *Enterprise* and *Saratoga* air groups. As it turned out, nearly all the marooned carrier aircraft, pilots, and aircrewmen would eventually be sent forward to fly from Guadalcanal. In addition, most of the *Wasp's* surface escorts, a force commanded by RAdm Norman Scott, were dispatched to Espiritu Santo to serve as a vitally needed surface force under the South Pacific Area command. They, too, would soon make an indelible contribution to the campaign to secure Guadalcanal.

The *O'Brien* reported that she was able to make 15 knots despite the loss of her bows, so she was dispatched alone at 1600 to nearby Espiritu Santo for emergency patching. She left there for a trip to the West Coast sometime later but came apart in heavy seas, from which her entire crew was rescued.

The blast on the *North Carolina's* port bow killed five sailors and opened a thirty-two-foot-long by eighteen-foot-high gash twenty feet below the waterline. A flash in the Turret-1 handling room caused the captain to order the forward magazines to be flooded. Nevertheless, the *North Carolina* easily kept station on the *Hornet* throughout the balance of the afternoon. She was dispatched at dusk with two escorting destroyers to Tongatabu. She eventually underwent complete repairs and an upgrading at Pearl Harbor. The *North Carolina's* departure left the *Washington* as the U.S. fleet's only modern fast battleship taking part in the Pacific War.

RAdm Kelly Turner's six heavily escorted transports steamed in circles through the night of September 15. Next day, Turner decided to make good his pledge to deliver the reinforced Marine regiment to Lunga, and he pressed on. The entire Marine regiment, an artillery battalion, and their supports, along with plenty of needed supplies, were uneventfully discharged on the beaches around Lunga Point on September 18.

As Turner was landing the Marines and supplies, the destroyers *Monssen* and *MacDonough*—two Eastern Solomons veterans—became the first U.S. Navy warships to bombard Japanese camps and supply dumps on Guadalcanal from Ironbottom Sound.

The landing was flawless, and Turner was able to leave with the empty transports at sunset—thus making way for that night's run of the Tokyo

Express, as the almost nightly Japanese troop-and-supply-carrying bombardment missions had been dubbed.

Now only the *Hornet* Air Group stood between the might of the Imperial Navy's Combined Fleet and the thin line holding Guadalcanal and nearby South Pacific bastions.

Part II

The October Offensive

Chapter 4

Task Force 61—now really only RAdm George Murray's Task Force 17—pulled in its horns following the loss of the *Wasp*. It had to. If the Japanese mounted a carrier offensive in the South Pacific, only the *Hornet* Air Group would stand between it and the Cactus Air Force.

For their part, the Japanese were strangely reluctant to press their decided advantage in carrier power. The *Shokaku* and the *Zuikaku*—the only Japanese fleet carriers that had started the war at Pearl Harbor and survived Midway—had just been joined on the Combined Fleet roster by two new fleet carriers and a new light carrier. The Japanese material advantage in carrier-based air was staggering, but it was not put to the test.

In mid September, the Guadalcanal Campaign entered a seesaw middle phase. Each side built up its infantry strength on the island, though Japanese mastery of the seas around Guadalcanal assured them of a more rapid build-up than the Americans could then achieve. Air strength rose on both sides but remained, on balance, about the same, even though each side poured in whatever new formations of fighters and bombers it could spare.

The Cactus Air Force fighters continued to dominate the daytime action, however, and that had a hobbling effect upon Japanese operations.

In strategic terms, the Japanese on land and in the air—and at sea—were predisposed toward mounting large operations that were meant to be decisive. This resulted in the episodic commitment to battle of large forces, and that resulted in a series of sorely needed breathing spaces for the hard-pressed U.S. forces.

For their parts, the U.S. ground and air establishments at Guadalcanal could never muster any meaningful strength to sweep the Japanese from the air or the close environs of Henderson Field. So they focused instead on chipping away at the Japanese, at keeping the enemy off balance by undertaking limited land offensives that were within their capabilities.

Once the fresh Marine regiment RAdm Kelly Turner delivered on September 18 had gotten its land legs, the 1st Marine Division was able to raid the strongly held Japanese side of the Matanikau River, which formed the distant western flank of the Lunga Perimeter—more a psychological dividing line than a real barrier. On the far side of the river from the Marine division, the Imperial Army was able over time to bolster the shattered 35th Infantry Brigade with a complete infantry division, the crack 2d "Sendai" Infantry Division, one of the best the Imperial Army had to offer. Moreover, LtGen Harukichi Hyakutake, the Imperial Army's senior commander in the Solomons and New Guinea, showed his increasing interest in winning back Henderson Field by taking steps to personally venture forward to Guadalcanal along with the headquarters of his 17th Army. (Despite this show of interest, Hyakutake's main focus remained on Papua New Guinea. He thus held back from Guadalcanal a second fresh infantry division to which he had access but which he hoped to commit whole to the "temporarily delayed" New Guinea offensive. To Hyakutake, Guadalcanal remained an irksome responsibility imposed upon him by headquarters far above his level.)

General Hyakutake's apparent new-found interest in Guadalcanal morally obliged the Imperial Navy to commit itself to mounting a huge killing blow against Henderson Field as soon as the 17th Army was able to concentrate adequate infantry and artillery on the island. The deal between the two services was struck by a representative of Imperial General

Headquarters seconded to Hyakutake's staff and Adm Isoroku Yamamoto himself.

Marine spoiling attacks in late September and early October unwittingly went a long way toward destabilizing the Japanese timetable for the desired killing blow. The Marines were unable to overwhelm the Japanese, but they killed or wounded many of them and even managed to put several crack Japanese infantry battalions out of commission. A number of spoiling attacks launched by the Sendai Division came a cropper, and that set the planned final blow back even further.

The air fighting over and around Guadalcanal, and extending northwestward as far as the Russell Islands and New Georgia, remained intense but inconclusive. Sometimes the Cactus Air Force was on top, sometimes the Rabaul-based Base Air Force (overseen by the Imperial Navy's Eleventh Air Fleet headquarters) was on top. Each side inflicted losses upon the other. But the impact of those losses was different for the sides.

The Japanese could more easily replace losses in aircraft than in pilots and aircrew. Every Japanese warplane that was severely damaged near Guadalcanal faced a 600-mile flight back to Rabaul or a somewhat shorter flight to one of several crude airstrips recently constructed along the way, but no closer than the southern end of Bougainville Island. If a Japanese warplane had to ditch or crash-land, there was a strong probability that the pilot or aircrew would never return.

On the other hand, the Marine, Navy, and Army Air Forces pilots operating out of Henderson Field and a new grass satellite strip dubbed Fighter-1 were most often close to home if they had to bail out, ditch, or crash-land. Though the scout-bombers frequently patrolled out to distances of 150 miles, a network of friendly islanders overseen by British, Australian, and New Zealand coastwatchers worked throughout the Solomons to provide both an early-warning network and a rescue infrastructure. Thus, the odds very much favored Cactus pilots and aircrewmen who survived bail-outs, crashes, and ditchings. Rescue boats were instantly dispatched from the friendly shore whenever any airplane ditched in Ironbottom Sound or adjacent waters, and a small number of two- or three-place float-observation planes could be sent farther afield to pluck downed aviators from the water or island beaches. As a result, many of the small fraternity of the Cactus

Air Force's top-scoring fighter aces survived multiple ditchings or crash-landings. (On the other hand, numerous pilots were killed or severely injured in the incessant bombings and shellings unleashed against their base.)

The Americans had a hard time making good their materiel losses—in particular, aircraft that had been damaged or destroyed. Had the *Saratoga* and *Enterprise* air groups and part of the *Wasp* Air Group not survived the damage done their departed ships, there is no telling where the Cactus Air Force might have found the minimal, over-worked assets it employed to fend off the Japanese strikes from land, sea, and air. By September 28—when LCdr John Eldridge's Scouting-71, from the *Wasp* Air Group, arrived at Cactus—fully half of the warplanes and aviators operating out of Henderson Field and Fighter-1 were from the Navy carrier air groups, and their number was in the decline because of battle losses, illness, and just plain physical and emotional exhaustion.

The *Hornet* hid out in port at Noumea during the last two weeks of September, and most of her aircraft were dispersed ashore at several airfields in the New Hebrides. The long layover was as much to rest the crew and airmen as to keep the precious carrier from harm. On October 1, VAdm Robert Ghormley, the lackluster South Pacific commander, decided to use the *Hornet* to strike Japanese-occupied advance anchorages in the Shortland Islands. The *Hornet's* sally was to be the first intentionally offensive action by a U.S. carrier since the start of the Solomons Campaign.

The Japanese could not lift the 17th Army to Guadalcanal or support it without amassing sufficient ships in relatively close proximity to the objective. Early on in the campaign, RAdm Raizo Tanaka, the Japanese destroyer-transport chief, had selected the Shortland Islands as his base of operations. Located at the southern cape of Bougainville, the several spacious anchorages in the area were ideal for Tanaka's purposes; they provided several superb harbors for vulnerable tankers, large supply ships, and transports well beyond the range of U.S. land-based bombers.

The Shortlands anchorages were close enough to Guadalcanal for fast troop-carrying warships to make an overnight dash straight down the Slot (New Georgia Sound) to Guadalcanal's Cape Esperance, or even far along the island's northern coast. The arrival of the Japanese warships usually came arrived at the extremity of the Cactus bombers' range at about dusk. If the Cactus searchers were alert, one hurried strike could be mounted. In any case, the Japanese warships could steam the rest of the way in relative safety—though several surprise night attacks were attempted by Cactus bombers with nil results. By dawn, the Japanese vessels would be long gone, far beyond the range of the frustrated Cactus bomber crews. Most nights, the Japanese warships compounded the frustration by hurling destructive 5-inch, 6-inch, and 8-inch high-explosive rounds at the air-base complex or Marine infantry positions.

The only danger Admiral Tanaka's ships faced at the Shortlands anchorages was from U.S. submarines or U.S. carrier air. The submarines were Tanaka's headache, and he had to hold back a number of precious destroyers and employ several tender-based amphibian aircraft units to counter the threat. The carrier air was beyond Tanaka's ability to counter, except at close range with antiaircraft fire, so he left that mission to the Combined Fleet, based at Truk, and components of the Base Air Force based at the nearby Buin airfield.

RAdm George Murray and his superiors up the South Pacific Area chain of command set their sights on the fat targets based at the Shortlands anchorages. The *Hornet* departed from her protracted revictualing at Noumea on the morning of October 2 in the company of four cruisers and six destroyers, and sailed into harm's way by a circuitous route well away from the Japanese submarines and scouts that daily patrolled around Torpedo Junction. The *Hornet* Air Group carrier aircraft—less twelve Bombing-8 SBDs held down by bad weather—rejoined the ship from the island air bases on which they had been dispersed for nearly two weeks. To help make good the loss of Bombing-8 and bolster Fighting-72, the *Hornet* air department placed in commission four spare F4Fs, six spare SBDs, and two spare TBFs.

As soon as she arrived in the Coral Sea after sunset on October 4, the *Hornet* turned northwest in the full of night and steamed swiftly toward the objective. The weather turned foul during the night, but there was nothing to do except keep going and hope that the skies would be clear in the morning. Bad weather the night before a major strike was not, after all, an entirely bad omen for a nation's only operational carrier sailing deep into enemy waters.

But the pre-dawn launch was marred by endless vistas of low clouds and foul air higher up. Cdr Walt Rodee, the *Hornet* Air Group commanding officer, had some second thoughts, but he elected to keep them to himself. LCdr Gus Widhelm, the Scouting-8 commanding officer, gloated a bit, for he had consistently warned against dawn strikes that required pre-dawn launches; the bad weather simply cemented his strongly held beliefs. LCdr Art Cumberledge, the *Hornet's* senior weather forecaster, looked into his crystal ball and told the senior decisionmakers, "Maybe over Bougainville it will be clear." Admiral Murray told the carrier's air officer to launch the strike.

Arrayed in two deck-load strike formations (eighteen SBDs and eight F4Fs in the first wave, and fifteen TBFs—each armed with four 500-pound bombs—and eight F4Fs in the second wave), the entire air group, less a strong combat air patrol, began launching into the unlighted sky at 0430, about ninety minutes before sunrise. The only guideposts the harried pilots had to mark the extremities of the flight deck were the reflections of the airplane exhaust flames off the faces of ship's crewmen watching the launch from the gunnery catwalks. The bombers were loaded to capacity, so they fell rather than flew off the end of the flight deck and had to be manhandled to altitude by the straining pilots, who also had to keep station on the plane ahead.

Lt(jg) Ivan Swope, of Scouting-8, was going through the usual mental and physical exertions when he was transfixed by the unexpected sight of a rapidly oncoming red light, dead ahead. This was the light atop the mainmast of the heavy cruiser USS *Northampton,* which was just then in the process of changing station from the carrier's starboard beam to dead ahead. Swope found the little something extra in his Dauntless's power plant to belly over the obstruction.

Amazingly, there were no accidents during the launch, and only one F4F missed the rendezvous and accidentally joined the combat air patrol over Task Force 17. The second deck-load launch was completed at 0524, after which the *Hornet* and her surface escorts turned southeast at 25 knots. The strikers would be recovered during the withdrawal, a safe plan given the target's proximity to the bomber-choked airfields at Rabaul and the new (but as yet unoccupied) Japanese advance fighter base at Buin in southern Bougainville, just across from the Shortland Islands

Once clear of the *Northampton,* Ivan Swope had to find the receding white light atop the plane ahead, which was piloted by LCdr Gus Widhelm, the Scouting-8 commander. If Swope lost sight of Widhelm's SBD, the first-strike group's formation would come unglued. Swope joined Widhelm without incident, and each succeeding warplane did the same.

The *Hornet* strike groups ran into a giant cloud as they neared Bougainville at 14,000 feet. The only thing to do was forge ahead. Gus Widhelm and Walt Rodee knew that their respective attack formations would naturally spread out in the murk, but they were confident that the strikers would re-form on the far side.

It was not to be.

Gus Widhelm emerged from the murk after flying nearly the entire length of Bougainville. In fact, when he got his bearings, he found that he was nearing Buka Passage—at the far northern end of the island! Worse, only he, Ivan Swope, and his other wingman were in sight; there was no sign of the whole rest of the first-strike formation.

Widhelm turned down Bougainville's east coast and flew directly to Kieta—he thought it was Buin—where he and his two wingmen cratered the local runway with their 1,000-pound centerline bombs and a pair each of small 100-pound wing bombs. They also destroyed several newly constructed buildings with machine-gun fire. Alas, like Buin, this newly built base had not yet been occupied.

Only five SBDs found Tonolei harbor, the first wave's intended target. It took repeated swooping dives for the SBD pilots to find targets for their bombs. Claims were made for hits on a heavy cruiser, a transport, and a cargo ship, but despite the brave display, there apparently were no hits scored by any of the five.

Cdr Walt Rodee, in his unarmed command TBF, was unable to locate any targets in the rotten weather, so he headed home as soon as he found some clear sky. Eight Torpedo-6 TBFs did the same, as did three of the second-strike F4Fs.

The rest of the *Hornet* Air Group groped into the clear singly and in small packets. Seven Torpedo-6 Avengers led by the squadron commander, Lt Iceberg Parker, plus five F4Fs, managed to locate the Buin anchorage in southern Bougainville beneath a 700-foot ceiling. Attacking what they believed to be two light cruisers, four destroyers, a 10,000-ton cargo ship, and a seaplane tender, five of the TBFs, each carrying four bombs, dropped one 500-pound bomb each during four glide-bombing attacks apiece. Claims were made for a hit and a near miss on the cargo ship and a hit on the seaplane tender.

The two remaining TBFs mounted separate attacks against targets in Tonolei harbor. One apparently scored a hit on a cargo ship, but the TBF piloted by newly promoted Lt(jg) Johnny Cresto was attacked by four floatplanes as Cresto lined up on a cargo ship. Two of the attackers—F1M Pete float observation biplanes—broke off after one pass, but two Nakajima A6M2-N Rufe float fighters stayed with Cresto as he fled south. In the end, Cresto's gunners drove off one of the Rufes, and Cresto lost the other in a cloud. Having evaded his pursuers, the plucky Johnny Cresto turned back to Tonolei and executed three bombing runs, which resulted in three near misses against a cargo ship.

While executing a strafing attack against a cruiser and a destroyer at Faisi, five of the eight Fighting-72 F4Fs that had accompanied the first strike wave crossed paths with a number of Petes that were scrambling into the air. The fighter leader, Lt Red Hessel, took a snap shot at one of the Petes, which snap-rolled into the water—Fighting-72's first kill of the war.

In all, the attackers damaged two Imperial Navy destroyers, destroyed one Pete in the air, and seriously damaged five four-engine flying boats.

Incredibly, and thanks in large part to a sodden runway at Buin that prevented the scheduled arrival of land-based Zero fighters, all of the strike aircraft safely returned to the *Hornet,* which used the foul weather to help cover her withdrawal. To further cover Task Force 17's withdrawal, a small strike by eleven Cactus-based SBDs and five TBFs went after the Japanese advance seaplane base at Rekata Bay on Santa Isabel. Bad weather caused the attack force to fragment, and results were negligible, but at least the Rekata Bay float fighters were kept occupied while Task Force 17 pulled out of range.

Japanese long-range patrol bombers were sent to find Task Force 17, and two of them got to within forty-two miles of the *Hornet.* A G4M Betty land-based medium bomber was downed by a full four-plane Fighting-72 Wildcat division at 1204, and another Betty fell to Fighting-72's Lt(jg) Henry Carey at 1249, following a long tail-chase away from the carrier. No other aircraft sightings were made, and the *Hornet* was not directly molested.

Although neither of the downed Bettys got off a sighting report, their failure to return to base from known patrol sectors, plus the Shortlands raid itself, pointed to the presence and the approximate position of an Allied carrier or carriers. The Base Air Force commander, VAdm Nishizo Tsukahara, ordered a strike force to be readied for a search and attack the next day, and a high-speed run to Guadalcanal by a Shortlands-based troop- and supply-laden seaplane carrier was postponed.

Damage to Japanese ships and facilities was minimal. Indeed, the Japanese considered themselves lucky to have been so mildly rebuked for their laxity. Admiral Tanaka wound up being the chief benefactor of the raid when he heeded the warning and dispersed his naval assets over a far wider area of the Northern Solomons. So, while American morale was given a boost by the audacity, if not the results, of the Shortlands raid, the Japanese gained the most by the inexpensive warning it afforded.

In the end, beyond holding back a resupply effort by one day, the rather bold Shortlands raid did nothing to delay the Japanese juggernaut that would push the Lunga garrison to the brink of defeat.

Following the raid, *Hornet* Air Group was brought to full strength by the addition of five former *Wasp* Air Group SBDs and aircrews to its roster, but the momentum gained by the Shortlands raid was dissipated when Admiral Ghormley returned to form and ordered Task Force 17 to patrol between Australia and New Zealand, which might as well have been a million miles from the war in the Solomons.

Beginning with the Shortlands raid by the *Hornet* Air Group, events on both sides of the Solomons battle lines moved rapidly toward the cataclysmic confrontation the Japanese hoped would rid them once and for all of the American interlopers at Guadalcanal. On the night of October 9, LtGen Harukichi Hyakutake landed at Cape Esperance with key members of his

17th Army staff and the bulk of the Sendai Division's artillery group. He immediately proceeded to the north-coast village of Kokumbona to establish his headquarters. As soon as Hyakutake was settled in, he ordered all the senior commanders ashore to his headquarters to plan what he intended to be the deciding land offensive of the Guadalcanal Campaign.

And not just the Guadalcanal Campaign. Before General Hyakutake had left his rear headquarters in Rabaul, he had revealed some new-found sentiments regarding Guadalcanal: "The operation to surround and recapture Guadalcanal will truly decide the fate of the Pacific War." Perhaps Hyakutake meant what he said, but he still planned to launch the decisive land battle without all but a few detachments of the fresh infantry division he was holding back for the resumption of the New Guinea offensive.

On the other side, replacements had been found to assume rear-defense duties from the U.S. Army's New Hebrides–based 164th Infantry Regiment, a National Guard unit that had been among the very first American infantry units to be sent to the South Pacific near the start of the war. Once relieved, the 164th Infantry was packed aboard a convoy of three troop transports guarded by three destroyers and three minelayers. As soon as the soldiers were aboard the ships, the convoy, which was directly commanded by RAdm Kelly Turner, steamed toward Guadalcanal. If successful, the deployment of 164th Infantry would be followed by additional reinforcement efforts built around several more regiments of the U.S. Army's Americal Division and the 2d Marine Division.

Guarding the troop convoy from a distance were separate battle groups built around the *Hornet* (RAdm George Murray) and the battleship *Washington* (RAdm Willis Lee). Closer in was a force of four U.S. Navy cruisers and five destroyers—many of them formerly screening vessels for the *Enterprise, Saratoga,* and *Wasp* task forces. This force, commanded by RAdm Norman Scott, who had formerly commanded the *Wasp* screen, was standing by off Rennell Island on the afternoon of October 11 in the event the Japanese dispatched a surface force to strike Kelly Turner's transports.

In fact, a Japanese surface force was located in the Slot by South Pacific long-range aerial searchers, but it was merely another—albeit quite large—troop-carrying effort bound for the beaches at Cape Esperance. (The transports were carrying seven Imperial Army infantry battalions and heavy weapons that included tanks and long-range, large-caliber artillery pieces.) What the searchers missed was a force of three cruisers and two destroyers that had been dispatched to bombard Henderson Field that night, to cover the landing of the troops, weapons, and supplies.

In the course of a wild, strange meeting engagement off Cape Esperance during the night of October 11–12, Admiral Scott's surface battle force utterly surprised and defeated the Japanese bombardment group. Scott lost one destroyer sunk, one light cruiser severely damaged, and one light cruiser moderately damaged. Against this, the Japanese lost one heavy cruiser and one destroyer sunk, and one destroyer crippled by Scott's warships. The Japanese flagship, a heavy cruiser, was damaged and the Japanese admiral commanding the bombardment force was mortally wounded.

Scott's nocturnal victory—the Battle of Cape Esperance—was considerably enhanced the next morning, October 12, when Cactus searchers found two Japanese destroyers running up the Slot, their decks packed to capacity with sailors they had tarried to rescue from the sunken and crippled warships. The Japanese ships—amounting to three rescue destroyers and one crippled destroyer by the time Cactus-based strikers arrived—were repeatedly bombed and strafed by relays of Cactus fighters and bombers throughout the morning. One of the rescue destroyers was sunk outright, and the cripple was left in sinking condition—later to be abandoned and scuttled with torpedoes.

The Battle of Cape Esperance was the U.S. Navy's first clear-cut victory since Midway. Occurring as it did within sight of Lunga Point, it was an immediate morale lifter for all the American forces ashore—not to mention all the Allied forces afloat throughout the Pacific. For the first time since the humiliating Savo debacle, the Imperial Navy was put on notice that the U.S. Pacific Fleet was willing to engage in surface actions if doing so would help secure the airfield complex at Lunga.

The message was heard and understood by the Japanese. Then it was Japan's turn to win one.

Chapter 5

Tuesday, October 13, dawned bright and clear at Guadalcanal. Marines and sailors on the beaches around Lunga Point saw a pair of fat U.S. Navy fleet transports drop their anchors in Lunga Roads and watched incredulously as battle-equipped men streamed down the cargo nets slung over the transports' sides to waiting landing craft. And they stood stupefied as the boats disgorged those men onto the beach. Reinforcements—the first U.S. Army regiment to be sent to Guadalcanal—had arrived. The long-promised relief of the beleaguered 1st Marine Division seemed to be under way. Once on the beach, the Dakota and Minnesota National Guardsmen of the 164th Infantry Regiment took the inevitable intramural ribbing good-naturedly and marched off to their bivouacks between the beach and Henderson Field.

At just two minutes past noon, twenty-four Rabaul-based Betty medium bombers, with eighteen Zero escorts, dropped in unannounced over Henderson Field. Cactus Air launched all of its forty-two operational Wildcats, which arrived at combat level too late to intercept the bombers. Seven 67th Fighter Squadron P-39s and six P-400s also took off to cover the lower altitudes. Numerous 250-kilogram bombs dropped from 30,000 feet struck both Henderson Field and Fighter-1; both runways were cratered, and the bombs destroyed 5,000 gallons of precious aviation gasoline stored in caches around the air-base complex. The Americans scored only one Zero destroyed and one Betty severely damaged for one Wildcat downed.

Black Tuesday had begun.

A second strike composed of fourteen Bettys and eighteen Zeros arrived over the airfield between 1330 and 1400. Unbelievably, the American fighters were again caught on the ground, still refueling after the earlier raid. Marine Capt Joe Foss, a green division leader serving with a newly arrived fighter squadron, VMF-121, led a dozen Wildcats after the Zeros, but the Bettys plastered both runways, causing only light damage this time. Only one American claimed a victory, and that was Joe Foss, who actually missed the Zero he claimed and whose damaged Wildcat piled up at the end of Fighter-1 at the conclusion of the raid. The two bombing missions were a complete success; both runways were cratered from end to end.

Japanese artillerymen had for days been hauling a newly committed regiment of 15cm howitzers to fresh emplacements west of the Lunga Perimeter. As the day's second air raid flew out of sight to the west, the Japanese gunners manning two of the howitzers registered their artillery pieces on the American enclave with slow, methodical precision. The new hazard, not yet fully grasped, made dead men out of more than one conscientious U.S. Navy Seabee or Marine engineer working in the open around the runways. The 15cm rounds were fired into the Lunga Perimeter until nightfall.

A Japanese surface battle force built around the battleships HIJMS *Haruna* and HIJMS *Kongo* steamed slowly and stealthily into Lunga Roads, undetected by American search aircraft grounded as the result of runway damage. Each dreadnought carried five hundred 14-inch high-capacity bombardment shells, a type never before used against land targets.

The attack began with the *put-putting* of an underpowered fabric spotter floatplane arriving over Lunga Point to drop flares for the battleship gunners. Once the target area had been sufficiently illuminated, the

Kongo's captain ordered his gunnery officer to begin registering the new 14-inch shells. The first salvos walked right up the beach toward a Marine regimental command post. There, numerous Marines and National Guardsmen who were passing through were killed or wounded; others were badly shaken. After several salvos had been fired, the Japanese task force commander ordered his flotilla gunnery officer to resume firing as soon as the moving warships could turn at the end of their firing leg and beat back up the channel off Lunga Point.

Ashore, chaos reigned amid scenes of dreadful carnage. Many men awakened by the massive explosions bolted from their sleeping places to the relative safety of underground shelters. Buildings, huts, and tents were ripped open, spilling their contents onto the quaking earth. Steel splinters, wreckage, and purple-dyed 14-inch baseplates cut through the air to slice holes in trees, tents, trucks, aircraft, and men. Gasoline—more precious fuel—went up in smoky conflagrations of unbearable heat, casting enormous shadows before the exulting Japanese gunners. In the target area, throughout the Lunga Perimeter, terrified men were beset by tens of thousands of terrified rats, which were dislodged from their burrows by the awful shelling and sent scurrying in their multitudes into the shelters and across the backs of cowering Marines, sailors, and soldiers.

A near miss beside the 1st Marine Division command post lifted MajGen Archer Vandegrift, the division commander, from his perch at the end of a bench and unceremoniously dropped him on the damp earth. Another blast injured men around the Marine artillery regiment's command post. Field telephones whose wire survived the pounding brought steady news of irreparable damage and mounting despair throughout the Lunga Perimeter. Two Marine infantry battalions occupying Bloody Ridge—just south of Henderson Field—took the brunt of the "overs" aimed at the main runway but were spared the worst possible fate by the soft, rain-soaked earth, which absorbed most of the killing effects of the huge rounds and smaller shells from accompanying cruisers and destroyers. A direct hit on the tent housing pilots from a newly arrived Marine Dauntless squadron, VMSB-141, killed the squadron commander and executive and flight officers and killed or seriously wounded most of the squadron's other senior pilots.

When the *Kongo* and *Haruna* and their cruiser and destroyer escorts had expended the last of their ammunition at 0230, they stood out of the channel, their wakes ineffectually dogged by four newly arrived American PT-boats. Next, before anyone in the Lunga Perimeter could organize damage-control parties, a chain of Japanese night bombers arrived to make matters worse. A direct hit on the garrison's main radio station prevented word of the disaster from going out until nearly dawn. By that time, forty-one Americans were dead, and dozens of others were wounded, some mortally.

The material damage was staggering. Thirty-two of thirty-seven Marine and Navy SBDs were damaged or destroyed, and all of Torpedo-8's remaining TBFs were put out of commission for the time being. Of all the Cactus warplanes dispersed around the bomber strip, only two new Army Air Forces P-39 and four old P-400 fighter-bombers survived the night intact. The Cactus Air Force's offensive capability was nil, though Fighter-1 had only been lightly shelled and bombed, and most of the American Wildcats had escaped serious damage.

On the morning of October 14, Henderson Field was incapable of supporting any sort of flight operations. Nearly every gallon of aviation gasoline had gone up during the night or was burning off in the light of the new day. Air operations had to be switched to Fighter-1.

Among the men affected by the bombardment were the crews of six 11th Heavy Bombardment Group B-17s. The heavy bombers had struck Japanese transports on October 13 in an unprecedentedly long mission to Buka Passage, north of Bougainville, and had been obliged to stop off at Guadalcanal to refuel. The bombers had been kept aloft by the October 13 noon bombing, then grounded by Marine BriGen Roy Geiger, the Cactus Air Force commander, who could not spare the required fuel from his burning stocks. As soon as it was light enough to work, the bomber crews went out onto the main runway to clear a path through the razor-edged shell splinters that littered the area. (As one of the B-17 crew chiefs prepared his airplane for the journey to Espiritu Santo, he boosted a seventeen-pound hunk of shrapnel out of the pilot's seat.) Only four of the six B-17s could be made airworthy during the day—one took off on only three engines—and they barely managed to fly off the abbreviated 2,000-foot patch of steel-mat-covered runway that was optimistically deemed operational. The B-17 group commander reluctantly ordered the destruction of the two grounded B-17s, which were crammed with super-secret devices.

With no fuel, there would be no defense. Someone remembered that small caches of aviation gasoline had been hidden here and there around the Lunga Perimeter weeks earlier. A search was given top priority and, as the day lengthened, the small horde was painstakingly assembled. Even the nearly empty tanks of the two derelict B-17s were drained. But it was not nearly enough.

Despite the night's calamities, several Cactus Air Force SBDs were launched at dawn to undertake a routine morning search up the Slot. And two F4Fs took off for the daily dawn patrol.

The morning search up the Slot revealed the whereabouts of the hitherto illusive Japanese convoy charged with delivering seven infantry battalions, tanks, artillery, and supplies to Guadalcanal. When located, the six transports and eight destroyers were only 140 miles from Cape Esperance. News of their presence caused MajGen Archer Vandegrift and BriGen Roy Geiger to deduce that the Japanese were about ready to launch a big push on land—perhaps including an amphibious attack against the Lunga beaches—and that all the attention being paid to Henderson Field by Japanese bombers and heavy artillery was the preliminary event.

Cactus fighters were scrambled at 1003, October 14, on the strength of a coastwatcher report and the return from an erratic radar set. No Japanese aircraft materialized, and one F4F cracked up on landing.

At 1157, twenty-five F4Fs scrambled to intercept a strike composed of twenty-six Bettys and eighteen Zero escorts. As the Wildcats climbed to altitude, nearly every flyable Cactus airplane on Henderson Field and Fighter-1 took off to get out of the way. The F4Fs were unable to reach the Bettys before both runways were severely cratered, and the attack force departed unscathed.

At 1303, a second Japanese attack force composed of twelve Bettys escorted by fifteen Zeros opened their attack against Henderson Field from more than 26,000 feet. Nine VMF-224 F4Fs at high altitude and eight 67th Fighter Squadron P-39s and P-400s lower down were on hand to intercept the bombers, and the F4Fs did so. On their diving pass through the Japanese formation, the Marines claimed five Bettys and two Zeros (they actually downed three Bettys and mortally injured a fourth). Then, as the remaining bombers split to attack both runways simultaneously from about 23,000 feet, a handful of Fighting-5 Wildcats entered the fray. Too late to influence the outcome of the bombing, the U.S. Navy pilots hit the bombers as they were coming off the target. Four F4F pilots claimed five Bettys, but they only crippled two that were ultimately lost in bad landings. Marine Wildcats at lower altitudes tangled with several Zeros and set a twin-engine reconnaissance plane on fire, but no kills were actually scored, though one Zero and the reconnaissance plane were claimed. One VMF-121 F4F was lost in the battle, and its pilot was killed.

An afternoon search to the north by several repaired Dauntlesses uncovered two separate Japanese ship formations. The first consisted of the six troop-laden transports and eight destroyer-transports already known to be heading for Cape Esperance. But two Imperial Navy cruisers and two destroyers were also coming on fast, undoubtedly to bombard the runways.

As 15cm artillery shells burst in and around their repair shops, Marine groundcrewmen wrestled with the damaged aircraft, cutting parts from the wrecks to assemble flyable bombers and fighters. The first offensive strike of four SBDs and seven P-39s and P-400s went after the transport convoy at 1445 but scored no hits. One of the P-39s was shot down, but its pilot eventually returned to Lunga. A second attack, mounted at 1545 by seven Navy SBDs escorted by several Wildcats, was met by heavy antiaircraft fire over the transports and six short-range Zeros out of Buin. The American dive-bombers came up empty, but the Zeros did not. One SBD and an F4F were shot down, and all three airmen in them were killed. (All six of the Zeros were lost when they ran low on fuel and were intentionally ditched in Rekata Bay.) Finally, a P-400 was lost in a landing accident after dark. For all their work, the Cactus airmen slightly damaged an Imperial Navy destroyer.

The only entry on the plus side of the Cactus Air Force's profit-and-loss statement for October 14 was the arrival of a mixed demi-squadron of eight former *Enterprise* Dauntlesses brought under the command of Lt Ray Davis and designated Bombing-6. This was to be the last contingent of dive-bombers and dive-bomber crews from the three carriers that had been damaged or lost since August 24.

News from elsewhere in the region was dismaying. In addition to the transports and warships the Cactus searchers had located in the Slot, PBY patrol bombers operating under the command of Aircraft, South Pacific (AirSoPac) headquarters had spotted Imperial Navy cruisers and destroyers moving into position from which they could sever the sea lanes between the New Hebrides Islands and Guadalcanal. Even worse, radio intelligence had pinpointed Japanese aircraft carriers and numerous surface warships about 400 miles northeast of Guadalcanal. Given the nature and power of all the sighting reports and radio intelligence, VAdm Robert Ghormley described the situation in a message to Adm Chester Nimitz, the Pacific Fleet commander-in-chief, as "critical."

Following his gloomy dispatch to Nimitz, Ghormley ordered RAdm George Murray's Task Force 17 to race toward Guadalcanal. The carrier task force, which had been refueling northwest of New Caledonia, completed the task at hand and turned toward the objective that evening. It would arrive in range of Guadalcanal on October 15. Also slated to arrive off Guadalcanal on October 15 were the U.S. Navy surface battle forces commanded by RAdm Norman Scott (cruisers and destroyers) and RAdm Willis Lee (cruisers, destroyers, and the battleship *Washington*). Lee and Scott were to unite during the evening and attack whatever Japanese ships they could find in proximity to Guadalcanal.

Although the Cactus fighters had done well against the second air raid of the day, the plight of the Cactus Air Force seemed so desperate that afternoon that General Geiger told his airmen that they would fly to the last, then join ground units to repel the anticipated land or amphibious assaults.

Beginning at 0150, October 15, two Imperial Navy heavy cruisers and two destroyers bombarded the Lunga Perimeter while the Japanese transports and destroyer-transports disembarked Imperial Army infantry and their equipment at Tassafaronga, well to the west of Lunga. During the thirty-minute bombardment, the cruisers alone fired 750 8-inch shells at Henderson Field.

In a way, the Marines at Lunga were happy that they were only bombarded; it had looked for a time as if the Japanese were going to mount an amphibious assault directly against the Lunga Perimeter.

Chapter 6

Dawn on Thursday, October 15, came as a relief. However, in the sunlit waters to the west, and in easy view of Americans at Lunga Point, the six Japanese transports were methodically and unhurriedly disembarking troops and supplies at Tassafaronga.

The first American aircraft aloft were two P-400s, each armed with a pair of 100-pound bombs for their routine dawn patrol. No sooner had the P-400 pilots gotten their wheels up than the Cactus Air operations center announced the arrival in the area of numerous Zeros. Both Army airmen turned inland and followed a line of clouds around toward Cape Esperance, where, Cactus Air said, there were ample targets. The two P-400s bombed and strafed the transports under the guns of several Zeros, but the brave Army pilots were forced to retire for lack of fuel. The results of this tiny strike, and several like it launched by Navy and Marine Wildcats, were negligible.

♦

Enraged by the pounding they had taken, BriGen Roy Geiger's air- and groundcrews worked nontop to drain every drop of fuel from the tanks of wrecked aircraft and gasoline drums for use by the Cactus Air Force's last three undamaged, flyable SBDs. Maj Joe Renner, the 1st Marine Aircraft Wing assistant operations officer, took charge of getting the three SBDs airborne and personally marked many of the obstructions and holes in the runway. When the pilots reported they could not see the path from their cockpits, Renner trotted ahead of the first taxiing bomber, which nevertheless nosed over into a shell crater before even reaching the main runway.

The second dive-bomber lost its undercarriage when it slammed into a shell crater. Unhurt and undaunted, 1stLt Robert Patterson, VMSB-141's senior surviving officer, drove over the field in a jeep with Major Renner, and then climbed into the last airworthy bomber on Guadalcanal. This time he managed to get airborne, only to discover that the hydraulic system had failed, preventing him from raising the landing gear. Nevertheless, Patterson delivered a wheels-down attack against one of the stationary transports—and missed.

Groundcrews pieced together more SBDs from the profusion of spare parts that littered the field and its environs. As the morning wore on, aircraft composed largely of other aircraft rolled off the reassembly lines one by one and took off to deliver solo attacks on the transports down the beach, which were protected at all times by shipboard antiaircraft guns and no fewer than thirty-two long-range Zero fighters. Hits were scored, and two of the ships were set afire and had to be beached amidst the cheers of the shell-shocked gawkers lining the beaches around Lunga Point. But the toll in airmen and aircraft became prohibitive, so General Geiger ordered the bombers grounded until a reasonable number could be collected for a coordinated strike.

Gasoline continued to be found throughout the Lunga Perimeter in forty- and fifty-drum lots, each drum representing an hour's flying time for a Cactus Wildcat. And word from rear area headquarters indicated that several large gasoline barges were being towed up and that several ships were on the way with deck-loads of aviation-gasoline drums.

General Geiger ordered literally everyone to work. He was out for blood.

Those who could fly would fly, those who could not would do what they could; Lt Swede Larsen, whose Torpedo-8 had no aircraft, took his pilots and groundcrewmen out to Bloody Ridge to stand by as infantry. And Geiger's personal PBY was pressed into service to launch a pair of aerial torpedoes against the Japanese transports. The Catalina was severely damaged in an attack more or less coordinated with a strike by seven baled-together Dauntlesses, but one of its torpedoes found a target. 11th Heavy Bombardment Group B-17s flying from Espiritu Santo scored three hits on the Japanese transports for dozens of bombs dropped from high altitude, and SBDs, P-39s, and P-400s caused additional damage at the cost of three Marine aircraft and crews.

With Cactus Air growing stronger by the hour, the Japanese decided to leave before the remaining three transports were sunk or severely damaged. Despite the very best efforts of the American aircrews, a company of medium tanks and nearly 4,000 crack infantrymen and technicians were landed with many tons of supplies.

Only one major air strike was launched by the Base Air Force on October 15, though harassment continued unabated through the day. At 1245, twenty-seven Bettys and nine Zeros were over Henderson Field without a Cactus fighter anywhere in the vicinity. Several fighters did get aloft, but only one Zero was downed, by the pilot of Fighting-5's only operational Wildcat.

The Cactus Air Force's strength changed continually during the course of October 15. Without aircraft to fly, fifteen exhausted Army and Navy fighter pilots and Marine dive-bomber pilots were evacuated by air from Guadalcanal that afternoon. On the other hand, six pilots from a rear-based Marine fighter squadron, VMF-212, ferried up the last six spare SBDs available in the South Pacific Area; these pilots were returned by air to Espiritu Santo to rejoin their fighter squadron, which was to fly to Cactus the next day.

In all on October 15, one Pete and six Zeros were downed over Guadalcanal at a cost of three SBDs, two P-39s, and an F4F. Four American pilots and three aerial gunners were killed.

♦

Farther afield but nonetheless of grave concern to Cactus Air operations was the approach through the early hours of October 15 of a small U.S. Navy resupply convoy composed of two cargo ships, a PT-boat tender, a fleet tug, and two destroyers. The latter three vessels were towing one barge apiece, each carrying 2,000 55-gallon drums of aviation gasoline.

Unfortunately, the Japanese were mounting an all-out search for American carriers in the same waters the convoy was traversing. During the morning, an island-based Japanese reconnaissance seaplane located the American vessels southeast of San Cristobal, and twenty-seven aircraft from the fleet carriers *Zuikaku* and *Shokaku* were quickly launched. Having spotted the seaplane, all but the tug (the USS *Vireo*) and one destroyer (the USS *Meredith)* turned back toward Espiritu Santo.

Harried by an attack mounted at 1050 by two reconnaissance planes, which were beaten off, the *Meredith* and *Vireo* reversed course until, at noon, the *Meredith's* thoroughly rattled skipper cast off his barge and ordered the *Vireo's* crew to abandon ship so he could sink it and the fuel barges to keep them from falling into Japanese hands. By 1215, the tug's crew had fled aboard the *Meredith* and the destroyer was about to fire its first torpedoes. At that moment, Japanese carrier aircraft arrived overhead. The Japanese attacked only the destroyer, which they quickly sank with bombs, bullets, and torpedoes. That left survivors of both American crews in lifeboats and rafts as the *Vireo* and both fuel barges rapidly drifted away from them.

One raft-load of survivors eventually reached the *Vireo*, but these sailors were unable to get the tug under way. The drifting *Vireo* was located by a PBY the next day, but it would be three days before ships could be released from other pressing duties to rescue the survivors. By then, only eighty-eight members of both crews were alive, the rest having succumbed to battle injuries, heat exhaustion, and shark attacks. In all, 185 members of the *Meredith's* crew and 51 members of the *Vireo's* crew perished in this lamentable incident. The *Vireo* and the drifting fuel barges were recovered, and the fuel was towed to Guadalcanal.

At the same time the *Meredith* was attacked by the main body of carrier bombers, two Japanese dive-bombers attacked the remainder of the convoy, which had fled much earlier. One of the supply ships was lightly damaged by near misses and the convoy sailed straight to Espiritu Santo, its cargo of absolutely no use to the hard-pressed men at Lunga.

Following the October 15 daytime action, Henderson Field was hit for the third night in a row, this time by a cruiser force sent down from the main Japanese fleet anchorage at Truk. Nearly 1,500 8-inch shells were fired beginning at 0030, but Fighter-1 and the repair shops were spared serious harm. It was by then obvious that the Japanese did not know the importance of the little grass strip, for they invariably fired at the main runway, Henderson Field.

At dawn on Friday, October 16, BriGen Roy Geiger counted ten SBDs on line with four P-39s and three P-400s, plus a reasonable number of Wildcats. While conferring early that morning with Fighting-5's skipper, LCdr Roy Simpler, Geiger blurted out in frustration, "Roy, I don't believe we have a fucking Navy." Since early September, Simpler had been through the worst of times with Geiger, but he retained his loyalty to his service. "General, if we have a Navy, I know where to find it." Geiger told Simpler to do that little thing, and Simpler climbed into the cockpit of one of Fighting-5's two remaining Wildcats. As soon as he was aloft, he flew southward, across Guadalcanal, and straight out to sea. He had about reached his point of no return when he spotted an American carrier task force, a sight to take the breath away on the best of days. Aircraft had been launched, so Simpler approached with caution, fighting the impulse to declare an emergency so he could land aboard the carrier and partake of a decent meal. But he could not; he flew to his home away from home and landed at Fighter-1. Once assured that a friendly, intact carrier air group was in the area, General Geiger arranged a little retribution.

First, the well-rested *Hornet* Air Group assumed responsibility for protecting the sky over Henderson Field—a relief of the first magnitude. While the bulk of the *Hornet* Air Group protected U.S. holdings on Guadalcanal, Scouting-8 was sent up the Slot to find and sink crippled Japanese warships. When nothing but a huge oil slick was located, LCdr Gus Widhelm led his Dauntlesses across Santa Isabel's central cordillera and threw in a quick strike against the Japanese advance seaplane base at Rekata Bay, a constant source of trouble for the carriers cruising Torpedo Junction as well as for the Lunga garrison.

Lt(jg) Ivan Swope, once again flying on Gus Widhelm's wing, found a Rufe float fighter in his gunsight—one of a dozen lined up on the beach. Swope unleashed a stream of rounds from his two cowl-mounted .50-caliber machine guns and clearly saw his bullets knocking chunks off the wings and fuselage of the Rufe, but no fire developed until Swope was below 300 feet. By that time, Swope was paying more attention to the coconut palms lining the beach than he was to his target. As he pulled out to the left, however, he saw that the Rufe had begun to burn. Before Swope completed his turn, he saw a cache of fuel drums hidden beneath camouflage netting. Concerned that another Dauntless pilot would beat him to the target, Lieutenant (jg) Swope climbed to only 1,000 feet, transmitted his intent to the other pilots, and initiated a low-level glide-bombing attack. His 1,000-pound bomb started a magnificent blaze in the middle of the fuel dump.

The Scouting-8 SBDs departed Rekata Bay without sustaining any damage following a wild ten-minute spree of destruction. They left twelve wrecked Rufes and a beach area marked by the thick black smoke of numerous fuel fires. It was an altogether satisfying catharsis.

Other *Hornet* warplanes mounted a succession of strikes against known Japanese dumps along Guadalcanal's northern coast and Imperial Army troop concentrations wherever they could be found. All returned safely to their ship.

One Marine SBD was lost to ground fire on October 16, and several P-400s all but fell apart from wear. Late that afternoon, the last pilots and aircrewmen of Fighting-5 were ordered to depart Henderson Field aboard Marine transport aircraft with the survivors of a Marine fighter and a Marine scout-bomber squadron, and the staff of the Marine air group that had been running Cactus Air since August 20 was replaced by a fresh Marine air-group staff. LtCol Joe Bauer, the unbelievably aggressive and inspirational VMF-212 commanding officer—his pilots called him "Coach"—was ordered to extend his squadron duties to become the head of the Cactus Air Force's new Fighter Command.

Five Fighting-71 pilots—the last marooned carrier airmen to reach Guadalcanal—arrived from the rear area and were attached to Maj Duke

Davis's almost fresh VMF-121. But the day's most important arrival was the seaplane tender *MacFarland,* a converted four-stack destroyer laden with twelve aerial torpedoes and more than 40,000 gallons of aviation gasoline carried in internal tanks and deck-loaded 55-gallon drums.

By 1745, the first several hundred drums of avgas had been unloaded from the *MacFarland* and dispersed ashore, more drums were being transferred to a tank lighter, additional fuel was being pumped from internal tanks into drums aboard a pontoon barge, and 160 evacuees were boarding the ship from several landing craft. All the activity inevitably attracted the attention of nine Base Air Force D3A Val dive-bombers as they arrived over the area. The Vals, which had been out all day vainly searching for the *Hornet,* were making a last-ditch pass over Lunga while on their way home to the Buin advance airstrip. Each Val was armed with two 60-kilogram bombs, which were useless under most circumstances.

There were many aircraft aloft as the Vals came up from the usually friendly south, so no alert was issued. LCdr Roy Simpler, who had decided to sail south aboard the *MacFarland,* noted the heightened activity over the field and told the ship's captain that he had better get some sea room fast, for Cactus airmen never went aloft for training. Next thing Simpler knew, several Vals were heading right for him.

As the ship cleared the fuel-laden pontoon barge, one 60-kilogram bomb detonated amidships, several more fell harmlessly astern, and one burst on the stern-mounted depth-charge rack. One or more depth charges were detonated, blowing off the *McFarland's* rudder and killing or maiming many crewmen and passengers, including nearly a dozen departing Fighting-5 groundcrewmen. The detonation also set off the 20,000 gallons of aviation gasoline that had been pumped into drums aboard the pontoon barge, and that killed all twelve men aboard the barge. As the rudderless *MacFarland* steered away on her engines, a 20mm gunner on her fantail cleanly shot down a Val, which crashed into the water.

The eight surviving Vals flew straight on from the *MacFarland* to Kukum, a seaside village near Lunga that the Marines used as a port facility. There they shot up whatever came into their sights before turning northwest for Buin.

Joe Bauer, who had knocked down four Zeros in one sortie during a familiarization flight on October 3, was in the traffic circle over Fighter-1. He was the last aloft of twenty VMF-212 pilots who had just flown up from Efate by way of Espiritu Santo for permanent duty at Fighter-1. Bauer went after the Vals alone as soon as he spotted the pillar of smoke from the burning fuel barge, and he caught them as they were recovering from their strafing pass at Kukum. Down they went: one, two, three. Minutes later, Bauer landed at Fighter-1 on the last of his fuel. He had earned a Medal of Honor for this and the four-kill sweep on October 3.

One other Val cracked up on landing, for a total of five lost from the nine engaged. But it was little enough revenge for the immense damage the Vals caused: Half of 40,000 gallons of vitally needed aviation gasoline was lost, twenty-one men were killed, twenty-eight were wounded, and eighteen were missing.

In the wake of the disastrous attack, as landing craft embarked the dead, wounded, and surviving passengers, the *MacFarland* limped out of the channel toward the Tulagi anchorage, steering on her engines. She lost power at 1950 while still eight miles from Tulagi and had to be towed the rest of the way. She was eventually towed up a river channel in nearby Florida Island and repaired over the next several weeks while under a camouflage of jungle greenery. On October 17, a U.S. Navy minesweeper carried out Roy Simpler and the used-up Navy and Marine groundcrewmen who had survived the attack on the *MacFarland.*

The night of October 16–17 passed more quietly than previous nights; most of the Japanese warships in the area were out looking for the *Hornet,* which was retiring from range on express orders from a badly shaken VAdm Bob Ghormley. During the night, Cactus Air learned that the crack Pacific Fleet signal intelligence section had pieced together Japanese plans to launch two massive air strikes the next day.

While on a routine dawn patrol around Cape Esperance in a P-400 fighter-bomber, 1stLt Frank Holmes chanced upon a find of incredible importance. Flying nearly at wave-top height, paralleling the beach, Holmes saw odd reddish shapes, the same color as the ground, humped up beneath the trees along the beach. Mindful that untoward curiosity might warn the

Japanese, Holmes highballed it for Fighter-1 and commandeered a ride to the air-operations center to tell of his find—hundreds of square yards of tarpaulin-covered supplies carried ashore from Japanese transports on October 15. Cactus Air at first thought to call in a B-17 strike, but a pair of American destroyers anchored off Tulagi were ordered across the channel to walk 5-inch shells from the inland side of the dump toward the beach. The ships' guns destroyed an enormous and irreplaceable portion of the goods the Japanese had landed at so much cost.

Nothing had been heard from the Combined Fleet's carrier force in many weeks, despite the fact that five Japanese carriers had sallied from Truk on October 11 to prevent the *Hornet* Air Group from intervening in the October build-up. Though their air groups might have done much to pare down the Cactus Air Force over the better part of a week, the Imperial Navy carriers merely hovered at the periphery of the battle arena, on the lookout for a need to be there, but serving no useful purpose beyond sinking the destroyer *Meredith* and disrupting the flow of aviation gasoline to Lunga on October 15.

Finally, on October 16, following the departure the evening before of Carrier Division 1—the veteran fleet carriers *Shokaku* and *Zuikaku* and the new light carrier *Zuiho*—RAdm Kakuji Kakuta's Carrier Division 2, composed of the new fleet carriers *Junyo* and *Hiyo*, was ordered to lay on a dawn strike on October 17 against U.S. Navy transports reportedly standing off Guadalcanal. The single hit-and-run strike force was to be composed of eighteen B5N Kate light bombers—nine from each carrier—armed with one 800-kilogram "land" bomb apiece. Escort would be provided by nine Zero fighters from each carrier.

Though the two new carriers had only reached Truk from Japan on October 9 and were undertaking their maiden combat sally, both air groups were led and to a large extent manned by veterans of aerial combat earlier in the war. On the other hand, though each of the new fleet carriers weighed in at a respectable 27,000 tons, they were actually converted passenger liners that sported short flight decks and constricted hangar decks. Even in the best of circumstances, neither ship could top 25 knots. Moreover, in contrast to the *Shokaku* and *Zuikaku*, with their seventy-two-plane air groups, the *Junyo* and *Hiyo* each embarked a forty-eight-plane air group. In sum, they were fleet-sized carriers that lacked one-third the offensive power of a standard Imperial Navy fleet carrier, and they were relatively slow to boot.

During the night, as Carrier Division 2 ran south to get within range of Guadalcanal, routine Base Air Force message traffic was being monitored by American listening posts, and the Cactus Air Force was apprised of the Japanese plan to mount the dawn strike. By strange circumstance, however, the American cryptanalysts failed to deduce that the strike was to be launched by a pair of carriers thought still to be in home waters; for all the Americans knew, the strike was to be carried out by light bombers and Zero escorts based at the Buin and Buka advance airstrips in the northern Solomons.

The slow fleet carriers launched the strike force at 0515 from a position about 180 miles north of Henderson Field. Within the hour, twenty-five American Wildcats were scrambled, in time, it was hoped, to gain an altitude advantage. At 0700 the Japanese pilots could see Savo Island from an altitude of about 9,800 feet. Shortly, the leaders of both Kate squadrons decided to attack two U.S. Navy destroyers that were running along the beach, shelling the supply dumps located only a short time earlier by 1stLt Frank Holmes.

The *Hiyo* Kates reached their targets first, at 0727, and all released their bombs without hitting anything. One Kate was destroyed and another was mortally damaged by 5-inch antiaircraft fire. The survivors withdrew.

At 0732, just as the *Junyo* Kates were lining up to attack, eight VMF-121 Wildcats led by Maj Duke Davis swooped on what the Marine pilots took to be land-based Aichi D3A Val dive-bombers. (These Marines had never seen Kates or Vals.) Before any more bombs could be dropped, three of the Kates were sent flaming toward the sea and two were driven off with severe damage (they eventually ditched). The last three Kates dropped their bombs, hitting nothing, and were shot down.

The Zero escorts, slow off the mark, retaliated by downing one Marine F4F, but one of them was struck by American bullets, and its veteran pilot was severely wounded; he eventually ditched at Rekata Bay. The pilot of the downed Wildcat was saved.

The only Japanese carrier strike of the period was a disaster. The *Junyo* Kate squadron was all but destroyed, and the *Hiyo* Kate squadron lost two of nine. The survivors landed aboard their carriers, which withdrew to Truk for revictualing. The Marine fighter pilots never realized they had tangled with carrier-based light bombers, nor even that the bombers were Kates.

Following the dawn strike, three Cactus-based SBDs spotted targets for the destroyers, which, assisted by a succession of Army P-39 and P-400 fighter-bombers and a flight of six 11th Heavy Bombardment Group B-17s up from Espiritu Santo, blasted the dumps to oblivion.

Numerous Japanese destroyers and cruisers managed to reach Guadalcanal unnoticed during the night of October 17–18, but while most unloaded troops and supplies at Cape Esperance and Tassafaronga, only five destroyers fired an ineffectual ten-minute barrage at Fighter-1.

On October 18, the Base Air Force mustered approximately forty-nine Betty medium bombers, thirteen Val dive-bombers, forty-five Zeros, and six reconnaissance aircraft. Many of these were committed to a six-day bomber offensive aimed once again at suckering the Cactus fighters—estimated by the Japanese at being only fifteen-strong—into a hopelessly one-sided battle of annihilation.

The October 18 air action started with a fighter sweep. After topping off their fuel tanks at Buin, nine Rabaul-based Zeros were intercepted over Guadalcanal at 1215. One Wildcat was shot up and forced to ditch. Marine pilots claimed five kills, but only two Zeros were knocked down, and a third ditched off Santa Isabel, where its pilot was eventually captured.

While the main body of Wildcats was dealing with the nine-plane Zero sweep, fifteen Bettys and seven Zero escorts attempted to slip in to attack Henderson Field. These formations were intercepted by four Wildcats, which claimed three Bettys but actually scored none. Nevertheless, the Bettys were obliged to salvo their bombs early—right over the Seabees' bivouac, where seven sailors were killed and eighteen were wounded.

As the bomber formation turned back to the northwest, it was assailed by five VMF-121 Wildcats whose formation was broken up when it flew through the escort Zeros trailing the Bettys. Three Wildcats turned into the Zeros, while the remaining two bored on after the rear section of Bettys. One of the Marines blew up a Betty in midair, but debris damaged his wingman's Wildcat. At the same time, four late-arriving VF-71 pilots hit the bombers. One Betty was badly damaged and had to ditch in the channel, from which two crewmen were rescued. By then, more Wildcats were piling on. Capt Joe Foss, who had already shot down one of the sweep Zeros, flamed the engine on one Betty, which eventually crashed in the Slot. In all, three Bettys and four Zeros were definitely shot down. Cactus losses were one pilot killed and one Wildcat destroyed in a a take-off accident, two Wildcats shot down (both pilots rescued), and several Wildcats damaged.

With plenty of gasoline in stock and on the way, and fresh aircrews in operation or coming up, Cactus Air was clearly resurgent.

On October 19, Marine and Navy Wildcat pilots launched to intercept a morning sweep by Base Air Force Zeros failed to locate the quarry, and one of the Wildcats and its pilot were lost in a crash probably attributable to oxygen starvation at altitude. A second fighter sweep arrived before sixteen Marine Wilcats could gain the altitude advantage. One Wildcat was shot down, though its pilot parachuted safely into the jungle, and a VMF-212 pilot was severely wounded by a 20mm explosive round. No Zeros were shot down, though two were claimed from the latter sweep.

On October 20, the Base Air Force mounted two fighter sweeps followed by a bombing mission. Fifteen short-range Zeros based at Buin led off and were met by only fifteen of twenty-three available Wildcats. (The remaining eight were held back by LtCol Joe Bauer, who wanted to try a new tactic for taking on multiple strikes.) One Zero of five claimed was actually destroyed, and one Marine pilot was shot down and killed.

Meanwhile, Coach Bauer launched the eight remaining Wildcats as a second fighter force reportedly closed on Lunga. One F4F turned back with mechanical problems, but the remaining seven went for twelve fresh Zeros that had bounced the Wildcat division led by VMF-121's Maj Duke Davis. Before the fresh Wildcats could get into the Zero-versus-Wildcat duel, they ran smack into nine Bettys escorted by an additional thirteen Zeros. Claims were typically high on both sides—nine Zeros and three Bettys versus ten F4Fs, but only one Zero was actually downed against the loss of two Wildcats.

The October 21 pattern differed from that of earlier days in that nine Bettys escorted by thirteen Zeros led off, followed in a half-hour by twelve Zeros. Joe Bauer sent seventeen Wildcats aloft barely in time for them to gain an altitude advantage. Three Marines went after the escort, of which one Zero of two claimed was actually shot down against the loss of a veteran F4F ace, Marine Gunner Tex Hamilton, who bailed out wounded and was never recovered. The pilot of the downed Zero was PO1 Toshio Ota, whose thirty-fourth kill was Tex Hamilton. Ota was himself killed by VMF-212's 1stLt Frank Drury. The nine Bettys were not challenged, and their bombs killed nine and wounded forty-four around Fighter-1 before one of the bombers was claimed by Marine antiaircraft gunners.

The follow-on fighter sweep was met by VF-71, VMF-212, and VMO-251 Wildcat pilots. Two Zeros were claimed (but none was actually lost) against the loss of one Marine shot down and killed and one Marine wounded.

When an urgent call went out for reserve F4Fs to be brought up from Espiritu Santo, LCdr Roy Simpler led eleven VF-5 volunteers from Efate to pick up the fighters and fly them to Guadalcanal. On the way, veteran pilot Lt(jg) Will Rouse reported engine trouble and ditched. Rouse was seen climbing into his life raft, but he was never recovered. The eleven remaining Wildcats were delivered in good order, and the VF-5 pilots were back on Efate that evening.

Bad weather over Rabaul held down the Base Air Force on October 22, but twelve carrier-type Vals and twelve short-range land-based Zeros based at Buin made it all the way to Lunga without being spotted by coastwatchers or radar. Nevertheless, there were no apparent targets, and the Japanese aircraft milled around until someone spotted a U.S. Navy destroyer. As the Vals made a beeline for the ship, they were bounced by Marine F4Fs, whose pilots claimed five shootdowns. Five of the Vals completed attacks on the destroyer, but no hits were scored. The Zeros never got in on the action. Of the five Vals claimed, one Val had been shot down on the spot, one was lost with its crew in a crash on an island near New Georgia, and two were badly damaged.

Condition Red sounded at Henderson Field at 1114 on October 23, and twenty-eight F4Fs and four P-39s scrambled to meet the incoming force of twelve short-range Zeros followed by sixteen Bettys escorted by seventeen Zeros. Three of the leading Zeros were knocked down on the spot, and a fourth cracked up, killing the pilot, when it ditched in Rekata Bay. Then the main bomber force was hit for the loss of one Betty and two Zero escorts. One Wildcat was badly damaged and seven others were merely holed.

Despite inflated claims and jubilation on both sides, victory in the week's air battles had gone to the Cactus Air Force. It appeared on the afternoon of October 23 that Henderson Field and Fighter-1 had weathered yet another of the periodic storms that had plagued the Cactus Air Force since late August. But that was not quite the case. The Cactus fighters had done well enough against the Base Air Force fighters and bombers, but the Japanese air effort had been at once a diversionary and supplementary effort. The real danger to the Cactus Air Force, to Henderson Field and Fighter-1, to the entire Lunga Perimeter, and, indeed, to the Allied South Pacific war effort lay much nearer to hand, on the ground, and not in the air.

Chapter 7

Adm Chester Nimitz, the U.S. Pacific Fleet commander-in-chief, had landed at Henderson Field on September 30 as part of a lengthy and ambitious effort to take stock of the forces deployed under his command. The Nimitz trip had begun some weeks earlier with a journey to San Francisco for ultra-high-level consultations with the Chief of Naval Operations, Adm Ernest King, and the Navy officers directing the Pacific War. The conferees detailed a series of sweeping command changes, almost worldwide, aimed at bringing the effort in the Pacific, and particularly in the South Pacific, to some sort of order.

While stopping over at his Pearl Harbor headquarters on September 20, Nimitz hosted Gen Henry "Hap" Arnold, commander-in-chief of the U.S. Army Air Forces. Arnold told Nimitz that he had been greeted in Hawaii by MajGen Delos Emmons, commander of Army aircraft in the Pacific, who was just back from a tour of the South and Southwest Pacific areas, which included a stopover at Noumea to meet with VAdm Bob Ghormley. Emmons had reported that Ghormley spoke and acted as if he thought the defeat of the American force on Guadalcanal was a foregone conclusion. Emmons was not alone in this perception; other senior officers had noticed in their meetings with the area commander that Ghormley had seemed unrelievedly pessimistic about the outcome of the campaign for Guadalcanal.

On September 25, Nimitz departed Pearl Harbor with members of his senior staff. A fortuitous meeting at Canton Island with the departing South Pacific aircraft commander, RAdm John McCain, gave the theater commander a fair understanding of what he might find in Noumea.

A day was gained in crossing the International Date Line, so the admiral's party arrived in Noumea on September 28, east longitude time. And there Nimitz met a tired, depressed Bob Ghormley. Part of the area commander's attitude had been formed, Nimitz guessed, by his remaining cooped up for weeks at a time aboard his command ship, the USS *Argonne*, a condition brought on by the refusal of his French "hosts" to offer more cheerful accommodations ashore. But the physical surroundings were only part of the story. Ghormley seemed mentally burned out by all the trials and tribulations of the past six months.

A top-level conference was convened aboard the *Argonne* in the afternoon, and it ran well into the evening. In attendance, besides Nimitz and Ghormley and members of their staffs, were General Arnold and MajGen Richard Sutherland, Gen Douglas MacArthur's Southwest Pacific Area chief of staff.

The discussion revolved largely around Guadalcanal. Nimitz was surprised to learn that numerous Army Air Forces and combat aircraft had been amassed in the South Pacific but that most were being held in reserve. Arnold was so dismayed that he stated that no additional Army Air Forces aircraft would be deployed in the area until those in reserve had been put to use against the Japanese.

Nimitz wanted to know what Ghormley planned to do with several U.S. Army infantry regiments stationed in the rear; why, he asked, had none yet been transported to Guadalcanal? And he asked several pointed questions about the singular lack of aggressive surface patrolling by Allied naval units in the waters adjacent to Guadalcanal—why the Tokyo Express was allowed to operate there with impunity.

Nimitz was deeply affected by Ghormley's reaction to two urgent messages from Guadalcanal that arrived during the session. In both cases, Ghormley muttered, "My God! What are we going to do about *this?*"

Nimitz spent September 29 touring Noumea, New Caledonia, and Espiritu Santo and speaking at length with RAdm Aubrey Fitch, the new AirSoPac, and MajGen Alexander Patch, whose newly formed Americal Infantry Division was slated to eventually replace Marine units on Guadalcanal.

Then Nimitz flew to Guadalcanal aboard an 11th Heavy Bombardment Group B-17. Following some excitement when the bomber was nearly lost in a storm, the admiral's party arrived at Henderson Field in the midst of a downpour.

Despite the rain, Nimitz insisted upon touring Bloody Ridge, just south of the airfield, and a trip to the hospital, where he spoke to the ill and wounded Marines who filled the tents. Though he saw much that disturbed him, Nimitz also saw how confident the Marines were; nothing he heard warranted the depression he had seen in Noumea.

After a pleasant dinner, Nimitz and MajGen Archer Vandegrift at last found an opportunity to hold a frank private discussion on a wide range of issues. Asked to comment upon what he considered the most important lesson learned thus far on Guadalcanal, Vandegrift referred to the tendency of senior naval officers to place the safety of individual vessels above the outcome of the mission, of the tendency of many commanders to hold back rather than fight through. Vandegrift referred to the need for a new set of naval regulations he knew Nimitz wanted to write: "Leave out all reference that he who runs his ship aground will suffer a fate worse than death. Out here, too many commanders have been too leery about risking their ships."

By the time the meeting broke up, Archer Vandegrift was certain he had found a new and willing ally. The days ahead were to show the accuracy of that surmise.

Despite Admiral Nimitz's very best intentions, it would take time to weed out the faint of heart before truly aggressive actions could take place. The shocking losses at Savo, the sinking of the *Wasp*, and the damage sustained by the *Enterprise* and *Saratoga* militated against truly bold use of what remained of the U.S. Fleet.

The Japanese had also fixed themselves on a relatively conservative course, though their stand was based on a view somewhat different from that taken in the United States. Whereas American admirals were fighting a waiting game and would eventually marshall the assets of an unprecedented fleet expansion, the Japanese never expected to fully replace their shipping losses, and they certainly had no expectation of exceeding them, as would in time their American adversaries.

The result was that both navies were loath to engage in surface actions near Guadalcanal. Rather, each was looking for a larger stroke involving a decisive, massive naval battle in open waters. Small fights off Guadalcanal would gain no strategic advantage for either side, though Nimitz was coming to realize that important tactical considerations could and had to be fulfilled by picking fights with Japanese surface vessels.

Over time, a bizarre modus vivendi had been established. The opposing sides merely worked their schedules out so that Japanese transport destroyers could unload at night, when American aircraft were ineffective, and American transports worked by day, when their own aircraft could cover them.

Almost daily, RAdm Raizo Tanaka's fast Imperial Navy destroyer-transports loitered in the Shortland Islands until the late afternoon, and then steamed the final 200 miles to Guadalcanal's Cape Esperance, where most of the unloading took place. American aircrews might have just enough time before sunset to launch a single strike upon the Japanese ships, which maneuvered erratically as the aircraft approached. Few hits were scored, and few ships were sunk, and all but a few airmen refused to strafe the troop-laden vessels.

While the Japanese destroyer-transports were landing troops and cargo, those that had already unloaded, and their escorts, often ran up to Lunga Point and fired salvoes at the runways and defenses. Nightly, Japanese four-engine flying boats from Rekata Bay dropped parachute flares, as much to disturb the sleep of men on the ground as to light the target area for ships' gunners. The flying boats nearly always dropped a sprinkling of 100-kilogram antipersonnel bombs, again as much to keep men awake as to hurt them.

Each Japanese destroyer-transport was able to comfortably carry at least 150 combat-equipped infantrymen to Guadalcanal, so runs of five or six ships each night were gradually shifting the odds even more in favor of LtGen Harukichi Hyakutake's 17th Army. So successful was the effort that, by early October, the cocky Japanese were landing within ten miles of the Lunga Perimeter. There was little short of night patrols by strong American surface forces that could stem the flow.

Still, while numerous fresh units were being committed to the fight at Guadalcanal, the Imperial Army had yet to view the campaign as being of decisive importance. Many of its high-ranking officers still saw the stalled Papua New Guinea offensive as being the more crucial, a view which precluded for a time their total commitment to a crushing offensive. They allowed Guadalcanal to become a sinkhole; Japanese war might was disappearing on and about Guadalcanal a little at a time.

Japanese strength would increase to 20,000 effectives by mid October. The Marines could field a force of roughly equal size. In September, the arrival of the 7th Marine Regiment from Samoa and the transfer of several Marine infantry battalions from Tulagi had considerably bolstered the Lunga Perimeter's strength, but by the end of September there seemed to be little hope that the U.S. Army would assist and ultimately relieve the 1st Marine Division before the Japanese could mount a major land offensive.

American garrisons far from Guadalcanal had gained little strength since the redeployment of the 7th Marines a month earlier. To make matters worse, while Admiral Nimitz was visiting Lunga, an on-again, off-again occupation of Ndeni in the Santa Cruz Islands was being actively supported by the U.S. Joint Chiefs of Staff. No one seemed inclined to support Archer Vandegrift's view that the diversion of precious combat units and other resources to Ndeni would doom the Lunga Perimeter. As the haggling over the availability of troops continued, and despite assurances from Nimitz, Vandegrift continued to witness an erosion in the effectiveness of the forces already on the island.

More than 800 air and ground personnel who had suffered wounds had been evacuated by early October, perhaps 3 percent overall of the men who had been committed. But another nearly 2,000 had come down with malaria, dengue fever, beri-beri, and other exotic illnesses that impaired their ability to patrol and fight.

MajGen Millard Harmon, the commander of all U.S. Army forces in the

South Pacific, had long been unhappy with the way things were going, and, while he controlled too few troops to provide relief and reinforcement of the Marines just yet, his contacts at the War Department included some of the highest policymakers.

In a letter to Admiral Ghormley, dated October 6, Harmon had vented some of his feelings about what he saw as a declining situation on Guadalcanal. He pointedly asked Ghormley to permanently scrub the Ndeni operation, which had by then been resurrected to employ a Marine regiment still in Samoa and a Marine defense battalion. Harmon questioned the logic of readying troops for the operation when they and many, many others were urgently needed at Lunga. He questioned the value of Ndeni as a base, since the Japanese would undoubtedly bypass it in a move upon Espiritu Santo once Guadalcanal had been won back. And then he hit upon the very essence of the matter—if Guadalcanal could not be held, there was absolutely no need to take Ndeni:

> In the final analysis [plans for taking Ndeni] are not . . . vital to the success of the main offensive operation . . . of maintaining security of South Pacific bases and lines of communication. . . .
>
> It is my personal conviction that the [enemy is] capable of retaking [Guadalcanal and Tulagi] and that [they] will do so in the near future unless [our garrison is] materially strengthened. I further believe that appropriate increase in strength of garrison, rapid improvement of conditions for air operations and increased surface action, if accomplished in time, will make the operation so costly that [the Japanese] will not attempt it. . . .

Archer Vandegrift could not have said it better. Bob Ghormley endorsed Harmon's views, though he retained a fascination for the Ndeni occupation. More to the point, however, Ghormley ordered Harmon to prepare a regiment of fresh infantry—*Army* infantry—for deployment on Guadalcanal, and RAdm Kelly Turner, who had a special fondness for the Ndeni plan, was ordered to transport it to Lunga as soon as possible. There was even a faint promise that more Army units would follow.

The reinforced 164th Infantry arrived at Guadalcanal on October 13, just in time to be hit by the opening salvoes of the Japanese October offensive. The regiment's commitment to Lunga marked progress, but it did nothing to break through the decision-making logjam. This was the underlying problem in the South Pacific, and the only person who could solve it was the Pacific Fleet commander-in-chief, Adm Chester Nimitz.

While the Americans battled over philosophy and vision, the Japanese were rapidly moving toward what they believed would be the decisive confrontation of the Guadalcanal Campaign and, perhaps, the entire Pacific War.

The American combat forces arrayed in the South Pacific Area, though materially weaker than the Japanese, were made stronger in a very real, if non-material, sense by superior intelligence-gathering capabilities. U.S. Naval Intelligence had long since decrypted vital Japanese fleet codes, and the U.S. Pacific war effort had been run largely upon the gleanings of that effort. The Midway battle had been planned by the U.S. Navy almost entirely on the basis of information the Japanese unwittingly but quite literally telegraphed ahead.

The combination of the punishing blows administered against Henderson Field in mid October and decrypted Japanese message traffic pointed to the unmistakable conclusion that the major effort at and around Guadalcanal would begin—and end—on "Y Day," which was thought to be October 21 or 22, 1942.

And the Japanese indeed *planned* to mount and win their three-dimensional—air, land, and naval—offensive on October 21 and 22, 1942, but last-minute operational glitches prevented them from doing so. The offensive was postponed by means of a rolling delay; when all of its many and complex elements were in place, it would be mounted on short notice.

For its part, the U.S. Pacific command was in turmoil caused by Admiral Nimitz's late-September command inspection. As a direct result of Nimitz's stopover at Guadalcanal to meet with Archer Vandegrift, and an overnight stay at Noumea to confer with the overwrought and indecisive Bob Ghormley, Nimitz had decided to replace Ghormley with a more aggressive leader. The decision had been an agonizing one for Nimitz, who thought well of his old friend, Ghormley, but who also realized that Ghormley had burned out under the pressures of his onerous job.

When Admiral Nimitz returned from his tour of the South Pacific, he put the lessons he had learned to good use. It was evident from his own findings, and more so from the naval action off Cape Esperance on October 12 and the massive bombardments of the following days, that the battle for Guadalcanal was approaching the critical stage. Pacific Fleet Intelligence estimated that the 17th Army had achieved front-line strength nearly equal to that of the reinforced 1st Marine Division. A command summary put it succinctly: "It now appears that we are unable to control the sea in the Guadalcanal area. Thus our supply of the positions will only be done at great expense to us. The situation is not hopeless, but it is certainly critical."

Mid October 1942 was a difficult time for the Allies worldwide. In Asia and the Pacific, and not withstanding the American offensive at Guadalcanal and defeats in the Coral Sea and Midway battles, Japan still held the strategic advantage, and with it the possibility that it could fight the war to a draw, if not win it outright. In Russia, the German *Wehrmacht*, terribly mauled in the previous winter's fighting, had undergone a dramatic recovery leading to its overrunning vast territories by the end of September. In North Africa, Axis forces were well entrenched near El Alamein, less than sixty miles from Alexandria. In Europe, Britain remained free but sorely beleaguered, while Germany maintained a firm grip on the Continent. Having concluded that Germany posed the greater threat to their survival, the Allies had made the defeat of the Third Reich their primary obective, with resources in men and materiel to be allocated accordingly. For Nimitz, this meant in practical terms that he would have to make do with what he already had, and with the little he could expect to receive at least until American industry could cope with the demands of supporting a global war.

Nimitz ordered the bomb-damaged *Enterprise* out of drydock and on her way to the South Pacific with her new air group, Carrier Air Group 10. The new fast battleship USS *South Dakota*, which had been damaged when she hit a reef, was also ordered out of Pearl with the *Enterprise*, though like the aircraft carrier's, her repairs were incomplete. The U.S. Army's 25th Infantry Division, on garrison duty on Oahu, was alerted for shipment to the South Pacific. And RAdm William Halsey, an aggressive and knowledgeable carrier commander, was ordered to replace the injured RAdm Leigh Noyes as commander of Task Force 61.

But rushing ships, troops, and senior officers to the South Pacific was, in many ways, cosmetic. A more fundamental change, or series of changes, was needed to get at the root of the problems in that area.

Nimitz called a special meeting at Pearl Harbor on the evening of October 15. It was attended by the small group of staffers that had accompanied him on his South Pacific tour. Most of the men present—all Nimitz intimates—noted that the ordinarily jovial commander-in-chief had an icy cast to his usually merry blue eyes. He was getting down to business.

It was clear, Nimitz noted, that the Japanese were about to open a major land offensive against the Lunga garrison, so he wanted to hear impressions regarding the situation in the South Pacific. He asked if anyone thought VAdm Bob Ghormley was capable of handling the pressure in a way that would inspire his subordinates.

After some discussion, the staff officers were unanimous in their opinion that Ghormley was not cutting it; he had become bogged down in minutiae, and was overwhelmed by pessimism.

Nimitz asked each officer in turn: "Is it time for me to relieve Ghormley?"

The answer from each man: "Yes."

The talk turned to possible replacements. Though Kelly Turner was a junior rear admiral, he seemed an obvious choice. He was a brilliant strategic thinker who had headed the Navy's War Plans division before the war. But his cantankerous and overbearing manner had him at direct odds with the ground commander at Guadalcanal. No, Turner probably needed a more-senior officer to arbitrate his inevitable disputes.

Halsey's name came up. There was an initial positive reaction. He was a fighter, and well respected throughout the U.S. Fleet. It was said that the carrier sailors had cheered aloud the announcement of his imminent return to sea duty following a lengthy illness. Nimitz, however, wondered whether the combative Halsey had the administrative savvy to handle the post.

Unwilling to commit himself either on the question of eventual relief of Ghormley, or on whom he might choose as a replacement, Nimitz adjourned the meeting.

Late that evening, while resting in his private quarters, Nimitz was called to the phone. A staff officer who had not been in on the meeting, and who did not know what had transpired, was calling to ask whether the admiral would grant a brief interview; he represented a small group of staff officers who had an opinion to express. Nimitz invited the man over.

The entire group of staffers arrived to find Nimitz dressed in pajamas and dressing gown, ready for bed, so they came immediately to the point: While Nimitz undoubtedly had feelings for Ghormley as a brother officer and friend, the situation clearly warranted a change. The group recommended that Halsey replace Ghormley.

Without committing himself, Nimitz expressed his appreciation for the group's concern and said that he would give its views every consideration.

The next morning, October 16, Nimitz radioed Adm Ernest King, the chief of naval operations, to ask permission to replace Ghormley with Bill Halsey. Nimitz promptly received a message authorizing him to proceed with the command change.

The impact of Admiral Nimitz's decision to replace Ghormley was nearly instantaneous. Halsey, who was on an inspection tour of the South Pacific preliminary to his assuming command of Task Force 61, was aboard a launch taking him from his seaplane to Ghormley's command ship when a sealed envelope was presented to him by a member of Ghormley's personal staff. The envelope contained a terse message ordering Halsey to immediately relieve Ghormley and assume command of the South Pacific Area and all Allied forces therein. "Jesus Christ and General Jackson," Halsey exclaimed when he had read through the secret dispatch from Nimitz. "This is the hottest potato they ever handed me!"

Halsey and Ghormley were both thunderstruck by what appeared to them to be a precipitous decision on Nimitz's part. Nevertheless, Ghormley appeared to be relieved by the change.

As soon as Halsey established his command in Noumea—a promotion to vice admiral accompanied the assignment—he asked for a briefing by

South Pacific staffers who had been to Guadalcanal. When he learned that not one of Ghormley's men had yet been to the front, his first impulse was to make the trip himself. But he realized that he would need the coming days and weeks to hammer the supporting services into shape, and that the task would require every waking minute until it could be completed. So he did the next best thing to going by inviting Archer Vandegrift to Noumea.

Halsey also sent word back to Hawaii that he wanted an inner circle of trusted aides to be dispatched immediately to Noumea. He needed to replace many among the morally spent Ghormley insiders with men of his own fiery ilk. These personnel changes helped matters in the long run, but they also deprived Task Force 16 and the *Enterprise* of battle-hardened experts just as the carrier was preparing to depart Pearl Harbor to join the *Hornet* in the South Pacific.

For his part, Archer Vandegrift was totally immersed in the reorganization of his defenses and in clearing up the debris of the bombings and shellings of the preceding week. It would be nearly a week, he thought, before he could get away, and only if the situation warranted his departure.

Arriving at Henderson Field on October 21 was Vandegrift's most welcome guest to date, the venerated Commandant of the Marine Corps, LtGen Thomas Holcomb. The PBY carrying Holcomb and MajGen Ralph Mitchell, the director of Marine Corps Aviation, was targeted by a pair of 15cm howitzers whose shells struck the fringes of Fighter-1 as the airplane was landing there. While Vandegrift understandably feared for Holcomb's safety, he was nonetheless thrilled to mark the arrival of the one man to whom he felt he could completely unburden himself. Beginning with a tour of the lines and talks with troop commanders, Vandegrift happily noted that Holcomb, whom he considered the Marine Corps' best tactician, seemed enthused over the troops and their deployment.

Inasmuch as Holcomb was leaving the region next morning via Noumea, Vandegrift decided to avail himself of Bill Halsey's request for a meeting; he would fly to Noumea with the Commandant, who would thus participate in the talks.

The next evening, following a cordial dinner with Kelly Turner aboard the admiral's flagship, Vandegrift went over to the *Argonne* to meet Bill

Halsey. Besides Vandegrift and Halsey, the meeting included General Holcomb, Admiral Turner, MajGen Ralph Mitchell, MajGen Millard Harmon (the Army's South Pacific commander), MajGen Alexander Patch (the Americal Division commander), Halsey's chief of staff, and several key members of the respective staffs. Each man in the room was waiting to see what the others had in store for him.

Halsey began by asking Vandegrift to outline the situation on Guadalcanal. The commanding general did this, stressing the poor physical condition of his troops due to a restricted diet over a period of more than two months. He further stressed the need for material support and added the obvious request for reinforcement and eventual relief. He specifically recommended that General Patch's division be committed in its entirety and added that the bulk of the 2d Marine Division might be sent in (one reinforced regiment having been landed in August).

Generals Harmon and Patch fully concurred with the troop requests, adding that the Americal Division would be ready to move just as soon as it could be relieved of garrison duties. With Harmon's vigorous concurrence, General Holcomb wholeheartedly endorsed every one of Vandegrift's requests.

Halsey patiently listened. When the tall, patrician-looking Marine division commander had completed his presentation, the new area commander lifted his bushy gray eyebrows and asked Vandegrift, "Can you hold?"

"Yes," the reply came, "I can hold. But I have to have more active support than I've been getting."

Halsey nodded. "You go on back there, Vandegrift. I promise to get you everything I have."

A direct result of the conference that evening was the final cancellation of the Ndeni operation, which for months had been a bad dream for Vandegrift, troubling his thoughts with visions of the disaster it might precipitate.

While the higher order of command decisions was being debated aboard the *Argonne*, fighting on Guadalcanal continued to rage. With BriGen Roy Geiger temporarily minding the store at Lunga, American forces on Guadalcanal were facing the most serious threat of the campaign.

Chapter 8

By the time VAdm Bill Halsey sat down with MajGen Archer Vandegrift, more than 5,500 Imperial Army veterans had nearly completed a secret march around the western flank of the Lunga Perimeter. Halsey and Vandegrift knew some sort of major attack was in the cards, but neither of them knew where or when it would come, and there was nothing either man could do to prepare for it that hadn't already been done.

The Japanese commanders in the South Pacific learned by doing. Earlier attacks against the 1st Marine Division bastion in August, September, and early October had failed, chiefly because they had employed enough ground troops and supporting arms in sufficient strength to crack the defenses. For his all-out October offensive, the 17th Army's LtGen Harukichi Hyakutake had opted for an attack against the interior perimeter line, the least defensible ground around the Lunga Perimeter and, once breached, the shortest distance to Henderson Field. In order to bring heavy infantry weapons to bear, Hyakutake dispatched engineers to cut a trail for the assault forces.

It was hoped that the main body of LtGen Masao Maruyama's 2d (Sendai) Infantry Division would be in position to launch a two-regiment assault against Bloody Ridge on the night of October 21, the date Imperial General Headquarters had set for the attack. To support Maruyama's main assault General Hyakutake decided that the Sendai Division's crack but somewhat used-up 4th Infantry Regiment would mount a tank-supported assault against the 1st Marine Division's western flank across the bar of the Matanikau River, both as a diversion and a serious effort in its own right. While the main force would haul some light artillery with it, the coastal force would be supported by 10cm and 15cm artillery based well beyond the range of the 1st Marine Division's 75mm and 105mm howitzers.

General Hyakutake was so confident of success that he withheld an order that would have brought the main body of the 38th (Nagoya) Infantry Division to Guadalcanal. There seemed to be no need for the reinforcements, which the 17th Army commanding general hoped to divert to Papua New Guinea.

The plan for the assault was complete in every detail. In fact, Adm Isoroku Yamamoto's Combined Fleet staff had thoughtfully provided instructions for the surrender ceremony, detailing the precise time and place at which MajGen Archer Vandegrift would relinquish his sword to Hyakutake.

The vanguard of General Maruyama's inland assault force moved out from camps west of Lunga on October 16, several days behind the trailblazing engineers. The main assault force was built around the fresh 16th and 29th Infantry regiments. Elements of the 38th Infantry Division's 230th Infantry Regiment were in reserve.

Despite the best efforts of the Japanese engineers, the going was extremely tough for everyone. Transport was left entirely to the bent backs of soldiers trudging single-file for up to sixteen hours a day along the narrow, winding, undulating jungle path. No cooking fires were permitted, so everyone subsisted on a half-ration of cold rice. When sheer cliffs barred the way, nimble men climbed them to secure ropes for those who followed. Dismantled 70mm infantry battalion guns, mortars, and machine guns were hauled up the steep, slippery hills, and then hand-carried to the next obstacle, an endless process, it seemed. The gooey muck left by each downpour pulled at the feet of the toil-worn infantry, taking their shoes from them, leaving them exhausted and in need of rest every few hundred yards. The nights were chilly, forcing men in rotting clothing to huddle together for warmth. Only the hardiest could keep pace by the third day in the rain forest. Gun after gun had to be abandoned, and so did many of the sick.

The vanguard lost its way, so it did not reach the upper Lunga valley until October 19, a few days behind schedule. General Maruyama decided to postpone the offensive until the night of October 22, but he did not send word of the delay to the Combined Fleet even though liaison officers had been provided for that eventuality.

When it became clear that the main assault could not be launched before the night of October 23, Maruyama sent a message to that effect to MajGen Tadamasu Sumiyoshi, the Sendai Division artillery commander, who had been left in tactical command of the diversionary coastal assault. There was no reply, so it was hoped rather than known that Sumiyoshi had received the vital signal.

The first probe was made on October 20, from the west, near the coast. A Japanese combat patrol accompanied by two medium tanks ventured into view of the Marine infantry holding a new outpost line on the east bank of the Matanikau. As soon as the small Japanese force came within range, a Marine 37mm antitank gun facing the sandspit disabled one tank with a single round. The other tank fled from sight along with the accompanying infantry. The 1st Marine Division headquarters did not quite know what to make of the tanks, but it had been preparing for the worst for some time.

Artillery salvoes struck throughout the Lunga Perimeter during October 21. The shelling became hotter as the day wore on and reached a climax when nine tanks supported by a large infantry force made a dash for the sandspit at the mouth of the Matanikau. When the 37mm guns covering the sandspit disabled one of the tanks, the Japanese once again turned tail.

Twice rebuffed, the Japanese on the coast refrained from mounting probes during October 22, preferring instead to augment the heavy artillery fire with that of their 90mm mortars. This was also the day on which General Maruyama attempted to contact General Sumiyoshi about a further twenty-four-hour delay.

It was quiet through most of October 23, except for the by-then-usual artillery fire from the west. At about 1800, mortars began bombarding the Marine outpost line. The bombardment soon intensified, with most of the shells directed at an 800-yard line along the river and back along the Government Track (coastal road) for several hundred yards. General Sumiyoshi was clearly trying to pin the American troops on the line while preventing reinforcements from using the road. He had not received the news that General Maruyama's inland assault had been postponed.

Shortly, nine light tanks supported by an estimated 600 Japanese infantrymen attempted to cross the Matanikau via the sandbar at its mouth, but twelve hurriedly redeployed 75mm and 105mm howitzer batteries—forty-eight guns in all—managed to pin the infantry west of the river while an outpost line manned by several Marine antitank guns supported by several infantry platoons stalled and then disabled the tanks. By 2200, the gunners were ordered to stand down for lack of targets.

Overall on the evening of October 23, the 1st Marine Division lost twenty-five Marines killed and fourteen injured. Only one of them died on the sandspit. Sumiyoshi had attacked, Maruyama had not, and hundreds of Japanese officers and men had died. For nothing.

October 24 was also a quiet day at Lunga. Marines bolstered the eastern flank, where another night attack was expected, but Maruyama's force finally found itself in position south of Bloody Ridge. The main assault went in at 2200 against a single Marine battalion holding a line it had formerly shared with a battalion transferred to the Matanikau front on October 23. In one of the hottest infantry actions of the Pacific War, in which a green battalion of the 164th Infantry was fed into the hard-pressed Marine line at the height of the action, American infantrymen defeated a Japanese force that outnumbered it two or three to one. Several penetrations were accomplished, but the thin Marine platoons sealed each one and pushed the enemy back. Having lost hundreds of men for no gain whatsoever, the Japanese commanders ordered their assault units to withdraw and regroup for another try the next night.

While Maruyama's force staggered back to regroup south of Bloody Ridge, the Imperial Navy's Base Air Force received orders to mount an all-out offensive with its carefully hoarded and newly arrived bombers and fighters.

Chapter 9

In the Guadalcanal Campaign's rich lore, October 25, 1942, is known as Dugout Sunday. Henderson Field came under steady, heavy long-range artillery fire through the day and, combined with the damage caused over more than a week, the big runway was most often closed down. Fighter-1, less intensely bombarded, had been transformed into a fairly muddy quagmire by the steady rains of the preceding two days.

VMSB-141 SBDs on the routine morning search located three Japanese destroyers only thirty-five miles northwest of Cape Esperance and coming on fast—in broad daylight! But the Cactus Air Force could do little enough to defend the Lunga Perimeter against attacks by the Base Air Force, much less against the oncoming surface warships.

Unable to defend themselves against the long-range artillery salvoes that hit the Lunga Perimeter every ten minutes, many Marines simply sat the day out in their bunkers, waiting for the Japanese to make their next move.

The first Japanese airplane to appear over Lunga was the very first Imperial Army warplane ever to operate in the South Pacific Area, a

Mitsubishi Ki-46 Dinah twin-engine command reconnaissance plane. The crew's mission was to determine the progress of General Maruyama's inland assault. The pilot had been told to expect to see the Rising Sun battle pennant flying over Henderson Field. As the Ki-46 made its first pass in search of victorious friendly troops, it was blown from the sky by unfriendly antiaircraft guns. And every Marine in range cut loose to vent his anger and frustration.

The Japanese were so emboldened by false reports of victory on the ground that the Base Air Force sent down relays of four seven-plane Zero flights that were each to orbit over Lunga for two hours until certain it was safe to land. The first of these special flights was spotted early and tracked by coastwatchers, and so were all the succeeding flights.

In response to the first coastwatcher sighting, and despite treacherously muddy conditions on Fighter-1 that could have caused deadly pile-ups, LtCol Joe Bauer scrambled six VMF-121 Wildcats under Capt Joe Foss to get aloft for an intercept. The F4Fs were slow getting airborne and had thus reached only 1,500 feet when they were bounced by the first flight of Zeros. The fight rose to 6,000 feet, where the Marines claimed three Zeros at the cost of one F4F lost. Actually, two Zeros were downed.

The next flight of Zeros was met by seven VMF-121 Wildcats led by Maj Duke Davis. No one made any claims, and there were no losses.

To meet the third Zero flight, Bauer scrambled six VMF-212 F4Fs led by 1stLt Tex Stout at 1030. One F4F got stuck in the mud and another's engine malfunctioned. The four remaining Wildcat pilots became embroiled in a naval battle between Lunga and Tulagi.

To help stave off naval bombardments from the channel, the Navy had decided to base a squadron of PT-boats at Tulagi. Six of the new boats were towed from Espiritu Santo by the USS *Trever* and USS *Zane*, a pair of World War I–vintage destroyer-minesweepers. The two old ships put into the wharf at Tulagi early on October 25. After untying the PT-boats and offloading two full deck cargos of aviation gasoline drums, Cdr Dwight Agnew, the task-unit commander as well as the *Trever's* skipper, was prevailed upon to carry a Marine surveying team to a potential new airstrip site on Guadalcanal's northern coast, well east of Lunga Point.

The *Trever* was about to sail at nearly 1000, when Commander Agnew was informed by the signal station ashore that three Japanese "cruisers" were standing in toward Lunga Point. Agnew saw that his only route out of the area through the restricted channel would bring the *Trever* and *Zane* close to the Japanese track. But there was no alternative.

Closer inspection revealed that the three "cruisers" were three modern destroyers. This was a small consolation, for two of the Japanese vessels mounted guns that far outranged the 3-inch main guns of the elderly American destroyers.

As the two groups approached to within three miles of one another at 1030, Commander Agnew ordered his helmsman to "chase salvoes" when the Japanese opened fire. This maneuver sent the *Trever* toward the Japanese when they fired short and away from them when they fired over. Though only one of the *Trever's* main guns could bear—and even it could not reach the enemy—Agnew ordered his gunners to commence firing, more to bolster morale than in the hope of drawing blood.

The sparring continued for about ten minutes. The *Zane* lost three killed when she was hit amidships, but the *Trever's* starboard waist gun set off ready ammunition aboard one of the Japanese warships. At this moment, 1040, 1stLt Tex Stout's four VMF-212 Wildcats bounced the Japanese warships, allowing the *Trever* and *Zane* to get clear and head out for Espiritu Santo at full speed.

As the Wildcats withdrew, the Japanese destroyers continued to sail along a curving southerly and southwesterly track. At about 1100, their guns flamed an American yacht-patrol boat as it towed a barge loaded with aviation gasoline toward Kukum.

The USS *Seminole*, a seagoing tug, had been ordered out of Tulagi Harbor earlier in the day, also to deliver a deckload of aviation gasoline drums as well as several 75mm pack howitzers to Kukum. It was a routine mission, similar to two others the *Seminole* had undertaken in the past two days.

Most of the tug's crew was at mess below decks when General Quarters was sounded. Gunners immediately rushed topside to man the *Seminole's* main armament, an antiquated 3.5-inch naval rifle and several .50-caliber machine guns. As the gunners watched three smoke plumes on the horizon growing larger by the minute, the tug's captain ordered his helmsman to steer for the nearest land. With no hope of putting up a serious fight, he did not even order his gunners to commence firing.

Shells from one of the Japanese destroyers set the aviation gasoline on the *Seminole's* deck ablaze and killed one sailor. The exploding fuel drums forced the tug's entire crew to abandon ship.

Emboldened by their string of victories over the U.S. Navy, the Japanese warships swung in toward Lunga Point to have a go at some U.S. Marines. Several 5-inch coast-defense guns manned by 3rd Defense Battalion crews appeared to score several hits. This pleased the American gunners no end, for they were usually on the receiving end in clashes with Japanese warships. The chastened Japanese retired behind a smoke screen.

Meanwhile, the four VMF-212 Wildcats led by 1stLt Tex Stout flew into the landing pattern at Fighter-1, where they were attacked by a fresh eight-plane Zero flight that had just arrived from Rabaul. As the three lead Zeros strafed the landing ground, 1sLt Jack Conger got on the tail of the third one and flamed it. Conger proceeded on up the line as the two survivors turned over the beach. Conger fired at the nearer Zero, which crashed, then went on after the climbing flight leader. The F4F's gun bays came up empty during a head-on pass at 1,500 feet, but Conger decided to hack the Zero up with his propeller ("a crazy thing to do"). This he did, but it cost him his F4F, too, and he had to bail out over the channel. When he landed in the water, he was nearly brained by wreckage from the Zero, but he was picked up by a landing boat and aided the crew in capturing the pilot of a Zero downed by one of his squadronmates.

In the end, the pilots of Tex Stout's VMF-212 division claimed only three of the four Zeros it actually knocked down. Only Jack Conger's Wildcat was lost.

The next Cactus fighter team was launched at 1130, a mixed crew of five VMF-121, VMF-212, and VF-71 Wildcats led by Capt Joe Foss. The quarry was six Zeros flown by veteran pilots that had refueled at Buka after taking off from Rabaul.

The Zeros arrived over Lunga at 1245, looking for friendly ground troops or signs of enemy activity. Foss's fighters were above them, ready to pounce. In a classic dogfight in which the Americans used up most of their ammunition, the Wildcat pilots claimed four Zeros shot down and the Japanese claimed five Wildcats, of which two Zeros were really lost with their veteran pilots and two Wildcats were only slightly damaged.

The biggest single air action of the day over Guadalcanal began with the arrival of sixteen Base Air Force Bettys at about 1400, an appearance that coincided with the arrival of the final relay of Zeros from Rabaul. The Bettys brought their own escort of twelve carrier Zeros now based at Buin.

Rising to meet the mixed force were eleven VMF-121 and VMF-212 Wildcats led by Maj Duke Davis. A wild, wild melee over Henderson Field and its environs produced claims by the Marine fighter pilots that four Bettys and five Zeros had been downed at no cost to themselves. The Japanese had actually lost two Bettys and a Zero, and the leader of the Rabaul-based Zeros crashed his malfunctioning fighter at Gizo Island and was later captured.

The Cactus Air Force's busiest day ever was capped by an attack undertaken by a large element of the fleet carrier *Junyo's* air group—twelve Vals escorted by twelve Zeros. The *Junyo* had launched the strike at 1435 on the express order of Adm Isoroku Yamamoto from a position only 200 miles northeast of Guadalcanal, amidst a huge surface fleet of which the Cactus command had no reliable information.

The strike force arrived at 1550 and met no opposition whatever; the attack came as a complete surprise. The Japanese bombers and fighters strafed Henderson Field at will and then retired unmolested and intact. Their target had been the aircraft boneyard adjacent to the main runway; the strike did no damage whatsoever to the Cactus Air Force.

The day's action had cost the Cactus Air Force two Wildcats destroyed (both pilots safe) and four damaged. These losses and operational wear and tear left Joe Bauer's Cactus Fighter Command with only eight flyable Wildcats.

Of eighty-two Japanese aircraft dispatched to Guadalcanal throughout the day in six tactical formations, one Imperial Army reconnaissance plane, two Bettys, and eleven Zeros were lost to enemy fire and two Zeros were lost operationally.

Dugout Sunday turned out to be the Base Air Force's last best gasp. Rising that morning in the hope of occupying Henderson Field, the Japanese airmen dispatched from Rabaul and elsewhere had experienced as spirited a defense as they had ever encountered, and that caused morale and moral purpose to plummet, not only among the airmen, but among the air commanders. RAdm Sadiyoshi Yamada, the second-ranked air commander at Rabaul, noted ruefully in his official report of the day's action, "Employing positive tactics, the enemy has recently reinforced his fighter strength." This conclusion was not correct, but the fact that it seemed so to Yamada was all the more telling.

In addition to locating the three Imperial Navy destroyers that battled through the channel between Tulgi and Lunga, the morning search by Henderson-based SBDs had located a second force composed of five troop-laden destroyer-transports escorted by the light cruiser HIJMS *Yura*. The first sighting was made at 0830 only 100 miles off Cape Esperance.

At the time of the *Yura* sighting report, the Cactus Air Force had just twelve flyable SBDs left on Henderson Field, which like Fighter-1 was waterlogged. It was not until the noon hour that five of the Dauntlesses, led by Scouting-71's LCdr John Eldridge, could get off the field without being endangered by the various Zero flights being engaged by Cactus F4Fs over Lunga.

At 1305, while the F4Fs based at muddy Fighter-1 fought over Guadalcanal, Eldridge's SBDs found the *Yura* and the five destroyer-transports just thirty miles northeast of Florida Island. There were more targets than SBDs, but Eldridge split his force to attack four of the ships, hoping at the very least to throw the fear of God and the Cactus Air Force into their captains.

John Eldridge, a consummate leader with consummate skills, went first. He dropped his single 1,000-pound bomb from 3,000 feet and scored a direct hit. The *Yura* lost way and began drifting. One of the other Scouting-71 pilots near-missed the destroyer HIJMS *Akizuki*, and a third near-missed the *Yura*, no doubt causing additional structural damage. The SBDs left the *Yura* dead in the water.

Next up, at 1435, three 67th Fighter Squadron P-39 fighter-bombers attacked the *Yura* with light bombs. Two near misses were claimed.

At 1500, Lt Ray Davis, the commanding officer of Bombing-6, led three other SBDs into the attack. Davis near-missed the *Akizuki,* and one of the other SBD pilots near-missed the *Yura* once again. As the attackers flew from sight, the battered cruiser's captain reported to the flotilla commander that the ship was flooding and asked that he be allowed to beach her on nearby Fara Island. Permission was granted, but the *Yura* was out of time.

At 1630, a mixed group of four Scouting-71 SBDs, three P-39s, and three F4Fs, all led by LCdr John Eldridge, located the hapless Japanese flotilla and attacked forthwith. One of the P-39s planted a 500-pound bomb dead on the failing *Yura,* and another bomb near-missed the damaged *Akizuki*.

As Lieutenant Commander Eldridge's SBDs were pulling up through a heavy antiaircraft screen, six 11th Bombardment Group B-17s under Maj Jim Edmundson arrived over the milling warships. Edmundson, who had hit a Japanese destroyer with bombs in mid August, waggled his wings to signal the other pilots to close formation and then ordered his bombardier to open bomb-bay doors and line up on the largest vessel, the *Yura*.

It was 1700 and the light was failing, even at the 13,500-foot altitude at which the B-17s were approaching. Two of the heavy bombers sustained minor damage from the antiaircraft fire, but the lead bombardier in Edmundson's airplane made a perfect run on the target. When he called "Bombs away!" his payload of eight 500-pound bombs left the aircraft at sixty-foot intervals. As the remaining heavy bombers followed suit, two bombs in one of them hung, so a total of forty-six were dropped. The bombers remained on course over the target so photographs could be taken. The antiaircraft fire seemed impenetrable, but the photographer finally said, "Photos taken," and Major Edmundson pulled away. His crewmen, who could see the bombs explode, cheered and yelled over the interphone, congratulating the pilot and bombardier for scoring at least three hits, and possibly as many as six.

It was by then too late for another strike against the *Yura,* but the Japanese ended the matter by removing her crew and torpedoing the hulk off Cape Astrolabe on Santa Isabel. The *Akizuki* had sustained severe damage to her boiler room and her starboard engines were disabled, but she was able to retire under her own power.

The upshot of the death of the *Yura* and the *Akizuki's* rough handling was the postponement of a landing that night by Imperial Army troops that was to have been undertaken from the destroyer-transports under the *Yura's* guns at Koli Point, east of Lunga. Or, as the Eighth Fleet's account of the action out it, "[Adm Gunichi Mikawa, the Eighth Fleet commander] decided to assemble his forces in the rear area until the recapture of the Guadalcanal airfield was definitely reported."

On the southern perimeter that day, the Marine battalion on Bloody Ridge tightened up to the right while the battalion of the 164th Infantry that had joined it in the midst of the previous night's battle took over the Marines' former positions on the left. Once reorganized, they and another battalion of the 164th Infantry that was on line to the east of Bloody Ridge dug in deeper and prepared for a new round of fighting.

The Sendai Division's weaker but no-less-resolute October 25 attack against Bloody Ridge was smashed. Here and there, individuals and small groups of Japanese actually penetrated the American line, but the Marines and Guardsmen held more easily than they had the previous night; the outcome was never in doubt.

Also that night, a second force of Japanese veterans struck a Marine battalion occupying a new and isolated screening position along a ridge between the main western Lunga Perimeter line and the Matanikau River. This battalion was less well prepared than the American battalions on Bloody Ridge, and the ground was more favorable to the attackers than it was to the defenders. The Japanese overran several Marine positions during the initial surprise assault, and it took the efforts of a bravely led ad hoc reaction force to regain the ground, but in the end this attack, like all the others that week, went for nought. Indeed, even if the Japanese assault force had overrun the Marine battalion in its way, it would have had nowhere to go. The attack was ill planned, its objective was unclear, and it just plain failed.

The Imperial Army's October assaults against the Lunga Perimeter had accomplished nothing. In all, ninety Americans died in the ground actions, and another two hundred were injured. To accomplish that, one of the two or three finest infantry divisions in the Imperial Army had been ground to dust and as many as 3,500 Japanese soldiers were left dead, wounded, or missing. Probably, more Imperial Navy participants died aboard the *Yura*, other warships, and in the air over Guadalcanal than Americans died in the week's ground battles.

Against all expectations, October 26 dawned an American dawn at Guadalcanal. That dawn, also, awaited the results of 1942's—and History's—fourth carrier-versus-carrier naval and air confrontation.

Part III

Carrier Operations

Chapter 10

The world's first true aircraft carrier, HMS *Furious*, launched the world's first carrier air strike against German Zeppelin sheds in northern Germany on July 19, 1918.

America's first true aircraft carrier, a converted collier, was recommissioned USS *Langley* on March 20, 1922, and designated CV-1 (*C* for carrier and *V* for heavier-than-air, a common designator for non-gas-filled flying machines). During the six years it took the United States to build two additional carriers, the *Langley* served as the test bed for the development of carrier-based air operations. Most of the techniques employed in launching and recovering carrier aircraft were developed and refined during the *Langley's* watch as the U.S. Navy's only operational flattop.

While the *Langley* pilots and aircrewmen were developing and learning their trade, the U.S. Navy was building two new fleet carriers. Both were converted from the newly built hulls of huge 43,500-ton battlecruisers that were proscribed at the Naval Disarmament Conference held in Washington, D.C., in 1922. The first of the new electric-powered carriers to be launched was the USS *Saratoga* (CV-3), which was commissioned on November 16, 1927. On December 15, the USS *Lexington* (CV-2) joined the United States Fleet. Both of the carriers were powered like the swift battlecruisers they were originally intended to be; both could run at nearly 33 knots (more than double the *Langley's* top speed of 14 knots). Moreover, both of the new carriers were large enough to operate at least seventy-five warplanes from their 900-foot-long, 160-foot-wide steel flight decks, and both were capable of sailing vast distances between refuelings. Both were considered strategic weapons of the first order, and their appearance on the high seas carried the potential for U.S. naval aviation well into the late first half of the twentieth century.

Only two years after the *Lexington* and *Saratoga* joined the United States Fleet, the U.S. Navy authorized construction of a small fourth carrier, the USS *Ranger* (CV-4), which was to be the namesake of a class of inexpensive but numerous new constructions. Though the *Ranger*, which was commissioned in 1934, was the first American carrier to be designed as such from the keel up, her marginal performance (top speed of 29 knots, deficient arresting gear, and elevators between the flight and hangar decks that did not quite fit the bill) forced naval strategists to opt for larger, more expensive carriers that could do the job required of them.

The designers amassed all the information that could be gleaned from the four previous efforts, and in 1932 the Navy requested two new swift, 20,000-ton carriers. Though the original request was turned down by Congress, the 1933 naval appropriations budget contained authorization for two slightly smaller but thoroughly modern fleet carriers.

The new ships, the USS *Yorktown* (CV-5) and the USS *Enterprise* (CV-6), were to be the prototypes for most of the fleet-type aircraft carriers that eventually carried the U.S. Navy through World War II. There were numerous changes made along the way, but the *Yorktown*-class carriers set the pace.

Each of the new carrier decks was constructed of teak or Douglas fir laid over a steel frame (similar to the *Langley's* and *Ranger's*, but unlike the *Lexington's* and *Saratoga's* steel platform flight decks). Both could get up to operational speeds of 32 knots, and both had plenty of built-in underwater anti-torpedo protection. The underwater protection was considered crucial for avoiding and defeating submarine- or air-launched torpedoes, and the high speed would aid in the launch and recovery of airplanes as well as in the avoidance of torpedoes and bombs. Each new carrier had three built-in elevators to speed the stowing and readying of airplanes between the flight and hangar decks. And both were fitted out with numerous antiaircraft weapons—up to 5-inch guns—mounted in gun galleries edging the flight deck. Each of the new carriers was capable of operating approximately seventy-five warplanes.

The *Langley* was downgraded to tender status in 1934, which allowed the United States to replace her within the 135,000-ton allocation provided for fleet carriers under the 1922 arms-control treaties. The lobby that had brought forth the *Ranger* as a precursor of small, inexpensive carriers got another chance. Thus the seventh U.S. carrier, the USS *Wasp* (CV-7), was something of a throwback. She was an improved *Ranger*-type carrier, capable of operating a full seventy-five-plane air group (the standard of the day) as efficiently as her larger sisters. Numerous delays and ongoing upgrades prevented the *Wasp* from joining the United States Fleet until 1940.

The 1922 Washington Naval Disarmament Treaty lapsed at the end of 1936, but the U.S. Congress did not authorize any new carrier constructions until 1938, when a third *Yorktown*-class carrier, the USS *Hornet* (CV-8), was more or less forced upon a Navy that, strangely, desired no new carriers. The *Hornet* was commissioned on the eve of the Pacific War. A much-improved ninth fleet carrier, the USS *Essex* (CV-9), was authorized in 1938, but due to ongoing design changes, she and the rest of her new class would not begin appearing until 1943.

The need for other types of carriers besides standard fleet carriers was seen, but little was done before the outbreak of the Pacific War to get them into service. A number of cruiser hulls were set aside for a makeshift breed of light carriers (CVLs), but none would be operational until 1943. Also, a breed of small auxiliary carriers to be used as aircraft ferries or convoy escorts was authorized, and the first of these, a converted merchant ship renamed the USS *Long Island,* was commissioned in June 1941. Eventually dubbed escort carriers (CVEs), the auxiliary carriers would have been useful on all the war-torn oceans from the first day of the war. Nevertheless, the numerous delays commonly associated with ironing out bugs in a new system and establishing a doctrine resulted in a slow start on new constructions.

Other world powers experimented with aircraft carriers during the interwar years. The Royal Navy, which was the first to employ carrier air power, built just three carriers between the wars but had four modern carriers under construction when war broke out in Europe in 1939. The Germans began building just one carrier, but it was never completed.

The U.S. Navy's only real competitor in the field of carrier-based aerial operations was Japan, a maritime nation whose position in the world depended to a great extent upon the strength of her Imperial Navy. Shackled like the U.S. Navy with the fruits of the 1922 naval disarmament accords, Japan was allotted tonnage in each category of warship at a rate only 60 percent that allotted the United States. Thus, the Japanese concentrated on getting more bang for the ton than did the Americans.

Japan's first true carrier, tiny HIJMS *Hosho*, which weighed in at only 7,470 tons, was commissioned in 1922. Like the *Langley*, she served as the test bed for future constructions and the proving ground for Japanese carrier flight operations.

Japan's next two carriers—HIJMS *Akagi* and HIJMS *Kaga* (commissioned in March 1927 and March 1928, respectively)—were built upon the incomplete hulls of proscribed capital ships, just like the *Lexington* and the *Saratoga*. The *Kaga* weighed in at 38,200 tons, and the *Akagi* displaced 36,500 tons. (The *Lexington* and *Yorktown* were each rated at 36,000 tons.) The Japanese announced, however, that each of the new carriers was rated at 26,900 tons, thus saving the Imperial Navy 21,000 tons in its overall carrier construction allotment.

Neither of the big Japanese carriers had a superstructure, which was a familiar feature of all the American fleet carriers. Both also featured innovative upper and lower flight decks, which allowed for more rapid or simultaneous launch and recovery of airplanes. On the negative side, the two giant Japanese carriers could each operate air groups of only sixty warplanes, as compared to the American standard of seventy-five warplanes per carrier air group. (The *Kaga* and the *Akagi* were both extensively remodeled between 1935 and 1937 to increase their capacities to ninety warplanes each.)

The fourth Japanese carrier, HIJMS *Ryujo*, was completed in 1931. At 10,600 tons, she was rated a "light" carrier (CVL in U.S. naval parlance). She was capable of operating forty-six warplanes.

HIJMS *Soryu* and HIJMS *Hiryu* were authorized at 10,050 tons each when their keels were laid, but they wound up weighing in at 15,900 and 17,300 tons, respectively, when they were launched in December 1937 and July 1939, respectively, long after the expiration of the terms of the 1922 naval disarmament accords.

Following the termination of the naval construction accords, Japan went into the business of building floating gunnery platforms—battleships and large cruisers. She did so pretty much at the expense of new carrier constructions. While geared up to almost manic levels, the Japanese shipbuilding industry was severely limited in its ability to churn out new ships. Rather late in the game, when some spare capacity became available, the Imperial Navy placed orders for a pair of thoroughly modern new carriers. These were HIJMS *Shokaku* and HIJMS *Zuikaku*, both rated at 26,675 tons, about 5,000 tons larger than the American *Yorktown*-class carriers. Each of the new Japanese carriers could steam at 34 knots (versus 32 for the *Yorktown*) and could operate ninety-six warplanes (versus seventy-five for all the American fleet carriers). The *Shokaku* was commissioned on August 8, 1941, and the *Zuikaku* was commissioned on September 25—just months before their air groups participated in the Pearl Harbor attack along with the air groups from the *Kaga*, *Akagi*, *Hiryu*, and *Soryu*.

Smaller Japanese carriers available on December 7, 1941, included the light carriers *Hosho* and *Ryujo* and the escort carrier (CVE) HIJMS *Taiyo*. Light carriers HIJMS *Shoho* and HIJMS *Zuiho* were nearly ready for a wartime role, and two carriers built on passenger-liner hulls, HIJMS *Hiyo* and HIJMS *Junyo*, were also being readied to go to war by late 1942. Though weighing in at 29,000 tons apiece, and thus rated as fleet carriers, the *Hiyo* and *Junyo* would embark air groups each numbering only forty-eight warplanes.

♦

The United States began the war with six operational fleet carriers (not counting the marginal *Ranger)* and one operational auxiliary carrier—plus several hybrid conversions used exclusively for ferry work. Japan opened the war with six fleet carriers, four light carriers, and one escort. The opponents traded the light carrier *Shoho* for the fleet carrier *Lexington* at the Coral Sea on May 7–8, 1942. That trade accrued some additional advantage to the Japanese side in relative numbers of carrier decks, tonnage, and numbers of operational carrier warplanes. Midway more than redressed the imbalance. There, the U.S. Navy lost the *Yorktown*, but Japan lost the fleet carriers *Kaga*, *Akagi*, *Hiryu*, and *Soryu*.

By the end of the first week of June 1942, the U.S. Navy was left with four operational fleet carriers and their air groups, and Japan was left with two fleet carriers, three light carriers, and one escort. Two new Japanese fleet carriers were about to be commissioned, but neither would be fully operational for some months. Similarly, several American light and auxiliary carriers under construction or about to be launched could not be made operational before the end of 1942 or by mid 1943.

Chapter 11

U.S. Navy and Imperial Navy fleet carrier air groups in mid 1942 each were composed of three basic warplane types: light torpedo/horizontal bombers, light scout/dive-bombers, and fighters. The mix of airplanes within a fleet carrier air group reflected the similar—but not identical—offensive and defensive doctrines employed by the two warring powers.

The U.S. Navy's standard fighter of the period was the Grumman F4F-4 Wildcat. First employed at Midway as a replacement for the underpowered four-gun F4F-3 variant, the F4F-4 featured six .50-caliber wing-mounted machine guns, a fairly modern gunsight, improved performance characteristics, and, as important as anything else, folding wings. It had a top speed of 318 miles per hour at 19,400 feet and a combat radius of well under 250 miles, quite a bit less than half the 770-mile maximum range. While the enhanced performance and fighting characteristics improved the chances of individual fighters to triumph and survive in aerial combat, the innovative folding wings allowed the U.S. Navy to pack more

Wildcats aboard the fleet carriers of the day—an extremely significant development. In July 1942, the typical fleet carrier fighter squadron carried thirty-six Wildcats on its roster.

Basically a defensive weapon—an interceptor—the carrier-based Wildcat was marginally designed to accompany carrier-launched bombers to their targets in order to fend off enemy fighters. The real function of the carrier-based F4F was to patrol above friendly carriers and other ships in order to fend off enemy bombers and fighters. A distinctly tertiary role—after bomber escort—was the provision of ground strafing during hit-and-run raids of the type that had characterized U.S. Navy carrier operations very early in the war. And there was an as-yet-nascent role in the field of support for forces ashore.

The Wildcat fighter was a mixed blessing, but the full extent of the mixture was still not completely known, even after the type had weathered a fair number of fighter-versus-fighter engagements during its second carrier battle, at Midway in June 1942. The Wildcat's strength and weaknesses were not adequately understood until large numbers of the type had taken part in the defense of the American carriers during the August 24 Battle of the Eastern Solomons or, even more so, until Wildcats were engaged in protracted defensive operations over Henderson Field between late August and mid October 1942.

There was an initially unperceived weakness arising from the placement of oil coolers in either wing. As were all U.S. Navy aircraft throughout World War II, the Wildcat was powered by an air-cooled radial engine, but oil was vitally important as a lubricant, and so oil coolers were vital, too. There was no place to put them except in the wings, but the wings were big targets in an aerial engagement, and so the coolers were vulnerable. If one was shot full of holes, the engine would eventually seize for lack of oil. Another mixed blessing was the F4F-4's six wing guns. The four guns in the F4F-3 had not had sufficient killing power, whereas the six guns in the F4F-4 certainly did. But the added weight and space requirements of the two extra guns meant that each gun was armed with fewer bullets, which translated to less time that the guns could be fired, which of course influenced the airplane's overall killing power. On balance, six guns with fewer bullets were probably better than four guns that could fire longer, but it was a very close call.

On the other hand, every Wildcat in the U.S. Navy inventory had a reasonably modern two-way radio. This was a tremendous boon, for individual fighters could be precisely controlled from afar, and fighter pilots could warn one another about impending danger. Also, the Wildcat could absorb a terrific beating. Some performance was sacrificed to the likes of radios, self-sealing fuel tanks, and heavy armor plate behind the pilot's seat, but all these things added appreciably to the overall effectiveness of the fighter and the survival capability of the pilot, so the sacrifices in performance were seen as trade-offs that by far favored the Wildcat's overall ability to fight and survive.

The U.S. Navy's standard scout/dive-bomber of the day was the Douglas SBD-3 Dauntless. Earlier versions had entered active service with the U.S. Marine Corps in mid 1940 and become operational aboard U.S. Navy carriers in March 1941. The SBD-3 had a top speed of only 250 miles per hour (actually quite speedy for a dive-bomber of the day), and its combat radius, when fully loaded, was 300 miles; but it boasted a substantial search range—up to 1,750 miles under ideal conditions. Its payload was usually a 500-pound bomb or 325-pound depth charge on patrol, and a 1,000-pound bomb on a strike mission. The extremely maneuverable SBD-3 was well adapted to defending itself with two forward-firing, cowl-mounted .50-caliber machine guns fired by the pilot and two .30-caliber machine guns mounted on a free-moving ("flexible") frame fired by the rear-facing radioman-gunner.

Designed as an offensive dive-bomber and a long-range scout, the SBD was also typically employed close to a friendly carrier deck for antisubmarine defense or, in extreme cases, as a last line of defense against low-flying torpedo bombers. The SBD was a fine airplane and loved by its pilots and aircrewmen because of its sheer survivability in aerial combat.

The third and newest U.S. carrier plane was the Grumman TBF-1 Avenger torpedo bomber. The Avenger was just coming into operational service in early June 1942, so only a handful appeared at Midway, and they had all been land-based. By far the largest carrier-based airplane type of mid 1942 and, indeed, of the Pacific War, the TBF was sturdy and long-ranged. The first carrier pilots to fly the Avenger operationally appreciated it for its ability to get into the air fully loaded long before running out of flight deck. The crew of three had adequate, if not ample, defensive firepower; the pilot could fire one cowl-mounted .30-caliber machine gun through the propeller disc, the radioman could fire a single power-turret-mounted .50-caliber machine gun, and the bombardier could fire a single tunnel-mounted .30-caliber stinger across the lower rear quadrant.

Used offensively, the Avenger could carry one aerial torpedo or up to four 500-pound bombs in the first internal bomb bay featured by any carrier bomber in the world. The TBF was also designed to fill in as a long-range scout and was often employed in tandem with SBDs. The TBF's only reasonable defensive role was on patrol against submarines, in which case it could carry up to four 500-pound aerial depth charges.

The Japanese fleet fighter of the day was the Mitsubishi A6M2 Model 21 Zero. This fast but very small and lightly built long-range airplane was, in its early career, simply the finest fighter available to any of the world's military powers. Its edge was its extreme maneuverability and exceptionally high rate of climb. Simply stated, in a one-on-one fight anytime in 1942, a well-flown Zero could almost always get away from nearly any adversary.

The Zero was armed with a pair of wing-mounted 20mm cannon and a pair of cowl-mounted 7.7mm machine guns. The two sets of guns could be fired separately or together. Usually, the 20mm cannon were used sparingly because of limitations in the number of 20mm rounds that could be carried (sixty) and because of the weapon's relatively low rate of fire and low muzzle velocity. The 7.7mm machine guns were used at longer ranges, mainly to get on target, whereas the 20mm cannon were usually used only for killing blows. In general, the carrier-based Zeros were used the same way as their American counterparts, for escorting bombers and to defend friendly warships under attack by enemy aircraft. But the Zero was longer ranged than the Wildcat, so it almost always accompanied carrier-launched bombers, while the Wildcat did so far less frequently.

Many Imperial Navy land-based fighter units were also equipped with A6M2 Model 21s, but there was also a new shorter-legged version that began appearing in mid 1942: the A6M3 Model 32. This airplane, with its shorter wingspan (for denser stowage aboard carriers), turned out to be unsuitable for long-range operations and was thus to be used mainly in a point-defense interceptor role in proximity to friendly bases. There were no Zero 32s aboard Japanese carriers in late 1942, but many were based at Rabaul and newer airfields in the northern Solomon Islands, from which they could just reach Guadalcanal.

The Zero's maneuverability was its best and, at times, only defense. The Japanese designers had sacrificed all manner of ruggedness and pilot amenities to the concepts of range and maneuverability. Land-based Zeros were not equipped with radios, because radios weighed too much. And the added weight of self-sealing tanks was avoided. When asked if they would like to have radios and other amenities, Zero pilots were quick and unanimous in saying no! They wanted nothing that would sacrifice a scintilla of maneuverability.

The Japanese counterpart to the American SBD was the Aichi D3A1 Type 99 Val "carrier bomber." (Name designations such as *Val* were not widely employed until late 1942, but they are used in this volume for convenience and familiarity.) The Val, which became operational in 1939, could lug up to 370 kilograms (816 pounds) of payload. For convoluted doctrinal reasons, however, carrier-based Vals usually flew with one 250-kilogram centerline bomb, and land-based Vals were usually armed with only two 60-kilogram wing-mounted bombs. Vals could fly up to 1,250 miles at a cruising speed of just under 250 miles per hour. Unlike its newer American counterpart, the Val featured old-fashioned spatted fixed landing gear. Its usual combat dive was undertaken at an angle of no greater than 60 degrees (as opposed to the SBD's steeper, faster 70-degree dive).

Crewed by a pilot and observer-gunner, the Val's defensive armaments consisted of a pair of cowl-mounted 7.7mm machine guns and a single rear-facing flexible 7.7mm machine gun. Like the SBDs, the Vals were employed in the dive-bombing and antisubmarine roles, but rarely as scouts.

The Nakajima B5N2 Type 97 Kate "carrier attack bomber" was accepted for fleet operations in 1937 and was thus a full generation older than its American counterpart, the TBF Avenger. A highly innovative model when first introduced, the Kate was a low-wing monoplane with retractable landing gear capable of lugging the superb 800-kilogram (1,764-pound) Type 91 18-inch aerial torpedo at the relatively high attack speed of 160 miles per hour. It had a 300-mile-plus combat radius. In addition to its primary role as a torpedo bomber, the Kate had proven itself in China and even at Pearl Harbor as an effective light horizontal bomber. In this role, it could carry up to 800 kilograms of bombs.

The Kate's three-man flight crew occupied a single cockpit covered with a distinctive, very long greenhouse canopy. The Kate's only defensive armament was a single 7.7mm flexible machine gun manned by the rear-facing gunner. Neither the pilot nor the man in the middle, the observer, had anything with which to contribute to the defense of the airplane. The observer was often the aircraft commander.

Other naval aircraft types that might be available to either side were land-based and amphibian scouts, bombers, and patrol bombers.

The American surface-ship-based scout of the day was the flimsy, underpowered Curtiss SOC scout-observation floatplane. The SOC's main function was observing naval gunfire against land targets. Constructed mainly of fabric and wire, and impeded in all but level flight by its bulky pontoon, the lightly armed SOC was in no way able to defend itself against any enemy aircraft.

The Consolidated PBY Catalina patrol bomber, powered by a pair of powerful engines mounted on a distinctive "parasol" wing, had been successful thus far in the war—up to a point. This tender- or land-based patrol bomber could stay aloft at a cruising speed of 117 miles per hour over distances of more than 2,000 miles. The Catalina was marginally capable of defending itself with its pair of .30-caliber bow-turret guns, a single rear-firing .30-caliber stinger, and single .50-caliber machine guns mounted in each of two waist blister turrets. If nothing else, the Catalina had proven itself to be extremely rugged in the face of enemy attack, and it most often carried its crew—and vital information—home. When on patrol, the Catalina could carry up to 4,000 pounds of payload and was variously armed with a pair of wing-mounted 500- or 1,000-pound bombs, a pair of wing-mounted 500-pound depth charges, or a pair of wing-mounted aerial torpedoes.

The Japanese fielded a somewhat larger array of scouts, bombers, and patrol bombers, including several types of reliable, rugged reconnaissance floatplanes launched from surface warships or based alongside tenders. Several of the float fighters—including the nimble A6M2-N Zero variant (Rufe)—were capable of holding forth against Wildcats.

The Japanese premier long-range patrol bombers of the day were the Kawanishi H6K Mavis and the brand-new H8K Emily four-engine flying boats. The Mavis featured single-mount 7.7mm machine guns in the bow, two side blisters, an open dorsal position, and one 20mm cannon in a tail turret. The thoroughly modern Emily, which had come on the scene in mid 1942, could defend itself with five single-mount 20mm cannon (one each in bow, dorsal, tail, and two beam positions) and three 7.7mm machine guns (in two side hatches and a ventral hatch). The older Mavis was at least as good as any U.S. Navy patrol plane in a forward area in mid 1942, but it was of startlingly flimsy, flammable construction. The Emily provided some armor protection, partially self-sealing fuel tanks, and a carbon dioxide fire-fighting system, but it proved to have little more staying power against fighter attack than the more vulnerable Mavis.

Unlike the U.S. Navy, the Imperial Navy had long fielded land-based bombers. The best by far was the new Mitsubishi G4M1 Type 1 Betty "land attack bomber," which had become available in very small numbers over China in August 1941. The Betty—rated a medium bomber by Americans—was capable of carrying up to 1,000 kilograms of bombs (typically four 250-kilogram or two 500-kilogram bombs) or a single 800-kilogram Type 21 aerial torpedo. The Betty had a combat radius of more than 1,200 miles, a cruising speed of 195 miles per hour, and a service ceiling of more than 30,000 feet, and it was extremely maneuverable. Like most of the lightly constructed Japanese warplanes, however, the Betty was highly flammable and could not take much abuse from a Wildcat's six .50-caliber machine guns. Its defensive armament consisted of one 7.7mm machine gun in the nose, one 7.7mm machine gun in each of two beam mounts and a dorsal blister, and a 20mm cannon in a tail turret. Most of the Bettys knocked down over Guadalcanal from August 7 onward succumbed to fires started by machine-gun bullets fired into vulnerable fuel tanks in the root of each wing.

Thus, aside from scout types and the singular niche filled by the Japanese Betty, both navies deployed roughly equivalent aircraft in mid 1942. Japan had, by far, the better, more reliable aerial torpedo, and its carrier aircraft were longer ranged than their American counterparts. On the other side, however, all of the American carrier models were far and away more rugged and better armed than their Japanese counterparts—a tremendous, often decisive, advantage in combat.

The organization of carrier air groups, squadrons, and smaller formations employed by the two sides was quite different.

American fighter squadrons, employing up to thirty-six airplanes each by mid 1942, were organized into more-or-less-standing four-plane divisions of two two-plane sections each. Because of their limited range, Wildcat fighters were not usually expected to undertake escort duties for air strikes; if enemy targets were well within the Wildcat's combat radius, four or eight fighters might be sent along all or part of the way. Or none might be sent with the bombers. The Wildcat was primarily an interceptor: At all times during the day, four to eight Wildcats were aloft over the friendly carrier, and four or eight were ready to take off at short notice. On rare occasions, Wildcats might supplement the bombers on antisubmarine patrols around the friendly carrier.

Doctrinally, American carriers depended mainly upon their own fighters to stave off enemy bombers. This meant that few fighters would be used to escort air strikes even against targets within the Wildcat's operational range. U.S. Navy surface ships accompanying the carriers could certainly put up a formidable antiaircraft defense, as could the carriers themselves, but the main burden of defense fell upon a distant barrier of radar-vectored interceptors whose primary mission was to fend off incoming enemy air attacks.

In the rapidly emerging, ever-changing doctrine of the period, the fighter division was the basic maneuver element, its two two-plane sections operating as an integrated team, attacking enemy airplanes and defending themselves in tandem. The reality of swiftly moving aerial combat often resulted in the sections—and even the teams of section leader and wingman—becoming unglued. Training included all possible permutations, and every pilot could perform in every slot used in all formations up to a full squadron formation. No pilot was so senior that he could not take over the wing slot on a junior pilot, if that was what the situation demanded.

SBD and TBF squadrons used as offensive strike forces were organized into three-plane sections built up into six-, nine-, twelve-, fifteen-, or eighteen-plane units, depending on availability, the mission, and the array of targets. SBD airplanes and crews nominally organized into separate scouting and bombing squadrons were completely interchangeable. Since the doctrine of the day called upon Dauntlesses to undertake arduous long-range searches and close-in patrol missions, there were always a number of Dauntlesses that could not be launched for attacks, either because they were busy elsewhere, had to be held back for other missions, or were down for maintenance. The same was essentially true for the less numerous Avengers. To help mitigate shortages and maintain unit integrity, carrier air groups operating together usually shared the patrol and ready roles on alternate days; one air group was essentially running defensive and search missions while most pilots and crews in the other were either resting or standing ready to mount strikes against naval or land targets.

The American scout and torpedo bombers of the day were solid, maneuverable airplanes with enough firepower to hold off Japanese fighters, though rarely to defeat them. The standard stepped-down vee-of-vees formation employed on the way to and from strike targets was defensive in nature. Awesome firepower in the form of massed forward- and rear-firing machine guns presented attackers with a formidable deterrent. In a few extreme cases, lone Dauntlesses had shot down Japanese fighters and bombers in one-on-one combat.

One overriding shortcoming of the U.S. Navy's carrier doctrine was that there had not yet evolved a means to smoothly combine and integrate the offensive or defensive capabilities of two or more carrier air groups operating together. Only the crudest control could be exerted by a carrier's Fighter Direction Officer (FDO) over his own defending fighter divisions. Handling more than one squadron at a time was beyond the capabilities of the crude radars and evolving fighter-direction systems then available. The same was true for coordinated air strikes. There was simply no means for having a designated strike commander oversee air strikes by more than a single carrier air group.

The Japanese carrier air group *(hikokitai)* was similar in organization to its American counterpart, but it was doctrinally dissimilar in a number of ways, both in capabilities and in outlook.

Japanese carrier-based fighters were organized into sections—*shotai*—of three airplanes and then into flights—*chutai*—of six to nine airplanes. The three-plane fighter *shotai* operated as a nearly inviolate unit, with a senior pilot and two wingmen. In most cases, one wingman was stationed off either of the senior pilot's wings, and just to the rear. Also, the *shotai* often operated in left- or right-echelon formations. In a left echelon, for example, the first wingman was stationed off and behind the leader's left wing, and the second wingman was stationed off and behind the first wingman's left wing. In most cases, also, the three launched coordinated attacks against targets selected by the senior pilot, and they operated as a team when on the defensive. But defense was not one of the roles for which the Zero fighter was built, nor were Japanese pilots as defense minded as they were finely honed hunters.

Carrier defense by fighters was problematic. A paucity of radar meant that Japanese fighters rarely had access to even the rudimentary carrier-based fighter direction enjoyed by the Americans. In general, Japanese combat air patrols were smaller than the American combat air patrols, but their ready fighters could get to altitude a good deal faster than American ready fighters. Japanese carriers depended upon fighters to keep American bombers at a distance; but if the carrier group was away on a strike of its own, most of the fighters would be with the strike. Thus the burden of Japanese antiaircraft defense lay with the escort vessels. Strangely, the Japanese carriers themselves were woefully undergunned to provide a meaningful self-defense, and few surface warships were ever designated to undertake close-in defense of the carriers.

There were twenty-one to twenty-seven Zero fighters available to each Japanese fleet carrier air group, both because of a shortage of aircraft and pilots and because there was no folding-wing variant available for denser stowage. (The A6M2 Model 21 had folding wingtips, which saved a little space.) Offsetting this particular disadvantage was the habitual pairing of Japanese fleet carriers in offensive operations. Unlike their American counterparts, the Japanese fighter pilots were used to operating under the senior fighter command pilot—from any ship—in the air at the time of offensive or defensive operations. Only the basic maneuver element, the three-plane *shotai*, was more or less structurally inviolate.

The Val and Kate squadrons also were organized into three-plane *shotai* and thence into *chutai* of six to nine airplanes, which usually flew in inverted vee-of-vees formations. As with the fighters—and unlike their American counterparts—Japanese offensive strike groups were highly flexible. Mixed groups from two or more carriers were often placed under the senior strike commander on the scene.

An unusual feature of the Imperial Navy's air-command setup was that a senior bomber commander—from air group commander to strike leader to *chutai* leader—was not necessarily a pilot. Very often, the commander rode as an observer in a Val, Kate, or Betty. This was never the case in any U.S. Navy flight formation; every American commander in the air was a rated pilot who flew his own airplane.

In many ways, American fighter doctrine was superior in the defense, and Japanese fighter doctrine was superior in the offense. And the more flexible Japanese strike doctrine was generally superior to American strike doctrine. Ultimately, however, any decision in a battle between carrier air groups would be determined by the size of the competing forces and by the staying power of the airplanes and the men who flew them.

Chapter 12

Until 1935, almost all U.S. Navy officer pilots were Regular line officers, usually graduates of the U.S. Naval Academy, and all enlisted pilots (Naval Aviation Pilots, or NAPs—no more than 30 percent of all pilots) were specially selected from the Fleet. Because the U.S. Navy promoted only qualified pilots to command its carriers, many senior officers, up to the rank of captain, attended flight school throughout the 1920s and 1930s.

When the Navy and Marine Corps began to vastly expand the strengths of their separate air arms in 1935, it was realized that the pool of qualified Regular line officers could not fill all the available billets, so the Aviation Cadet Act of 1935 provided for the selection and training of specially qualified Reserve pilots. Recruiting took place mainly among college graduates between the ages of twenty and twenty-eight. The initial AvCad course was extremely rigorous, including one year at flight school at Pensacola, Florida (465 classroom hours and 300 flight hours to qualify for wings). Once the AvCad earned his coveted Wings of Gold, he spent three years flying with the Fleet ranked between warrant officer and ensign. The AvCad finally received his commission as a Navy ensign or Marine second lieutenant four years after qualifying for flight school. At the same time that he was commissioned, however, the early AvCad was placed on *inactive* status with the U.S. Navy or Marine Corps Reserve.

The AvCad program was substantially upgraded by the Naval Aviation Reserve Act of 1939. This provided for six thousand trainees who would receive commissions upon completion of flight training at Pensacola and who would serve a total of seven years on active duty. AvCads who had earned their wings prior to the inception of the new act were immediately commissioned, and those who had gone on Reserve status were given the opportunity to return to active duty.

In 1940, Congress expanded the act to train enough pilots to man 15,000 Navy and Marine aircraft. On December 7, 1941, the Navy and Marine Corps had a total of 6,500 qualified active-duty pilots. About half of them were AvCads trained at Pensacola or newer flight schools at Corpus Christi, Texas, and Jacksonville, Florida. In addition, many hundreds of additional AvCads were in the pipeline, days or months away from graduation.

As the AvCad program expanded alongside flight training programs for Regular officers and enlisted cadets, the vastly expanded needs of the day resulted in relaxed entry standards. Early in the program, only perfect physical specimens were selected (no dental fillings, no broken bones). This was to help reduce the vast pool of otherwise qualified applicants clamoring for admission to a very small program. When more cadets were needed than the perfect-specimen pool could provide, some of the most extreme physical criteria were relaxed, and the educational requirement was rolled back to two years of college. As an added inducement, AvCads were to earn a bounty of $500 per year for four years, payable when they mustered out. Many a Depression-deprived college sophomore signed up in the hope of earning enough in four years to pay his junior- and senior-year tuition bills.

At the same time that entry qualifications were being relaxed, cadets were required to weather fewer and fewer classroom and flight hours. Ultimately, the scaled-down twenty-six-week course called for just 207 flight hours prior to commissioning and assignment to advanced specialized training. Even the truncated syllabus barely provided enough qualified—which is not to say "seasoned"—pilots to man the carrier air groups following the attrition resulting from the war's early carrier battles at the Coral Sea and Midway. Older AvCads, Regular officer pilots, and NAPs held the line as the new wave of AvCads, along with a sprinkling of qualified Regulars, learned the art of survival in the air, literally on the fly. In the weeks after Midway, more than one rookie pilot undertook his first real carrier landing upon reporting to his first operational squadron.

By the summer of 1942, as the Midway battle losses were being made good in active carrier air groups, the U.S. Navy found some breathing room and redoubled its effort, begun in early 1942, to commission new reserve carrier air groups. These reserve groups, which were composed largely of unproven rookies led by small numbers of veterans, were slated to go aboard new carriers still under constructio, or to replace carrier air groups that needed to be rested or reorganized following combat tours at sea. The first reserve group, Carrier Reserve Air Group 9, was destined to take part in the North Africa invasion in November 1942, but Carrier Reserve Air Group 10 shipped out to Hawaii on August 8 to complete its training. There was no telling at the time where it would be used, but the return of the damaged *Enterprise* and her beaten-up and parceled-out Air Group 6 following the Eastern Solomons Battle provided the reserve group with a new home in very short order. Since the *Enterprise* went straight into drydock to be repaired and somewhat modernized, Carrier Air Group 10 (which quietly dropped "Reserve" from its name) continued to work up from bases ashore.

Through mid 1942, the American genius for mass training barely won the battle of time in the case of carrier-based combat pilots. But that particular genius enabled the Navy to hold the line, and now the Navy air arm was getting ahead of the curve with more carrier pilots than it could deploy at the moment. The same was not true for the Japanese survivors of the vicious early carrier battles.

Nearly all Japanese officer carrier pilots were graduates of Eta Jima, Japan's naval academy. Because Japanese carrier captains and carrier-fleet commanders did not need to be qualified pilots, however, few older officers undertook the rigors of flight training. (A notable exception was

Capt Isoroku Yamamoto, who was to command the Imperial Navy's Combined Fleet during the first eighteen months of the Pacific War.) Each young Eta Jima graduate was commissioned following a rigorous three-and-a-half-year course and before beginning flight training. Far from following the American model of compressing the flight-training syllabus, the Japanese in 1940 lengthened their officers' course from about eight months to a full year. Also, whereas American pilots in the prewar years might be called upon to fly all types of airplanes available to the United States Fleet, most Japanese pilots specialized in just one type.

The vast majority of Japanese carrier planes were flown by enlisted pilots who either came from the Combined Fleet, following several years' service, or were recruited directly from the population. During the 1930s, the naval aviation community recruited many fifteen- and sixteen-year-old boys, which obliged the Imperial Navy to undertake secondary education as well as flight training. An emphasis in selection was placed upon physical strength, coordination, and agility. Pre-flight training discipline was particularly brutal as a conscious means to weed out *most* candidates.

The selection, schooling, and training process was comprehensive but glacial in speed. Belatedly, the Imperial Navy streamlined the system in August 1941, when it set a goal of training 15,000 pilots.

By the time the war started, some early enlisted pilots had been commissioned as special-duty ensigns, and many were warrant officers. By the time an Eta Jima graduate reached an operational squadron following theoretical and flight training, he was usually a newly promoted lieutenant junior grade.

By the time the Japanese enlisted pilot reached an air group, he had spent seven to nine months undergoing flight training, including rudimentary instruction in his specialty. In that time, nearly two-thirds of his classmates washed out of flight school. (Pensacola graduated about two-thirds of its cadets.)

The differences between the two naval services became more pronounced at the operational level. American pilots were largely interchangeable, though there was a trend toward placing an individual pilot in a job for which he had the most aptitude. The average Japanese pilot was specialized early in his training. American pilots were all selected for leadership traits, whereas only Japanese officers, warrant officers, and very senior enlisted pilots could lead other pilots into combat. The vast majority of Japanese enlisted pilots were merely taught to follow the leader.

The most important difference was the permanence of postings. Japanese rookie pilots were more or less permanently assigned to a particular air group, which served as his advanced-training command. If the group to which the rookie was assigned happened to be engaged in combat, he very often learned the finer points of his profession under the gun—or he died trying. If the rookie's air group had been gutted by combat losses—as was the case for many once the Pacific War got under way, but also during the long years of the so-called China Incident—there was a chance that he would rise to a key level of intermediate responsibility before he was quite ready. This tendency was not reinforced by the creation of many new carrier- and land-based air groups in late 1941 and early 1942, which tended to siphon off many of the skilled senior pilots, who also served as trainers, mentors, and examples to younger pilots.

The rookie American naval aviator usually underwent advanced training in his specialty before joining an operational air group. For example, all fighter pilots honed their skills and probably flew the latest fighters at the Miami Naval Air Station. Also, the fledgling U.S. Navy pilot bound for carrier duty trained for several weeks to a month or two with an advanced carrier training group (ACTG). There, he simply learned to take off from and land on a carrier deck (most often a simulated carrier deck superimposed on a land-based runway). If there was time, he stayed with the ACTG until he mastered carrier operations or, if he could not, until he was sent elsewhere, usually to fly multi-engine planes.

When it was formed in early 1942, Carrier Reserve Air Group 10 received a draft of battle-experienced veterans, some older pilots who had thus far missed combat (mostly due to training duties), and a large component of recent ACTG graduates. There would always be a need to directly replace individual pilots lost in combat and operational accidents, but through the balance of the Pacific War, the reserve carrier air groups and their successors would provide the majority of young American rookies with the time and the place to learn the ropes from veterans. It was a golden opportunity most Japanese rookies missed.

The clear implication of the vastly different "polishing" phases was that the U.S. Navy was turning out pilots to spare while the Japanese were under the gun from the start. The Americans had staying power the Japanese lacked.

Of equal importance was that the formation of new U.S. Navy carrier air groups and the burgeoning number of training billets at home would eventually provide large numbers of veteran American carrier pilots with an opportunity to recuperate from the rigors of war cruises, whereas the veteran Japanese carrier pilots would have to keep flying and fighting as long as their home carriers were in the war zone. Veteran American pilots could train rookies far from the sound of the guns, but Japanese veterans often could not. The potential for simple fatigue to have a negative impact on group operations was greater on the Japanese side. And because the Japanese squadrons were manned by increasing numbers of raw fledglings, an increasing share of the burden inevitably fell upon the declining population of veterans. It was virtually impossible for the decimated Japanese carrier groups to draw experienced replacements—particularly command pilots—from land-based groups, and vice versa, because of early and ongoing specialization in mission training.

If the war was not decided quickly—in a matter of months—the small number of operational Japanese carrier air groups stood the better chance of simply being ground down.

Chapter 13

The only reason for building, maintaining, and defending aircraft car-riers was the mobility they afforded airplanes in moving across vast ocean distances. The heart of the aircraft carrier and the carrier task force was air operations.

Prior to taking off on a typical search or combat mission, duty pilots gathered in their squadron ready rooms, which were steel cubes located on the deck just beneath the flight-deck level. They were like very small theaters with eight rows of four upholstered seats per row. On the forward bulkhead, to the left, was a teletype machine fitted with a red typewriter ribbon. A large chartboard dominated the center of the forward bulkhead. On a table set against the rear bulkhead was a perpetually filled coffee urn and white enamel mugs. The room was usually hazy from cigarette smoke and was invariably dimly lit. At night the lights were red to prevent night blindness.

When a pilot was to leave for a search or patrol mission away from the task force, the teletype clattered out a message to keep him abreast of the speed and planned course of the carrier, known magnetic variations, and other navigational data that would help him to a safe return.

If a long flight by all or most of the squadron was planned, the squadron engineering officer—a senior pilot with that additional squadron duty—might brief on how to get maximum gas mileage by leaning out the fuel mixture to the point where engine temperature rose to the allowable limit.

In the event of a strike mission, the carrier's air officer—a senior pilot on nonflying duty as part of the ship's company—would usually come down from the bridge to cover special points and answer questions. As data continued to be updated via the teletype, individual pilots jotted down their own navigational notes on their plotting boards—16-by-18-inch navigational devices that fit under the airplane dashboard and could be referred to and updated during flight. Fighter pilots and the radiomen assigned to the bombers were given radio call signs and a schedule of frequencies and emergency bands for the mission and nearby bases.

When all had been said and done and it was time to leave, pilots and aircrewmen proceeded from their separate ready rooms to the flight deck, usually to the accompaniment of tinny voices sounding orders over the ship's public address system: "Pilots, man your airplanes."

Once on the flight deck, a mission pilot might walk around his airplane to inspect it and the load of ordnance slung beneath it. Then he would climb aboard by way of the left wing. Once in the cockpit, the pilot shrugged into his seat and parachute harnesses, usually with a helping hand from his plane captain. Then he plugged in his helmet-mounted earphones and microphone. Following a briefing from the plane captain on quirks and potential problems—invariably followed by a thumbs-up for luck from the man who would stay behind—the pilot waited for clearance to run up the engine to check it and the magnetos. If there was a problem and the plane had to be scrubbed from the mission—the decision was the pilot's—the pilot had to signal the plane captain and then shut down the engine. If that happened, plane handlers would swarm around the airplane in a race to get it out of the way before the launch was thrown completely off schedule. If all seemed well with the power plant and the electrical system, the pilot waited his turn until signaled by the deck boss or the deck boss's assistant to taxi his airplane forward to the take-off spot. Within seconds, as the engine wound up to full power, he had to get his fully loaded fighter or bomber airborne—from a standing start to fully airborne within a few hundred feet. As soon as the airplane was steady on the take-off spot, the pilot pushed both feet into the brakes and nudged the throttle forward with his left hand until the engine was running at full power.

At a signal from the flagman, the pilot lifted both feet simultaneously from the brake pedals and gently set them on the rudder pedals. The plane was rolling. To keep it steady, the pilot alternately nudged first one rudder pedal and then the other as he held the control stick steady with his right hand and pushed the throttle forward with his left.

To increase the lifting power of aircraft wings, the carrier steamed at top speed directly into the wind during the launching operation. Depending on how full the flight deck was, any given airplane would be able to use more or less than one-half the total length of the flight deck for takeoff.

Predawn or evening launches were always thrilling because, in addition to normal perils, carriers in operational areas showed no lights whatsoever on the flight deck or superstructure. The total darkness did nothing to enhance depth perception ahead or to the sides. About all most pilots had to guide on in predawn or evening launches was the flickering blue flames emitted from the engine exhaust stacks of the airplane just ahead. From time to time, a pilot became disoriented during a launch in the dark and flew toward lights that were in fact reflections on the surface of the ocean. At other times, day or night, the airplane engine did not have enough power to keep the airplane airborne. And sometimes the air was too humid for the physics of a launch to quite work out. Airplanes were lost and men were killed in carrier launches; it was an occupational risk.

Seasoned pilots with a decade or more of experience in carrier flight operations were only just slightly less prone to operational accidents than the rawest novice. In addition to inexperience and exhausting schedules that often muddled judgment or slowed reflexes, work-weary airplanes and the inexperience of recent additions to the flight-deck and ground crews were factors contributing to high operational losses.

A fully loaded SBD with a 1,000-pound bomb, four hundred .50-caliber rounds and twelve hundred .30-caliber rounds, plus a full load of gas, had a tendency to waddle down the flight deck and more or less fall off the bow of the ship. If, by that time, the airplane had not powered up to 65 or 70 knots of air speed, it was not a flying machine and would fall into the water.

At a moment only the inner ear could gauge, the pilot smartly pulled the stick in his right hand toward the pit of his belly to get the nose up. He was committed to flight.

If the warplane did become airborne, the pilot immediately had to pull up the landing gear and flaps. These tasks—coupled with keeping the nose high and turning leftward away from the ship—were made more difficult by the need to accomplish both jobs more or less simultaneously through cross-hand actuation or by shifting the stick from one hand to the other and back again. Dropping the left wingtip into the water was an easy mistake to make while performing these gymnastics, and the sudden drag thereby generated could easily flip a fully throttled airplane into the sea.

Wildcat pilots had to turn a hand crank twenty-seven times to pull up the landing gear while fighting the airplane's marked tendency, caused by high engine torque, to pull too far and too quickly to the left. Turning the hand crank usually caused the newly airborne Wildcat to undulate as it ascended until the landing gear was safely up and secured.

Avenger pilots had the best airplane by far for carrier takeoffs: the huge-winged TBF was often airborne long before it reached the bow, and it was usually uphill all the way. If the Avenger had one failing it was a distinctly sluggish engine on very hot days. If the ambient temperature was too high, the plane could become airborne but could not climb.

A typical daily mission for carrier scout- and torpedo bomber crews was a dawn or afternoon search for enemy vessels. Each search sector usually consisted of a wedge of ocean 200 to 250 miles in length covering ten degrees of a 360-degree circle centered on the carrier. Depending on the needs of the moment, anywhere from eighteen to thirty-six 10-degree sectors would be searched. And depending upon the availability of SBDs and TBFs, each pie-shaped sector would be searched by one or two airplanes.

The searcher had to know his position at all times, both as a means for returning safely to his ship and in order to accurately report the position of whatever he might encounter. Each searcher was typically armed with a single 500-pound general-purpose bomb, though his mission was less to engage enemy ships than to find, track, and report on them. Only in extreme circumstances, or if the opportunity was too good to pass up, was a search pilot to launch an attack upon, primarily, an enemy carrier—and only after he was dead certain he had made an accurate position report that had actually been received by a friendly vessel or base.

Most of the hundreds of daily search sorties were simply boring. Most of the search pilot's energy went into scanning the endless sea and checking his position relative to his carrier, which was usually on the move to a position far from the point at which the searcher had been launched.

Usually, the search pilot flew out from the task force just off the surface, because climbing to altitude used up a great deal of fuel. In any case, it was impossible for the pilot to read the play of the wind on the surface of the ocean at altitudes higher than 150 feet. By knowing the strength and direction of the wind, the pilot could determine which way and how far the airplane was being blown off course. This was the only way he could fly out to distances of 250 miles and expect to find his way back home with reasonable assurance.

All carrier planes had small radio receivers that could pick up homing signals in every direction from the carriers. Depending upon the code the pilot and radioman could hear, the pilot could fine-tune his final approach to the left or the right to find the carrier. If an airplane flew past the carrier in bad weather or at night, the homing radio would tell him so—if he was in line-of-sight VHF range. The key to the system was letter signals; the pilot knew which way to fly based upon which Morse code letter he was receiving on the radio.

Once settled on the first search leg, the pilot could stop watching his compass and air-speed indicator to the exclusion of all else and look around. Indeed, the search crew's main purpose was looking far and wide to see what was out there. If the pilot and crewmen saw anything of note on the search leg or cross leg—enemy ships or an inbound hostile strike force—they were to report all the details to their ship, and keep on reporting for as long as possible.

The third, or intercept, leg of the three-legged pattern was the most crucial to the crew of the search plane. If all the navigational computations—mainly direction and wind speed—had been correct, the search pilot would find his way home to Point Option—the place the carrier would be four to five hours after the searcher had been launched. In the words of one carrier pilot at sea in mid 1942, "If he has done his navigation correctly and Point Option has not changed without his knowing it, the fleet will appear at the proper time. If not, there is still only water and more water."

Once the returning pilot found the carrier, he had to undergo the stress of landing upon what invariably looked like a short, narrow flight deck that was moving *away* from him at high speed.

As soon as the pilot had sighted the carrier, he would wheel into the imaginary oblong landing traffic pattern down the port side toward the stern of the ship. If landing operations were under way, the planes in the landing traffic pattern would pace themselves to begin final approaches at 40-second intervals. Airplanes with fuel or mechanical problems would receive priority clearance if there was time.

Each pilot in the landing traffic pattern would tick off his prelanding checklist: canopy back and locked (for quick escape in the event he somehow hit the water), fuel on rich mixture (for immediate added power if he suddenly needed to fly away from the groove), fuel coming in from the fullest internal tank (so his engine would not suddenly die from fuel starvation while his mind was on other matters), cowl flaps partly open (to keep the engine cool), and prop in low pitch (so it could bite the maximum amount of air at the low landing speed).

If the checklist checked, he was ready to land.

In the case of landing a Wildcat, for example, the pilot next reached across his torso with his left hand, found the required lever, and dropped the tail hook. He had by then slowed his fighter to an indicated air speed of 120 knots. Next he lowered his landing gear and landing flaps, the latter causing a slight downward pitching motion. As he slowly flew up the carrier's wake, right in the groove, his air-speed indicator should have registered the desired 90 knots, and the fighter should have been in a perfect nose-high attitude. The experienced carrier pilot was able to fly by feel alone, which totally freed his eyes to follow the motions of the most important man in the carrier pilot's world, his landing signal officer (LSO).

In its essence, a carrier landing was phased to consist of the following sequence: While the carrier sailed at top speed into the wind, the pilot lowered his airplane's tail hook and approached the carrier flight deck from dead astern; guided by the LSO, the pilot lined up on the flight deck at just the right altitude, attitude, and speed; if the LSO was satisfied that the airplane was in the correct position relative to the deck, he signaled the pilot to land. If the airplane was not in the correct position and could not be guided into the groove in the time remaining, the LSO would wave it off for another try. If the pilot was allowed to land, he quickly dropped to the deck in what can only be described as a controlled stall with the intention of catching the extended tail hook on any of the nine stout cables running the width of the deck; if the tail hook caught a cable, the cable gave a bit while the airplane was pulled to a rapid stop; if the tail hook missed all the cables, and if the deck was clear, the pilot gunned the engine and took off for another try; if the tail hook missed the cable and the deck was obstructed, the nose of the plane was arrested by a flexible barrier, which usually damaged the propeller but prevented a flaming collision between the airplane and whatever obstructions lay ahead.

Only the LSO could determine when an approaching pilot was ready for the carrier. He would signal his opinions with his two outstretched luminous paddles.

By that time, the pilot was reviewing his landing litany: A one-second delay in cutting the throttle makes the difference between a normal cable-arrested landing and a crash on the flight deck. Never touch the throttle until safely on the deck. If you miss the cables, immediately push the throttle forward to acquire lift-off speed. If the airplane is properly arrested, cut power to the absolute minimum and taxi off as soon as the hook and the cable have been separated by a deck crewman.

The pilot had to totally concentrate on altitude, attitude, propeller pitch, throttle setting, landing gear, flaps, tail hook, the rapidly approaching LSO, and the motion of the tossing, twisting postage-stamp-size flight deck.

The LSO stood tall in front of his protective windscreen on the starboard aft corner of the flight deck. A pilot who had once naively asked the

LSO what the screen was for had received a sarcastic answer that the ship would be doing 18 to 20 knots, which, combined with a wind-speed factor of anywhere from zero miles per hour to infinity, usually created enough of a breeze to pitch a sturdy LSO into the drink. The dark-colored screen also aided the pilot in finding and following the motions of the LSO, who was clad in light-colored clothing.

On the far side of the screen was the LSO's assistant. It was his job to see if the tail hook, landing gear, and flaps of the approaching plane were down. If so, he would yell above the wind, right into the LSO's ear, "All clear." Then he would turn to watch the deck as the landing plane hurtled past the LSO platform into the cable.

Many LSOs waved their paddles with a great deal of energetic flair, but most passed the standard thirteen landing signals in a straightforward manner. Ten of the signals told the pilot of some specific error in technique or procedure—wrong height, wings not level, approach speed too fast or too slow, even that the tail hook was not deployed or the main landing gear was not down. The remaining three signals were Roger, Cut, and Wave-off.

Pilots wanted a Roger on the first pass. If the plane was correctly lined up, the LSO would hold his paddles straight out from the shoulders to signify that the airplane was "in the groove"—that the approach was satisfactory.

Just as the pilot sensed that his airplane's nose was hovering several feet over the fantail, the LSO dropped his left arm to his side. Then his right arm lifted and the right paddle abruptly slashed across his throat. That was Cut.

The pilot immediately chopped back his throttle and held the control stick rock steady. The airplane was now in a perfect three-point landing attitude, which meant that all three wheels would strike the deck at the same instant. Things happened fast from that point. There was nothing for the pilot to do; the laws of physics were running the show.

The pilot next felt the shock of the landing gear as they hit the solid flight deck. Then he felt the tail hook grab hold of the wire. If it was the first wire, the landing was perfect. The mass of the fighter rapidly decelerated and came to an abrupt no-brakes near stop. Immediately, the tension on the arresting cable eased, and the fighter's remaining momentum pulled it forward about forty feet with the hook still attached. This brought the fighter to a controlled stop. At that point, the pilot came under the direction of the deck crew and plane handlers. No more than five seconds had elapsed from "cut" to the rolling stop.

Once the pressure was off the tail hook, the pilot and his airplane became the center of furious activity. A quick glance into the rearview mirror would reveal a deck crewman ducking beneath the tail to release the hook from the cable. At almost the same instant, another deck crewman took charge of the taxi routine by passing up his unique set of signals. First, on signal, the pilot retracted the tail hook. Then he had to get lined up with the centerline of the deck to get into taxi position. The vertical barrier, which looked like an oversized tennis net and was raised for all landings, was dropped as soon as the tail hook caught the cable. The instant the tail wheel was clear of the barrier, the obstruction was raised again in preparation for the next landing.

As soon as the airplane cleared the barrier, the LSO's assistant, who was standing with his back to the LSO, turned aft and yelled "All clear!" into the LSO's ear.

If the recovery operation was perfect, the succeeding airplane was in position to take the Cut just as the previous airplane cleared the deck barrier.

Often, in a large landing operation, the LSO had to pass the Wave-off signal to two or three pilots as they felt their way into the groove one after another. To pass this signal, the LSO simply waved both paddles over his head. The wave-off had the force of absolute law. Even if the pilot was in fact right in the groove and lined up for a perfect landing, he had to obey the wave-off signal, as there might be an emergency beyond his knowledge or range of senses—such as an imminent enemy attack. Pilots were not given the option of overruling an LSO's orders, especially in the case of a wave-off.

Maintaining and servicing the warplanes of a carrier air group required endless hours of work by dedicated groundcrewmen.

The plane captain—usually a rated aviation machinist's mate permanently assigned to a particular airplane—oversaw an ad hoc crew of specialists consisting of rated petty officers and seamen strikers—younger seamen working their way up the rungs of the promotion ladder, trying to get their own specialty ratings. The plane crews worked on everything from hydraulics to fuselage repairs to maintaining the guns, engine, gas lines, radios, navigation aids, and so forth.

The permanence of the flight crews was fairly well established during a combat situation. During routine operations, however, many of the senior groundcrewmen flew on training missions to qualify for standby aircrew duty and to enable them to receive flight pay, a sort of reward for extra services.

Typically, the commanding officer (CO), executive officer (exec), and flight officer of a carrier bomber squadron had their own personal airplanes and crews. The junior officers often flew any airplane assigned to them, often with a strange crew.

The ship's company did the plane handling on the hangar and flight decks, plus refueling and respotting airplanes.

Most of the aircrewmen in the torpedo, scouting, and bombing squadrons held radioman ratings, but a small percentage were aviation machinist's mates or even aviation ordnancemen.

A typical torpedo squadron numbering twelve to fifteen airplanes consisted of approximately twenty-four pilots, fifty aircrewmen, four ground officers, and twelve to fifteen nucleus groundcrewmen serving as plane captains. The scouting and bombing squadrons mustered more men because they each consisted nominally of eighteen airplanes. Attrition was through combat and operational losses and maintenance problems, but spare planes of all three types were stowed on the hangar deck, and extra ground personnel could be assigned from the ship's company if needed.

In addition to flying duties, everyone assigned to a carrier air group, including the pilots, had certain squadron or shipboard duties.

Part IV

In Search of a Battle

Chapter 14

The orders that sent the Imperial Navy's Combined Fleet into action at the end of October 1942 were inextricably linked with the same general directives issued by Imperial General Headquarters in Tokyo that launched the 17th Army's abortive land assault on Guadalcanal.

Although the Imperial Army and Imperial Navy had been making some small attempts within the Solomons battle arena to arrive at a mutually beneficial working relationship, the long-term effects of a bitter traditional interservice rivalry had proven too ingrained to be overcome by even the realities of the life-and-death Guadalcanal struggle. On the broader plane, both partners were equally at fault. Imperial Army officers had had to wring personal concessions from Adm Isoroku Yamamoto, the Combined Fleet commander-in-chief, in order to get the navy to support its Tokyo-ordained October offensive. Nevertheless, once the concessions were becoming reality, the 17th Army dealt the Combined Fleet out of the operational planning. Even more important, the 17th Army did not share the details of its final plans—nor even its intelligence estimates—with the Combined Fleet. Except for sharing key dates and making requests of one another, each service went ahead with its own planning without consulting the other. The result was the birth of a pair of non-identical twins: two separate battles based upon two different strategies that would be undertaken at roughly the same time in two separate but overlaid venues.

For its part, the Combined Fleet was less interested in helping the 17th Army win back Guadalcanal than it was in achieving mastery over the U.S. Navy in the Eastern Solomons and, by extension, in all Pacific waters. The Imperial Navy was no longer certain how many American carriers remained operational, but its most-senior commanders felt that the number was very small, two or three at most. On the rather broader strategic plane upon which those commanders operated, the objective was the destruction of the *will* of the U.S. Navy to conduct meaningful strategic operations. For, without a viable navy, the United States could not implement an offensive—or much of a defensive—policy in the broad Pacific expanses. Thus, the upcoming operation was seen as a global imperative, and the commitment to it was as nearly total as had been the commitment at Midway. But it was also seen as a clean-up operation, which is a role that had never seriously been contemplated for Midway.

The U.S. Navy would certainly be obliged to commit all or nearly all of its few remaining carriers to the showdown, and that could lead to the ultimate victory the flagging Japanese war machine urgently required in mid 1942.

At the local level, the Combined Fleet for once did its best to live up to the personal oath Admiral Yamamoto had made to a senior 17th Army representative. Indeed, senior Combined Fleet staffers based at Truk had rather naively timed their entire operation as if the 17th Army would flawlessly live up to its timetable and assurances of ultimate victory.

Several naval actions that had been undertaken in daylight on October 25 by the Rabaul-based Eighth Fleet in Ironbottom Sound and adjacent waters—actions that resulted in damage to several destroyers and the loss of the light cruiser *Yura*—had been an unusual sign of good faith on the part of the Navy. So had the Base Air Force's all-out plan of action for October 25. This exhibition of good faith—and the movement of vast Combined Fleet battle units from Truk—was met with stoney silence from the

17th Army. The Combined Fleet was not even informed by any Imperial Army sources that the land assault against the Lunga Perimeter had failed at every point and that the 17th Army was withdrawing from the assault.

In support of the 17th Army's "victory" at Guadalcanal, the largest force of Japanese carriers assembled since the Midway battle was sailing in waters between Truk and the Eastern Solomons, and Admiral Yamamoto had committed it to another iteration of his final-battle strategy.

The entire Japanese naval combat force—dubbed the Guadalcanal Support Force and commanded at sea by VAdm Nobutake Kondo—was divided into four groupments: Kondo's Advance Force, VAdm Chuichi Nagumo's Striking Force, VAdm Gunichi Mikawa's Outer South Seas Force, and VAdm Teruhisa Komatsu's Advanced Expeditionary Force (submarines). Admiral Yamamoto, with still other naval units at his immediate disposal, would oversee the operation from his flagship, which would remain at anchor in Truk Lagoon.

The Advance Expeditionary Force, an operational component of Vice Admiral Komatsu's Sixth Fleet, was composed of eleven fleet submarines strung along a vast screening line. As always, the submarines were to monitor U.S. fleet movements and report sightings, as well as attack Allied ships when possible.

Vice Admiral Mikawa's Outer South Seas Force, an operational subsidiary of his own Eighth Fleet, operated out of Rabaul and the Shortlands anchorages. Its role was to directly support the 17th Army land offensive with troop lifts and naval bombardments, and it suffered for its devotion to these missions when it bore the brunt of Cactus-based daylight air attacks on October 25.

The Advance Force, which was directly commanded by Vice Admiral Kondo, was divided into the Main Body (five cruisers and six destroyers), the Air Group (two fleet carriers and four destroyers), and the Support Group (two battleships and six destroyers). If the U.S. Navy carriers could be pinpointed, it would range ahead of the other major Combined Fleet formation, the Striking Force, by only 100 to 120 miles. With any luck, Kondo's Advance Force would both draw off some of the power of the expected U.S. carrier air attack and be in a position to dash forward to directly engage U.S. Navy warships, including American carriers.

Nagumo's Striking Force was divided into the Carrier Group (two fleet carriers, one light carrier, one cruiser, and eight destroyers) and the Vanguard Group (two battleships, four cruisers, and seven destroyers). As its name implies, this was the force that the U.S. naval forces were to reckon with.

In all, the Advance and Striking forces comprised four fleet carriers, one light carrier, four battleships, eight heavy cruisers, two light cruisers, and thirty-one destroyers.

The scheme devised by the Combined Fleet under Yamamoto's guidance was quite different from the defeated Coral Sea, Midway, and Eastern Solomons concoctions, but it had similar elements. For once, no landing force was tied directly to the naval operation, and no bait was put out. Also, the main Japanese battle formations were within supporting range of one another.

Another quite different feature was that a very powerful surface battle force was placed *in front* of the carrier striking force. It is clear that the Japanese planners hoped that the Advance Force would serve as a buffer between the expected American retaliatory air strikes and the main body of Japanese carriers. But this is not to say that the planners were using the Advance Force entirely as a means of drawing off American air strikes. The Advance Force was an extraordinarily powerful battle force well able to fend for itself; it was, in every way, a formidable mobile striking force in its own right, and it had a meaningful mission that was central to the Japanese master plan. That mission was to track down and destroy the main U.S. Navy battle force operating in support of the Lunga garrison.

Initially, the Guadalcanal Support Force had four fleet carriers and one light carrier. Two of the fleet carriers—the *Shokaku* and *Zuikaku*—and the light carrier—the *Zuiho*—made up the Carrier Group of VAdm Chuichi Nagumo's Striking Force. The two new fleet carriers, *Junyo* and *Hiyo*, made up the Air Group of VAdm Nobutake Kondo's Advance Force. But on October 21, the *Hiyo* was disabled by an engine-room fire and the next day had to be dispatched under escort to the Truk anchorage for repairs. Her air group was partly broken up to provide fillers for *Junyo* Air Group aircraft lost in operational accidents and the disastrous October 17 attack against Lunga. (Most of the rest of the *Hiyo* Air Group was sent to Buin, from which it mounted the uncontested and unproductive strike against Henderson Field on the evening of October 25.) In a radical departure from previous ill-starred plans, the idea was for the *Junyo* Air Group to provide the Advance Force with close-in air cover and remain within easy support range of Nagumo's larger Carrier Group. Its job was to support the advance surface force and not—*specifically* not—to draw American carrier strikes away from the larger carrier force, which had been the fate of the *Ryujo* force on August 24 at Eastern Solomons.

Oddly, many senior Japanese officers were not informed that their side was initiating the action, nor even that it was in support of the 17th Army's grand assault against the Lunga Perimeter. Cdr Masatake Okumiya, a seasoned staff officer embarked in the *Junyo,* heard from senior briefers that the second foray from Truk in two weeks was merely in response to a U.S. Navy initiative involving several its carriers.

Notwithstanding Commander Okumiya's ignorance of his own service's strategic imperatives and initiatives, the essence of his information was correct: the U.S. Pacific Fleet *was* seeking a confrontation with the Combined Fleet. The germ of the bold U.S. plan was conceived by Adm Chester Nimitz during his rather disheartening South Pacific tour of late September. Nimitz's decision to name Bill Halsey to head the South Pacific Area was emblematic of his desire to breathe life into the psychologically stalled Solomons offensive. Halsey was known for his combative offensive traits, and he had been active in the early part of the war striking at Japanese bases throughout the Pacific at the forefront of his nation's limited carrier force. His chief contribution had been as commander of the two-carrier task force that had raided Japanese island bases in February and March 1942 and from which LtCol Jimmy Doolittle's small force of Army Air Forces B-25 medium bombers had been launched against Tokyo in April 1942. Great things had been expected of Halsey until he was laid low by medical problems on the eve of Midway. His reinstatement as Fletcher's permanent replacement with Task Force 61, and his ultimate elevation to the South Pacific Area command, had sent gleeful shivers of anticipation right through the heart of the Pacific Fleet.

On October 16, the very day he forwarded Halsey's name to Washington as his choice to replace Ghormley, Nimitz implemented a bold gamble aimed at giving the combative Halsey the means for seizing anew the initiative that had been so ignominiously lost at Savo and therafter. Though the wounds the *Enterprise* had suffered at Eastern Solomons were by no means fully healed, that ship stood out from Pearl Harbor, and Task Force 16, the battle group of which the *Enterprise* was the center, made all speed to the south to join the *Hornet* battle group, Task Force 17. Once Task Force 61 had been reconstituted as a multi-carrier battle force, it was to sweep into Japanese-dominated waters to seek out and bring to battle the main elements of the Combined Fleet. Thus, the two surviving *Yorktown*-class triplets were to be reunited for the first time since Midway, and they were to operate again under the combative Bill Halsey for the first time since the breathtaking Tokyo Raid in April.

Once installed at Noumea, Halsey set himself the task of either bringing his carrier force in contact with the Japanese carrier force or launching some equally forceful operation. Halsey later wrote to Nimitz, "I had to begin throwing punches almost immediately."

The *Hornet* battle force (Task Force 17, commanded by RAdm George Murray) was on station in the South Pacific region, as were the new fast battleship *Washington* (Task Force 64, commanded by RAdm Willis Lee) and a fairly large assortment of cruisers and destroyers doled out to several of the battle forces. Along with the oncoming *Enterprise* battle force, these ships, and the area's flotilla of submarines, would be used to locate and strike the two Imperial Navy carriers *(Zuikaku* and *Shokaku)* known to be in the region, stave off Imperial Navy surface forces, or, if possible, mount a devastating strike against Japanese advance anchorages and air bases around Bougainville and the Shortland Islands.

What the various components of the South Pacific Force did, and when they did it, would depend upon what the Japanese did first. Thus, the battle plans emerging from either side placed great emphasis on the movements of the other side. In short, if the opposing battle fleets came into range of one another, there would be a battle. If not, one side or the other—or both—would pummel the opposition's advance land bases.

Chapter 15

The wounded *Enterprise* had made her way to friendly Tongatabu immediately after the bloody ordeal at Eastern Solomons. There, her war-weary crew had been allowed to intersperse the hours of grueling repair work with deserved shore leave in a true South Pacific paradise. The damaged carrier was still at Tongatabu when the news reached her that the *Saratoga* had been torpedoed.

During the stay at Tongatabu, the *Enterprise's* air component was reduced to a mere dozen warplanes. All the rest that had survived Eastern Solomons were flown off to make good the climbing losses at Guadalcanal or to help bolster the defenses at bases immediately to the rear of the Solomons battle arena. The *Enterprise* Air Group was disbanded in all but name.

When the *Enterprise* was deemed seaworthy for a long journey, she was dispatched to the superb Pearl Harbor Navy Yard—a real disappointment to all hands, who were certain that the only repair facility capable of handling the carrier was at Bremerton, Washington, from which home leave could be taken. Except for a rampant epidemic of dysentery, the long sea journey, undertaken in September, was relaxing for just about everyone aboard the carrier. All hands faced a rigid refitting and training schedule that they knew would be ameliorated by the first decent liberty schedule they had gotten since the previous December.

The *Enterprise* entered the Pearl Harbor Navy Yard on September 10, 1942. Five days later, the *Wasp* was sunk by three Japanese torpedoes. The news further energized the already frenetic pace of the repair work.

The men returned from the war found some strange attitudes among the men supporting the war. LCdr Orlin Livdahl, the carrier's gunnery officer, was greeted upon his arrival at Pearl Harbor by a representative of the Navy's Bureau of Ships who had brought along a comprehensive plan, complete with drawings, for the replacement of four of the carrier's five mediocre quad-1.1-inch antiaircraft mounts with modern director-guided quadruple-40mm mounts. The new Swedish-designed Bofors guns had a slower rate of fire than the despised 1.1s, but they were more reliable, had greater range, and could cause more damage. That was fine with Livdahl, but he was not happy with the planned placement of the 40mm guns. From the standpoint of gunnery alone, the placement of the new mounts would reduce the firing arc that had made the dismal 1.1-inch guns as successful as they had been. Equally important, the ship's executive and air officers determined by means of a scale-model mock-up that the proposed placement of the 40mm guns would eliminate four precious aircraft parking spaces. After exhaustive consultations with the ship's air officer, Lieutenant Commander Livdahl redrew the plans—and ran into an immediate roadblock when the bureaucrats running the Navy Yard told him they were not authorized to change Bureau of Ships plans. So Livdahl went to his ship's outgoing captain, Capt Arthur Davis, who arranged a conference with the yard officer and the senior officer whose employ Davis had left months earlier to assume command of the carrier—Adm Chester Nimitz. Next morning, the Pacific Fleet commander patiently listened to both sides of the argument. The yard engineers said that it would take weeks to prepare new plans and have them approved by the Bureau of Ships. The *Enterprise* people said that the 1.1-inch guns had already been removed and that the proposed placement of the new guns and their ammunition stowage had already been marked out on the decks, that work could begin immediately. Admiral Nimitz asked the yard engineers one question: Could they place the guns where Livdahl wanted them without going beyond the scheduled completion date. The engineers allowed as they could, to which Nimitz said, "Do it." And they did.

Other modifications included the installation of a radar direction system for the carrier's 5-inch antiaircraft guns. The radar could "see" targets through cloud cover. New men with strange new rates usually arrived with the newfangled gear, and, as the modern weapons and machinery were being installed, selected officers and sailors were sent to school to learn how to use and care for them.

All hands who would be sailing back to war aboard the *Enterprise* were super-critical when it came to undertaking, overseeing, or checking repairs to their ship. Every weld was examined and critiqued, every placement was measured and re-measured for accurate dimensions and smooth movement, every yard worker was pushed by the crew to the limits of his ability and endurance. In the words of Lt(jg) Jim Kraker, an Eastern Solomons veteran, "We had to fight this ship, and we wanted a perfect weapon."

The grueling task of repairing and refitting was made yet more grueling by the need to absorb all the new people, familiarize everyone with new equipment and weapons, and generally keep crew honed to a fine edge of combat readiness. The immediate lessons of Eastern Solomons drove home the need for all hands to be able to function in the dark or in smoke-filled spaces. To the extent possible, drills were realistic. Gunners and others drilled until they dropped, then drilled again, often as not with blindfolds on. Everyone, even the crustiest old sea dog, was eager to practice, and the new kids were eager to learn from the blooded veterans. The time at Pearl was used by many to cram for exams that would win coveted promotions, or even to change specialties within the Navy's dizzying array of new ratings.

Every day, old hands were called over the loudspeakers to receive orders to new billets, mainly new carrier constructions in the States. The good-byes were painful, even for the men who were departing for the cherished home leaves that went with the new orders. Daily, new officers and men reported aboard.

During the stay at Pearl Harbor, the nominal *Enterprise* Air Group was replaced by Air Group 10, the first reserve carrier air group to report for carrier duty in the Pacific. A small number of *Enterprise* Air Group alumni were transferred to the new group—including Lt(jg) Hal Buell, who had not only flown at Coral Sea, Midway, and Eastern Solomons, but had just returned from Guadalcanal, where he had flown for an entire month. For the most part, the new air group was composed of youngsters whose first combat still lay ahead. But many of the new air group's senior officers and flight leaders were combat veterans of the Coral Sea or Midway, or both. Others were expert pilots who had until recently filled instructional billets in the States, turning out some of the green pilots they would ultimately lead in battle. Most of the green pilots and aircrewmen had far more training and flying time than many of the veterans of the earlier battles, a definite early payoff of the reserve carrier air group program. With their new home tied up at the Navy Yard, the Air Group 10 pilots and crewmen had to content themselves with ongoing field carrier training at nearby airfields associated with the Pearl Harbor complex.

During the refit, also, the *Enterprise* Air Department was expanded to incorporate the ground crews of the air squadrons. Formerly, each squadron had carried its own ground echelon on its rolls. Under the new plan, nearly all groundcrewmen were carried on the rolls of the ship's company, thus reducing paperwork for squadron pilots assigned to secondary administrative chores. The entire groundcrew operation was streamlined.

The *Enterprise* underwent sea trials on October 10 in order to provide Air Group 10 with an opportunity to qualify all of its many novice pilots with actual carrier landings, the first many of them had ever attempted. In two days, 274 landings were completed without a single mishap.

On October 16, the Task Force 61 commander-designate, RAdm Bill Halsey, left the *Enterprise* and Task Force 16 in the hands of RAdm Tom Kinkaid in order to join an inspection team heading to Noumea and other South Pacific bases. Halsey expected to rejoin the *Enterprise* at sea, as both Task Force 61 and Task Force 16 commader, and Kinkaid was slotted to replace RAdm George Murray in command of the *Hornet* battle force, Task Force 17.

When at last the *Enterprise* was ordered back to sea on October 16, 1942, she had greater defensive firepower than any carrier afloat, and she was manned by a crew as thoroughly trained and dedicated as there was aboard any warship in the world.

The ten-day journey from Pearl Harbor was filled with hard work. Rough edges left from the frantic repair job had to be dealt with, and training continued at maximum levels. Moreover, the wearing routine of watches had to be reinstituted. That meant that, in addition to hard work and hard training, all hands had to learn or relearn the art of getting by on inadequate rest and hurried meals.

At daylight, October 23, Task Force 16 rendezvoused with the fleet oiler USS *Sabine*, and all ships topped off their fuel tanks in preparation for what seemed to be an immiment contact with the Combined Fleet. During the refueling, several key Task Force 61 staff officers were transferred from the *Enterprise* to the *Sabine* to be carried to Noumea, where they would join VAdm Bill Halsey's South Pacific staff. These key staffers would arrive too late to help Halsey during the upcoming battle, and the absence of several—notably the U.S. Navy's leading fighter direction officer and the *Enterprise's* experienced radar officer—would be keenly felt as soon as the battle was joined.

Chapter 16

RAdm Tom Kinkaid's mission, which had been transmitted to him aboard the oncoming *Enterprise* by VAdm Bill Halsey on October 22, was to "sweep around north of [the] Santa Cruz [Islands]." That is, Task Force 61 (along with RAdm Willis Lee's Task Force 64) was to interpose itself between the Truk-based Combined Fleet and Henderson Field. As it turned out, according to Halsey's post-battle letter to Adm Chester Nimitz, dated October 31, it was Halsey's intention that Task Force 61 sail north of the Santa Cruz Islands only if "no enemy comes down." This detail was never communicated to Kinkaid, who thus planned to sail north of the island group no matter what.

Almost on the heels of sending his October 22 initiating dispatch to Kinkaid, Halsey learned from Pacific Fleet Intelligence that the anticipated major Japanese offensive could start as early as a day or two hence. The cryptanalysts had pieced together several mentions of "Y-Day" in Japanese dispatches, but they were unable to say what it was or when it might take place. Yet it was clear on October 22 that something big was in the offing, so Halsey allowed time for Task Force 16 to join Task Force 61, and for Kinkaid's carriers and Lee's surface ships to snoop out the enemy forces no doubt closing on Guadalcanal.

On October 23, the cryptanalysts informed Halsey that at least eight Imperial Navy long-range submarines had received orders to "form a scouting line in the Solomons area." This Halsey knew was consonant with unvarying Imperial Navy battle doctrine. If the submarines were forming a "scouting line," they could well be doing so in advance of a sally by the Japanese carriers. This surmise was bolstered when the cryptanalysts added that the submarines were being ordered to "sweep for [U.S. Navy] forces," a sign that seemed to point to a Japanese fleet offensive. Later that day, the cryptanalysts raised to ten the number of Japanese submarines covering the Solomons and New Hebrides, and they added their surmise that the Japanese would attempt to initiate a fleet action within two or three days, October 25 or 26.

The pieces seemed to be falling into place, but Pacific Fleet Intelligence persistently underestimated the number of Japanse carriers operating out of Truk. As far as the Americans knew, only the fleet carriers *Shokaku* and *Zuikaku* were operating outside of Japanese home waters.

Unbeknown to Pacific Fleet Intelligence, the South Pacific Area command, or any Americans serving with Task Force 61 or Task Force 64—but in complete affinity to their expectations—Adm Isoroku Yamamoto had finally grown impatient with the 17th Army's slipping timetable. The Combined Fleet commander-in-chief was understandably nervous. His submarines and reconnaissance aircraft had lost track of the American carrier force on October 16 and, in the ensuing week, had not been able to reestablish even an inferential fix upon it. The only potential carrier sighting anywhere during that week was by a patrol bomber based in the Gilbert Islands, which spotted a diversionary force of two U.S. Navy destroyers sent out to make it appear that a carrier strike in the Gilberts might be imminent. That sighting was not as revealing of American plans as it was worrisome with respect to the ultimate size of the otherwise invisible American force.

The only U.S. naval force of consequence whose position was regularly monitored that week—on October 21 and 22—by Japanese long-range reconnaissance aircraft was Task Force 64, the surface battle force built around the battleship *Washington*. Task Force 64, primed to screen Task Force 61 from a Japanese surface attack or to rush to the aid of the Lunga defenders, had been sailing for days in the area between Rennell and San Cristobal islands, frustratingly out of the range of Japanese strike aircraft.

During that week, Yamamoto's own carriers were at sea and thus vulnerable to an American surprise attack. But the Americans knew neither the number nor the position of the Japanese carriers.

The status quo—the search for a battle by no means certain—abruptly changed on October 23.

After a quiet week, the Japanese noted a sudden intensification of U.S. reconnaissance flights throughout the area. These aggressive searches, combined with the disappearance of the American carrier force, alerted Combined Fleet to a possible renewal of U.S. offensive naval operations in support of the ground forces that, the 17th Army still claimed, would be swept from Guadalcanal.

For their part, beyond pulling Japanese plans and dispositions from the ether, Halsey intelligence advisors began to get some hard eyeball information to bolster their estimates. During the morning of October 23, a Patrol-91 PBY crew located a large Imperial Navy force about 650 miles north of Espiritu Santo—the first definite sighting in many weeks. This was RAdm Hiroaki Abe's surface Vanguard Group operating ahead of VAdm Chuichi Nagumo's Carrier Group. That evening, a Patrol-91 radar-equipped night PBY located two small surface flotillas—a heavy cruiser, a light cruiser, and two destroyers in one group, and a larger force only ten miles to the rear. The second force appeared to include a carrier—and, indeed, it was Nagumo's Carrier Group itself.

As soon as news of the evening sighting came in, AirSoPac launched three night PBYs armed with aerial torpedoes. At 2030, Lt(jg) George Enloe, piloting a Patrol-51 PBY, reported a possible hit on a Japanese cruiser.

From the Japanese perspective, evidence of aggressive American intentions had begun mounting shortly after 0200 on October 23, when three bomb- and torpedo-armed AirSoPac PBYs based at Espiritu Santo launched a surprise strike in bright moonlight against Tonolei Harbor in the Shortlands. This attack severely compounded the discomfort inflicted that same night—and for the next two nights—by small harassing strikes undertaken by New Guinea–based Fifth U.S. Air Force bombers against ships anchored off Rabaul. And of course, the October 23 PBY sightings of and attack against Nagumo's Striking Force caused no end of dismay.

As a result of the moderately active day and night throughout the region by American long-range reconnaissance and land-based bombers, Admiral Yamamoto's headquarters informed General Hyakutake's 17th Army headquarters that, unless Henderson Field fell that night or the next night, a pending fuel shortage at sea would oblige the Combined Fleet to cancel its part of the overall operation.

On October 24, Japanese units at sea picked up an American commercial radio broadcast that said "a major sea and air battle is expected in the near future in the Solomon Islands area." This contributed to a feeling of increasing uneasiness by the Japanese even as it reinforced their belief that the Americans were initiating the forthcoming clash.

At 1245 on October 24, Task Force 61 was reconstituted when the *Enterprise* task force (Task Force 16) joined the *Hornet* and her consorts (Task Force 17). Now in command of Task Force 61was RAdm Tom Kinkaid, aboard the *Enterprise*.

At 1500, October 24, the U.S. Navy's offensive thrust began when, in accordance with what Kinkaid understood to be Halsey's will, Task Force 61 turned northwestward to follow a track beyond the Santa Cruz Islands. Hopefully, the swing north would carry Task Force 61 out of range of Japanese aerial snoopers and beyond the Japanese submarine scouting line.

That night, October 24–25, the initial 17th Army main assault south of Henderson Field was beaten back, but the 17th Army nevertheless radioed Yamamoto's Truk headquarters in the wee hours of October 25 to announce the fall of the airfield and the ongoing mop-up of shattered U.S. ground forces.

The outright lie—which was amplified and corrected too late, after dawn of October 25—irretrievably set the Combined Fleet in motion. VAdm Gunichi Mikawa's Solomons-based Outer South Seas Force mounted its planned (and ill-fated) daylight surface sally to Guadalcanal, and the carriers of the Advance Force and the Striking Force were released from their tethers to hunt for the lurking American fleet.

A clash at sea was inevitable.

Chapter 17

The cat-and-mouse game between the opposing carrier forces began in earnest early on October 25. At the outset, it appeared that the confrontation both sides desired would take place that day, too.

VAdm Nobutake Kondo's Guadalcanal Support Force, composed of Kondo's own Advance Force with VAdm Chuichi Nagumo's Striking Force 120 miles to the rear, had been sailing toward Guadalcanal all night in order to be on hand to cover the final 17th Army assault on the Lunga Perimeter. News was received at 0500 on October 25 that the land assault had been successful, but by 0730 it was evident that the reports of victory were incorrect or, at best, premature. As soon as the bad news was in, Kondo ordered all the warships to turn north and sail beyond the range of Allied aircraft that were presumably stalking them. Kondo still hoped to attack the American carriers, but for the moment he felt he needed some sea room—and a definite sighting!

In the meantime, RAdm Aubrey Fitch's AirSoPac (Task Force 63) searchers were out in force, looking to fix the position of Japanese warships they had begun locating on August 23. Well before dawn, Fitch's force dispatched ten PBYs and six 11th Heavy Bombardment Group B-17s to search sectors ranging 650 to 800 miles in an arc to the north. Home base for the PBYs was the seaplane tender USS *Ballard,* which was anchored off Vanikoro, the southernmost of the Santa Cruz Islands. The B-17s operated out of Espiritu Santo.

The first break of the day came at about 0930, when 1stLt Mario Sesso's B-17 crew spotted Kondo's Advance Force 325 degrees (roughly northwest) and 525 miles from Espiritu Santo. According to Sesso's report, the Japanese ships were tracking to the east. As soon as Admiral Fitch had Lieutenant Sesso's report in hand, he ordered the launch of twelve B-17s to attack the Japanese surface ships.

At about 0940, a Patrol-91 PBY piloted by Lt(jg) Warren Matthew discovered RAdm Hiroaki Abe's sizeable Vanguard Group, which was sailing ahead of the carrier arm of Nagumo's Striking Force. While the patrol bomber's radioman reported the position to all friendly bases eavesdropping on the search frequency, Matthew circled around to get into position to attack a battleship he incorrectly identified as the HIJMS *Haruna* (it was either the HIJMS *Hiei* or the HIJMS *Kirishima,* but it was definitely a battleship). Matthew's aggressive move was largely quixotic, for PBYs on daylight searches did not carry aerial torpedoes, a policy aimed at increasing their productive search ranges as well, perhaps, as obviating an attack such as the one Matthew decided to carry out with the only weapons he did have, a pair of 500-pound depth charges.

The glide-bombing approach was flawlessly executed, though the projectiles were hurled well short of the target. As soon as the depth charges were released from their shackles, Matthew pivoted his surprisingly nimble parasol-winged patrol bomber into a tight escape turn and ran from the area. Two nimble F1M Pete observation float biplanes launched from the *Kirishima* bounced the Catalina well before it got clear, but they were beaten off by the PBY's gunners, who claimed credit for downing at least one F1M and damaging the other. The PBY was shot full of holes during the encounter, and its port engine was damaged, but it returned to base in due course. Matthew's initial sighting report had reached friendly ears when first transmitted, but follow-up reports describing course changes by Abe's surface force—a reaction to the PBY's presence—were never heard.

At 1000, shortly after Lieutenant (jg) Matthew's crew spotted Abe's Vanguard Group, a Patrol-24 PBY piloted by Lt(jg) Robert Lampshire ran across "unidentified task forces" (plural!) while searching the 338- to 344-degree sector adjacent to Matthew's. In a follow-up report, the PBY crew noted that a force composed of two battleships, two light cruisers, and four destroyers had been pinpointed at 8°5' South Latitude, 164°20' East Longitude. This message was rebroadcast to all friendly bases by the seaplane tender *Ballard*.

Lampshire clung to the enemy battle force, plotting and reporting course changes for the next hour. Then, at 1100, while broadening the search somewhat, the PBY crew noted by radio that a small carrier—the *Zuiho*—was launching fighters. At 1103, Lampshire's radioman reported the thrilling news that two more carriers had been located as they sailed on course 145 degrees (nearly southeast) at 25 knots.

The Japanese sighted and correctly identified at least two American PBYs, at 0907 and 1003. And at 1030 the Japanese fleet commanders received news of a radio intercept indicating that one of the PBYs had correctly reported their position. Kondo ordered his entire battle force, and especially Nagumo's, to turn north at top speed as soon as the moment's routine air operations had been completed. Though Kondo was itching to bring the Americans to battle, there was no way he was sailing in harm's way without knowing where the American carriers were lurking.

The first news RAdm Tom Kinkaid had of any of the morning sightings came at 1025, from a rebroadcast by the seaplane tender *Curtiss* (RAdm Aubery Fitch's Noumea-based AirSoPac flagship) of 1stLt Mario Sesso's 1000 sighting report. The position given for Kondo's surface force placed it 150 miles northeast of Guadalcanal, which was 375 miles northwest of the American carriers—well out of range. Alert to a Japanese move on Guadalcanal, Kinkaid's Task Force 61 remained on its base course to the northwest at 22 knots. The *Enterprise's* Air Group 10 was responsible for routine patrols over the task force as well as launching search missions in the event the longer-ranged AirSoPac searchers located any suitable targets. The *Hornet* Air Group had the day's strike duty; a full deckload of carrier bombers were gassed, armed, and ready to go.

While Task Force 61 sailed northwest of the Santa Cruz Islands and waited for news of targets within range of its strike aircraft, Air Group 10 crews delivered three SBDs and two TBFs to the *Hornet* to make good some of her air group operational losses of the past few weeks. This slight adjustment left both carrier air groups with more than enough ready aircraft and spares to get through a day of battle.

Once the *Hornet* air department had signed for the spare SBDs and TBFs delivered by the *Enterprise*, the *Hornet* had eighty-five aircraft aboard: thirty-one SBDs, sixteen TBFs, and thirty-eight F4Fs. Unfortunately, due to deck-space limitations, the *Hornet* Air Group was not allowed to operate all of these airplanes, even though it had enough pilots and crewmen to do so. The air group was held to an operational strength of all sixteen TBFs (Torpedo-6), twenty-four SBDs (twelve each for Scouting-8 and Bombing-8), and thirty-three F4Fs (Fighting-72). The balance. including a preponderance of "war-weary" birds, were stowed in overheads above the hangar deck.

Fresh from Hawaii aboard a newly refitted ship, Air Group 10 had more aircraft at its disposal—forty-one SBDs, thirteen TBFs, and thirty-six F4Fs—but fewer in service: all thirteen TBFs (Torpedo-10), twenty-seven SBDs (Scouting-10 and Bombing-10), and twenty-nine F4Fs (Fighting-10). The Fighting-10 Wildcats had a modest range advantage over the Fighting-72 fighters in that they could each carry a pair of 58-gallon wing tanks rather than the single, somewhat smaller belly tank the Navy Wildcats had been using to that point. The thought at the moment was that the Fighting-10 Wildcats might be able to provide a deeper escort than the Fighting-72 Wildcats, but the range enhancement was actually negligible when taken against the flying—and thus fuel-conservation—experience even the junior Fighting-72 pilots had over most of the Fighting-10 novices.

Trouble struck Air Group 10 late in the morning, when Fighting-10's Lt(jg) William Blair reported a propeller malfunction while taking part in the combat air patrol over the *Enterprise*. At 1119, the *Enterprise's* new skipper, Capt Osborne Hardison, approved an attempt to get Blair and his fighter back aboard. The nature of the problem was such that Blair would have only limited control of his fighter once he lowered the landing gear.

The bad situation was made worse when, in the pressure of the moment, Blair neglected to drop his tail hook and the LSO's spotter failed to note Blair's mistake. Unarrested, the F4F barreled through the barrier and ran straight into a nest of parked SBDs, knocking one overboard and damaging three. When control was regained, it was discovered that four plane handlers had been injured and two SBDs and the F4F were damaged beyond repair. The three were hurriedly stripped of useful parts and pushed over the side.

The pile-up on the *Enterprise's* deck had yet to be untangled when, at 1150, Admiral Kinkaid received one of Lt(jg) Robert Lampshire's sighting updates. The message stated that two carriers and supporting surface vessels were 130 miles to the northeast of the position at which 1stLt Mario Sesso had first spotted a Japanese surface force at 0930. The Japanese were holding to a base course of 145 degrees and coming on at a speed of 25 knots.

After replotting the sighting report, Kinkaid and his staffers saw that the Japanese carriers were 355 miles from Task Force 61, and just slightly to the north of west. This position corresponded to 250 miles northeast of Henderson Field, nearly within striking range of the Cactus runways. Since Imperial Navy surface forces had been spotted in the same area, it was reasonable to assume that the Japanese carriers might be out to cover a direct amphibious assault against Lunga.

Kinkaid and his staff had not finished assessing the situation before an urgent and succinct message arrived from ComSoPac, VAdm Bill Halsey. Based on his own assessment of the available information, Halsey ordered Kinkaid to "Strike. Repeat, strike. ComSoPac sends Action CTF61 and 64."

In the earnest hope that the Japanese carriers would continue on course toward Guadalcanal, closing the range as they did, Kinkaid saw that there might be an opportunity to join the fight during the afternoon. There was a major glitch, however, in that the prevailing winds favored the Japanese, just as they had at Coral Sea, Midway, and Eastern Solomons. The Japanese carriers were sailing into the wind, which allowed them to launch and recover aircraft without backtracking. Task Force 61, on the other hand, had to reverse course—sail away from the oncoming Japanese—each time planes had to be launched or recovered. Among other tactical advantages, the arrangement increased the effective range of the longer-legged Japanese carrier aircraft, because they could be launched at a great distance and recovered after the carriers had closed the distance. The short-legged American aircraft suffered from the wind pattern in that the distance from which they were launched against enemy ships was pretty much the distance they would have to fly on the return leg. Other operational considerations were enhanced for the Japanese and subtracted for the Americans, but the effective range of strike aircraft topped the list. The upshot of it all was that the Japanese might be able to strike the American carriers and withdraw even before the Americans could get within range of the Japanese carriers.

The main advantage the Americans enjoyed this noon hour was that they knew the position of the Japanese carriers whereas the Japanese had yet to locate Task Force 61.

As soon as Kinkaid had all the facts he could gather, he ordered Task Force 61 to up its speed to 27 knots and set course directly for the quarry. Then, perhaps because the Fighting-10 Wildcats had slightly more range potential than the Fighting-72 Wildcats, Kinkaid ordered Air Group 10 to ready itself to mount the first strike of the day. It further appears that Kinkaid had carefully studied the results of the three earlier carrier battles and felt that every U.S. offensive strike had lacked the advantage of the follow-up or second-wave strikes the Japanese usually managed to mount. If all went well, the veteran *Hornet* Air Group was to be the second wave.

Uneasy in the certain knowledge that his carriers had been ferreted out by an American PBY, VAdm Chuichi Nagumo turned his Striking Force to the north. The final Japanese move of the day was made at 1300, only minutes after the *Zuikaku* launched an area search composed of four Kates, an antisubmarine patrol composed of two Kates, and three Zeros to shoot down the American searchers, or at least to drive them off.

At 1415, VAdm Nobutake Kondo received word from the Base Air Force that one of its patrol planes had located "two battleships, four heavy cruisers, one light cruiser, and twelve destroyers" 170 miles southeast of Tulagi.

This was undoubtedly RAdm Willis Lee's Task Force 64, a much smaller force than reported, and not a particularly important one in the day's global scheme.

At 1430, on the assumption that the American surface force might be screening the elusive American carriers, Kondo ordered Nagumo to ready a large strike force—as much to go after Lee as to be heading in the right direction in case the American carriers were located. Nagumo calculated that the American surface vessels were 340 miles from his own carrier decks, and he responded to Kondo's order by saying that he felt, even if the American carriers were in proximity to the American surface force, they were too far out to launch an attack of their own. Kondo allowed the attack order to lapse, and both his and Nagumo's battle forces continued to sail northward. They were already well beyond the range of the American carrier air groups, and getting farther by the moment.

Chapter 18

RAdm Tom Kinkaid was determined to strike the elusive Japanese carriers—or any other warships that crossed his path. He was so set upon an aggressive course that he was willing to engage in a late-afternoon or early-evening attack that would bring his strike aircraft home at dusk or even after dark.

Twelve Scouting-10 Dauntlesses were launched in pairs from the *Enterprise* at 1348 to search outward 200 miles along a fan of sectors from due west to north-northeast. It was Kinkaid's plan that Bombing-10, Torpedo-10, and Fighting-10 aircraft—thirty-five planes in all—would follow the median line of the search sectors out to 150 miles and either attack Japanese warships pinpointed by the searches or return to the *Enterprise* in time for a landing before dusk.

Due to a combination of errors, failures, and faults, the strike force ended up at only twenty-three aircraft—five Bombing-10 SBDs, six Torpedo-10 TBFs, the unarmed Air Group 10 command TBF, and only eight Fighting-10 F4Fs. The first of the strike aircraft barreled down the *Enterprise's* flight deck at 1408, and the last took off at 1425.

Ens Jeff Carroum, who was flying on the wing of LCdr James Thomas, the Bombing-10 skipper, was in many ways typical of the young pilots launched on that afternoon "search-and-strike" mission. Above all, Carroum was scared to death of what the strike might encounter; he did not truly believe he was quite ready for combat, and he doubted that so small a strike force would accomplish much even if it did find the Japanese carriers.

The plan was for the strike group to fly out 150 miles along the median line of the search sectors—325 degrees—until it received word—or did not receive word—of firm sightings by the scouts. If no word was received, the strike group was to return to the ship followed by the pairs of searchers. Nevertheless, once the strike force had formed between 15,000 and 17,000 feet, Lieutenant Commander Thomas led it out at 287 degrees, because his reading of the day's sighting reports suggested that the Japanese would be located farther to the south, assuming they were still coming on at high speed. (Although the Air Group 10 commander, Cdr Dick Gaines, was along on the strike—in an unarmed TBF—Thomas was the strike commander. Current U.S. Navy doctrine forced the air group commanders into the role of "strike evaluators" and denied them the opportunity to directly engage the enemy.)

Even as the Air Group 10 searchers and strikers were fanning out in search of targets, a small but growing number of Americans already knew that it would be impossible for them to locate or attack the main body of the Japanese battle force. At about 1450, six 11th Heavy Bombardment Group B-17s led by 1stLt John Buie, sighted the surface warships of RAdm Hiroaki Abe's Vanguard Group of VAdm Chuichi Nagumo's Striking Force as they retired from range of Task Force 61 at 25 knots. By 1510, the six B-17s were in position to execute level bombing runs against the largest target they could catch, the battleship HIJMS *Kirishima*. After scoring no hits on the ship, the B-17s had to fight their way out through three *Zuikaku* Air Group Zeros that barred their escape.

While flying into the clear, Lieutenant Buie's radio operator notified SoPac that enemy ships had been located and were retiring to the north at high speed. The message was received, authenticated, and passed across the chain of command. When Tom Kinkaid heard the news, he decided to do nothing. The Scouting-10 searchers would find nothing and arrive home in due course, and the strike group commander had firm orders to fly out only 150 miles and then turn for home. Given all the known factors, all the Air Group 10 aircraft would be back aboard ship well before dusk.

It was not to be. LCdr James Thomas had already deviated from his orders by leading the strike group out along a more southerly track than ordered. As the force came up on 150 miles without hearing any news from the searchers, Thomas gave in to what Admiral Kinkaid later characterized as "excess zeal;" he ordered the strikers to fly an additional 50 miles in the hope of giving the searchers more time to locate targets. Then, when the extra 50 miles of empty sea had passed beneath his wings, Thomas angled off to the north to fly an additional 80 miles. Nothing was seen, and no news came in, so Thomas finally called it a day and angled southeast, into the wind, to find the *Enterprise*. He had taken what he felt was a reasonable risk, and in doing so he had made a terrible miscalculation. The strike force had flown about 280 miles and was at the extremity of its operational range.

Ens Jeff Carroum was one of many Air Group 10 pilots who was gladdened by the order to turn for home. It was late in the day, and the night sky was closing in. Carroum had made only fifteen actual carrier deck landings in his life, none at night, so the darkening sky was cause for considerable concern. He had flown a total of ten hours that day, including a fruitless four-and-a-half-hour morning patrol, so he was dog-tired. Because his oxygen system had developed a leak on the outward leg of the search-and-strike mission, he had flown without oxygen at about 17,000 feet for three hours, an extremely dangerous situation. He had a killer headache and could barely keep his eyes open, the inevitable results of oxygen deprivation.

The many inexperienced pilots in the strike formation were having fuel-consumption problems. The junior pilots had been exactingly trained to maintain formation on their leaders, so they tended to waste a lot of fuel executing small maneuvers aimed at keeping station. Moreover, the green junior pilots had not yet developed the veterans' knack for conserving fuel, which entailed various tricks to control engine performance in order to eke out range. The rather short-legged F4Fs had real fuel problems much earlier than the SBDs and TBFs despite the fact that each of the Wildcats carried a 58-gallon auxiliary fuel tank. Indeed, in several cases, the wing tanks all but failed because of suction problems. The Fighting-10 pilots also began running out of oxygen much earlier than the bomber crews.

The strike force was still in the air after sunset. Scattered cumulonimbus clouds obscured the horizon, adding a sense of vertigo to the fatigue everyone was feeling by then.

As the strike group was nearing the end of the mission, Ens Jeff Carroum discovered that his YE/ZB homing device had apparently malfunctioned, for he received no comforting directional signals from *Enterprise*. But Carroum was not overly concerned; he assumed that Commander Gaines—or someone—would be able to find Point Option without difficulty.

Fighting-10's Lt Fritz Faulkner knew exactly where he was. The veteran former SBD pilot knew from experience that the YE/ZB device was often less reliable at shorter distances than at longer ones. Taking that into account, and adding his excellent plotting-board work, Faulkner felt he knew where home base lay. He flew up alongside the fighter leader, LCdr Bill Kane (the Fighting-10 exec), and motioned that he was taking the lead. Kane appeared to motion an affirmative, so Faulkner turned to the correct heading. But Kane did not follow. By the time Faulkner realized he was alone, it was too late to find Kane or the strike group. Fritz Faulkner landed aboard the *Enterprise* while there was still light, the first and so far the only striker to get home.

As Fritz Faulkner was landing, the strike force was feeling its way lower in the darkening sky, trying to pick up some sort of visual directional cue. At 1814, Lt Don Miller reported that his Wildcat was running on fumes. The fighter swiftly fell back in the formation, and then Miller bailed out, never to be seen again.

At length, Lt Doc Norton, who was leading the second section of Torpedo-10 Avengers, heard the faint homing signal. Norton had by then become separated in the clouds from the leading Avenger flight, so he was responsible for navigating on his own. He had not closely followed Lieutenant Commander Thomas's turns during the outbound phase of the flight, so he was not sure of his position relative to anything. There was not enough light from the cockpit instruments to read the teletyped YE/ZB interpretation code, which was stuck onto a strip of aluminum riveted to the dashboard. Norton had to work the aluminum strip loose from the rivets, a tedious chore that took his attention away from his flying and flight leadership of three other Avengers and a pair of escorting Wildcats. Once the code strip came free, Norton had to slide it around in the glow of the instruments, also at the expense of attention to his flying.

Maintaining the formation in the clouds was extremely difficult and, in Jeff Carroum's case, a matter of life and death because of his Dauntless's malfunctioning ZB receiver (YE was the carrier's transmitter). Things got a little better when a bright moon rose an hour after sunset, but Carroum began wondering if there was still a carrier on which to land. Maybe the Japanese had struck a deadly blow during the late afternoon. Maybe that was why all the flight leaders seemed to be milling around in confusion. Maybe he was not receiving the homing signals because home had been sunk.

Though the sky was hazy with clouds, Commander Dick Gaines did find Point Option. But there was nothing there. Following one circuit of the area, Gaines led the entire strike formation directly into the wind, a pretty safe bet in that sort of a situation. The SBDs jettisoned their 1,000-pound bombs in the hope of gaining some range, and the flash of one of the exploding bombs gave the first hint of salvation.

While getting airborne for the strike, Lt Swede Vejtasa, a veteran Fighting-10 division leader, had noticed that the *Enterprise* was trailing fuel from a leak. When Vejtasa spotted fuel on the surface in the light of an exploding bomb, he knew which way the ship had gone. He took over the group lead and headed straight into the wind for home.

All the *Enterprise* warplanes returned to the vicinity of Task Force 61 beginning at 1830, more than an hour after sunset. As Swede Vejtasa led the formation in, the *Enterprise* showed a blinker light that ordered the fighters to land first. Lt Robin Lindsey was already on the LSO platform, decked out in a reflective "skeleton" suit and equipped with reflective paddles.

There was confusion borne of inexperience, fatigue, and jagged nerves. Very few of the pilots waiting to get aboard had ever performed a carrier landing in the dark. Swede Vejtasa landed okay—he was an old hand—

but his wingman, Ens Whitey Feightner, came in on the same Cut and nearly plowed into Vejtasa's tail. The only thing that saved them from a deck crash was a lucky early snag by Feightner's tail hook. The four remaining F4Fs made it aboard in due course, but the time-consuming process forced a fuel-starved SBD to ditch at 1905.

Jeff Carroum was coming up the groove with all his gas gauges reading empty when he received a Wave-off for being a bit too high. There was no way, he knew, to go around again on no fuel, so he gave himself the Cut, confident that he could mitigate the offense by making a good landing. But the Dauntless kept floating in high, right over the Number-9 arresting wire, right on into the island. The right wing crumpled and fell off, and so did the right wheel. Carroum and his rearseatman climbed unsteadily from the wreckage and made a sheepish exit from center stage. No one ever mentioned the accident to Carroum, even though wreckage of his airplane flattened the tail of another SBD, and both planes had to be junked. Also, another Bombing-10 SBD was forced to make a water landing while the flight deck was being cleared.

Lt Scoofer Coffin, the Torpedo-10 exec and torpedo-flight leader this day, was in the lead TBF and only five seconds from touchdown when his engine died. He could not even turn aside from the *Enterprise's* wake before sliding into the water, from which he and his crewmen were plucked by one of the plane-guard destroyers.

Doc Norton finally thought he saw the *Enterprise's* dim night-recovery illumination and blinked his TBF's blue formation-flying wing lights before breaking out of formation at 500 feet to take advantage of a gap in the ragged recovery formation just below. Though Norton was a 1939 Annapolis graduate—as was the missing Lt Don Miller—he had only been flying since early in the year. (Annapolis graduates served two mandatory years with the fleet before they could attend flight school.) He had been accelerated through the latter stages of training because of a command-pilot shortage early in the year, though he had had as much finishing as any of the junior pilots. This was Doc Norton's first night carrier landing. He came up the groove okay, and took the Cut, but his tail hook caught the wire far to the right of center. The heavy TBF was just coming to rest when its right wheel dropped over the edge of the flight deck into the starboard aft 20mm gun gallery. Landing operations were briefly shut down as a deck tractor tugged the damaged Avenger back up on deck by the tail. When Norton was safely parked, he checked the fuel gauges and found that his Avenger had come to rest with only a gallon or two of aviation gasoline aboard.

The last strike plane to get aboard the *Enterprise*—a TBF—landed at 1927, but the two TBFs that were in line behind it ran out of gas and ditched nearby. Both pilots and three of four crewmen were rescued from the water.

Of the forty-one search and strike warplanes, one fighter crashed at sea, two dive-bombers were wrecked in a landing mishap, and two dive-bombers and three torpedo bombers were obliged to land in the water when they ran out of fuel in the traffic pattern. One F4F pilot and one TBF crewman were lost.

The eight warplanes written off that night had to be added to a tally of four F4Fs that had been destroyed on the *Enterprise's* flight deck in a landing accident early in the day, so the score for October 25 was twelve Air Group 10 warplanes damaged or destroyed and one pilot and one aircrewmen lost in operational accidents. The only mitigating factor was that the *Enterprise* had plenty of spare planes aboard, for she had been carrying a number that were otherwise destined to serve as replacements for the Cactus Air Force. These were broken out of storage and reassembled to make good some—but not all—of the day's very high operational losses.

Later that evening, the *Enterprise* air officer, Cdr John Crommelin, gathered the weary Air Group 10 pilots together in the wardroom and gave them an inspiring pep talk in which he revealed his certainty that the next day, October 26, would find them in battle:

> This may be the beginning of a great battle.
>
> You men do not need to be babied, and I don't intend to hold your hands. We know that the Jap task force we are looking for will have a three-to-one superiority over us. Four of our PBY patrols sighted the Jap task force. . . .
>
> You men will have the privilege tomorrow of proving the worth of your training, your schooling, our way of life as against the Japs'.

> The offensive strength we have in the Pacific is at this moment in the hands of you men in this room and of those on the *Hornet*.
>
> On you rests the safety of our Marines at Guadalcanal who have fought magnificently. Last night, they were bombarded again, and the Japs made an assault upon our position, but they held, proving their worth.
>
> Wherever we have met the Jap at sea with our carriers, despite overwhelming odds, we have stopped them.
>
> The Japs are determined to drive us out of the South Pacific. If they get through to Guadalcanal with their carriers tomorrow, the Japs will take it. If Guadalcanal falls, our lifeline to Australia will be menaced.
>
> To stop them, you must knock out their carrier force.
>
> . . . We are on the right side of this war. God is with us. Let's knock those Jap bastards off the face of the earth.

The Japanese also received a sort of a peptalk that evening—an operations order from Adm Isoroku Yamamoto that reached the Guadalcanal Support Force at 2118:

> (1). Army units plan to storm Guadalcanal airfield this evening at 2100; accordingly, there is great likelihood that the enemy fleet will appear in the area northeast of the Solomons.
>
> (2). The Combined Fleet will seek to destroy the enemy fleet on October 26.
>
> (3). All forces will take appropriate action to (2) above.
>
> (4). [Guadalcanal] Support Force will operate as designated by Commander-in-Chief.

Yamamoto's order was rewritten and transmitted by VAdm Nobutake Kondo to all ships of the Guadalcanal Support Force at 2240: "Commander-in-Chief, Combined Fleet, orders that since there is a great possibility that we will engage in a decisive action, aircraft of all units continue searching and tracking operations regardless of weather and enemy planes, in an attempt to discover the size and nature of the enemy forces."

Chapter 19

Despite the harrowing recovery of Air Group 10's ill-starred strike force, the Allied effort to locate the Japanese carriers did not close down for the night. Tender- and land-based reconnaissance aircraft were abroad after dark, six of them probing the night skies and darkened sea with the aid of airborne radar sets. If something of substance was found, RAdm Tom Kinkaid was determined to launch a night strike, which is why he had held back the experienced *Hornet* Air Group while risking Air Group 10 on a possible dusk or night recovery. If any of the night searchers found a suitable target within 150 miles of the *Hornet*, Kinkaid was prepared to send off fifteen SBDs, six TBFs, and even eight F4Fs. Underscoring this intent, at 2115 Kinkaid ordered Task Force 61 to come about to 305 degrees—northwest—at a speed of 22 knots. He was closing on the enemy!

None of the pilots or crewmen manning the *Hornet* Air Group strike aircraft were happy with the honor bestowed on them. The bright moon would help them fly and find targets, but who could know when clouds might obscure the moon. The least happy of the strike airmen were the eight Fighting-72 Wildcat pilots, whose orders included instructions to strafe enemy carrier decks in the hope of setting fire to fueled and armed enemy airplanes. The fighter pilots felt that the proposed mission was a one-way affair; if they survived the strafing attack, they did not expect to make it home on the fuel their fighters could carry.

At 1201, October 26, the operator of a new radar set aboard the Patrol-51 PBY piloted by Patrol-11's Lt(jg) George Clute, found what Clute's subsequent radio report labeled merely "the enemy" at a point some 300 miles northwest of Task Force 61. After skulking about for another twenty minutes, Clute followed his radar operator's directions to attack a "cruiser"—actually the destroyer HIJMS *Isokaze*—from among the throng of warships making up RAdm Hiroaki Abe's surface Vanguard Group. Beginning twelve miles out, Clute allowed himself to be coached to the release point for his torpedoes by the radar operator—the first time a radar-guided torpedo attack had ever been attempted in combat. At an altitude of under 100 feet, Clute conducted a straight-in approach until he visually acquired the *Isokaze* dead ahead. He released both of the aerial torpedoes slung beneath the Catalina's parasol wing. But it was not to be. In his excitement, Clute had flown too close to the target for the torpedoes to arm themselves, and the *Isokaze,* which had spotted the PBY at a distance of six miles, took evasive action. The torpedoes missed, and Clute and the *Isokaze* both ran from the scene.

At 0250, October 26, the main strength of the Guadalcanal Support Force was sailing southward again. It had run northward, out of range, until sunset and then had turned again to race through the night to within range of the American carrier task force.

Suddenly, the drone of aircraft engines was heard above the noise of machinery and ships' engines. The drone was coming closer. It passed overhead. Then it seemed to recede. Suddenly, the stillness was shattered by ear-splitting explosions from two pairs of 500-pound bombs. Debris and seawater washed over the superstructure of the fleet carrier *Zuikaku*. Then the darkness was pierced by a blinding white photo flare as, high above and farther out, the racing engines of a lone U.S. Navy PBY carried Patrol-91's Lt Glen Hoffman and his brave crew to safety.

Capt Toshitane Takata, the senior staff officer serving with VAdm Chuichi Nagumo's Striking Force, made his way from the *Shokaku's* bridge to report details of the attack to Nagumo and his chief of staff, RAdm Ryunosuke Kusaka. Nagumo had not yet arrived at a decision when he also learned of the earlier torpedo attack on the *Isokaze*.

The Striking Force commander concluded that he was sailing into an American trap. Immediately, Admiral Kusaka shot off a message to all ships of the Striking Force: "Emergency turn, together, 180-degrees to starboard." Then, "All ships, execute turn. Speed 24 knots." Aboard the *Zuikaku* and *Shokaku*, hangar-deck crews began disarming and degassing strike aircraft that had been readied for a predawn launch. Nagumo had lost one carrier fleet—at Midway—to bombs set off among fueled and armed carrier planes, and he was not going to risk doing so again even if it meant delaying his first strike of the new day.

Meanwhile, at 0310, as soon as Glen Hoffman's Patrol-91 Catalina had cleared the Japanese Striking Force, Hoffman's radioman broadcast details of the sighting that had culminated in the spectacular glide-bombing attack against the *Zuikaku:* "One large carrier, six other vessels on a southerly course, speed 10 [knots]." The message was received and authenticated, but the report took two hours to get from the tender *Curtiss*, based at Espiritu Santo, to Task Force 61, because someone in the communications chain incorrectly assumed that Admiral Kinkaid's staff would be monitoring the original sighting broadcasts. Thus, as Hoffman's PBY broke contact, the most important element of the Guadalcanal Striking Force slipped from American view.

The delay getting Hoffman's sighting report into RAdm Tom Kinkaid's hands would be decisive.

Cdr Masatake Okumiya was the senior staff officer on watch aboard the fleet carrier *Junyo*, which was part of Kondo's Advance Force, sailing sixty to eighty miles south of the Striking Force before Nagumo's turn. Okumiya was thus one of the first of Kondo's officers to learn of Nagumo's turn. He informed RAdm Kakuji Kakuta, commander of the Advance Force's Air Group (i.e. the *Junyo* force), and Kakuta transmitted the news to Kondo's chief of staff, Capt Mineo Yamaoka, who was with Kondo aboard the heavy cruiser HIJMS *Atago*. Kondo took only a few moments to decide his next move before issuing an order for the Advance Force to turn northward and follow the Striking Force out of the area at high speed. Kondo's Advance Force executed its turn at 0400. Like Nagumo's Striking Force, Kondo's Advance Force, including the *Junyo*, disappeared from American view.

Kondo's turn to the north left only RAdm Hiroaki Abe's Vanguard Group still sailing south toward Guadalcanal. At 0415, Abe's surface flotilla reached a point 250 miles northeast of Lunga, whence it was to follow Nagumo and Kondo back north. Just before the turn was made, the heavy cruisers HIJMS *Tone* and HIJMS *Chikuma* launched seven reconnaissance seaplanes in a fan that would carry them south of Guadalcanal, to waters in which the American carriers were known to seek haven.

Beginning at 0445, at Nagumo's order, the *Shokaku, Zuikaku,* and *Zuiho* launched four, four, and five Kate torpedo bombers, respectively, on headings ranging from 050 degrees to 230 degrees. The Kates were to search out to 300 miles. As soon as the Kates were airborne, the three carriers began preparing twenty-two Zeros to undertake the day's combat air patrols and twenty-two Kates, twenty-two Val dive-bombers, and twenty-five Zeros for the day's first strike. The first patrol fighters—three *Zuiho* Zeros—would begin launching at 0520, a half-hour before dawn.

Nagumo's turn to the north at 0300 had been made as the Striking Force was coming to within 250 miles of Henderson Field. Nagumo had been planning a night launch at full strength for a dawn attack against enemy carriers or surface forces. Now he would have to settle for a daylight engagement, for if there was no battle on October 26, the Guadalcanal Support Force would have to break contact and refuel.

Tom Kinkaid had also decided to call off the proposed night launch of the *Hornet* strike force. It had become clear that the Japanese would not be sailing into range that night, and there was a potential strategic edge to leaving the fueled and armed *Hornet* strikers on deck, ready to go at a moment's notice after daybreak. Kinkaid was quick to take RAdm George

Murray's advice that the *Hornet* Air Group remain on strike alert on October 26 while Air Group 10 performed the patrol and search duties for another day. In the event the hoped-for battle shaped up during the day, the *Enterprise's* more experienced fighter directors thus would be in charge of overseeing the defense of Task Force 61.

For his part, as overseer of all Allied assets in the region, VAdm Bill Halsey allowed matters to continue on their own. Halsey had not intended to bring Japanese carriers to battle so early in his watch as SoPac commander, nor to do so at the extremity of his land-based air assets. Nevertheless, the events of October 25—including the desperate night battles on Guadalcanal that bracketed it—had led Task Force 61 ever northward, toward the tantalizing prospect of a carrier-versus-carrier fleet confrontation that might well relieve the hard-pressed and dwindling Cactus Air Force of the burden of defending Lunga against an overwhelming onslaught by both land-based and carrier-based air strikes. Caught between a desire to mitigate the dangerous situation at Cactus and his own aggressive instincts, Halsey moderated his concerns over the possible relative strength of the opposing forces, Air Group 10's painfully obvious inexperience, and the day's many operational losses. In the end, realizing that matters were beyond his personal control, he tacitly allowed Kinkaid to remain on the prowl.

If there was any way the two sides could engage one another on October 26, there would be a battle. The Japanese had to get it done or break contact to refuel, and the Americans had to get it done or stop advancing from beneath their umbrella of land-based long-range patrol bombers.

Part V

The Battle of the Santa Cruz Islands

Chapter 20

The American and Japanese carrier forces north of the Santa Cruz Islands had avoided a confrontation on October 25 only because the Japanese had been unable to precisely pinpoint the position of the American carriers and, as a result, sailed back and forth just outside of the operational range of the American carrier-based bombers. The operational commanders on both sides—RAdm Tom Kinkaid and VAdm Nobutake Kondo—desired a clash, and both sides were determined that it would take place on October 26. To that end, the Japanese had prepared to launch a skyful of search planes from land bases, the carriers, and several of the large surface warships that carried reconnaissance seaplanes. Even a specially equipped fleet submarine or two were to launch reconnaissance planes before dawn.

Task Force 61 had also been steaming forward to join battle with the Japanese. Except to turn southeast into the prevailing wind to launch and recover airplanes, the American carriers had been heading north for two days. Through the night, in clear weather, beneath scattered clouds, in bright moonlight with visibility at fifteen miles, Task Force 61 had been zigzagging northward at a speed of 23 knots.

During the night, Tom Kinkaid and his staff reviewed everything they had learned about the Japanese fleet dispositions: Two separate battle groups had been reported by land-based search planes; one—portions of Kondo's Advance Force—was reported to have been eighty miles south of the other, which included at least one of VAdm Chuichi Nagumo's three carriers.

It was incorrectly assumed by the Americans that the two Japanese battle groups were positioning themselves to support a thus-far-undiscovered reinforcement group composed of transports and surface warships. The incorrect surmise was understandable; the Japanese had dispatched ground elements or reinforcements in all of the war's three previous carrier confrontations. In fact, the mid October crisis at Guadalcanal had arisen out of the early dispatch of the reinforcements. Nevertheless, all the Japanese ground troops that were going to be sent had for the time being been sent.

Anticipating that far-ranging night patrols would be able to reestablish contact with the Japanese carrier force—no one suspected that there might be *two* Japanese carrier forces—Admiral Kinkaid had ordered the rested *Hornet* Air Group to stand ready to launch an immediate strike mission, beginning as early as sunrise.

At 0512, as the search planes on the *Enterprise's* flight deck were going through their final checks just before the dawn launch, Task Force 61 received an important dispatch from AirSoPac sources: Lt Glen Hoffman's 0310 sighting report of Nagumo's Striking Force.

The two-hour delay in getting the critical news to Admiral Kinkaid found the Task Force 61 commander less sanguine than he had been earlier. As the first Air Group 10 searchers were being launched, Kinkaid's chief of staff, Capt Country Moore, urged that the *Hornet's* ready strike force be launched at once to undertake a search-and-strike mission in the most promising direction. But the bad luck Air Group 10 had experienced on October 25 had probably affected Kinkaid by then, and perhaps fatigue played a part, for the Task Force 61 commander decided to withhold his strike forces until after sunrise, by which time Air Group 10 would have dispatched eight pairs of searchers in *all* the likely directions. The *Hornet* Air Group and the remainder of Air Group 10 would await a firm sighting report. Kinkaid's decision was thus to expend more rather than fewer Air Group 10 SBDs on sector searches instead of committing some of them to the air group's back-up striking potential. If Kinkaid had known in time what Lieutenant Hoffman had found at around 0300, he probably would not have ordered Air Group 10 to search as far or as wide as he felt he had to at 0512.

Committing that extra handful of Air Group 10 SBDs to the search rather than to an all-out attack against the Japanese carriers was going to make all the difference in the world to the outcome of the day's unfolding carrier engagements.

To the west, Nagumo's Striking Force, once again preceded by Abe's Vanguard Group, was sailing directly at the American carrier task force.

On the Japanese side, the only news of note following the night's final turnabout to the south was a report to Combined Fleet headquarters at Truk from Guadalcanal indicating that the 17th Army's assault on the Lunga Perimeter had been unsuccessful. By then, the 17th Army's failure was beside the point for the Guadalcanal Support Force. The American carriers seemed to be closing to within range, and that was all the reason Kondo and Nagumo needed for being there.

Just before dawn, Nagumo's Striking Force had launched thirteen Kate torpedo bombers from the *Shokaku*, *Zuikaku*, and *Zuiho*. Their mission was to undertake extended sweeps across sectors centering on due south, to find the American carriers no matter what stood in their way.

The *Enterprise* came about into the wind at 0510—just before the Hoffman sighting report was handed to Admiral Kinkaid—and began launching her first CAP of the day, eight Fighting-10 Wildcats. Next in line on the crowded flight deck was the first search mission of the day, sixteen Bombing-10 and Scouting-10 Dauntlesses, each armed with a 500-pound bomb. Each pair of searchers was assigned a 15-degree sector out to 200 miles. The area covered was from due north to west-southwest. Right behind the searchers were six Dauntlesses for the antisubmarine patrol. At 0551, the *Hornet* launched two Fighting-72 Wildcat divisions to bolster the Fighting-10 CAP.

The two fleets were very close to one another; the Japanese were less than 200 miles due west of Task Force 61.

Lt Vivian Welch and Lt(jg) Bruce McGraw of Bombing-10 had the 266–282-degree search sector. They were outward bound at 1,200 feet and only eighty-five miles from the *Enterprise* when they both spotted a *Shokaku* Kate heading past them three miles to starboard and on a course precisely opposite to theirs. Both pilots at once surmised that the carrier attack bomber would be heading straight out from a carrier, so they flew on, their excitement mounting.

Welch and McGraw flew for only another twenty minutes before they saw vessels in the distance. It was 0617. Welch led McGraw up to 2,000 feet to take advantage of the scattered clouds at that altitude and then headed around to a spot about ten miles east of the Japanese ships.

Except for a few fast-moving squalls, Welch and McGraw enjoyed unlimited visibility. The sun was behind them, and the Japanese lookouts would certainly be concentrating on the westward approaches to their fleet. Both pilots and both rearseatmen began counting and identifying the array of warships below. They checked and rechecked, but it was clear that there were no carriers in sight. At 0630, Welch ordered his radioman, ARM1 Harry Ansley, to key a sighting report on the Morse transmitter: "Two [battleships], one [heavy cruiser], seven [destroyers]. Lat[itude] 08–10S, Lon[gitude] 163–55E. [Course] north. [Speed] 20 [knots]."

Welch and McGraw had found RAdm Hiroaki Abe's Vanguard Group of VAdm Chuichi Nagumo's Striking Force.

Still intent upon locating the Japanese carriers, Welch and McGraw headed north to the extremity of their 200-mile search, but they found nothing. At about 0700, they again passed over Abe's Vanguard Group on the return leg. This time, as a second contact report was being transmitted, Welch and McGraw were spotted and fired on by the nearest surface warships. The gunfire was heavy but it fell well short of the Dauntlesses. With that, since they were nearing the extremity of their search sector, Welch led McGraw back toward the *Enterprise*. When they were on the way back, about 100 miles from home, the *Shokaku* Kate they had seen on the outbound leg passed them again only one mile away heading in the opposite direction, but, as before, none of the warplanes opened fire. (Welch was later criticized for not taking this Kate on the first time he and McGraw encountered it, but this Kate's crew never saw an American ship on its search mission.)

Welch's position reports were only a little bit off. Abe's two battleships, four cruisers, and seven destroyers were actually twenty-five miles south of the reported position. For once, the sighting message was directly picked up by the *Enterprise* and rushed to the flag bridge to be placed in Admiral Kinkaid's hands.

As soon as Welch and McGraw passed over Abe the second time, the Japanese admiral ordered his force to alter course to the left, to 300 degrees, and raise speed to 30 knots, the better to evade an attack by American carrier strike aircraft.

Rank hath its privileges.

LCdr Bucky Lee, the Scouting-10 commander, was the senior searcher sent aloft on the morning of October 26, so he selected the center search sector—298–314 degrees—the one where everyone thought the Japanese carriers would be found.

Lee and his wingman, Ens William Johnson, were at 1,200 feet at 0640 when they approached the end of their 200-mile search leg. No enemy carriers had been sighted. Were they up ahead, or somewhere else in the sector?

Just as the two Scouting-10 Dauntlesses reached the end of the outward leg at 0645, Lee saw vessels dead ahead—he reckoned thirty-five miles ahead. The squadron commander adjusted his course, and Johnson followed. At 0650, they were only fifteen miles from the enemy force when both pilots and both rearseatmen definitely identified at least two carriers busily launching airplanes—seventeen Zeros, as it turned out, scrambled to join the three-plane *Zuiho* CAP in order to shoot Lee and Johnson out of the sky.

Lee's radioman, ACRM Irby Sanders, keyed the transmitter: "Two [fleet carriers] and accompanying vessels at Lat[itude] 07–06S, Long[itude]

163–38E." The message was sent four times in as many minutes, but no friendly base acknowledged it.

Lee was only ten miles off in his fix on the *Shokaku* and *Zuikaku*. The *Zuiho* was also in the area, but she was not sighted.

Lee and Johnson were climbing through 3,000 feet to get into position for a bombing attack when Johnson reported that seven Zeros were overtaking the Dauntlesses from the starboard beam. Lee assumed the Zeros would try for a head-on attack before he and Johnson could reach some nearby clouds, and that is exactly what happened. As a Japanese 7.7mm bullet starred his windscreen, Lee fired his two fixed cowl-mounted .50-caliber machine guns and reported sending the lead Zero diving away in flames. Ensign Johnson claimed two more Zeros with his fixed guns. (No Zeros were actually lost.) A moment later, the Dauntlesses reached the clouds, which were disintegrating in the heat of the rising sun.

When Lee and Johnson flew out of the cloud, the Zeros were waiting. The Dauntlesses ducked back in, but they almost immediately flew into the clear. A three-dimensional guessing game ensued as the Dauntless pilots tried to stay in the dissipating clouds and the Zero pilots tried to find the spot where they would inevitably leave the cover. At length, the Americans became separated during one wild maneuver, and they were unable to reestablish contact. Lee thought of making a try at the carriers, but the game became futile and he eventually was able to get clear and head for home—hopefully to refuel in time to join the strike he knew his contact-report message would generate. He arrived safely and found that Ensign Johnson had arrived minutes earlier.

The immediate consequence of Welch's and Lee's separate sighting reports was the spontaneous rerouting of search teams in the adjacent sectors.

Lt(jg) Howard Burnett, an Eastern Solomons veteran now serving with Scouting-10, was leading Lt(jg) Kenneth Miller in the 272–298-degree sector—between Welch and Lee—when he heard Welch's sighting report on Abe's Vanguard Group. Burnett immediately turned toward the reported coordinates and led Miller up to 14,000 feet in preparation to launch a dive-bombing attack on one of the large targets.

The two Scouting-10 pilots easily found Abe's force at 0645 despite its altered course and speed. Burnett's radioman reported the sighting, and Burnett quickly led Miller in an attack against the heavy cruiser *Tone.* The antiaircraft fire put up by the *Tone* and nearby vessels was intense and accurate. As Miller's Dauntless passed below 10,000 feet, a near miss by a large-caliber shell sent it spinning out of control. Miller was below 6,000 feet when he regained control of his airplane and resumed his attack. Though neither Dauntless was shot down or seriously damaged, the intense antiaircraft fire had the next-best effect; it threw off the pilots' aim. Both 500-pound bombs narrowly missed the *Tone,* which was shaken but unscathed. Both Dauntlesses emerged from the maelstrom in flyable condition, joined up, and headed for home.

The search team immediately to the north of LCdr Bucky Lee's sector was composed of two more Scouting-10 Dauntlesses, flown by Lt(jg) Les Ward and Lt(jg) Doan Carmody. Carmody was particularly tense this day; he was certain he would find Japanese ships. After about two hours in the air, he kept seeing what he thought was black smoke on the horizon, but closer inspection invariably revealed that the "smoke" was merely the reflection of clouds on the surface of the ocean.

Ward and Carmody were nearing the end of their outward leg when both heard Bucky Lee's sighting report. The two pilots studied their chartboards and came up with identical solutions: the Japanese carriers were eighty to one hundred miles west of their position, well within range. Ward led Carmody around to the new heading and began a slow, fuel-conserving climb to attack altitude. The pair flew on for thirty minutes and were just topping 8,000 feet when Carmody saw black smoke—*real* black smoke—on the horizon fifty or sixty miles dead ahead. The two pilots, conversing by means of well-rehearsed hand signals, agreed to stay close to the fluffy clouds in order to cover their approach. If all went well, their attack would come as a complete surprise to the Japanese.

Minutes later, and quite far from the carriers, both Dauntlesses temporarily ran out of cloud cover. They were only partway across the large gap on the way to the next nearest cloud when they were spotted and attacked by at least six Zeros. As Ward and Carmody jerked their SBDs around in radical and unorthodox evasive maneuvers—they nearly collided several times—the two American rearseatmen—ARM3 Nick Baumgartner, with Ward, and ARM2 John Liska, with Carmody—each claimed one Zero. The wild melee lasted only a few minutes, the time it took Ward and Carmody to reach the nearest clouds and sneak away from the area. Despite claims by both sides, neither of the Dauntlesses was damaged, and no Zeros were lost.

Chapter 21

At 0630, as ARM1 Harry Ansley was transmitting the Welch-McGraw sighting report on RAdm Hiroaki Abe's Vanguard Group to Task Force 61, a *Zuikaku*-based Kate pilot peeked over the horizon and spotted the *Hornet's* Task Force 17. At 0658, he reported, "Large enemy unit sighted. One carrier, five other vessels." Though visibility was hampered by an undercast, the Kate pilot turned north to shadow the quarry. In due course he amplified the initial sighting report: The carrier appeared to be a *Saratoga*-class ship escorted by fifteen other vessels, all bearing 125 degrees from the Striking Force at a distance of 210 miles.

The Japanese did not waste a moment pondering the implications of the reconnaissance report. As soon as Admiral Nagumo heard of the sighting—at 0658—he ordered his force's first strike group to be launched. First, however, Nagumo wanted verification of the contact report, so he ordered the carrier force's only dedicated reconnaissance plane, a Kugisho D4Y, to be launched from the *Shokaku*. Within minutes, the D4Y was airborne, followed at 0710 by the first strike aircraft, eight *Shokaku* Zero escorts commanded by Lt Hisayoshi Miyajima followed by twenty *Shokaku* Kate torpedo bombers commanded by the squadron's *hikotaicho*, LCdr Shigeharu Murata.

Beginning at 0715, the little *Zuiho* launched five Zeros to bolster the CAP, one torpedoless Kate to serve as a strike liaison plane, and nine escort Zeros commanded by Lt Saneyasu Hidaka. Next, at 0725, the *Zuikaku* launched eight escort Zeros commanded by Lt Ayao Shirane, followed by twenty-one Vals led by the group *hikotaicho*, Lt Sadamu Takahashi. One torpedoless Kate was also launched to track the strike force to the target.

Murata's strike force consisted of twenty-one Vals, twenty torpedo-armed Kates, two torpedoless Kates, and twenty-one escort Zeros—an imposing sixty-four aircraft. The *Shokaku* and *Zuiho* contingents joined up and departed at 0730, and the speedier *Zuikaku* Vals and their escorts left at 0740 but soon caught up with leading elements.

As soon as the last of Murata's first-strike aircraft had cleared the task force, a three-plane Zero CAP *shotai* landed aboard the *Shokaku* for fuel and ammunition following its running fight with the American Dauntlesses. Likewise, the *Zuiho's* three-plane combat air patrol landed to rearm and refuel. At the same time, the *Zuikaku* began moving armed second-strike aircraft from the hangar deck to the flight deck. Twenty-one Zeros remained aloft to keep more American snoopers at bay or to fight off an expected American carrier strike force.

No one ever said much about it, but Lt Birney Strong had been under something of a cloud since August 24, the day he had found the light carrier HIJMS *Ryujo* but had stood off monitoring her position while other searchers had launched attacks. When Strong had returned to the *Enterprise* with his bomb that day to file his formal report, the ship's air boss, Cdr John Crommelin, had flown into a rage, had questioned Birney Strong's nerve, and had thrown Strong into "hack"—confinement to quarters—until he, Crommelin, calmed down a few days later.

No one knows quite what occurred when the *Enterprise* returned to Pearl Harbor for repairs. Strong was still aboard as acting skipper of the small remnant of Scouting-5, and he stayed aboard when Air Group 10 arrived to replace the *Enterprise* Air Group. Many thought that Birney Strong, newly married just before he shipped out at the start of the war, should have gotten some good home leave after a long combat tour beginning in February 1942, on a raid against Japanese bases in the Marshall and Gilbert islands; on into March in raids against Japanese bases in New Guinea; through an attack on the Japanese carriers during the Coral Sea battle; then on to the invasion of Guadalcanal; and culminating in his ill-received judgment call at Eastern Solomons. Moreover, Birney Strong's reassignment to Scouting-10 placed him in a subordinate role to two or three other senior lieutenants, something of a blow to a man who had commanded a squadron, even on a temporary basis.

A 1937 Annapolis graduate and a superb flyer, Birney Strong was "Old Navy" all the way. His first and middle names—Stockton and Birney—were the names of early American naval heroes. He was a quiet, serious young man, known by all as an unremitting perfectionist who set the highest personal standard imaginable.

Whatever the reasons or reasoning, Birney Strong had sailed to the war once again when the *Enterprise* left Pearl Harbor on October 16. As far as anyone was concerned, the August 24 question was past history.

When LCdr Bucky Lee assigned himself the choice center search sector, Birney Strong drew him aside and said, "I think you'll find the yellowbellies are in your sector. When you discover them, give us the word, loud and clear."

Before the flight, Strong gave his radioman, ARM1 Clarence Garlow, a cheerful "Good morning!" and admonished him to keep the radio carefully tuned to the search frequency.

On October 26, Strong was flying into the prevailing wind in the 330–335-degree search sector, with Ens Chuck Irvine on his wing, when he heard Lt Vivian Welch's sighting report on Abe's surface Vanguard Group. Though he and Irvine were only five minutes from the end of their 200-mile outward leg, Strong turned his Dauntless southward at 0640. He was determined to fly nearly 150 miles to drop his 500-pound bomb on one of the Japanese battleships. If his estimates were correct, a long climbing approach would leave him with just enough fuel to reach home after throwing in a quick dive-bombing attack—but only if the battleships were where Welch said they were, and only if his navigation was perfect.

Strong and Irvine were thirty minutes along the down-leg when their earphones crackled with another sighting report. As promised, Bucky Lee's radioman was filling the air waves with the loud-and-clear news that the carriers had been spotted. A quick navigation check revealed that Nagumo's carriers were about fifty miles closer than Abe's battleships. But it was no conflict in any case; Strong wanted a carrier if he could get one.

The two Dauntlesses altered course slightly to chase down Lee's contact report. They flew on for only another twenty minutes and arrived dead-on. Ahead, filling a break in the intermittent cloud cover, were two carriers—the *Shokaku* and *Zuiho*. The *Zuikaku* was nearby, but she was obscured by the clouds.

Irvine drew up as close to Strong's Dauntless as he dared and followed the leader from cloud to cloud as Strong sought the best way to sneak up on either of the carrier flight decks. At that moment, out of sight behind other clouds, the entire Japanese CAP was going after Les Ward and Doan Carmody.

At 0740, Birney Strong signaled Chuck Irvine that he was set to commence the attack. Irvine slowed down a bit as Strong tilted his own Dauntless's nose up just a hair, began slowing down, and plunged away from 13,000 feet toward the nearest orange-painted flight deck. Irvine waited for just a moment before following Strong after the same carrier.

The Japanese were totally surprised and utterly unable to counter the Dauntlesses' swift descent with more than a desultory burst or two of small-caliber antiaircraft gunfire.

As Strong dived through a last layer of cloud and went through all the ingrained motions on the way down, he tried to identify the carrier from his odd angle of approach. He thought it was the *Shokaku* or, perhaps, the *Zuikaku*. In fact, his target was the *Zuiho*.

Strong was pulled back to the job at hand as he dived clear of the obscuring cloud layer when his rearseatman, ARM1 Clarence Garlow, called out the altitude readings. Strong knew that the altimeter was unwinding far behind the actual altitude, so he checked his aim one last time and then released his 500-pound bomb. Garlow's last call was at beneath 1,500 feet. Next, Strong closed his dive flaps, flattened out the dive, and ran for safety at full throttle just above the waves. An instant later, Chuck Irvine exactly repeated Strong's actions.

"Your bomb was a hit, Mr. Strong," Garlow said; "Mr. Irvine got one, too."

Both 500-pound bombs had driven into the *Zuiho's* flight deck between the island and the stern.

During their recovery to the west, Strong and Irvine received all the gunfire they had avoided during the approach and attack. But they flew through the instantaneous eruption without ill effect and swiftly got beyond the range of most of the gunfire. There, at the edge of the ring of fire, they were met by several Zeros.

The two Dauntlesses executed a close approximation of the weaving, scissoring pattern designed to draw attackers intent upon one airplane into the fire of another airplane. Designed for fighters with forward-firing wing guns, the weave was superb under these conditions for a pair of warplanes equipped to fire to the rear as well as forward. The rear gunners—ARM1 Clarence Garlow, with Strong, and ARM3 Elgie Williams, with Irvine—did their share, and more. When one Zero misjudged and swung too wide on a firing pass, Garlow got his twin-.30-caliber guns to bear before the Zero could whip out of range, and he nailed him; the Zero's belly took most of Garlow's fire, and the plane burst into flames as it skidded all the way into the sea. Williams smoked another Zero and watched it fall toward the water.

When Garlow found a moment that was not filled with attacking Zeros, he reached for his voice-radio transmission key and passed the vital news that a Japanese carrier had been hit, along with position and course information. Then he went back to fending off Zeros.

During a forty-five-mile tail chase, the Japanese shot up Irvine's tail and holed his starboard main fuel tank. Of equal importance was the amount of fuel both Dauntlesses sacrificed during the full-power chase. When at last the pursuing Zeros withdrew at about 0800 after chasing the Dauntlesses into a large cloud, Strong and Irvine both chopped back to minimum power and leaned out their fuel mixtures as much as they dared. It was by no means certain that they would reach a friendly flight deck.

Later, when the effects of the battle had dissipated somewhat, Cdr John Crommelin was instrumental in writing a recommendation to award Birney Strong a Medal of Honor. In the end, Strong received a Navy Cross, which was nothing compared to the unyielding respect he earned this day.

The Japanese were severely shaken by Birney Strong's and Chuck Irvine's swift, sudden appearance and attack, and they lost no time launching every available strike airplane before new misfortunes arose in the form of a mass attack by American carrier bombers. Even as the *Zuiho* was being hit, deck crewmen aboard the *Zuikaku* and *Shokaku* pushed their fuel carts straight into the water, lest their contents be set on fire by bombs amidst armed and fueled carrier aircraft. Then, when no follow-on attack was forthcoming, all available hands pitched in to get the second-strike aircraft safely into the air.

By about 0805, the *Shokaku* was ready to launch five escort Zeros commanded by Lt Hideki Shingo (the *Shokaku* fighter *hikotaicho*), the rearmed and refueled CAP *shotai*, and twenty Vals commanded by the group *hikotaicho*, LCdr Mamoru Seki. The *Zuikaku* contingent was delayed by the need to arm fourteen Kates with torpedoes, so the *Zuikaku* used the time to bring aboard four Kates just back from the morning search, of which two would be retained and two would be relaunched to take part in the second strike.

The delay aboard the *Zuikaku* caused Nagumo and his staff to think about delaying the *Shokaku* launch for thirty minutes, so the entire strike could proceed together, but many of these Japanese naval officers had survived Midway, and not one of them favored leaving armed and fueled aircraft on a carrier deck whose whereabouts were known to the enemy. The *Shokaku* got her launch under way at 0810, and Lieutenant Commander Seki departed the task force at 0818 with eight Zeros and twenty Vals, of which one Val later aborted. As soon as the strike force had departed, the *Shokaku* recovered two of her morning searchers.

During this busy time, also—at 0740—Admiral Kondo ordered Abe's Vanguard Group to depart from its screening station in front of Nagumo's Striking Force and race ahead to intercept the American carrier task force.

Abe split his force, sending RAdm Chuichi Hara ahead with the heavy cruisers *Tone* and *Chikuma* and two fleet destroyers, and coming on himself at 26 knots with the battleships *Kirishima* and *Hiei,* the heavy cruiser HIJMS *Suzuya,* the light cruiser HIJMS *Nagara,* and four destroyers.

As Abe's surface ships formed themselves into two units and surged away from the main carrier force at 0925, the main body of Kondo's Advance Force, including the *Junyo* force, raced to close the distance between itself and Nagumo. In addition to providing protection for Nagumo's carriers, the move would bring the *Junyo* Air Group to within distant striking range of the American carriers.

Until Kondo closed on Nagumo, the *Junyo's* air group was too far distant to take part in strikes against the American carriers, but it would eventually be in place for follow-on missions, a luxury of the first order. Far from the eyes of American snoopers, the *Junyo* readied a twenty-nine-plane strike. Even as she did, the Japanese situation was eased somewhat when the *Zuiho's* engineering officer informed her captain that their ship would soon be able to launch warplanes, though recovery on the damaged after flight deck would be out of the question until the light carrier had undergone major repairs at a naval shipyard in Japan.

Chapter 22

The first American strike bombers—seven Scouting-8 and eight Bombing-8 Dauntlesses under Scouting-8's LCdr Gus Widhelm—did not begin launching until 0732, nearly twenty minutes after the first Japanese launch. Following the Dauntlesses were six Avengers under the Torpedo-6 commander, Lt Iceberg Parker. Last aloft were two divisions of Fighting-72 under the squadron commander, LCdr Mike Sanchez. This strike, under the overall command of Lieutenant Commander Widhelm, was vectored directly against the last-reported position of the Japanese carriers.

The next strike group began launching from the *Enterprise* at about 0750, nearly twenty minutes after Widhelm's strike began launching. This force was led by Cdr Dick Gaines, the Air Group 10 commander, who was flying his own command Avenger. It consisted of just three Bombing-10 Dauntlesses flown by Scouting-10 pilots; seven Avengers under the Torpedo-10 commander, LCdr Jack Collett; and eight Wildcats under the Fighting-10 skipper, LCdr Jimmy Flatley.

There were several Avengers available aboard the *Enterprise* that could not be launched on this makeshift mission, because three Avenger aircrews were stuck aboard the plane-guard destroyers that had fished them out of the water during the night-landing fiasco. In addition, two Torpedo-10 crews were temporarily marooned aboard the *Hornet*, having been forced to stay overnight after ferrying two replacement TBFs over late the previous afternoon. The inconsequential showing by the *Enterprise* dive-bombers was the result of the requirements of both the morning search and maintaining antisubmarine patrols for the entire task force.

The *Enterprise* strike group, such as it was, took an extremely long time getting airborne. Torpedo-10's Lt Doc Norton, who was one of the last in line, saw that each pilot ahead of him was stopping to read from a chalkboard held up by one of the flight-deck crewmen. When Norton's turn came, he read, "Proceed without Hornet." Norton, who took off a few minutes later, did not even see any *Hornet* aircraft, though that ship was starkly visible on the horizon.

Beginning at 0810, about forty minutes after Widhelm's strike commenced launching, the *Hornet* Air Group commander, Cdr Walt Rodee, piloting his command Avenger, led off the second *Hornet* strike: nine Dauntlesses under Lt Johnny Lynch, the Bombing-8 exec; eight Avengers under Lt Ward Powell, the Torpedo-6 exec; and seven Fighting-72 Wildcats under Lt Warren Ford. This was the clean-up formation; it would strike what there was left to strike, carriers or surface warships.

The problem with the cobbled-together attack plan was that it was not cohesive. Both carriers initially launched the bombers and fighters they had available on the flight deck or at the ready and within easy reach on the hangar deck. Because each strike group was obliged to fly up to 200 miles to reach the Japanese—a circumstance was made worse by the need of the U.S. carriers to sail *away* from the Japanese during launches into the prevailing wind—forming the first *Hornet* and *Enterprise* groups into a single unit was deemed too demanding on fuel supplies. Moreover, there was no U.S. doctrine allowing the subordination of one air-group commander to another, nor the meshing of squadrons of one air group with like squadrons of another.

So, the U.S. strike groups went off as a stream of separate mixed units, each one composed of whatever aircraft happened to be available at the time of the launch. Indeed, each of the three strike groups lacked internal cohesion; each was itself strung out over distances of several miles.

Throughout 1942, the U.S. Navy had been working hard to develop types of formations that would cluster the bombers in such a way as to make them mutually supporting and to take full advantage of the forward- and rear-firing machine guns, but there was no doctrine for mixing dive-bombers and torpedo bombers in the same formation. Fighter-escort procedures were also relatively crude, but even the crude methods were obviated by the distance that had to be covered between each strike group's lead and rear bombers. The Wildcat divisions—two to each strike group—tended to stay high because the Wildcats needed an initial altitude advantage to effectively combat faster-climbing Zeros. In the case of the two fighter divisions escorting the lead *Hornet* strike, one division had to fly cover with the higher Dauntlesses, while the other had to fly at only 2,000 feet with the Avengers. The mixed *Enterprise* strike planes all flew at roughly the same altitude, with the two fighter divisions split up to guard either flank just ahead of the bombers.

The opposing strike formations began passing one another at about 0830, when Gus Widhelm's lead strike group was only sixty miles out from the *Hornet*. The low group of Wildcat-escorted Avengers actually passed directly beneath the larger Japanese formation. Widhelm and his pilots warily eyed LCdr Shigeharu Murata's strike group, and Murata and his pilots reciprocated. Many individual gunners in both forces trained out their machine guns, but no one opened fire and none of the fighters broke formation to molest the enemy. Within minutes, the strike groups had passed one another other. Assuming the Japanese had warned their ships of their presence, and thus feeling no need to maintain radio silence, both Widhelm and Mike Sanchez radioed Task Force 61 that a large Japanese strike was inbound. Murata did the same; he radioed the Carrier Group that fifteen enemy bombers were inbound. High above the passing bomber formations, twenty-nine *Zuikaku* Zero pilots failed to spot the American aircraft.

Next up—about ten miles behind Widhelm, 5,000 feet lower, and somewhat to the east—was Dick Gaines's smaller *Enterprise* strike group, which had been launched only twenty minutes earlier and which was only forty-five miles from the ship. The *Enterprise* group was still low and climbing very slowly to conserve fuel—except for Commander Gaines, who had more fuel aboard than the other pilots and who rapidly climbed far higher than anyone else.

The Dauntlesses, which were the slowest of the three American aircraft types, had the lead so that the swifter Avengers could hold station on them. This required the Avengers—flying in newly contrived stepped-down diamond-shaped, four-plane defensive formations—to weave a little in order to keep from overrunning the straining SBDs in the long, slow climb. The two fighter divisions—LCdr Jimmy Flatley's on the right and Lt(jg) John Leppla's on the left—were weaving back and forth 1,000 feet above and just ahead of the bombers in an effort to match speed with the much slower Dauntlesses.

Flatley and Leppla were both veterans of the Coral Sea. Indeed, both had won Navy Crosses in history's first carrier-versus-carrier battle—Flatley for his superb fighter leadership and Leppla for being the most aggressive Dauntless pilot anyone could remember. (Leppla's rearseatman at Coral Sea, also a Navy Cross holder, was ARM2 John Liska, who was returning home to the *Enterprise* at that very moment with Scouting-10's Lt(jg) Doan Carmody.)

Few of the *Enterprise* strike aircraft had turned on their radios yet, the better to preserve radio silence. They were still climbing when Gus Widhelm and Mike Sanchez broadcast their warnings to Task Force 61—which intercepted neither message—and no one in any of the *Enterprise* aircraft heard the alert.

Lt Saneyasu Hidaka, leading nine *Zuiho* Zeros, was frustrated by the lack of orders from Lieutenant Commander Murata to attack the passing *Hornet* strikers, so he did not wait upon word from Murata when he spotted the climbing *Enterprise* force. Though bouncing the second wave of American bombers would deprive Murata's force of close-in support, Hidaka apparently thought that a quick hit-and-run pass from 14,000 feet would leave him with plenty of time to rejoin the bombers before the attack on the American carriers commenced.

At 0840, Lieutenant Hidaka signed to the eight other *Zuiho* Zero pilots to follow him down in string formation against the American carrier bombers. After the Zeros had completed a descending 180-degree turn, the attack would be launched against the rear of the *Enterprise* formation and from out of the sun.

Hidaka's attack completely surprised the Americans. Ironically, only moments before the Japanese struck, LCdr Jack Collett, in the lead Avenger, had wondered aloud about the total absence of chatter on the radio—radio silence was seldom perfectly maintained—and had asked ARM1 Tom Nelson whether the radio was functioning. Nelson indeed found that someone had turned the frequency selector from the torpedo channel, and he made the necessary change. But it was too late.

The first American warplane to be struck by the Japanese fighters was Collet's. ARM1 Tom Nelson had just heard a bleat of "Bogeys!" over the radio and was cranking back his tunnel-mounted .30-caliber machine gun when he heard the throaty voice of the .50-caliber turret gun overhead. An instant later, the Avenger shivered right down her air frame and involuntarily fishtailed. Then the starboard wing went down a bit. Nelson realized that the torpedo bomber was gliding toward the ocean. A quick peek out the starboard porthole revealed a sick sort of look on the face of Lt(jg) Robert Oscar, the pilot of the TBF stepped off Collett's starboard wing.

Oscar's expression told Nelson that it was time to go. He was just beginning to move when he realized that smoke was pouring through the fuselage of the airplane. He grabbed the interphone mike and yelled into it to get Collett's attention, but there was no answer. It looked more and more like the engine had been damaged or destroyed and the pilot had been injured or killed.

By the time Nelson called to warn Collett, the latter had already exited the cockpit. Lt(jg) Raymond Wyllie, the pilot of the rear TBF in Collett's division, saw the squadron commander climb out onto the right wing and jump. He was never seen again.

Meanhile, Tom Nelson crawled into the radio compartment and pulled the locking pins on the hatch, which he kicked out into space. AM1 Steve Nadison was still in the turret, so Nelson had to get his attention and hand him his parachute. As he did, he realized that Nadison had balked at wearing even his parachute harness in the cramped turret. So, while all Nelson had to do was clip his emergency parachute to his harness, Nadison had to climb into his harness and then clip on the chute. It was a life-and-death difference.

Nelson tarried for a moment to help Nadison into the harness, but it was too cramped in the radio compartment for so much frantic movement, and it was all the more difficult because the Avenger was turning out of control to the right. Evidently realizing that Nelson couldn't help him, Nadison looked right into Nelson's eyes and cocked his head, a signal for Nelson to give him room by bailing out. With that, Nelson clipped on his chute and stood in the hatchway. The slipstream was powerful, and the airplane was still accelerating as it dived in a tight right spiral toward the ocean. It took a real concentration of energy for Nelson to dive through the tiny hatchway, but he did. The last thing he saw in the Avenger was the altimeter, which showed a reading of 2,000 feet.

Tom Nelson instantly yanked the D-ring on his parachute pack, far too soon for inertia to overcome his momentum, which was the same as the falling airplane's. The force of the pilot chute's impact with the rushing air tore it away from the main chute and knocked Nelson out. When the radioman came to, he was floating beneath a beautiful white silk canopy. He saw a large burning fuel slick on the surface of the ocean about a quarter-mile away. This was certainly his airplane. He quickly looked around for more parachutes, but there was none. At that moment, a Zero made a firing pass on Nelson, and the chute was badly riddled. Nevertheless, Nelson slipped into the water a moment later and ducked beneath the surface. The respite was short-lived; he had bluffed the Japanese pilot, but one of the parachute shroud lines had become entangled with the buckle of his flight suit. He was being dragged down by the sodden, heavy parachute when he found the tangle and pulled it free. He yanked the twin D-rings on his Mae West life jacket, but only one side automatically inflated. He blew the other side up by the mouth tube and discovered that it had a hole in it, which gave him something upon which he could focus his attention. He had no idea what to do next.

AMM3 Tom Powell, the turret gunner aboard Lt(jg) Robert Oscar's TBF, located on the right wing of LCdr Jack Collett's lead Avenger, was watching on the right side of the formation when the Zeros hit. This was his role in a new method of formation defense known as concentrated cone fire. All the turret gunners on the right watched and fired to the right, and all the turret gunners on the left watched and fired to the left. The area overhead and between the right and left airplanes was a free-fire zone. The tunnel gunners directed their attention and fire by the same method. From the first moment the Zeros broke out of the sun firing all their weapons, Powell was engaged up to his eyeballs in returning the fire. He never even noticed that the lead Avenger had fallen out of the formation.

During one sweeping firing pass by a Zero *shotai,* Powell thought he saw one of the enemy fighters explode in mid air, but his attention was instantly diverted elsewhere. A few moments later, during a fast peek over the side of the airplane, he definitely saw another Zero smoking as tracers from another Avenger passed all the way through it. The ensuing kill was credited to ARM3 Charles Shinneman, the turret gunner aboard Lt Tommy Thompson's TBF, the lead plane in the stepped-down second torpedo element. Powell had no fewer than three Zeros in view at all times throughout the brief engagement.

The tail-end Avenger in the first section, piloted by Ens John Reed, was mortally hit by the second Zero *shotai* passing from ahead to astern. AMM3 Murray Glasser, the turret gunner, barely had time to fire a few bursts at the passing Zeros before the intercom crackled with Ensign Reed's screams, "Bail out! Bail out!" At precisely that moment, Glasser realized that pieces of the airplane were flying back past the turret, and he thought he saw the tip of flames licking around his post. He instantly locked the turret and dropped into the large radio compartment.

The gunners' chest parachutes, which were too large to wear in the confined turret and tunnel, were secured by large bungee cords to the bulkhead directly above the starboard hatch. Glasser was the first to get to them, and he threw one to the radioman-bombardier, RM3 Grant Harrison, who was sitting in the jump seat in front of the bombsight. It took Glasser another instant to realize that Harrison was already pushing the hatch open against the slipstream, though he did not have his parachute on. Glasser was about to say something to Harrison, but he saw that the radioman was glassy-eyed and realized that he had drifted off into a catatonic state.

Glasser dived through the open hatchway and pulled his parachute's D-ring. As the chute billowed above him, he saw a Zero knife straight into the water. Minutes later—he had lost track of time—he gently entered the water and climbed out of the encumbering parachute harness without any difficulty. When next he looked, the sky was empty and eerily quiet.

It took several seconds after the initial attack on the lead Avengers for the rear Zero *shotai* to strike Lt Doc Norton's airplane, which was next-to-last in the rear Avenger formation. Both Norton's plane and the rearmost, piloted by Lt(jg) Dick Batten, were riddled by 20mm cannon and 7.7mm machine-gun fire. Nevertheless, both of the turret gunners got rounds into one of the Zeros as it flashed on by from astern to ahead, and the Zero ignited like a torch just before it grazed Norton's right wingtip. Though all the gunners probably got a piece of the destroyed Zero, the entire kill was credited to Batten's tunnel gunner, AM2 Rex Holmgrin.

Batten's Avenger was hit by the passing Zeros. A fire erupted in the hydraulics line controlling the port aileron, which stood straight up. Holmgrin yelled a warning to Batten, who responded, "Get ready to jump. I'll put her in the water," and then went on the open radio channel to say that he was on fire and setting down in the water. The burning TBF dropped out of formation, but the damaged aileron fell off the wing and the hydraulics fire burned itself out. The bomb bay doors could not be opened, and thus the torpedo—which was probably damaged, too—could not be jettisoned. Batten found he could keep the damaged Avenger flying, so he gingerly turned back toward Task Force 61, hoping to nurse it all the way home.

The first American fighters into the fray were John Leppla and his Fighting-10 Wildcat division—Ens Al Mead, Ens Dusty Rhodes, and Ens Chip Reding. All save Leppla were novices. Leppla flew directly into the oncoming Zeros. The four Wildcats instantly received hammer blows from hundreds of 20mm and 7.7mm rounds.

Chip Reding, Leppla's second-section leader, saw only the rear Zero *shotai* as it closed on the Avengers. He immediately charged his guns and dropped his wing fuel tank. The transition from the drop tank to the main tank did not go well, however, and Reding temporarily lost air speed. In a second or two, the fuel-starved engine sputtered and died, and the Wildcat spiraled toward the ocean as Reding desperately tried to restart the engine.

Dusty Rhodes, Reding's wingman and the division's tail-end-Charlie, also had a problem with his wing tank. It stuck in place when he tried to jettison it, and a Japanese incendiary or tracer round set it aflame. Rhodes nevertheless stayed on station above Reding while the latter fluttered toward the sea and until he got his engine restarted. During those few bleak moments, oncoming Zeros riddled Rhodes's canopy, shot out most of his instruments, and clipped his pushed-up goggles from his forehead—all without injuring him. Meanwhile, the wing tank continued to spew dangerous flames.

As his engine restarted, Chip Reding distinctly saw two Avengers struck by Zeros diving from above and both sides, from directly out of the sun. He led Rhodes straight at the attackers, but other Japanese fighters intervened and pressed home their own attacks at such steep angles and in such quick succession that neither Reding nor Rhodes was able to get any of the Zeros in his reflector gunsight. At some point in the swirling fight, however, the fire in Rhodes's wing tank went out, by then a small consolation.

John Leppla was gone. The last person to see him was Dusty Rhodes, who had looked back just once to see Leppla making a head-on run at one Zero with a second Zero clinging to his tail. A few moments later, Rhodes saw a partially deployed parachute streaming toward the water and thought it might be Leppla, but there was no way to be sure because by then several Avengers had been culled from the formation.

Long before Rhodes's last sighting, and only an instant after the action got under way, Leppla's wingman, Al Mead, had evacuated his disabled Wildcat. He safely parachuted into the water.

After a minute or two, Reding and Rhodes became separated. Each of their fighters had suffered severe damage. Rhodes had no instruments, and Reding's electrical system was gone, which meant he could not use his radio or fire his guns. Each pilot instinctively looked around for the other, and they managed to get back together. They had been flying as a team for months and simply fell into a smoothly executed scissor weave, less as a means of suckering in Zeros—for neither Wildcat was able to fire its guns—than as a way of evading Zeros. Slowly, the two Wildcats were being pulverized. But neither pilot had yet been injured.

Then Rhodes's engine burned out and froze. He was at 2,500 feet. He put the nose down for speed and turned upwind preparatory to ditching. A Zero dead astern opened fire, and the 7.7mm bullets severed the rudder-control cable. By then, Rhodes was approaching 1,000 feet. It was time to leave. He threw back the remains of the Wildcat's canopy, stood up, kicked the joystick right into the instrument panel, and yanked the D-ring on his parachute. The unfurling silk canopy neatly plucked Dusty Rhodes from his dead fighter and carried him gently to the sea, where he made a hard landing. When Rhodes next looked up, Chip Reding was zooming away with three Zeros glued to his tail.

Reding tried to stay over Rhodes, but the Zeros on his tail quickly drove him away. He dived toward the water and was below 100 feet before he was able to break away from the attackers. The strike group was long gone, and the Japanese seemed to be gone, too. Chip Reding turned the nose of his scrap-heap fighter toward the *Enterprise's* last known position.

LCdr Jimmy Flatley's division did not initially see the Zero attack nor Leppla's response because Leppla's division was weaving away from the main formation when the attack was sprung. By the time Flatley realized that his group was under attack, the relative position of Leppla's division had shifted from the formation's port vanguard to well astern. At the same moment, Flatley saw one Zero take position below and ahead of the TBFs.

As soon as Flatley saw the attack on the Avengers get under way, he turned into the main formation to harass the nearest Zero, which was by then well along in its approach from beneath the Avengers. Flatley executed a diving turn, came up with a full-deflection shot, and unleashed a stream of .50-caliber bullets. The Zero pulled up and turned away from the Avenger as Flatley recovered above and to the side to begin a second run. Flatley again got the Zero in his sights and instantly flicked the gun-button knob on his joystick while still at extreme range; a Zero hardly ever stayed put long enough for a perfect set-up. The gamble paid off: the Zero began smoking. A third, high-side, attack sent the Japanese fighter hurtling into the waves.

When Jimmy Flatley looked up for more targets, he saw that the Zeros were gone and that the group of Torpedo-10 Avengers had been reduced from eight to six. Leppla's Wildcat division had vanished.

The score for this unanticipated contest was four of nine Zeros downed by TBF gunners and F4F pilots, two of eight TBFs downed, and three of eight F4Fs downed. The human toll was four Japanese pilots lost, five American pilots and crewmen killed, and two Wildcat pilots and two Avenger crewmen in the water.

When the Zeros were gone—they made only the one sweeping pass—Doc Norton checked his riddled TBF for damage and discovered that he had no hydraulic power. This meant that the bomb-bay and .50-caliber turret were inoperable. The Avenger's right aileron was flapping in the slipstream, its control cable severed, and there was a large hole in the right wing disturbingly close to the locking mechanism. A closer check of the right wing revealed that the red warning tab was projecting, a pretty fair indicator that the locking pin was not properly seated and that the folding wing might fold at any moment. Fortunately, no one aboard Norton's plane had been injured.

Norton conducted a brief internal argument with himself. It was certain that Japanese carriers lay ahead, and getting Japanese carriers was what he was drawing pay to do. But the fact that the bomb-bay doors were locked tight by the disabled hydraulic system, and that the rear turret could not be worked at optimum performance for the same reason, militated against continuing. The clincher was that projecting wing-lock warning tab. There was a better-than-even chance that the right wing would fold back if Norton pulled too many negative gees, and doing so was a virtual certainty in a combat torpedo approach. So, Norton gave the section leader, Lt Tommy Thompson, the hand signal for "sick airplane" and gingerly peeled into a turn for home. By then, Lt(jg) Dick Batten had fallen out of the formation, and the two damaged TBFs joined up for the trip back to the *Enterprise*.

It naturally occurred to many of the six airmen aboard the returning Avengers that they were behind the Japanese strike group. All of them had an uneasy feeling about what they might find when next they saw Task Force 61.

For their part, the *Zuiho* Zeros were done for the day. Four of nine had been shot down, and one or two others, possibly including Lieutenant Hidaka's, were badly damaged. Feeling there was no way any of his Zeros could catch up with Lieutenant Commander Murata's receding strikers, Hidaka turned for home with the four remaining Zeros of his squadron. The *Zuiho* Zeros had done much to blunt the power of the *Enterprise* strike group, but Lieutenant Hidaka's rash decision to attack was going to bear bitter fruit when Murata's force came within range of the Wildcats protecting Task Force 61.

Chapter 23

At about the time *Enterprise* was turning into the wind to launch her search teams, Lt(jg) George Poulos of Patrol-11 was 500 miles down his outward search leg from Espiritu Santo. Poulos and other AirsoPac patrol pilots and crewmen had been fully briefed about the probability of a carrier battle taking place that day, and he and the others had been exhorted by their superiors to turn in a maximum performance.

The sun had barely begun to rise when one of Poulos's crewmen reported seeing a submarine submerging about five miles ahead. He also said he saw a float biplane taking off from the water. Poulos realized that he was too far away from the submarine to attack it, and he did not want to take on the biplane, which seemed insignificant in view of what might be sailing just over the horizon. So, to the disappointment of his crew, Poulos flew on. As he did, he thought about the position of the biplane, which was in a direct line between his base at Espiritu Santo and the probable location of the Japanese carriers. PBYs out of Espiritu Santo would be flying into the sun on the outward leg, so the biplane fighter would be able to approach them before it could be seen. If that was the case, the only thing that had saved Poulos's PBY from being attacked was its launch two hours before AirSoPac PBYs were usually launched. The Catalina had just been passing up-sun of the submarine when the biplane had been sighted.

All of the little decisions made that morning by George Poulos and his superiors paid off at 0830, when one of the lookouts called out that he had spotted many vessels. The cruising warships far ahead slowly resolved themselves into what appeared to be four carriers and their escorts. The nearer carriers, at least, seemed to have launched their attack planes, for their flight decks were clear.

George Poulos's entire purpose in life came down to evading the Zeros guarding the Japanese fleet and gaining some altitude so his sighting report would be heard at distant bases. As Poulos climbed through antiaircraft shell bursts, he ordered his crewmen to count the ships below, identify them by type, and report to the radioman. There was some disagreement about the number and types, but all agreed that there were four carriers. When the best count the crew could get was in, the radioman trailed a long antenna designed for long-range transmissions and sent the first of many reports on the size, position, and heading of the Japanese battle force. Unfortunately, but rather true to form, Poulos's initial sighting reports were not picked up at any friendly base. A report was finally fielded and acknowledged by the seaplane tender USS *Curtiss* at 0925, but it was not retransmitted to Task Force 61 until late in the day.

As soon as the 0925 message had been sent, Poulos turned back toward the Japanese fleet for a better count. This time, the crew came to quick agreement about the ships' size and types, so Poulos decided to leave the area. He was just turning away when four Zeros attacked. This frankly surprised the American pilot; he had by then been within sight of the Japanese for an hour, and he had been shot at early on by several ships. The Zeros had had plenty of time to attack him. Moreover, Poulos was surprised that the Zeros—the only line of defense against a possible American air strike—were being compromised for the sake of harassing a patrol bomber that had certainly already reported its findings to its base. The pilot radioed, "Enemy [carrier] aircraft," as he began evasive maneuvers.

Poulos took his slow amphibian bomber as low as he dared, just above the fifteen-foot swells on the surface of the ocean. At least the Zeros would not be able to launch attacks on his PBY's vulnerable belly, and they would have to pull out of their firing passes early to avoid plunging into the sea.

As Poulos maneuvered from side to side, from swell to swell, the Zeros came on. As each fighter began its firing run, Poulos flicked the patrol bomber to the right or left, into the line of flight of the approaching fighter. This forced the Japanese pilots to tighten their own turns, and reduced the amount of time they had to spray bullets at their huge target. The nearest any of the Japanese were able to get their bullets to the Catalina was twenty feet. After several passes each, the four Zeros departed.

Later, Poulos's PBY encountered a Japanese four-engine patrol bomber on a reciprocal course. The American pilot yielded to the loud pleas of his crew and gave chase, but the Japanese eventually drew ahead and escaped into thick cloud cover. With that, Poulos called it a day and plotted a course directly for his base at Espiritu Santo.

Between the time George Poulos's PBY crew first sighted the Japanese carrier force and the *Curtiss's* acknowledgement, the *Zuikaku* had launched a strike force composed of seventeen Kates (sixteen armed with torpedoes) and four Zeros. Poulos's crew never saw the launch, which was completed at 0900, and never realized that the four Zeros that attacked the PBY were the four escorts. The Zero pilots were certain that they had downed the PBY, and they rejoined the Kates in due course.

While the Zeros were chasing Poulos's PBY, the Kate crews spotted a second PBY entering the area. This was a Patrol-24 airplane piloted by Lt(jg) Enos Jones. Its crew spotted three vessels, which were identified as a large cargo vessel and two destroyers. The "cargo vessel" was the *Zuikaku*. Before Jones's crew could get a better view, the Kate *hikotaicho*, Lt Shigeichiro Imajuku, dispatched three torpedo planes to chase it off. The lightly armed Kates were practically useless for attacking enemy planes, but they acted aggressively during their overhead approch, and Jones indeed fled the area.

Although Jones's sighting report was picked up like Poulos's, it was not immediately forwarded to Task Force 61. But that hardly mattered, for the first *Hornet* strike group was by then closing on Nagumo's Striking Force.

♦

The lead American attack formation—seven Scouting-8 Dauntlesses, eight Bombing-8 Dauntlesses, six Torpedo-6 Avengers, and eight Fighting-72 Wildcats commanded by LCdr Gus Widhelm—found Japanese ships at about 0850, only twenty minutes after passing Lieutenant Commander Murata's attack force. A pair of Japanese cruisers—the *Tone* and *Chikuma*—escorted by at least two destroyers were sighted first, off to starboard, only 150 miles from the American warplanes' launch point. This was RAdm Chuichi Hara's Cruiser Division 8, which had earlier lost contact with the rest of Abe's Vanguard Group during high-speed maneuvering.

Feeling he might have missed something vital, Widhelm went to the radio with a call to LCdr Mike Sanchez, the Fighting-72 skipper: "Gus to Mike. Do you see carriers?"

The response Widhelm and most of the other strike pilots heard damaged their good impression of Sanchez: "Mike to Gus. No carriers in sight. Let's return."

When Widhelm next faced Sanchez, he threw a roundhouse punch for this cowardly response. But the words did not come from Sanchez. The Japanese were monitoring the *Hornet* strike frequency, and one of them had spoken for Mike Sanchez.

Withal, Gus Widhelm elected to forge ahead. He knew for a fact that Japanese carriers lay ahead. Twenty miles beyond Hara's Cruiser Division 8, someone reported what appeared to be a pair of battleships to port; closer inspection revealed two battleships plus two cruisers and as many as seven destroyers—the main body of Abe's Vanguard Group. Far to port, someone spotted another large force of ships partially cloaked by haze.

Widhelm started to climb for a better look at the distant formation and called out to Mike Sanchez: "Gus to Mike. I'm going up. Help me dive-bomb."

As soon as the battleships were spotted, a Zero *shotai* from the *Zuiho* reached out at the *Hornet* Air Group formation from almost dead ahead. For some reason, the four Wildcats escorting the fifteen *Hornet* Air Group Dauntlesses had fallen far behind the dive-bombers and were slightly below them, hardly the best spot from which to parry a challenge from the agile Zeros. The four Wildcat pilots, led by Mike Sanchez, had not yet acted to follow Widhelm higher when, at 0910, an SBD pilot called, "Tally ho, dead ahead. Tally ho, down below. Two Zeros." By then, the lead Zero had rolled into a high-side run on the unsuspecting Wildcats.

Instantly, the second section of Sanchez's Wildcat division—Lt(jg) Tom Johnson leading Ens Phil Souza—was separated from Sanchez's section. The lead Zero pounced on Johnson and Souza across from the left, over the top of both F4Fs. Souza, who had shared credit for a Japanese four-engine patrol bomber on October 16, was spellbound by the enemy carrier fighter's quick passage until it occurred to him that the man flying the gorgeous fighter out there was trying to kill him. He attempted to jettison his 42-gallon auxiliary tank—it failed to drop—and began weaving to throw off the Japanese pilot's aim, but too late. About seventy-five 7.7mm rounds and numerous 20mm shells struck Souza's Wildcat, mainly in the right wing.

The Wildcat's slow speed, Souza's adrenalin-induced strength, and the impact of so many bullets caused the Wildcat to snap-roll several times. Souza's erratic flying undoubtedly caused the Japanese pilot to assume that Souza was dead or dying, so he eased off and pulled out of his dive ahead of Mike Sanchez, who fired and thus forced the *shotai* leader to continue his dive. In the meantime, Souza recovered to find that his right aileron was about shot off, making the Wildcat extremely difficult to maneuver. Nevertheless, the second Zero came up dead ahead, a perfect target as it went to work on Tom Johnson's Wildcat. Souza quickly checked his reflector gunsight and applied pressure to the gun-button knob beneath his thumb. The Zero staggered and began throwing large chunks into the air as it rolled away. An instant later, the sky in front of Souza's fighter was empty; both the Zero and Johnson's Wildcat were gone.

As Souza looked for other airplanes, he noticed that the third Zero, which was nearly obscured by his wings, was working over the Wildcat piloted by Lt(jg) Willie Roberts, Sanchez's wingman. Souza fired a burst at long range, which chased the Zero off. As Souza flew up beside Roberts's Wildcat, he saw that its fuel tanks were holed and that the other pilot was bathed in blood from a life-threatening shoulder wound. Souza's earphones came alive: "We better go home," Roberts called. There was no sign of Mike Sanchez or Tom Johnson, and Souza was barely able to keep his damaged airplane level, so he and Roberts turned for home at 0915. As Phil Souza had initially feared, Tom Johnson had been shot down.

After losing track of Willie Roberts, LCdr Mike Sanchez outmaneuvered one of the attacking Zeros and fired on it. He was given credit for a probable, but his quarry was not downed by him. Failing to locate a single member of his division, Sanchez turned back to find the other Fighting-72 division, which was escorting the Torpedo-6 Avengers.

After recovering from their attack on Sanchez's Wildcat division, the two surviving *Zuiho* Zeros joined up and soon spotted Lt Jack Bower's Fighting-72 Wildcat division, which was at 2,000 feet, escorting the first group of *Hornet* Avengers. The attack was perfect, and Bower was sent diving into the water, probably before he knew what hit him. Bower's wingman, Lt(jg) Robert Jennings, and the second section, Lt(jg) Bob Sorenson leading Ens Roy Dalton, swung in to avenge Jack Bower. Jennings and Sorenson fired at the passing Zeros, and each claimed a probable. In fact, the *shotai* leader was shot down and killed.

The Torpedo-6 Avengers charged to the care of Bower's Wildcat division took no part in the fighter-versus-fighter action; their crews were not even aware it had taken place. It would be some time before the squadron commander, LCdr Iceberg Parker, even noticed that he had no escort.

After emerging from the initial melee and unable to locate the remainder of his division or the *Hornet* SBDs, Mike Sanchez took over the lead of Bower's division, which by then had turned for home. Because of bad positioning and questionable tactics—not to mention the three bold, aggressive *Zuiho* Zero pilots who so completely neutralized the Fighting-72 escort divisions—there was no fighter escort for the *Hornet* carrier bombers when they opened their attack on Japanese warships through the main body of the Japanese combat air patrol.

Chapter 24

As LCdr Gus Widhelm was beginning to climb for a better view of the distant, haze-obscured groupment of warships and the sea all around the main mody of VAdm Hiroaki Abe's milling Vanguard Group, he chanced to see the *Zuiho* Zero *shotai* opening its attack on LCdr Mike Sanchez's Wildcat division. Fearing that other Zeros might at that instant be pouncing on his vulnerable dive-bombers, Widhelm turned almost due north toward a bank of clouds—and the haze-obscured vessels. Down on the water, Lt Iceberg Parker failed to notice Widhelm's turn with all fifteen of the Scouting-8 and Bombing-8 SBDs, so he continued to lead his six Torpedo-6 TBFs on their assigned heading, 300 degrees.

Five minutes after turning, as the SBDs arrowed out of the cloud cover, an eagle-eyed pilot reported seeing two carriers, a light cruiser, and four destroyers. Closer scrutiny revealed that one of the carriers—the *Zuiho*—was smoking. The other, larger, carrier was the *Shokaku*. The third carrier, the *Zuikaku*, was hidden safely beneath a rain squall when the *Zuiho* and *Shokaku* were spotted by the American carrier bombers.

Without a flicker of hesitation, Widhelm had his radioman broadcast a sighting report to all ships and planes within hearing—"Contact bearing about three-four-five [degrees]." As the report was going out, Widhelm selected the larger of the two visible carriers, the undamaged *Shokaku*, which was about twenty-five miles off and slightly to port.

In keeping with standing doctrine, the dive-bombing attack was to have been coordinated with an attack by the six Torpedo-6 Avengers, but the Avengers had never climbed above 800 feet and their pilots and crewmen had entirely missed Widhelm's fortuitous turn toward the Japanese carrier formation. As the fifteen SBDs, each equipped with a 1,000-pound bomb, climbed and turned to find the optimum attack position, four *Shokaku* Zeros flew out to look them over.

The Japanese had been following the *Hornet* Air Group contingent's progress since 0840, when the *Shokaku's* experimental air-search radar team had located it on bearing 135 degrees at a range of seventy-eight miles. At that moment, the Japanese CAP was composed of twenty-three Zeros, including the *Zuiho shotai* that eventually turned back the Fighting-72 escorts. The Japanese fighter directors and their charges had the doctrine to meet the oncoming strike force far out from the carrier decks, but few of the Zeros were equipped with radios, and few pilots or directors considered the radios very reliable. Thus, the Japanese preferred to conduct the defense of their carriers close in, where visual control could also be exerted. Fighters were prudently stacked at high, low, and medium altitudes, but there were only twenty of them after the *Zuiho shotai* expended itself on the Wildcat escorts.

A moment after the first Zeros turned to meet the Americans, two bursting antiaircraft rounds marked the Dauntless formation for yet more Zeros. The Dauntlesses were then at 12,000 feet and still many minutes from climbing to the point at which they could begin their dives. At the approach of the first Zero, Gus Widhelm patted the side of his airplane: "Close up."

The American pilots tightened their defenses and coolly plowed on. The defensive formation they used was new. Rather than the old vee-of-vees formation, the SBDs were organized into four-plane sections and arranged in stepped-down diamond formation so defensive fires could be powerfully concentrated. Actually, Widhelm's own Scouting-8 flight was short a plane, so Widhelm flew with two wingmen in a vee formation, and the other four Scouting-8 SBDs formed a stepped-down diamond below and to its rear. Farther back, Lt Moe Vose's eight Bombing-8 SBDs were able to form into two complete, mutually supporting diamonds.

As the four *Shokaku* Zeros commenced runs from overhead and dead ahead at 0918, Gus Widhelm lifted his lead dive-bomber's nose and drew a bead on the lead Zero. When the gunsight pipper fell on the Zero's engine cowling, Widhelm pressed the gun-button knob on his joystick and unleashed his twin cowl-mounted .50-caliber machine guns. He had a fleeting sensation of flame as he flew past the oncoming fighter.

The Dauntless pilots following Widhelm had all they could handle just trying to maintain formation on the weaving, bucking, bobbing flight leader. The Zeros appeared to Lt(jg) Ralph Hovind, Widhelm's left wingman, to be coming directly out of the sun. As each one came into view, Gus Widhelm violently turned in toward it, and the entire Dauntless formation followed, guns blazing as the Zero passed overhead from ahead to astern. About all Hovind took time out to do was keep an eye on Widhelm, whose moves would be duplicated by the entire formation. Hovind had enormous confidence in the flight leader; he was placing his life entirely in Widhelm's hands. Indeed, his major concern was that he would be catching the 7.7mm and 20mm rounds meant for Widhelm's SBD.

Each attacking Zero—now including two *Zuiho* Zeros that had joined the fray—ran into the concentrated fire of as many of the guns as the Dauntless defensive formation could bring to bear. No amount of gunfire, no amount of diving and twisting and weaving by the Japanese fighter pilots could break the integrity of the American formation, though the Bombing-8 flight fell back and to the right of Widhelm's because of the strike leader's vigorous maneuvers and recoveries.

As the Japanese fighter leader directly challenged Gus Widhelm in a second diving head-on attack, Widhelm lifted his Dauntless's nose and poured .50-caliber bullets into the Zero's engine cowling. One hundred yards from the lead SBD, the Zero's engine exploded. The Japanese pilot attemped to ram Widhelm's SBD, but Widhelm slipped beneath the burning fighter, which then disintegrated. The Zero pilot, PO1 Shigetaka Omori, so impressed his fellow Zero pilots with this attack—they all thought he had crashed into the Dauntless leader—that he was posthumously promoted two ranks to special duty ensign, an extremely rare act.

So far, only six of Nagumo's twenty CAP Zeros had been drawn in after the American dive-bombers. Now five *Zuikaku* fighters joined in the defensive attacks, for a total of eleven, but five *Shokaku* Zeros stayed low to ward off torpedo planes, and a pair each from the *Zuiho* and the *Zuikaku* held themselves over their own ships.

As Ralph Hovind followed the progress of yet another approaching Zero, he distinctly saw a pattern of 7.7mm bullets penetrate the cowling of the strike leader's bomber. Widhelm's SBD took at least one round in the oil tank, whose contents immediately began leaking, soon to be followed by thin wisps of smoke. It would be just a matter of time before the engine suffered a complete failure. For the time being, however, Widhelm doggedly held his place at the head of the formation, still plainly visible as the strike leader, still leading the charge, still setting an example.

The pace of the action was unremitting. Far back in the formation, Lt Fred Bates, the Bombing-8 flight officer, glanced ahead at Lt(jg) Phil Grant's Dauntless just in time to see a fresh belt of .30-caliber ammunition ripped from the gunner's hands by the slipstream and lost over the side. A moment later, Bates's attention was redirected at a Zero making a steep diving run on the four-plane section he was leading. As all the nearby gunners trained out their free guns to bear on the intruder, the Zero came on so fast that its wingtips were pulling white vortices. Suddenly, both of the fighter's overstressed wings flipped off, and the fuselage knifed straight toward the sea.

Following a series of attacks—too many firing passes for the beleaguered Dauntless pilots or gunners to count—the first victim fell away; Lt(jg) Phil Grant and his radioman-gunner rode their mortally damaged SBD from Moe Vose's right wing all the way into the sea. They both perished.

A minute after Phil Grant's Dauntless was shot down, Lt(jg) Clay Fisher's Dauntless rolled away from Fred Bates's right wing and glided toward the waves. Unable to continue because of a hydraulic break caused by a 20mm shell, Fisher headed for the nearest cloud. A Zero followed him down and nearly finished the SBD off before ARM3 George Ferguson chased it away with fire from his twin-.30-caliber guns.

Lt(jg) Ken White, the trailer in Bates's section, was shot in the left hand and shoulder. He had to abort because his Dauntless's port aileron was shot away in the same burst. Though the Dauntless was virtually uncontrollable, White managed to head out of the battle area without ditching or being downed. All of the other Dauntlesses had been damaged to one degree or another.

Ralph Hovind was certain his airplane had over a hundred bullet holes in it; all the wing tanks had been holed. A 7.7mm bullet from a Zero Hovind never saw entered the cockpit and shattered a plastic control knob, which sent slivers of the bullet and the plastic into Hovind's right leg.

The loss of Grant, Fisher, and White left twelve Dauntlesses, which closed ranks behind Gus Widhelm as each new loss was counted. The running fight had carried the evading Dauntlesses too low for an optimum dive-bombing attack, but there was no way to regain altitude in the little distance remaining; to do so would mean going around in the face of the unremitting Zero attacks.

Finally, at 0925, as the reduced bombing formation was swinging into its final approach, the last of the oil drained from the breached cooling system of Gus Widhelm's SBD, and the engine immediately overheated. Widhelm held position through another set of gunnery runs by the Zeros, but the engine froze as overheated bearings visibly began burning. Widhelm patted the top of his head—"Take over"—and pointed his right forefinger at a thoroughly startled Ralph Hovind, who had begun the mission as a stand-in for Widhelm's regular number-two pilot, who was ill.

The bomber formation passed just overhead as Widhelm jettisoned his 1,000-pound bomb and began his long glide toward the sea. As he went, Widhelm cursed a blue streak over the communal strike channel, lest he never have another opportunity to make his opinions known. He cursed the innocent Mike Sanchez for a coward and gave a rather rough write-off to all the escort fighters; where were they when he needed them the most?

As soon as the Scouting-8 skipper was clear of the formation, the

Bombing-8 skipper, Lt Moe Vose, surged ahead with his remaining Bombing-8 Dauntlesses. As Vose passed Ralph Hovind's lead Scouting-8 Dauntless, he gave Hovind a broad grin and signed that Hovind was to relinquish the lead. Thankful to be relieved of this responsibility, Hovind nodded his assent and eased off the throttle a bit so that he could drop back with the surviving Scouting-8 Dauntlesses.

Gus Widhelm's Dauntless must have seemed like buzzard meat to the only Zero pilot who bothered to follow it as it corkscrewed away from the main dive-bomber formation. But as Widhelm tried to find a small patch of unoccupied ocean amid the surging, circling Japanese battle formation, his rearseatman, ARM2 George Stokely, duelled the Zero to a draw.

Widhelm was flying at extremely low altitude, nearly ready to pancake into the water, before the Zero finally broke off. At the last moment, Widhelm popped his dying airplane's landing flaps and dropped the tailhook—to let him know when he was about to enter the water as well as to slow the otherwise uncontrollable Dauntless when it did strike the waves. The former strike leader's riddled Dauntless came to a smooth stop and the pilot and rearseatman quickly climbed onto a wing and deployed the life raft.

The Zeros kept hammering away at the eleven remaining Dauntlesses through the final approach. Two American gunners were severely wounded, and all the Dauntlesses were damaged by the time they arrived over the *Shokaku's* flight deck—at 0927. Up to that point, the excited American pilots and gunners had counted fifteen Zeros downed, and the Japanese pilots later claimed fifteen Dauntlesses.

At nearly the last moment, Lt(jg) Joe Auman saw a Zero streak by his Bombing-8 Dauntless from high right to low left, firing all the way. Shrapnel from a 20mm cannon round stung Auman in the back of the head and riddled the radio set between the cockpit and the gunner. As Auman reflexively wiped blood from the back of his flight helmet, he instinctively banked his Dauntless around to the left in the slim hope of hitting the departing Zero with his cowl-mounted machine guns. As the Zero pulled up and away, Auman tried to follow the maneuver, which nearly stalled the Dauntless's engine. The abrupt maneuvers and near stall caused Auman to miss the final group maneuver before the dive. When Auman finally looked up, he was alone.

Moe Vose armed his 1,000-pound bomb and pitched his Dauntless into the nose-down diving attitude. The others followed at regular intervals. Thousands of feet below, the *Shokaku's* Capt Masafumi Arima used 30 knots of speed and all his ship's formidable maneuvering capability to try to slip from beneath the American bombsights.

Midway back in the bomber stream, Fred Bates's gunner warned Bates that a Zero was approaching from dead astern. Bates was trying to concentrate on following the SBD dead ahead into the dive. He shrugged off the news, spread his dive flaps, and pushed over.

Ralph Hovind's Dauntless, which was leading the Scouting-8 team, was struck by a Zero just as Hovind executed his dive. A stream of bullets carried away the rear canopy and blew the guns from the hands of Hovind's radioman-gunner.

Lieutenant Vose dropped his bomb at low altitude and zoomed down to hug the waves. Each of nine remaining Dauntless pilots did the same. Vose got a confirmed hit; a large charred splinter of one of the two remaining flight decks to launch warplanes against Pearl Harbor was blown by the detonation of Vose's bomb into the open cockpit of Fred Bates's Dauntless just as Bates was pressing his own bomb release. As Bates pulled away just off the surface, he looked back in time to see the *Shokaku's* after elevator heaved high above the flight deck in a cloud of flames and smoke.

Ralph Hovind was unable to contact his radioman-gunner on the intercom and assumed the gunner had been killed or injured. He had no idea how badly his Dauntless had been damaged. The Zeros were gone, but the antiaircraft fire from the carrier and her consorts was extremely intense. By the time the remaining Scouting-8 SBDs began their dives, the Japanese gunners had the range and deflection all worked out. The oncoming rounds looked to Hovind like roman candles. He was certain that each new burst was going to strike his dive-bomber, but each blob of rising red light fell away at the last moment. Hovind decided that if he was badly injured before he reached his bomb-release point, he would dive straight into the carrier's flight deck, bomb and all. As it was, his bomb narrowly missed the carrier's island.

Joe Auman, who had become detached from the Bombing-8 group, entered his dive alone a few moments after he saw the tail of the last Scouting-8 Dauntless pitch up and over. He was able to follow the plane ahead to the bomb-release point by keeping his dive brakes closed and flattening out his dive to only 60 degrees, as opposed to the usual 70- to 75-degree dive. Doing so also meant he would have to find an aiming point fast and get his bomb detached at fairly high altitude if he was to have a chance to recover over the water. Auman's concentration was perfect; nothing else in the world mattered as much as that onrushing flight deck. As Auman angled across the carrier from the starboard bow to the port quarter, a detached part of his mind saw that the flight deck was already burning, that smoke was spreading back from about midships, abreast the island. The rest of Auman's mind was scrolling through an endless set of barely perceived mental calculations aimed at precisely matching his dive, the pitch of the bomb, and the momentum of the carrier. The bomb was released at below 2,000 feet, dangerously low. As Auman used the speed of his no-brakes dive to get away, his gunner sang out with the news that their bomb had solidly struck the *Shokaku's* flight deck.

The American pilots and gunners counted three hits, but the Japanese reported as many as six, and Gus Widhelm, who was bobbing nearby in his life raft, also counted six. Whatever the actual number of hits, the *Shokaku's* flight deck was riddled and had to be shut down, and her innards had suffered grievous harm. Neither she nor the *Zuiho* would be lost this day, but both would be in repair yards for very long refittings.

Lt(jg) Stanley Holm, the last man in the Bombing-8 formation, was unable to line up on the *Shokaku,* so he attacked the antiaircraft destroyer HIJMS *Teruzuki,* on which he scored a near miss. While pulling out, Holm shot up the heavy cruiser HIJMS *Kumano* with the last of his .50-caliber bullets.

The retirement of the SBDs was nearly as eventful as the approach. Three SBDs were worked over by an enthusiastic Zero pilot who shot them up, rear to front, as they formed up at wave-top height. Lt Ben Moore, of Scouting-8, was cut up by 20mm shrapnel that passed through his armored seat, and Moore's radioman-gunner, ACRM Ralph Phillps, was hit in the arm. ARM2 Richard Woodson, in Lt(jg) Don Kirkpatrick's Scouting-8 SBD, was wounded in the same pass. To top it off, the Japanese pilot joined on the wing of Lt(jg) Roy Gee's Scouting-8 Dauntless and snapped a salute at Gee before leaving the Dauntlesses to themselves.

As he exited the area, Fred Bates saw large-caliber shells detonating on the water dead ahead and on both sides of his recovering Dauntless. Joe Auman pulled out of his no-brakes dive to the northeast, so he had to turn back and pass around the edge of the Japanese task force. He was so low over the water that he had to dart between rather than over the screening warships. As Auman turned left just outside the screen, he finally met up with a half-dozen friendly bombers and joined on them as he chomped into a candy bar he had brought along for some quick energy. He was amazed at how much saliva his overexcited system was producing as he ate.

Eight of the surviving Dauntlesses formed on Moe Vose for the trip home, and the rest turned toward Task Force 61 on their own.

The six Torpedo-6 Avengers that had been accompanying Gus Widhelm's SBDs entirely missed seeing the carriers and did not pick up Widhelm's sighting broadcast. The torpedo squadron commander, Lt Iceberg Parker, resolutely led his flight to the appointed 210-mile extremity of the outbound search leg, then turned northwest to scout another 50 miles out. Nothing was seen during the extended search, so Parker led his torpedo bombers around to try to relocate the cruisers and destroyers they had passed up earlier. The carriers were again obscured by intervening rain squalls, so Parker decided to go after the surface targets. At no time during the long search was he or any of his pilots in radio contact with any of the other American attack elements.

Many of the pilots in the battle-depleted *Enterprise* strike group, now numbering three Dauntlesses and four Avengers escorted by four Wildcats, heard Gus Widhelm's initial report pinpointing the carriers. They were rushing to catch up at 0930 when, during a course correction, several of the bomber pilots and crewmen spotted two Japanese battleships and their escsorts. Lt Tommy Thompson, who had taken command of the Avenger flight following the loss of LCdr Jack Collet, radioed LCdr Jimmy Flatley, the fighter leader, to see if the Wildcats had enough fuel to fly on another ninety miles to the apparent location of the carriers reported at about 0920 by Gus Widhelm. Flatley's four remaining fighters were about wrung out; they had jettisoned their auxiliary tanks before plowing into the Zeros during the earlier ambush, and high-speed maneuvering had used up a great deal of the fuel in their main tanks. Flatley replied that he was sure the fighters could not fly the full distance. The decision was Thompson's, and he decided to briefly search in the immediate area for other carriers, which he correctly understood lay to the north of the first *Hornet* strike group's assigned track. During the search, the three Dauntlesses came unglued from the rest of the tiny formation and flew away to the northwest.

Unable to locate the carriers during a ten-minute search, Tommy Thompson's four *Enterprise* Avengers descended to wave-top height in a series of skid turns and there found the heavy cruiser HIJMS *Suzuya* crossing their path.

At 0937, as antiaircraft fire burst well behind the tiny torpedo-bomber formation, Lieutenant Thompson dropped his fish at a 45-degree angle off the cruiser's port bow, and his wingman, Lt(jg) Bob Oscar, dropped off the cruiser's port beam. The other element—Lt Jim McConnaughhay leading Lt(jg) Ray Wyllie—followed Thompson and Oscar toward the cruiser's port side, but McConnaughhay's torpedo hung in the bomb bay. Wyllie followed McConnaughhay off the target, saw then that the leader's torpedo had hung, and returned to make a second run on the *Suzuya*. The heavy cruiser veered away at the last moment, and Wyllie's fish went on by. Five tries, three drops, three misses. McConnaughhay had to haul his torpedo well clear of the Japanese formation before he was able to jettison it.

The four accompanying Fighting-10 Wildcats strafed the *Suzuya* while the torpedo bombers were still boring in. Undoubtedly, the many half-inch machine-gun rounds caused some damage and might have caused some deaths or injuries aboard the cruiser, but they had negligible lasting effect. As soon as Ray Wyllie completed his second torpedo run, the Wildcats joined on the Avengers and headed for home.

Though the torpedo attack against just one ship in VAdm Hiroaki Abe's Vanguard Group caused little or no damage, some good came of it. Abe found himself disheartened by all the American carrier bombers passing over his flotilla, so he continued along a northwesterly track—away from his quarry, Task Force 61.

Lt John Lynch, the Bombing-8 exec, unwittingly led nine of his squadron's Dauntlesses around the edge of the ambush of the *Enterprise* Avengers. The action itself was too far away to be seen, but Lynch saw three airplanes crash into the water as well as four parachutes descending. He had no idea whose planes or parachutes they were.

Lynch's flight was joined at 0900 by ten *Hornet* Avengers—nine from Torpedo-6 that were equipped with four 500-pound bombs each and one unarmed command Avenger piloted by Cdr Walt Rodee, the *Hornet* Air Group commander. Shortly, a transmission from Gus Widhelm, still leading the first *Hornet* strike formation, pinpointed the Japanese surface warships but indicated that Widhelm was boring ahead to try to locate the carriers. Lynch's group reached the Japanese surface force just as Widhelm's pilots copied the bogus message purportedly from Mike Sanchez: "No carriers in sight here. Let's return." There was absolutely no way for Lynch to know that he was monitoring a phony report. Lynch, who did not hear any of Widhelm's subsequent messages, knew that Widhelm was twenty minutes ahead of his flight, and he saw that visibility ahead was unlimited, so he reasonably deduced that there were no carriers within effective range. Accordingly, he radioed Rodee with news of his decision to immediately attack a heavy cruiser that was just then passing beneath his wings and firing its antiaircraft batteries at his formation. Rodee did not protest—he never heard the transmission—so Lynch proceeded with the attack.

As Lynch turned to mount his attack, Walt Rodee turned, too, as did two Wildcats that were escorting the command Avenger. But Lt Ward Powell's nine bomb-armed Avengers did not hear any of Lynch's radio messages, and they flew on to the northwest at 10,000 feet, accompanied by a pair of Fighting-72 Wildcats.

Covered by three Fighting-72 Wildcats led by Lt Warren Ford, John Lynch's dive-bombing attack against the heavy cruiser HIJMS *Chikuma* commenced at 0926 from 11,500 feet. The time of this attack coincided roughly with the attacks against the *Shokaku* and the *Suzuya*.

The *Chikuma* and three accompanying warships—RAdm Chuichi

Hara's Cruiser Division 8—put out an extremely large volume of antiaircraft gunfire during the entire approach and on into the Dauntlesses' dives. Lieutenant Lynch, in the lead, and Lt(jg) Clark Barrett, in the third SBD, each claimed a solid hit. Indeed, one of the two 1,000-pound bombs detonated on the cruiser's bridge, injuring her captain and killing or maiming all but a dozen of the numerous Japanese officers and sailors around him. A second 1,000-pound bomb ripped apart the cruiser's main battery control station, damaged torpedo mounts, and started several small fires.

Following a fruitless ten-minute search for the carriers, the three *Enterprise* Dauntlesses—three Bombing-10 airplanes flown by Scouting-10 pilots—arrived over Cruiser Division 8 just as Lynch's Dauntlesses were departing the scene in good order. At 0939, the three dived from 12,000 feet and released their bombs over the wounded *Chikuma,* which the three identified as a battleship. The section leader, Lt(jg) Glenn Estes, a veteran Scouting-5 alumnus, claimed that his bomb struck the starboard deck amidships. Lt(jg) John Richey, another Scouting-5 veteran, claimed a near miss, and Lt(jg) Skip Ervin, a 1940 Harvard graduate on his first mission, claimed a solid hit on a turret. A number of American pilots, including Jimmy Flatley, saw smoke issuing from the ship. One of the bombs penetrated the *Chikuma's* deck and detonated within the ship's engineering spaces, flooding a boiler room and putting an engine out of commission. Two near misses amidships caused underwater damage and pierced the cruiser's upperworks with numerous splinters.

The three Dauntlesses rendezvoused at wave-top height and fled for home. As they ran, three Zeros attacked Richey's Dauntless, which was bringing up the rear. Richey's radioman-gunner, ARM3 Jay Pugh, claimed a kill, but none of the fighters was lost. Farther on, the Dauntlesses encountered a lone Wildcat, which was described in reports as being "all over the sky." It was LCdr Mike Sanchez's plane, and Sanchez was lost. After Glenn Estes pointed the way home, Sanchez nonchalantly lit a cigarette and flew ahead over the horizon.

At 0945, the nine bomb-armed Torpedo-6 Avengers and two escorting Fighting-72 Wildcats commanded by the Torpedo-6 exec, Lt Ward Powell, were approached by two *Zuikaku* Zeros as the Americans neared the end of their outbound search leg. The first Zero executed a head-on attack, but the Avengers, which were cruising at 10,000 feet, merely opened out to let it pass through their formation. The combined speed of the Zero and the oncoming TBFs was so great that turret gunners traversing to follow the Zero had time to get off only a few rounds apiece before the fighter had zoomed out of range. The Zero fired countless rounds without apparent effect, and the American pilots and gunners did the same.

The second Zero attacked the Avenger formation from above, front to rear, and pulled out at 4,000 feet, below and ahead of the two Wildcats. Lt Jock Sutherland set up a perfect full-deflection shot and opened fire from 400 yards as he closed on the Zero. The Japanese fighter blew up when Sutherland was still 100 yards away.

During the attack by the Zeros, Lt(jg) Jerry Rapp, a Torpedo-10 pilot who had been temporarily dragooned into Torpedo-6 after ferrying a TBF from the *Enterprise* to the *Hornet* the evening before, saw a large formation of Japanese bombers high overhead on a reciprocal course.

Lieutenant Powell saw Japanese cruisers and destroyers a little farther on. This was Admiral Hara's Cruiser Division 8.

The weather was generally clear, but towering cumulus clouds obscured the view in some sectors. No carriers could be seen, so Powell decided to go after Hara's little force. Still at an altitude of 10,000 feet, Powell led the Avengers out to the northwest, around the curtain of antiaircraft gunfire. In the near distance, he was able to see a number of Dauntlesses—Lynch's flight—diving on one of the cruisers.

Powell selected the damaged *Chikuma* for his flight's target. The approach was made from astern, using as much cloud cover as there was. Relatively little antiaircraft fire rose to greet the Avengers as the pilots dropped their landing gear to help slow their 45-degree dives.

Powell's glide-bombing attack was marred by an electrical failure that both knocked his radio off the air and forced him to drop all four of his 500-pound bombs in one salvo. At least two of the following Avengers suffered similar failures, with the same results. Nevertheless, one of Powell's bombs struck the cruiser; it damaged a torpedo mount, and the floatplane on the cruiser's after starboard catapult was set on fire.

Lt(jg) Jerry Rapp found that he had to steepen his dive angle to keep the pipper of his bombsight on the rapidly oncoming target, which maneuvered frantically to evade him. Because of the tremendous pressure on his stick and rudder, Rapp was only able to make minor corrections after that. Rapp elected to pass through 1,500 feet, at which point he should have released his bombs. He kept diving through 1,200 and pickled the bombs one at a time with both the electrical and manual bomb releases. The TBF was diving at a 55-degree angle by then and was much too close to the water for a comfortable recovery. As soon as the bombs were away, Rapp retracted his landing gear and closed the bomb-bay doors to reduce drag. Then he leveled off and advanced the throttle to maintain the high speed he had accumulated in the dive. His next hurdle was an enemy ship, dead ahead. He finally came straight and level at about 300 feet and instantly began jinking maneuvers to throw off the aim of gunners ahead, abeam, and astern. He passed directly over the bows of a destroyer and finally broke free from the worst of the gunfire.

Altogther, Ward Powell and seven of his pilots claimed five bomb hits, but only one bomb, dropped by Powell, seems to have struck the *Chikuma*.

Lt(jg) Humphrey Tallman, a veteran fighter pilot who had been transferred into torpedo bombers to help make good losses at Midway, also executed a glide-bombing attack on the *Chikuma*, but none of his bombs could be released. Tallman then went after one of Hara's two destroyers and released his full payload. He claimed hits on a "light cruiser" but apparently hit nothing. Unable to locate the rest of the pack following his recovery, Tallman turned for Point Option alone.

Lt(jg) Jerry Rapp had become separated from the other Avengers during the recovery from his over-steep glide-bombing attack. He was able to pick up some chatter on the radio but nothing helpful. Remaining close to the base of the cumulus clouds so he would have a safe haven in the event he was found by prowling Zeros, the lone Torpedo-10 pilot steered a course for where he hoped home would be.

Joined by the two Fighting-72 Wildcats, which had strafed the bridge of one of the destroyers while the bombers were at work, the rest of the Avengers flew northeastward through heavy antiaircraft fire until they were out of visual range of the Japanese, and then they rendezvoused and turned for home. None sustained any significant damage.

♦

By sheer coincidence, Lt Iceberg Parker led his low-flying, torpedo-armed *Hornet* Avengers over Cruiser Division 8 at precisely the moment Ward Powell's *Hornet* Avengers were commencing their attack on the *Chikuma*. Parker's target was Admiral Hara's flagship and the *Chikuma's* sister ship, the heavy cruiser *Tone*.

Opening their attack at 0951 through extremely dense antiaircraft fire, Parker's six *Hornet* Avengers spread out across the *Tone's* bows and delivered a classic hammer-and-anvil attack. Theoretically, the cruiser should have been hit by torpedoes on one side or the other, no matter which way she turned to evade the onrushing fish. Two of the American aerial torpedoes were seen by American airmen to run erratically, and Parker's torpedo hung in its bomb bay. Of the remaining three fish, American airmen counted three hits: two on the cruiser's port side and one on her starboard side. In reality, the *Tone* combed the wakes of all three American torpedoes and sailed on with no damage.

Parker's six Avengers recovered without loss or damage and headed for Point Option.

So far, losses among the various American attack groups amounted to three *Enterprise* Wildcats, two *Hornet* Wildcats, two *Enterprise* Avengers, and two *Hornet* Dauntlesses downed.

Four of the six crewmen aboard the downed Avengers perished with their airplanes, and two—ARM1 Tom Nelson and AMM3 Murray Glasser—were eventually rescued by Japanese warships, as were Fighting-10 pilots Ens Dusty Rhodes and Ens Al Mead. Lt Johnny Leppla of Fighting-10, Lt Jack Bower of Fighting-72, and Lt(jg) Tom Johnson of Fighting-72 were all lost with their Wildcats. Scouting-8's Lt(jg) Phil Grant and ARM2 Floyd Kilmer were apparently killed when their Dauntless crashed. LCdr Gus Widhelm and ARM2 George Stokely would be rescued by a Catalina patrol bomber on October 29.

No Japanese ship was sunk, but, counting damage inflicted by the scouts, two carrier flight decks were down, and one heavy cruiser was out of action. Five Zeros were downed in engagements over the Japanese ships, and a sixth ditched. For so much effort and expense, the American strikers had not done at all well.

An Imperial Navy Aichi D3A Val dive-bomber. (Imperial Navy)

A U.S. Navy SBD Dauntless dive-bomber in action. (Official USN Photo)

A U.S. Navy F4F Wildcat fighter makes an arrested carrier landing. (Official USN Photo)

An Imperial Navy Mitsubishi A6M Zero fighter. (Imperial Navy)

An Imperial Navy Nakajima B5N torpedo bomber. (Imperial Navy)

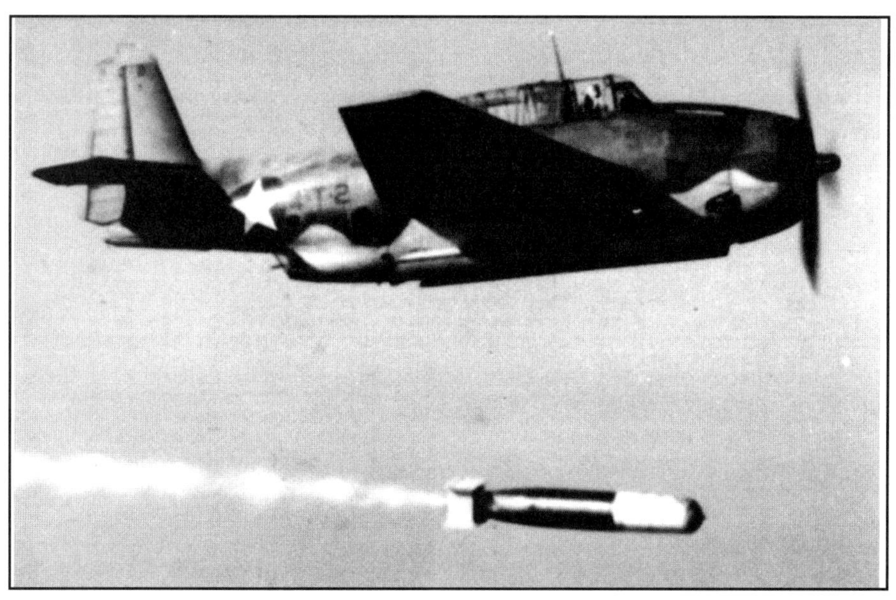

A U.S. Navy TBF Avenger torpedo bomber in action. (Official USN Photo)

The USS *Wasp* burns at sea after being struck by a spread of Japanese submarine-launched torpedoes. (Official USN Photo)

Wasp senior officers at a briefing session (l. to r.): Capt Forrest Sherman, LCdr Courtney Shands, Cdr John Shea, Cdr Mike Kernodle. (Official USN Photo)

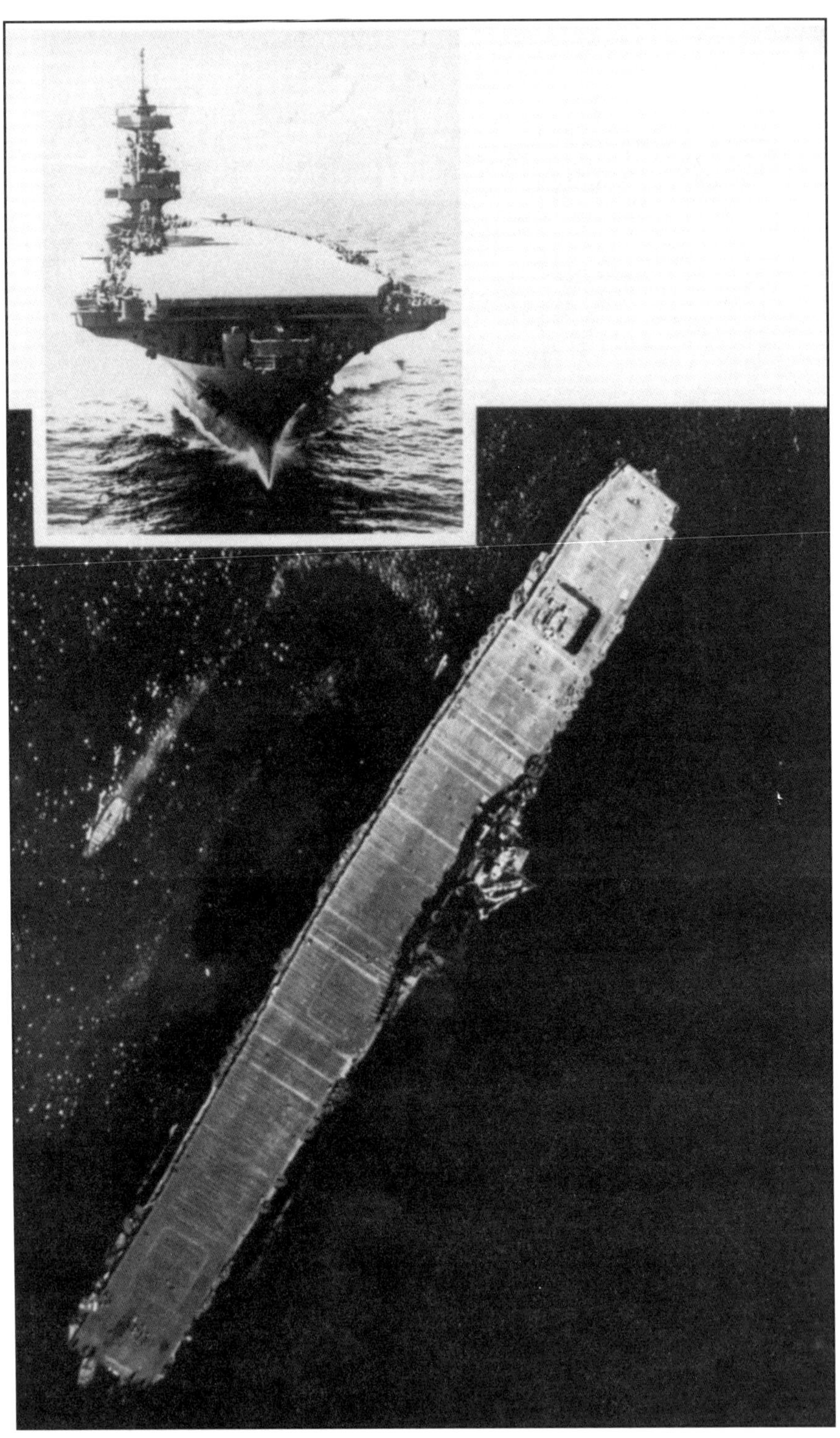

The USS *Enterprise* (CV-6). (Official USN Photos)

An LSO in Action: The *Wasp's* Lt Dave McCampell. (Official USN Photo)

An SBD makes an arrested carrier landing. (National Archives)

Torpedo-10 TBFs and Fighting-10 F4Fs on deck are being readied for launch from the *Enterprise*. (National Archives)

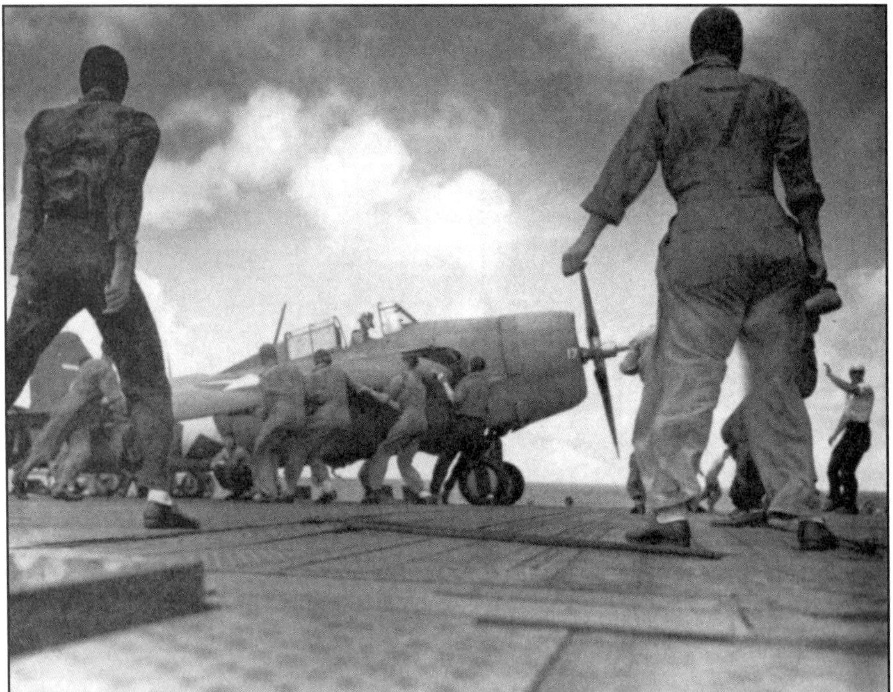

A VF-10 Wildcat is being prepared for takeoff from the *Enterprise*. Plane handlers are unfolding the airplane's wing. (National Archives)

Adm Isoroku Yamamoto (Imperial Navy)

VAdm Chuichi Nagumo (Imperial Navy)

VAdm Nobutake Kondo (Imperial Navy)

RAdm Tom Kinkaid. (Official USN Photo)

"Proceed Without *Hornet*" is the message flashed to a Torpedo-10 pilot as he prepares to take off from the *Enterprise* on October 26, 1942. (Official USN Photo)

Lt Birney Strong.
(Compliments of H. L. Buell)

Carrier Air Group 10 commanders (l. to r.): LCdr James Thomas, Bombing-10; LCdr Bucky Lee, Scouting 10; Cdr Dick Gaines, Air Group 10; LCdr Jack Collett, Torpedo-10; and LCdr Jimmy Flatley, Fighting-10. (National Archives)

LCdr Mike Sanchez.
(National Archives)

LCdr Gus Widhelm.
(National Archives)

Lt(jg) Ralph Hovind. (Compliments of R. Hovind)

HIJMS *Zuikaku*. (Imperial Navy)

The heavy cruiser HIJMS *Chikuma* after being struck by bombs on October 26, 1942. The direct hit near the bridge is clearly visible as a light smudge. (Official USN Photo)

The *Enterprise's* port aft 5-inch antiaircraft gun group. Note the LSO platform at the aft edge of the flight deck. (Official USN Photo)

Enterprise sailors and Marines practice firing stanchion-mounted 20mm antiaircraft cannon. (Official USN Photo)

The *Enterprise's* newly installed quadruple-40mm antiaircraft gun mounts, aft of the island. (Official USN Photo)

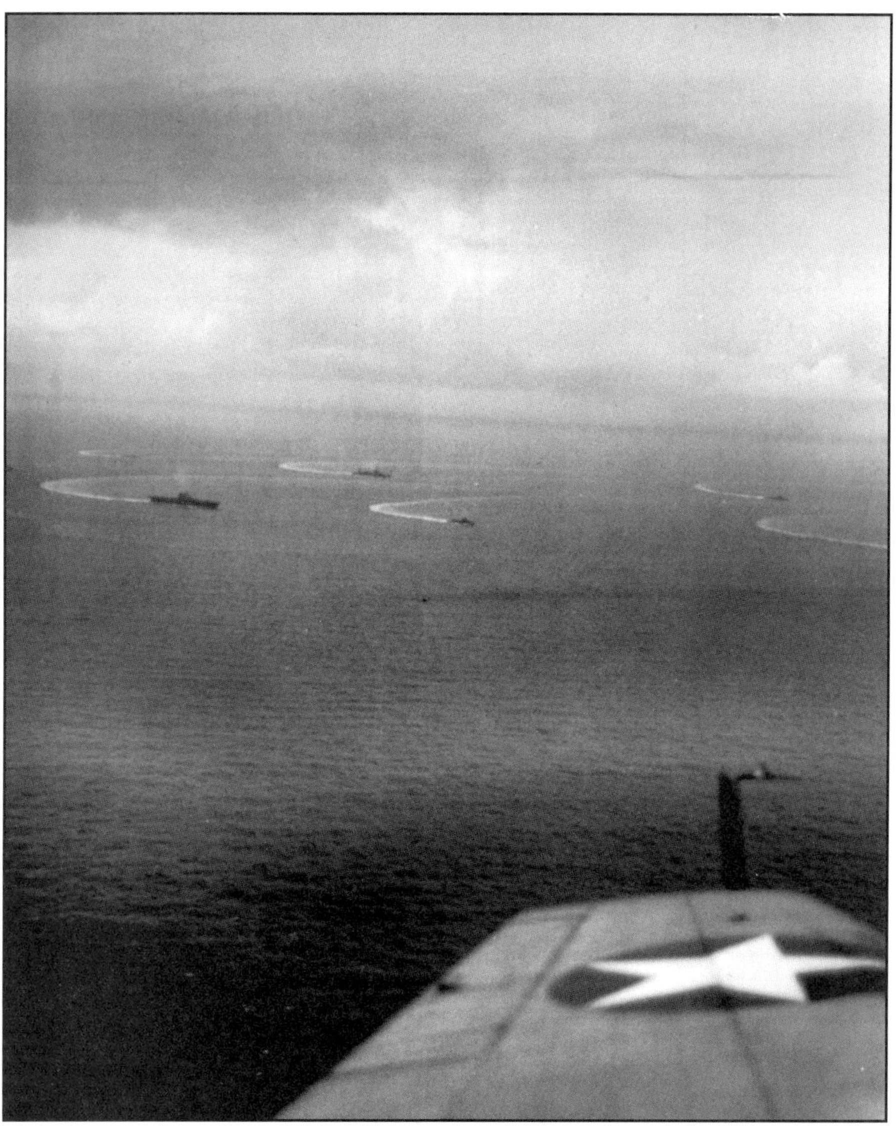

Task Force 17 maneuvers at high speed moments before the first Japanese bomber wave opens its attack against the *Hornet,* which is clearly visible to the left. (Official USN Photo)

WO Shigeyuki Sato's *Zuikaku* Val is about to crash into the *Hornet.* Also in the photo is Lt(jg) Takeo Suzuki's *Shokaku* Kate as it recovers after launching its torpedo at the *Hornet.* (National Archives)

Sato's Val at the moment of impact. (National Archives)

The *Hornet's* shattered signal bridge. (Official USN Photo)

Hornet fire fighters move to extinguish the blazes ignited by flaming gasoline from WO Sato's wrecked Val, parts of which are strewn across the flight deck. (Official USN Photo)

Enterprise plane handlers respot newly landed Wildcats and Dauntlesses at 0940, October 26. (National Archives)

Lt Doc Norton's battle-damaged Torpedo-10 Avenger comes under fire as it arrives over Task Force 16 at 1020, October 26. (National Archives)

Lt Swede Vejtasa. (National Archives)

Ens George Wrenn. (Official USN Photo)

A pair of *Zuikaku* Kates retire toward the USS *South Dakota* after launching torpedoes at the *Enterprise.* (Official USN Photo)

A bomb from a *Junyo* Val near-misses the *Enterprise.* (National Archives)

Ens Phil Souza's battle-damaged Fighting-72 Wildcat bounces toward the *Enterprises's* starboard aft gun gallery as *Junyo* bombers attack the ship. (National Archives)

F3 Ralph Morgan. (Compliments R. C. Morgan)

Smoke billows from the *Enterprise's* forward elevator well. (Official USN Photo)

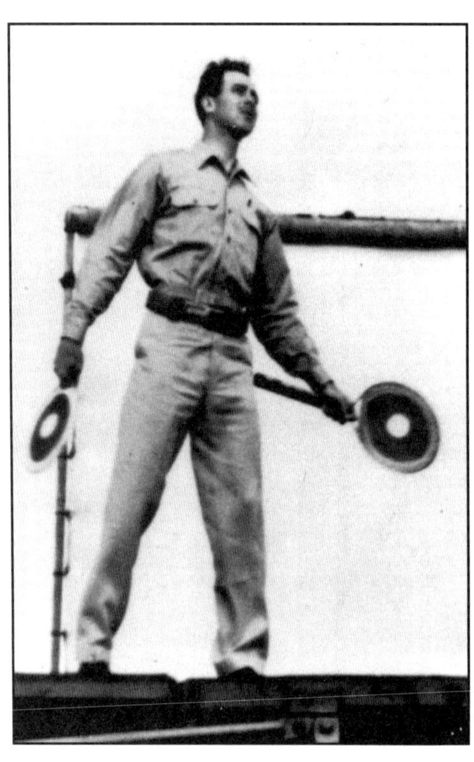

Lt Robin Lindsey.
(Official USN Photo)

The USS *Smith's* main deck forward was a charred ruin after the ship was struck by a Kate torpedo bomber. (Official USN Photo)

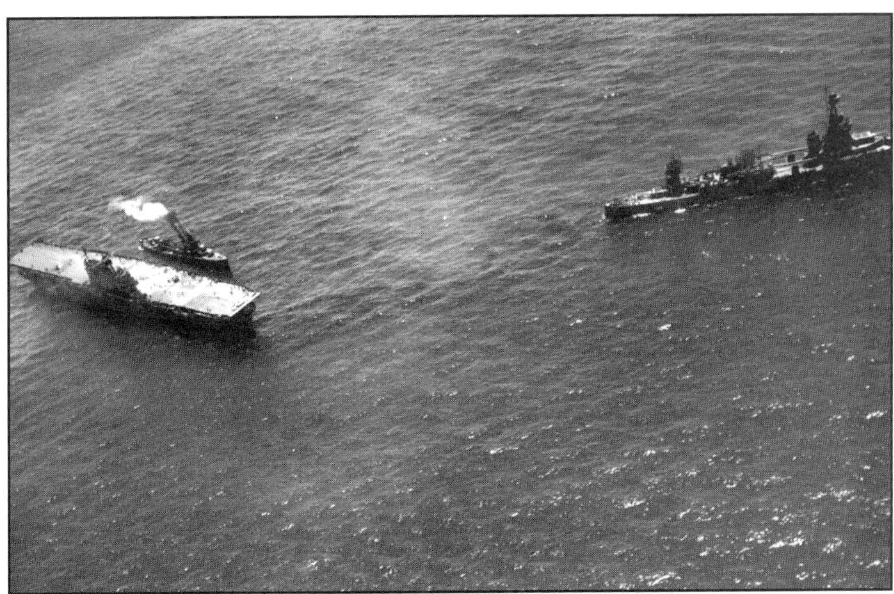

The USS *Northampton* maneuvers to resume the tow as the *Hornet* drifts helplessly at about 1100, October 26. The USS *Morris* is alongside the carrier. (National Archives)

WT1 Lyle Skinner. (Compliments of Mrs. L. M. Skinner)

The *Hornet's* crew abandons ship as fires burn out of control. (Official USN Photo)

Chapter 25

The defense of a U.S. Navy aircraft carrier in late 1942 was conducted across three interlocking spheres. The first line of defense was provided by carrier-based fighters, whose primary mission it was to intercept and engage incoming enemy bombers as far from the friendly carrier deck as possible. Next, any incoming bombers that got past the fighters were to be engaged by long-range heavy-caliber antiaircraft gunnery put up by the carrier herself and the warships accompanying her. The final defense lay in the hands of gunners manning medium- and light-caliber automatic weapons aboard the escorts and the carrier herself.

Task Force 61's first line of defense—the distant fighters—was controlled by fighter-direction officers (FDOs) based aboard the two carriers. Throughout 1942, the FDOs had access to radar sets, which were the key to the system. On October 26, the best-trained FDO in Task Force 61 was Cdr Jack Griffin.

Following the precipitous detachment of the *Enterprise's* veteran senior fighter direction officer to serve on VAdm Bill Halsey's South

Pacific staff, Griffin had been lent to the Task Force 16 staff from his regular job as director of the Navy's Fighter Direction School, which had recently been moved from San Diego to Hawaii. He happened to be in Hawaii when Task Force 16 sailed, and so he went with it.

A 1925 Naval Academy graduate, Jack Griffin had studied his craft in England under Royal Air Force radar officers during the late stages of the Battle of Britain. His assignment aboard the *Enterprise* was both to round out the training of her complement of FDOs and to be in a position to apply and assess the solutions to lessons gleaned from early defensive battles over U.S. carriers, to work toward a standard fighter-direction doctrine. As it turned out, Griffin's task was a long way from being accomplished. As of October 26, 1942, the system could not perform to the standards set for it.

The radar-assisted fighter-direction capability of the day was both experimental and crude. Indeed, it was Jack Griffin's mandate to act as a participating observer as a means of finding specific ways to improve sighting, tracking, communications, control, and interception techniques—all of which needed work, according to findings following the Coral Sea, Midway, and Eastern Solomons battles.

The system was based on the experimental CXAM air-search radars, which had been built by RCA since 1940. Since the operating end of the device looked to many like a bedspring, sets in use aboard ships of the United States Fleet were familiarly known as "bedspring" radar.

The FDOs were assigned to a small compartment known as Radar Plot, which was located on the third deck of the carrier's island structure. Armed with only a microphone on a long cord, the lead FDO—Jack Griffin—stood over a plotting table. On the far side of the table were two junior FDOs—two of the six trainees who made up the backup pool of FDOs aboard the carrier. The two assistants were equipped with earphones and chest-supported sound-powered microphones connected to the radar communications frequency. The radar repeaters and their operators were located in an adjacent compartment, so information was passed to the junior FDOs only by means of their sound-powered battle phones. Their job was to plot the progress of the incoming enemy flights, along with the relative positions of gaggles of friendly fighters, on the polar chart located on the table. A fourth member of the team was the gunnery liaison officer, who coordinated moves by fighters with the ship's gunnery department—hopefully to help fighters stay clear of friendly fire. The gunnery liaison officer was the only member of the team who had access to eyeball information from outside the windowless Radar Plot compartment.

Three radiomen and their radio receivers were also crammed into Radar Plot; one each of the radios was devoted to incoming traffic from the torpedo bombers, scout bombers, and fighters, which all usually operated on separate frequencies. A fourth radio was used to monitor talk between the task force commander and all his ships. These radios were the FDOs' only means of following the changing scene of the battle outside on the constantly revised and updated polar chart.

In theory the fighter-direction operation provided a controlling influence over defensive fighter operations, which tended to become diffused as enemy aircraft drew nearer and combat action erupted. Just as the landing signal officer's observations morally outweighed even those of the pilot coming in for an arrested landing, so the FDO's instructions were to outweigh the on-the-spot deployment decisions of the fighter leaders—up to when the point the battle was actually joined. In essence, the FDO was the commander of fighters and the orchestrator of defensive fighter tactics.

That was the theory. The reality was that the crude CXAM had limited range, and there were gaps in its vista.

Though the CXAM was designed to "see" a single airplane fifty miles out in any direction, it was known that it could pick up larger formations of incoming aircraft at ranges of up to ninety miles—if the airplanes were high enough and if the air was humid enough. (Moist air is a better conductor than dry air.)

As soon as the first radar sighting was made, the CXAM—rotating high atop a special mast over the island superstructure—was to be routinely stopped for a better fix and then rotated some more to search for other targets. All that the enlisted radarman answering to the FDO had to go on was a fuzzy ^-shaped interruption in an otherwise level horizontal white line running the width of his radarscope. The bearing of the target was easily determined by a gyro-controlled bearing indicator located right over the radarscope.

As soon as the radar sighting, bearing, and time of sighting had been confirmed, the information was fed via sound-powered telephone to the junior FDOs, who marked each sighting report on the large polar chart. The center of the chart represented the carrier, and each new mark represented the progress of various groups of aircraft. Enemy aircraft or unidentified "bogeys" were marked **X**, and friendly aircraft were marked **O**. The progress of each group was represented by lines drawn between each new time-annotated mark and the previous time-annotated mark. The polar chart was calibrated by means of degree-marked radii emanating from the center of the chart and concentric distance-marked circles.

The only way to separate enemy aircraft from friendly ones was by means of the IFF (Identification, Friend or Foe) transponder carried aboard every U.S. carrier-based fighter or bomber. Whereas each group of enemy or unidentified aircraft on the radarscope registered above the line as a **^**, IFF registered as a **V** below the line.

The size of a gaggle of incoming airplanes had to be estimated from the size of the **^** or **V**. Exhaustive testing had been conducted over the preceding year, and the experienced radarmen manning the scopes aboard the *Enterprise* and *Hornet* were considered so well versed in their esoteric trade that their judgments were not questioned.

The speed of radar-monitored aircraft was easily determined by the time it took the incoming or passing airplanes to get from one point on the polar chart to another.

The only variable that had to be purely estimated was the altitude of the incoming gaggles. Until incoming airplanes flew to within the twelve-mile range of standard gunnery radars, there was no way to provide hard information regarding that vital statistic. The CXAM had no means of providing an explicit altitude reading. It had been noted, however, that there were reliably permanent gaps in the readings of each individual radar set. These gaps had been calibrated by exhaustive use of friendly target planes flying at known altitudes and distances from the ship. Thus, each time a bogey disappeared, the "fade" chart that had been specially prepared for each radar was supposed to yield a confirmatory altitude. Because the charts had been drawn up in calm seas, however, any roll experienced by the ship heavily influenced the accuracy of the implied readings. In fact, the *only* way to be certain that friendly fighters had an altitude advantage over the incoming enemy was to direct the Wildcats to sufficient altitudes without recourse to radar estimates. It was easier for fighters to dive from above than to try to climb from below.

Another dangerous gap in the system was the inability of the CXAM to spot low-flying bogeys at distances in excess of twelve miles. This was caused simply by the effect of the curvature of the earth upon a line-of-sight technology.

The first news Task Force 61 had of the approaching Japanese air strike came at 0830, when LCdr Mike Sanchez broadcast "Stand by for dive-bombing attack" as the *Enterprise* strike group was being bounced by Lieutenant Hidaka's *Zuiho* fighters. The readout on the *Hornet's* crude CXAM radar—which had been salvaged from the battleship USS *California* after she was sunk at Pearl Harbor—showed no bogeys. Neither did the set aboard the *Enterprise.* Nevertheless, on the strength of Sanchez's warning, RAdm Tom Kinkaid ordered both ships to "launch all planes immediately. Jap planes coming in."

Most puzzling in all this was that no one aboard the carriers thought to get a third opinion, for the heavy cruiser USS *Northampton,* serving as Task Force 17's screen flagship, also had CXAM radar aboard. Indeed, from their position directly astern the *Hornet,* the *Northampton* radarmen had detected a large bogey at 0841 bearing 295 degrees and closing from seventy miles away. A query to that ship from the *Enterprise* or *Hornet* would have given the fighter directors crucial minutes in which to deploy their limited resources to better advantage. But they never thought to ask, and the screen commander aboard the *Northampton,* RAdm Howard Good, never thought to volunteer the information with the emphasis it deserved. Confident that both carriers had achieved similar radar contact, Good passed his news along by means of a routine flag hoist. The message was delivered to the *Hornet's* FDO, Lt Al Fleming, too late to do any good, and Jack Griffin never knew it had been posted.

At the moment of the *Northampton's* radar sighting, Task Force 61 was deployed in two separate carrier groups, each ten miles from the other. Only thirty-seven Fighting-10 and Fighting-72 Wildcats were aloft or ready to be launched as part of the Combat Air Patrol (CAP). Few of them were in an ideal position to defend the carriers.

The first of many tactical errors this day was the well-trained but inexperienced Cdr Jack Griffin's order to LCdr Bill Kane, the Fighting-10 exec, to head south to look for possible Japanese planes coming up from that direction. There was no basis for this order; Griffin merely wanted to cover the area between the two carrier task forces. But he sent the CAP's senior fighter pilot in the wrong direction with four fighters of a not-very-large defensive force.

Next up was the interception by the *Enterprise* of an errant radio message stating that there were bombers "off to port." Much later the message was traced to one of the outbound strike bombers, but Griffin was convinced it originated from one of the CAP fighters or a screening warship. At 0842—a minute after the *Northampton's* accurate radar fix—he issued this well-meaning but vague directive to the entire CAP: "Look for hawks [enemy bombers] on port bow and port quarter. Angels probably high. Look south of REAPER BASE [the *Enterprise*]." This got everyone looking the wrong way, but Griffin's response to the inexact radio mesasage was understandable in light of the fact that his air-search radar was telling him nothing.

At 0843, RAdm George Murray compounded Jack Griffin's rumor-mongering—for the basis of Griffin's warning was hardly more than that—when he warned the ships of Task Force 17 via TBS voice radio that an attack was coming in from 275 degrees, approximately due west. Tom Kinkaid felt that an attack force coming from the west would encounter Task Force 16 first, so at 0844 he radioed Murray to say that the *Enterprise* fighter-direction team would oversee the defense of both task forces.

The Wildcat division commanded by the Fighting-10 exec, LCdr Bill Kane, had been vectored south to look for incoming Japanese warplanes long before Jack Griffin's first all-CAP warning. At 0847, Griffin recalled Kane, but not before Ens Maurice Wickendoll, Kane's second-element leader, had spotted two unidentified warplanes as the division orbited at 6,000 feet well south of the friendly carriers. When Wickendoll rocked his wings to let Kane know that targets were close by, Kane led the division down. Moments later, the distant targets resolved themselves into a pair of *Enterprise* Dauntlesses returning from their search hop. This effort pretty much dissipated the defensive services of Kane's division, which represented more than ten percent of Task Force 61's fighter defense.

At 0852, Task Force 16 slid into a rain squall. At 0853, as the duty FDOs aboard both American carriers stared at empty radarscopes, a member of LCdr Shigeharu Murata's strike force spotted ships' wakes ahead—Task Force 17.

Murata, a highly regarded leader who had led the December 7 torpedo attack against Battleship Row, acted decisively. He ordered his radioman to transmit "*To-tsu-re*" to the other attack aircraft—radio shorthand for "Assume attack formation." At that moment, Murata's force of twenty torpedo-armed *Shokaku* Kates, a pair of unarmed control Kates, and four *Shokaku* escort fighters—all that remained following Lieutenant Hidaka's attack against the *Enterprise* strikers—was at 14,000 feet. Higher up, at 17,000 feet, were Lt Sadamu Takahashi's twenty-one *Zuikaku* Vals, and eight *Zuikaku* Zero escorts were at 21,000 feet.

At 0855, the *Hornet* CXAM came up with its first solid return of the morning. Lt Al Fleming took only a moment to analyze it and then ordered the two Fighting-72 divisions aloft to a vector of 260 degrees against a large bogey then thirty-five miles out. Within a minute, the *Enterprise* CXAM also came to life, showing a large bogey registering at 255 degrees and forty-five miles. Griffin ordered two Fighting-10 divisions to move out fifteen miles from Task Force 16 and climb to 20,000 feet.

The connection between the *Enterprise* FDO and his own and the *Hornet's* Wildcats was substantially below par. It was true that the best solution to the problem of controlling the two fighter squadrons was through the controller closest to the approaching enemy, but the entire system lacked integration—even in a standard terminology. It had been determined in earlier studies that the integration of separate squadrons under one FDO should not be undertaken if the carriers were more than ten miles apart. When fresh CAPs were launched from both carriers beginning at 0800, the carriers were well within this optimum range, but the *Hornet* had slipped farther behind the *Enterprise* during the approach of the Japanese strike group. From the start, all of Griffin's vectoring instructions to divisions of both squadrons referenced the position of the *Enterprise*. This was fine as long as both carriers were in plain sight and no more than ten miles apart, but the system endured while the carriers began undertaking evasive maneuvers, and even after the *Enterprise* became hidden from the view of all the friendly and enemy pilots by the rain squall it had entered at 0852. The factors of maneuver and the rain squall rendered Griffin's references useless for all the Fighting-72 and Fighting-10 Wildcat divisions. (In Griffin's defense, it must be said that he had no true radar bearing to work with until well after the errant report was received from the strike bomber at 0842. After that, for as long as he was able, Griffin transmitted true bearings to the fighters.)

Another of Griffin's options that went awry was the decision to send fighter divisions out only as far as fifteen miles from the carriers to investigate contact reports. Griffin's thinking was based on errors made during the August 24 Eastern Solomons battle, where roving fighter divisions had been vectored too far out and had not been able to get back in time to have an impact on the defense of the carriers. The down side of the decision, however, was that the divisions held back in this manner on October 26 would inevitably join the action too close to the friendly flight decks to be able to adequately defend them. In order for a balance to be struck between the options, the entire CAP should have been much larger. Nevertheless, the departing strike groups had included nearly one-third of the available fighters. Virtually every fighter left in Task Force 61—thirty-seven Wildcats—was aloft or ready to be launched when the first radar contact was made.

Another option that went awry was Griffin's decision to keep the bulk of the available fighters at or below 12,000 feet. Once again, his reasoning was sound. Flight at lower altitudes burns up less fuel, and pilots do not normally need oxygen below 12,000 feet. Again, the large fighter force accompanying the outbound strike groups forced Griffin to make this defensive decision. If Griffin had had more fighters available, the criticality of fuel supplies—of flight duration—and turnaround time aboard the carriers would have had less to no impact on the senior FDO's ability to marshall his forces. As it was, Griffin had to stretch his limited resources. He intentionally sacrificed an early altitude advantage for flight duration and numbers. At Eastern Solomons, CXAM radar had picked up the approaching Japanese strike group at a distance of more than eighty miles, so Griffin fully anticipated receiving adequate advance notice of the approach of the Japanese strike, either from the departing strike aircraft or by means of the CXAM radar sets aboard the two carriers (not to mention the *Northampton's* forgotten set). He received only inferential notice until the Japanese had already seen one of his carriers, and by then it was too late to make good all the logical and well-intentioned decisions that had gone so terribly wrong.

So, for all the intelligent application of technology and theory, not to mention lessons from the recent past, the fighter defense system broke down in Task Force 61 on October 26 as completely as it had on August 24. Only eight Fighting-72 Wildcats would be in position to meet either of the incoming Japanese strike formations before they broke up into smaller elements. The point of contact would be, at best, only fifteen miles from the *Hornet's* outer ring of screening warships.

As most of the American CAP pilots pointed their slow-climbing Wildcats at the enemy, Lieutenant Commander Murata angled the twenty-one Vals and twenty armed Kates at his disposal toward the *Hornet's* flight deck, the only one he could see.

Chapter 26

Following the fighter directors' initial confusion, Lt Red Hessel led his Fighting-72 division, and Lt Bob Rynd's, out on the vector provided by the *Hornet's* Lt Al Fleming. The result was a head-on confrontation by the eight Wildcats with a key element of LCdr Shigeharu Murata's strike force moments before the Val and Kate formations split off to launch their attacks.

When first seen at 0859 by Hessel's wingman, Lt(jg) Tom Gallagher, the Japanese were at the same altitude as the Wildcats—17,000 feet—and between ten and eleven o'clock from Hessel's course. As Gallagher called out his sighting, Al Fleming queried Hessel: "What have you got? To Red from Al. What is composition of tally-ho?" Hessel replied, "I think they are all hawks. Angels seventeen."

Fleming didn't miss a beat. He immediately ordered the *Hornet's* remaining CAP fighters, seven Wildcats in two divisions led by Lt Al Emerson and Lt Ken Bliss, to turn toward Murata's force and climb. At that moment, Murata was twenty miles from the *Hornet*. For good measure, Jack

Griffin ordered the Fighting-10 divisions led by Lt Swede Vejtasa and Lt Fritz Faulkner to "climb, climb!"

At 0858, Murata ordered the attack on Task Force 17, which at that moment was swinging to port in formation and passing through a southeasterly heading. Murata's radioman, who had broadcast the fateful "*Tora, tora, tora*" signal at Pearl Harbor, this time keyed "*To-to-to*" ("All forces attack"). Next, Murata ordered, "Attack Method B," which divided his aircraft to undertake a coordinated dive-bomber and torpedo attack employing a hammer-and-anvil tactic. As Murata commenced a high-speed let-down that would carry his eleven-plane Kate *chutai* to the southeast of Task Force 17, Lt Goro Washimi brought his nine-plane Kate *chutai* against Task Force 17 from a little north of west. As the Kates neared the target, each *chutai* would break up to surround the target, *shotai* by *shotai*. If the torpedo attack fell on the *Hornet* as planned, there would be no way for the American carrier to turn without being vulnerable to bombs and torpedoes.

Also descending to attack altitude, 12,000 feet, Lt Sadamu Takahashi's twenty-one *Zuikaku* Vals would take a straight-in approach against the *Hornet*, coming in more or less between Murata's and Washimi's Kates. Of twelve escort Zeros on hand, four would stay with Murata and eight would stay with Takahashi. Washimi would have no escorts.

All Lieutenant Red Hessel could do was lead his two divisions in a sweeping left turn to parry the oncoming cloud of Kates, Vals, and Zeros. As the Japanese formation split up, the lead Fighting-72 division went after the Vals. Hessel decided to go after the leader of the leading vee—Lieutenant Takahashi, the squadron *hikotaicho*. For this, he banked sharply to the left to hit the Val on a flat approach at its own altitude, 15,000 feet. As Hessel came into range, he opened fire and then climbed to make a second run from above. A third firing run finally caused Takahashi to take evasive action; he twisted out of Hessel's way so abruptly that his Val's rudder became jammed, forcing him to give up his leadership position and abort his attack. He later jettisoned his bomb.

Tom Gallagher, Hessel's wingman, went up against the nearest target to his airplane, the trailing Val in the two-plane second *shotai* of Takahashi's lead *chutai*. His attack forced this Val to evade and lose its place in the formation.

To the left of Hessel and Gallagher, Lt Claude Phillips, Hessel's second-section leader, lost track of the lead section during the turn against the Vals. Phillips thus eased out farther to Hessel's left to concentrate on the four-plane second *shotai* of the second Val *chutai*. Phillips was able to set up a flat 45-degree deflection shot on the second plane in the *shotai*, and he opened fire at extremely close range. The target, which was raked from nose to tail, made an immediate downward turn to the left to evade Phillips's guns. Rather than follow, Phillips went around and came up on the third *Zuikaku* Val *chutai*, fired into the leader of a two-plane *shotai*, and walked his bullets from nose to tail. This Val also dived away from the formation, either to evade Phillips's fire or because it had been fatally hit. (Phillips's first target was left badly damaged and trailing the Val formation, but the second Val appears to have been destroyed outright by the section leader. Phillips understandably claimed two definite kills.)

By the time Claude Phillips had forced two Vals from the Japanese formation, he had swept wide to the right of the remaining Vals. It was a good place and time to begin looking for his wingman, Lt(jg) John Franklin, to join up. Suddenly, he was rocked by the loud explosion of a 20mm round striking somewhere behind his armored seat back. The Wildcat's cockpit immediately filled with black smoke, which choked Phillips and obscured his forward vision. Though Phillips knew his Wildcat was on fire, his reaction was so cool it surprised him. He opened the plexiglas canopy hood and dived to facilitate his departure. This sucked the smoke out of the cockpit. Able to see again, Phillips decided to stay with the fighter, which seemed flyable.

A quick look around revealed that his wingman, John Franklin, was under attack by at least a *shotai* of Lt Ayao Shirane's eight-plane *Zuikaku* escort *chutai*. Phillips hauled back on his stick and maneuvered into a head-on run at the Zero closest to Franklin's tail. The force of the turn was so great that the Wildcat shuddered into a high-speed stall. Unable to get a good shot at the Zero, Phillips nevertheless fired in the hope of rattling the Japanese pilot. The ploy worked and the Zero ran.

Franklin's fighter was in bad shape; the fabric rudder was shredded and the Wildcat was rapidly losing altitude. Phillips tried to get closer to see if his wingman had been wounded, only to watch as the damaged fighter flew straight into the water. John Franklin did not escape.

Lt Bob Rynd's Fighting-72 division came apart as it swept in right behind Hessel's division on the Japanese vee-of-vees. Rynd's second section, led by Lt(jg) Ken Kiekhoefer, split off to the right as Rynd and Ens George Wrenn charged into the third Val *chutai*. Rynd fired on a Val that rolled right out of his line of sight and then ducked instinctively as a Zero passed over his Wildcat from above and behind. As the Zero pulled up in front of the division leader, Rynd reflexively pulled up steeply to try to get his gunsight on it. Wrenn tried to follow Rynd, but his airspeed bled off rapidly and he had to nose over to prevent a stall. As he did, a Zero settled on his tail and he had to keep diving to use his airplane's greater weight and power to pull away from the enemy fighter.

Rynd was unable to keep up with the steeply climbing Zero. He returned to shoot up another Val. Altogether, he claimed a victory and a probable but provided only sketchy details of the action in his debriefing report.

Rynd's second section—Lt(jg) Ken Kiekhoefer and Lt(jg) Paul Landry—tore into the Japanese with all their guns blazing. They teamed up on one Val in the rear *chutai* and left it trailing smoke; it was scored a probable. The next Val at which Kiekhoefer fired also dropped back, but it did not smoke, so no score.

As they dived through the Val formation, Landry lost Kiekhoefer in a swift turn and wound up alone, well behind Rynd's and Hessel's divisions. As he turned again to try to find his section leader, Landry's Wildcat came under the guns of a *Zuikaku* Zero, which caused it to dive out of control all the way into the sea, killing Landry in the crash. A second Zero attacked Kiekhofer but overshot. Kiekhoefer quickly fired a strong burst as the Zero passed in front of his gunsight, and the Zero rolled away trailing smoke. Kiekhoefer claimed this Zero as a victory, but it and its pilot survived the morning battle.

A moment later, the Zero that had downed Paul Landry fired at Kiekhoefer's Wildcat. As Kiekhoefer pulled into the tightest turn he could manage, he heard what sounded like solid rhythmic hits on his fighter, but he quickly realized that he was breathing so hard that his oxygen hose was banging against the side of the cockpit. Immensely relieved, Kiekhoefer laughed impulsively and inadvertently kicked his rudder over, which sent the Wildcat into an outside snap role. From there, Kiekhoefer sought a calming respite in a cloud.

Red Hessel and Tom Gallagher had come through their first encounter with the *Zuikaku* Vals in good shape. Indeed, they had done much to ruin the integrity of the formation by forcing the Val squadron leader, Lt Sadamu Takahashi, to take sudden evasive action that damaged his airplane. As Takahashi's lead *chutai* attempted to follow the leader through wrenching maneuvers, the entire Val formation came unglued. Follow-on attacks by Hessel's second section and Bob Rynd's Fighting-72 division broke the Vals up even more. Nevertheless, the second Val *chutai*, led by Lt Toshio Tsuda, was able to squeeze through unscathed.

After recovering from their first slashing attack, Hessel and Gallagher rejoined and went after the third Val *chutai*. They immediately encountered a straggler whose pilot bravely turned head-on into the two Wildcats. All three aircraft, firing as they came on, held their places until collision seemed imminent. The Americans blinked first; Hessel nosed down and Gallagher went high. Before the Wildcats could rejoin, the Val nosed over and dived straight into the sea. No doubt, bullets fired during the game of chicken had fatally damaged the airplane or its pilot.

The game cost Hessel the last of his ammunition. He flew clear of the melee in hopes of locating the *Hornet* so he could reload. Meanwhile, Gallagher climbed into a Val *chutai* and got himself into a duel with three of the dive-bombers. The Wildcat took many hits, and finally the engine quit. Gallagher was lucky to ditch in one piece and scramble aboard his life raft before the Wildcat sank. He and Red Hessel were each credited with one Val destroyed and two Val probables. The pair certainly destroyed one Val and almost certainly destroyed another.

In all, Hessel's and Rynd's eight Fighting-72 Wildcat pilots claimed four Vals and a Zero shot down, and seven Vals probably shot down. Three Vals were most likely downed, and three were most likely damaged by these pilots. No *Zuikaku* Zeros were downed at this stage of the fight. On the other hand, two Wildcat pilots—John Franklin and Paul Landry—were shot down and killed, and Tom Gallagher had ditched. For the time being, for various reasons, the five remaining Wildcats were out of the fight.

Lt Ken Bliss's Fighting-72 division had been on an early CAP and had only just refueled when the incoming Japanese first came up on the *Hornet's* CXAM radar. Bliss's four Wildcats immediately launched and, under orders transmitted at 0904 by Lt Al Fleming, climbed directly on a heading of 225 degrees toward the Japanese, whom they first saw as they passed through 12,000 feet. By then, the large vee-of-vees formation met by Hessel's and Rynd's divisions had broken down into smaller formations maneuvering to attack the *Hornet* from several angles. Bliss missed seeing the second Val *chutai* pass a thousand feet below, but his wingman, Lt(jg) Bob Holland, spotted them and called Bliss's attention to them. Bliss reversed into a diving turn, but he came up right behind a lone Val that was trailing the second *chutai*—the Val damaged earlier by Lt Claude Phillips.

As Bliss came up on the straggler's tail, this Val evaded by dropping into a steep dive. Bliss's entire division followed. The Val pilot was highly skilled; he kept the four Wildcats distracted and off target through a series of nimble rolls and turns that carried the Wildcats back down through 10,000 feet. Finally, Bliss, Bob Holland, and the second-section leader—Lt(jg) George Formanek—were able to get the Val in their sights. For Bliss, it was an easy zero-deflection shot right up the Val's tail. There was no question in Bliss's mind that he was scoring hits, but he saw no direct evidence of this until he was passing through 5,000 feet. At that point, thick black smoke began pouring from the Val, which jettisoned its bomb as it plunged straight into the water.

Lt Al Emerson's three-plane Fighting-72 division, which had taken off ahead of Bliss's, missed the Vals altogether and tooled off into empty space until Lt Al Fleming noticed its departure from the airspace over Task Force 17. At 0910, Emerson finally responded to Fleming's repeated calls to return with a bland "No contact." Fleming ordered the trio to return.

♦

Twenty-two Fighting-10 Wildcats arrayed in five uneven divisions never made it into the fight while the Kates and Vals were maneuvering into position against Task Force 17. Confused and at a loss because of the failure of his CXAM radar and what appeared to him to be conflicting radio reports, Cdr Jack Griffin lost control of the situation. In the critical moments it took Griffin to recapture a mental image of the unfolding battle, the ability to control events slipped from his grasp.

As Red Hessel's and Bob Rynd's Fighting-72 divisions were arrowing toward the *Zuikaku* Vals, Griffin queried Al Fleming to find out whether the *Hornet* was tracking more than one bogey. "Negative," Fleming replied. "One group spread out."

Then it dawned on Griffin that the Japanese had altered course to the south and that Task Force 17 was their target. He immediately dispatched two divisions numbering three and four Wildcats, respectively, to head out on vector 230 degrees—southwest from the *Enterprise*—and orbit ten miles from the center of Task Force 16, an arbitrary spot in space that was still well short of the big fight west and south of Task Force 17. Next, because his radar operators were getting no altitude return on the CXAM, Griffin asked Fleming for an altitude reading on the bogeys. Fleming replied curtly, "Angels seven."

Griffin next put out a call to the entire CAP, "Look south of base." Then he factored in the low altitude reported by Fleming and deduced that a torpedo attack was under way, so he called the three Fighting-10 divisions that were south of Task Force 16—Bill Kane's, which had been sent much earlier, and the two divisions sent minutes before: "Look for fish [torpedo planes]," Griffin admonished the mispositioned Wildcat pilots. What Griffin did not see on the *Enterprise's* radar return was that all but one of the Fighting-10 CAP Wildcats had slipped from his control and were racing south on their own to do what they could to save the *Hornet*. It was not Jack Griffin's fault that his enclosed Radar Plot compartment in the *Enterprise's* conning tower had become something of an ivory tower, it was that far from the reality of what men with an open view could see with their own eyes and react to in their own way.

♦

The ready Wildcats had done all they could to forestall the Japanese strike aircraft and fend off the accompanying Zeros—a good last-minute showing by a dozen of them against the *Zuikaku* Vals—but it was not nearly enough. Moreover, Lieutenant Commander Murata's deadly *Shokaku* Kates had not even been touched by the defending fighters.

Chapter 27

From the moment the first news of the Japanese approach was sounded at 0840, the atmosphere aboard the *Hornet* was one of undisguised excitement. Most of the men aboard the carrier were veterans, had been nearly to the gates of Tokyo in April, had endured a grueling but ultimately uneventful wait at Midway in June. Now, they awaited the inevitable, as had fellow sailors aboard the *Lexington* at the Coral Sea, the *Yorktown* at Midway, and the *Enterprise* and *Saratoga* at Eastern Solomons. The Japanese Vals and Kates were on the way; the ultimate test of their ship's fighters and gunners was at hand.

RAdm George Murray had commanded the *Enterprise* at the start of the war, through early raids on Japanese-held islands, and during the Tokyo raid, when his ship had escorted the *Hornet* to the gates of the enemy capital. When sailors came to his flag bridge aboard the *Hornet* to seal him in with steel shutters, he protested, "Leave them open. I want to see the show, too." In this simple request, Admiral Murray expressed a desire common to all his shipmates at that hour, for seeing the show was far better than enduring it in blind compartments throughout the vast ship.

As the last ready fighters were launched, as inert carbon dioxide was pumped into the aviation-gasoline fueling system, as a Marine chaser ran to the ship's brig to free the prisoners in the event the ship was set aflame or sunk, as three thousand sailors and Marines went to the highest stage of alert, as the *Hornet's* own fighters pitched into the oncoming waves of Vals and Kates, Capt Perry Mason passed the word to his senior gunnery officer, "Commence firing at any target in sight." Then, to his ship's senior engineer he said, "Make full speed and maintain it until further orders."

The first enemy aircraft—the seven surviving aircraft of the *Zuikaku's* second Val *chutai*—were spotted by *Hornet* lookouts at 0905. For the moment, clouds intermittently obscured the attackers, but the ships of Task Force 17 that could bear on the target trained out their weapons. At 0909, one of the screen destroyers opened fire. By then, according to the carrier's gunnery radar, the Vals were 10,500 yards away.

It was not evident that the *Hornet* was the focal point of a beautifully coordinated attack planned on the fly by LCdr Shigeharu Murata and executed by the sixteen surviving *Zuikaku* Vals and the twenty as-yet-unscathed *Shokaku* Kates.

The *Hornet's* gunnery department, which was essentially devoted to antiaircraft gunnery, oversaw three types of weapons. The most powerful and longest-ranged were eight 5-inch, .38-caliber dual-purpose guns (hereafter referred to as "5-inch" guns) arrayed in pairs of mounts at each corner of the flight deck. Four medium-range quadruple 1.1-inch mounts were located in pairs at flight-deck level just ahead and just aft of the superstructure, and a fifth quad-1.1-inch mount was located at the bows just beneath the leading edge of the flight deck. Finally, thirty 20mm cannon on stanchions—with several .50-caliber machine guns thrown in—were located on the catwalks just below and virtually all the way around the flight deck.

All defensive fires were formally coordinated by the gunnery and antiaircraft gunnery officers and their assistants from Sky Control, which was atop the island, 110 feet above the waterline. They all acted on the basis of what they saw for themselves, or from reports from the gunnery liaison officer manning the polar chart in Radar Plot, or from more than a hundred officers and sailors of L ("Lookout") Division, who were manning posts all around the flight deck and throughout the tall island structure on the starboard side of the flight deck. L Division was an integral part of the gunnery control system. Its lookouts had been painstakingly trained to keep their eyes riveted to particular sectors—no matter what was going on elsewhere.

Gunnery control was exercised largely by means of sound-powered battle phones once the sound of gunfire drowned out the ship's loudspeakers. Each battery had at least one talker connected to the primary and secondary gun-control centers. The gunnery officer's and antiaircraft gunnery officer's talkers could cut into any fire-control circuit by means of a rotary switch. When the various battery officers or lookouts reporting to them saw airplanes approaching, they deployed their forces in proportion to the threat and tried to hold something back for new threats. If no battery was firing at a new target, the gunnery officers, from their Sky Control vantage points, ordered particular batteries to switch targets.

One dubious advantage the *Hornet's* gunners counted on was the probability that their ship would be the main focus of most or all of the Japanese attackers. If that was so, they reasoned that their job would be made easier, for there would be no need to lead airplanes that were heading straight for them.

A real problem with the gunnery program lay in the fact that only a relatively small percentage of the gun crews were composed of full-time gunners, who were also primarily responsible for maintaining the guns. The majority of sailors and Marines assigned to the gun crews normally worked at a wide range of jobs in the ship's company or in the various air departments. For most of the men manning the *Hornet's* guns, shooting and learning to shoot was a vital but secondary duty.

Keeping the 1.1-inch guns on target was the job of the pointer, who was assisted in this task, as well as in target selection, by the battery officer, who was responsible for two mounts, and the gun captain, who was responsible for just one mount. The job of the loaders for each 1.1-inch mount was to extract empty magazines and load full magazines. The chamber serving the four guns in one mount held two magazines, so quick loaders could ensure that the guns were always armed.

The 5-inch guns were hampered by a much slower rate of fire. Each round, with its premeasured powder charge, had to be loaded by hand.

Though the guns were aimed and fired at long range and high altitude by a relatively sophisticated radar-assisted battery director, the system was fairly crude and quite slow in its own right. At low altitude and short range, the guns went on local control, which slowed them even more. About the best a 5-inch crew could hope for was a near miss that blossomed into a lethal burst of shrapnel in proximity to a diving or oncoming airplane.

The last line of defense lay in the hands of the 20mm gun crews. Each of these rapid-fire cannon was manned by two trained gunners. One, the senior gunner, was strapped into a shoulder harness right behind the gun. The other, the loader, worked at his shoulder and stood ready to take over the firing if the gunner was injured or killed. The gun was fixed on a flexible stanchion mount that was welded to the flight-deck catwalk; it operated as an extension of the man to which it was mated. Capable of putting out many rounds in short bursts, the 20mm cannon—which were grouped in four-gun batteries—were far more responsive and reliable than the 1.1-inch guns and generally a more useful weapon than either the 5-inch or 1.1-inch guns.

Of course, the *Hornet's* fate was also largely in the hands of gunners aboard the six destroyers, two light antiaircraft cruisers, and two heavy cruisers assigned to Task Force 17 on October 26. All of these surface vessels had gone into a circular defensive deployment 4,000 yards in diameter around the carrier at the first news of the incoming air strike. Ahead of the *Hornet* was the lethal light antiaircraft cruiser USS *Juneau*, mounting sixteen rapid-fire 5-inch dual-purpose guns in eight mounts, plus a battery of quad-1.1-inch antiaircraft guns and numerous 20mm cannon. The *Juneau's* sister, the USS *San Diego*, was off the carrier's port side. The screening warships and the *Hornet* got their speed up to 28 knots and had plenty of room to maneuver in order to throw off the aim of the Val and Kate pilots who would be loosing bombs and torpedoes in a matter of minutes.

At about 0900, AMM3 Chuck Beck, a Fighting-72 plane captain attached to a damage-control hose team on the flight deck forward of the island, had heard nearby Marine antiaircraft gunners talk about the incoming bombers and left his station to retrieve the blue-denim flash jacket he had stashed in the forward end of the island. When Beck stepped back onto the flight deck after putting on the jacket, pulling its sleeves and hood tight around his wrists and face, and pushing his trousers into his socks, he found that the fifteen-man hose team he had left moments earlier had disappeared. A quick look around revealed that every gun was pointed skyward. Before Beck could react, the most distant screen destroyer opened fire, and the entire screen—and the *Hornet*—followed suit. Beck began running straight down the middle of the flight deck, chided himself for not having the equipment to get airborne, and veered off toward the opening of a bomb shelter, a covered section of the catwalk rimming the flight deck. He tumbled in among at least a dozen other sailors who were all tucked up to prevent concussion damage to their innards.

At the last moment, the *Hornet's* loudspeakers advised all the men who could not see, but who could hear the pounding of her guns, "Stand by to repel attack." LCdr Oscar Dodson, the *Hornet's* and Task Force 17's communications officer, bounded up to the signal bridge from the flag bridge to check on the eighteen signalmen manning battle stations there. Dodson knew that nearly all of them and their young signal officer were facing first combat; he thought his presence would help settle them. He found that many of the enlisted signalmen had neglected to clap on helmets or pull on their protective flashproof jackets.

As soon as the signalmen were properly rigged out, Dodson trained his binoculars outboard and picked up incoming *Shokaku* Kates at maximum range from the west. When the Kates were about five miles from the *Hornet,* they split into two uneven formations and began circling the ship to find the best attack angles. The Japanese torpedo *hikotaicho,* LCdr Shigeharu Murata, fired a large smoke bomb over the tail of his dark green airplane. On that signal, the twenty Kates turned toward the *Hornet.* Murata, with eleven Kates organized into four *shotai,* was circling to attack the carrier from the southeast, and Lt Goro Washimi was coming in from the northwest with nine Kates.

Six Vals led by Lt Toshio Tsuda—the *Zuikaku's* second Val *chutai*—were the first Japanese aircraft to attack the *Hornet.* Tsuda angled his Val downward against the carrier at 0910. Emerging from the cloud base at 5,000 feet, the first three Val pilots found the carrier steaming away from them at 28 knots. Tsuda dropped his bomb from as low as he dared, and the projectile detonated just off the *Hornet's* starboard bow.

At 0912, the second Val planted its 250-kilogram bomb dead center on the flight deck, across from the island. This semi-armor-piercing projectile penetrated three decks and detonated in the forward crew messing compartment.

The third Val was struck by antiaircraft fire that might have killed the pilot or damaged its control surfaces. In any event, the Val, with its bomb still aboard, struck the water thirty feet from the *Hornet's* starboard bow.

EM1 Tom Kuykendall was prone on the deck in the forward crew messing compartment, one of sixty-five members of the forward repair party. The repair officer, who was wearing headphones, had been keeping the sailors abreast of events as they occurred, and the loud detonations of the antiaircraft guns easily penetrated to the compartment, though it was insulated on all sides and above by other compartments and decks. Suddenly, the deck beneath Kuykendall's body quivered as though an earthquake had struck. Kuykendall heard a huge muffled explosion, and the lights went out; he could sense but not see expanding points of red-hot metal and the smell of burning explosives. A searing heat passed over him. He knew right away that he had been severely burned, even though his nerves had not yet fully responded to the trauma. Kuykendall felt around in the dark to locate the men who had been lying near him. He couldn't find anyone, but he was able to crawl to a ladder he knew was only three feet away. The metal rungs, still hot from the explosion, seared Kuykendall's palms, but he pulled himself upward toward the hangar deck.

In all, at least sixty of the sixty-five members of the forward repair party were killed outright in the bomb blast.

The second Val *shotai,* led by Lt(jg) Yozo Shimada, had to flatten its dive as it came out of the clouds astern the rapidly receding carrier. The result was shallower than a dive-bombing attack and steeper than a glide-bombing attack.

Pfc Vic Kelber, one of sixteen Marines and two sailors manning the quad-1.1-inch gun tubs directly aft of the island, picked up several Vals as they followed through past their bomb-release points. Two or three of the Vals were clearly burning and about to fall into the sea. One of the dive-bombers was firing its twin cowl-mounted 7.7mm machine guns. As Kelber was about to unleash a curse at the strafer, a single 7.7mm round entered his mouth and exited his cheek. He did not know he was injured until someone yelled, "Kelber, you're bleeding." The thoroughly engrossed gunner raised his hand to his cheek, felt that it was wet, and spit out a mouthful of blood and teeth. Then he dopily pressed his eye to the gunsight to track yet another Val.

The Val that had hit Vic Kelber, or perhaps another that was firing its guns as it flew by the flight deck from ahead to aft, bracketed S1 Ed Knobel, the plane captain of the *Hornet* Air Group command TBF, as he was boosting a 1.1-inch magazine from the catwalk into one of the gun tubs. An indistinct peripheral view of the approaching stream of bullets impacting on the flight deck caused Knobel to fall to the deck. Two rounds clipped the legs of his trousers.

Seconds later, within the same minute as the first 250-kilogram detonation forward, a 242-kilogram "land" bomb struck the ship. It detonated on impact with the flight deck and blew out an eleven-foot hole about twenty feet in from the starboard edge. Pfc Vic Kelber was plucked from his seat and wrapped around his 1.1-inch gun like a wet rag. In all, thirty Marines and sailors were killed and many others were wounded. Though wounded and paralyzed, GySgt Eugene O'Connor, the gun-group chief, continued to issue orders to the surviving gunners by means of his sound-powered battle phones as he lay supine on the catwalk behind the gun tubs.

Though S1 Ed Knobel was only clipped on the back of his left knee by a tiny pinpoint of shrapnel, the blast in front of his eyes was so bright that it all but blinded him. It would be three days before Knobel could see much more than a red film before his eyes.

Immediately after Shimada's Val dropped its bomb, it was ripped apart by 20mm cannon shells. The pilot, PO1 Asataro Taka, managed to gain some altitude, at which point Shimada popped out of the rear seat and deployed his parachute. Taka did not make it out; he rode the Val into the water about 1,000 yards off the heavy cruiser USS *Pensacola's* starboard bow. Apparently nobody noticed Shimada land in the water, or nobody cared enough to try to pluck him out.

The two remaining Vals in the second *shotai* delayed their attacks to try to catch up with the fleeing *Hornet.* They flattened out and circled ahead of the carrier, where the pilots released their 250-kilogram bombs off the port bow. One of the bombs missed altogether, but the other angled into the flight deck near the first hit. It punched a twelve-inch hole in the flight deck and angled forward about fifty-three feet while penetrating two steel barriers on its way to the third deck. Though the blast breached the overhead and several bulkheads of the chief petty officers' messing compartment, penetrated to adjacent compartments, knocked out a 5-inch ammunition hoist, and set fire to upholstered furniture and other combustibles, it resulted in no direct loss of life. Nevertheless, the force of the blast was felt by all hands in the forward part of the ship. It added to Pfc Vic Kelber's woes by lifting him from his 1.1-inch gun tub and dropping him into a ready room beneath the flight deck.

WT1 Lyle Skinner was in the compartment just aft of the one occupied by the gutted forward repair party when the first bomb detonated. After a moment in which he lost all his senses, Skinner saw sparks flying through the darkness that had instantly engulfed his space, he heard groans and shrieks, and he smelled the strong odor of the vaporized explosives. As his senses fully returned, Skinner found that he was lying atop and beneath twisted rubble. At first, he was afraid to move, because he knew that the deck on which he lay was directly above a fuel-oil tank; if the tank ruptured, he feared he might fall in. He had lost all sense of direction except up and down and had no idea which way to go when he finally began easing out of the rubble. The fumes seemed to be growing stronger, and breathing became increasingly difficult. Skinner groped for his handkerchief and placed it over his nose and mouth, but it did not help. As he lay in the dark feeling the successive bomb detonations reverberate through the steel deck, he calmly reached the conclusion that he would eventually die in that compartment. His only question at that point was whether he would succumb to fire, suffocation, or drowning. He decided that all he could do was await the inevitable conclusion of his life.

Then fate intervened. An unknown crewman who was probably trying to find a way topside momentarily opened the hatch at the after end of the dark compartment and shined in a battle lantern. Apparently convinced that there was no escape by that route, the man closed the hatch and departed. The briefly shining light was Lyle Skinner's beacon to life, for it gave him back his sense of direction and showed him that he could safely make his way across the debris-strewn deck. Skinner wriggled out from the confining rubble and pushed open the hatch, which had mercifully been left undogged by his departing shipmate. He took only two or three steps before the ship was rocked by a vast explosion.

Of six second-*chutai Zuikaku* Vals to attack the *Hornet*, three scored bomb hits and two were shot down with the loss of two pilots and one observer. A seventh Val from this *chutai* had been shot down by Fighting-72's Lt Ken Bliss as the attack commenced, and its pilot and observer were lost. The three bombs to score hits thus far had killed at least ninety sailors and Marines, wounded many others, and started several fires. Nevertheless, the ship was yet in no mortal danger.

In the space of the next two or three minutes, bigger blows were about to fall.

Chapter 28

While the second *Zuikaku* Val *chutai* kept many of Task Force 17's guns busy to the west and north, the strike commander, LCdr Shigeharu Murata, led eleven *Shokaku* Kates on a long run from northwest to southeast of the *Hornet.* As they circled out to what amounted to the rear of Task Force 17, Murata's Kates lost altitude. Ahead, four *Shokaku* Zeros were in position to sweep American fighters from their path.

When Fighting-72's Lt(jg) Ken Kiekhoefer left the cover of a cloud into which he had earlier been chased by a Zero, it was in the hope of finding his wingman, the ill-fated Lt(jg) Paul Landry. Suddenly, large red popcorn balls—20mm rounds—passed Kiekhoefer's Wildcat from behind. He had been jumped by a Zero with a broad red stripe around its fuselage—the marking of the *Shokaku* Air Group. Kiekhoefer hunkered down behind his armored seat back and slowed his fighter. Sure enough, the Zero passed overhead. As quickly as he could get his gun pipper on the target, Kiekhoefer fired. Only one thin stream of bullets emerged from the left outboard gun as the Zero swung back to initiate a head-on run. The

Zero did not fire, and Kiekhoefer was out of ammunition in all but one gun, which sent forth a puny stream. Desperate, Kiekhoefer suddenly dropped his Wildcat's left wing in an attitude that must have appeared like an intentional effort to ram the oncoming Zero. The Japanese fighter pilot swung out and ran from sight. Kiekhoefer had had enough, too. He ran for the protection of Task Force 16's battleship *South Dakota,* whose many guns trained on his fighter and opened fire. He finally ducked into a nearby cloud and broadly cursed battleship sailors on the open fighter circuit.

Ken Kiekhoefer was only the first American fighter Murata's Kates encountered on their final run in to the target, and by far the least dangerous. Moments after detaching the one Zero to go after Kiekhoefer, the Zero flight leader, Lt Hisayoshi Miyajima, spotted another Wildcat.

Down at 5,000 feet, Lt Ken Bliss had just hammered a *Zuikaku* Val into the ocean and was thinking about getting his division re-formed when he was assailed by WO Yukuo Hanzawa, whom Lieutenant Miyajima had detached to do the honors. Before Bliss could react, many 7.7mm bullets had passed the Wildcat, and one had already penetrated halfway into Bliss's instrument panel. Suddenly, the lighter Zero passed the heavier Wildcat along the right side in a vertical dive and then made a shallow pull-through without taking evasive action. Bliss later learned that the rubber life raft he was carrying in a compartment behind the cockpit had been released by 7.7mm hits. Hanzawa probably mistook the departing raft for a departing Wildcat pilot and passed the Wildcat simply to gawk at it. Bliss only needed to fire a very short burst to blow Hanzawa's Zero out of the air.

The last two *Shokaku* Zeros, flown by Lieutenant Miyajima and PO1 Masashi Ishida, went after Lt(jg) George Formanek, the section leader in Bliss's Fighting-72 division. The two Zero pilots riddled Formanek's Wildcat, but they did not finish the job. Though badly wounded, Formanek was able to ditch his airplane and get out. He was picked up by the destroyer USS *Russell* at 0925.

Thus far, no American fighters had come close to laying a glove on Murata's Kate *chutai,* but some slick maneuvering by the *Hornet's* Capt Perry Mason came close to denying Murata a worthy target. Mason had reversed course to the north as Murata was positioning his Kates for the killing blow, and that left Murata with no option but to undertake a tail-chase after a receding target, the most difficult attack possible against a speeding warship.

As the Kates came down to their attack altitude and raced to catch up to the target, they slipped into a ragged right-echelon formation so each pilot would have a clear view and a clear shot at the American carrier. Meanwhile, the *Hornet* pitched into a turn that carried her still farther to the west, thus making the resulting going-away shot even more difficult for each Kate pilot to judge, given the time it would take the torpedoes to reach the carrier from the release points.

As Murata turned left to try to follow the *Hornet's* turn, each of the airplanes to his right rear had to pivot farther to the left, around the outside of Murata's turn, in order to align themselves on the carrier. Very quickly, the physics of the attack gave way to pure instinct. These were among the best torpedo pilots the Imperial Navy had left. If they couldn't hit the *Hornet* from where they had to launch, nobody could.

Murata's three-plane *shotai* passed between the heavy cruiser USS *Northampton* and the destroyer USS *Anderson* and came up on the speeding *Hornet's* starboard quarter at an altitude of 300 feet. One of these Kate pilots—it's not certain which—released his torpedo at a range of 1,500 yards and was immediately killed with his observer and gunner as the Kate was pummeled into the water by 5-inch and 20mm antiaircraft fire. The two remaining Kates pressed on to within 1,000 yards of the receding, corkscrewing *Hornet,* released torpedoes, and swung right to parallel the carrier. Antiaircraft fire ignited the left wing tank in one of the Kates, and the airplane streamed burning gasoline as it rolled to its left and crashed off the *Hornet's* starboard bow. The third Kate was also hit, but it escaped ahead of the *Hornet,* pulling thin trails of smoke from both wingtips as it went. LCdr Shigeharu Murata and his crew were killed in one of the two downed airplanes.

Next up was the three-plane Kate *shotai* led by Lt(jg) Takeo Suzuki, which came up astern the *Anderson* and penetrated the screen between that ship and the destroyer *Russell.* As the Kates flew up between the destroyers, 20mm fire struck one of them and caused the pilot to jettison his torpedo just before he veered sharply to the left. This airplane spouted flames and crashed into the water just ahead of the *Northampton,* which was holding station directly behind the *Hornet.* In the meantime, Suzuki and his remaining wingman released their torpedoes and ended up turning to the west directly astern the *Hornet.* As it turned out, the two had released their torpedoes too soon, and both fish missed the carrier well to starboard. Suzuki and his wingman withdrew up the *Hornet's* port side, drawing little fire because there were targets high up over the carrier.

The third Kate *shotai* coming up from the south turned in and penetrated the screen between the *Russell* and the heavy cruiser USS *Pensacola,* the latter of which was keeping station about 2,000 yards off the *Hornet's* starboard beam. The fourth *shotai*—two Kates—was a little to the rear, and it also passed between the *Russell* and the *Pensacola.* The lead *shotai* shaped a course that might bring it out ahead of the carrier, but antiaircraft fire downed the middle Kate and the other two released their torpedoes at what turned out to be an impossible angle that brought the torpedoes out well ahead of the *Hornet.*

The two remaining Kates split up. The *shotai* leader followed the third *shotai* past the screen, turned in, and dropped his torpedo against the *Pensacola,* which apparently was the only worthwhile target he felt he could hit. The last Kate ended up grazing the outside of the screen. Finding himself unable to get past the surface warships, and with the *Hornet* blocked by the *Pensacola,* the pilot decided to take his shot at the cruiser. He prepared to release his torpedo from off the turning vessel's starboard beam, but the ship came about head-on to the Kate, and her antiaircraft gunners fatally damaged the airplane. Aflame and only 1,000 yards from the *Pensacola,* the Kate retained its torpedo and wobbled on in what seemed like a last-ditch effort to crash into the cruiser. It missed the *Pensacola's* bows by a matter of feet and crashed into the water only 100 feet off the warship's port side. The splash from the crashing Kate was so big that, from his angle, the *shotai* leader assumed his torpedo had hit the cruiser.

Five Kates had been shot down with all aboard, and only eight of eleven torpedoes had been launched against the *Hornet.* Of these, only two had any hope of overtaking the carrier. But before this act could play itself out, the *Hornet* was assailed from the northwest by the remaining *Shokaku* Kates and *Zuikaku* Vals.

♦

The lead Val *chutai* had come unglued under the guns of Fighting-72's Red Hessel and his wingman, Tom Gallagher, who had earlier run the squadron *hikotaicho*, Lt Sadumu Takahashi, out of the fight. It took Takahashi's next-ranking officer, Lt(jg) Nobuo Yoneda, several minutes to reorganize the lead *chutai's* six remaining Vals, of which one had been damaged by the Wildcats. By then, Lieutenant Tsuda's second *chutai* had forged ahead to mount its attack.

To make up time as well as take advantage of the moves the *Hornet* was taking to evade Murata's Kates, Yoneda led his force to the north, in order to come down on the carrier's port side. It was a smart move, but it unintentionally carried the Vals into range of several elements of Fighting-10, which were bearing down from the northwest to protect the *Hornet*.

Several Fighting-10 divisions thus got within range of the six Japanese dive-bombers only a moment or two before they entered the curtain of antiaircraft fire put out by the *Hornet*, the light antiaircraft cruisers *San Diego* and *Juneau*, and the destroyers *Morris* and *Barton*.

Lt Swede Vejtasa, a veteran former dive-bomber pilot with several aggressive air-to-air kills already under his belt, was initially ordered by John Griffin to lead his Fighting-10 division to the southwest (from the *Enterprise*) to look for bogeys. The division was at 12,000 feet and climbing when Vejtasa looked up in time to see five Vals in a loose column glide to their push-over point above the *Hornet*. All the Vals were coming out of the sun when Vejtasa first noticed them. One last look around revealed that the *Hornet* was already under attack by at least one other Val *chutai*, which had approached from a different angle.

Vejtasa picked up a sixth Val—the airplane damaged earlier by Tom Gallagher—as it passed through the bottom of a cloud exactly at his altitude. He flipped the Wildcat into a sudden wing-over, executed a high-side run, and opened fire. The Val faltered in its dive and fell away in flames. By then, there were no more Vals preparing to dive on the *Hornet*.

The next Wildcats to find Yoneda's Vals were four of an ad hoc six-plane Fighting-10 division led by Lt Fritz Faulkner. Of the four, Faulkner and two others lost contact with the Vals as the dive-bombers entered a cloud, but Lt Mac Kilpatrick, the tail-end Charlie, attacked. In the end, Kilpatrick was unable to stay with the Val and pulled up before he could open fire.

Two more Wildcat pilots had a crack at the five remaining first-*chutai* Vals—Ens Maurice Wickendoll and Ens Whitey Feightner, the second section of LCdr Bill Kane's misdirected Fighting-10 division. The pair had come unglued from Kane's lead section and were regaining altitude to look for it when they stumbled upon the five diving Vals. Wickendoll, in the lead, latched onto one of the Vals, but his guns would not fire, so he pulled away with Feightner following.

The first three second-*chutai* Vals released their bombs over the twisting *Hornet* but scored no hits. The fourth plane in the string, piloted by WO Shigeyuki Sato, spouted flames on the way down, doubtlessly hit by the torrent of antiaircraft that was bearing on his Val.

At 0913, Warrant Officer Sato intentionally crashed his burning and disabled Val straight into the forward port corner of the *Hornet's* stack. After tearing through some signal halyards, the Val glanced off the stack and fell into the flight deck at the base of the island. Flaming aviation gasoline from ruptured fuel tanks poured directly down on the signal bridge, where most of the signalmen were bathed in the burning fuel, and seven were instantly killed. The burning gasoline also destroyed all the signaling apparatus and burned all the flags in the flag bags. By sheer luck, LCdr Oscar Dodson happened to be shielded from the burning fuel by one of the steel legs of the ship's huge tripod signal mast. He waded right into the circle of burning men and tried to beat out the flames, but his own gloves caught fire; he was helpless as soon as he pulled them from his hands, and he had to watch his subordinates writhe in agony and succumb to the intense heat and trauma. One terrible sight that Dodson missed was a rush by one uninjured signalman into the arms of his twin brother, who was in the center of a large pool of burning gasoline. The twins died together, locked in a final embrace.

Sato's unarmed 250-kilogram bomb passed through the wooden flight deck and a steel bulkhead and came to rest on a catwalk beside the island. It did not explode. A wing-mounted tank of aluminum powder used to help aircraft rendezvous passed through the flight deck and three steel bulkheads before coming to rest beneath a table in one of the squadron ready rooms. It was thought to be a 60-kilogram bomb, so the flight personnel in that ready room nimbly stepped into the nearest companionway as the steel projectile rolled from beneath the table to block the only available hatchway.

After falling away from the stack, Sato's Val—minus one wing, which stuck in the funnel—cracked open after penetrating the flight deck and the overhead of the Scouting-8 ready room. Burning aviation gasoline flooded down into the ready room, where about fifteen unengaged pilots and crewmen had been listening in total silence to the hammering of 20mm and 1.1-inch antiaircraft guns right outside. The flaming fuel quickly spread to the companionway outside the compartment. Already shaken by the impact of the three bomb hits, the squadron flight officer, Lt Ben Tappan, lurched to the the rear of the compartment and began undogging the emergency hatchway. All his fellow pilots scrambled after him.

CY Ralph Cotton, the Bombing-8 chief yeoman, was one of the last to leave the adjacent Bombing-8 ready room. As Cotton was moving toward the hatchway, he saw a large object fall from the overhead and felt a warm sensation across his belly. Certain he had been hit, Chief Cotton reached down and pressed his hand against a thick greasy substance, no doubt a dollop of hot oil from Sato's engine. Behind Cotton, a pool of burning aviation gasoline was spreading throughout the Scouting-8 ready room.

Scouting-8's Lt(jg) Ivan Swope, who had been blown out of the leather-upholstered high-back seat nearest the companionway, came to on his back to find flaming fuel within inches of his face. The entire Scouting-8 ready room seemed to be engulfed in flames as the fire spread to upholstered chairs. Before Swope's head quite cleared, someone reached in from the adjacent Bombing-8 ready room, grabbed him under the shoulders, pulled him to safety, and helped him toward the flight deck.

In the next ready room over, six Fighting-72 alert pilots were untouched while, high above, the last first-*chutai* Val dropped its bomb—which missed—and fled the scene at low altitude. As all this was happening, two of Murata's Kates, which had launched torpedoes moments earlier, passed down the port side of the ship, and a *Shokaku* Zero was strafing the carrier's bows. It was quite a show.

♦

The next hitters to approach the plate were Lt Goro Washimi and his *chutai* of nine *Shokaku* Kates, coming in from the northwest against the turning carrier. The Kates were deployed in left-column formation with Washimi leading from the extreme right.

Earlier, Fighting-10's Ens Don Gordon and Ens Jerry Davis had been vectored out to the southwest at 7,000 feet to find the incoming enemy bombers. Unable to do so, the pair had climbed to 15,000 feet and turned for home. They were still southwest of the *Hornet* when the sounds of battle erupted in their earphones. Gordon looked down and chanced to spot five Kates. He led Davis after the lead torpedo bomber—Washimi—and set his shot. Gordon had a fit of what he later described as buck fever. His aim was off, he fired too soon, and his bullets passed harmlessly over the Kate. Nevertheless, the sudden passage of Gordon's tracers spooked Lieutenant Washimi into jerking his airplane to the right, directly into Ensign Davis's gunsight. Davis fired, and Washimi's smoking Kate veered even farther from its path.

While Gordon and Davis were harrying Washimi, Lt Mac Kilpatrick had come up on the tail of the next Kate over. A bit at a loss as to the best way to take on an enemy bomber that low over the water, Kilpatrick simply parked on the Kate's tail and fired short bursts. One of these killed the gunner, but the Kate angled down to fifty feet. Before Kilpatrick could react, Don Gordon leading Jerry Davis pulled in on the Kate's tail. The two were going too fast to set up a decent firing run, but they both pulled around, overtook Kilpatrick, and came on again. This time Gordon was dead on target. From a height of only ten feet, the Kate fell into the water. By then, the three Wildcats were under fire from ships in Task Force 17, so they pulled around and flew away.

Ens George Wrenn had become separated from Lt Bob Rynd's Fighting-72 division during the first wrenching turns at the point of encountering the *Zuikaku* Vals at the opening of the battle. He had dived through the Val formation without doing any damage and had barely evaded a Zero as he did. Once he had lost the Zero, thanks to his Wildcat's superior diving speed, Wrenn planned to recover for another firing pass at the Vals, but he saw below him six of Lieutenant Washimi's nine *Shokaku* Kates—the center and left *shotai*—as they began descending for their low-level torpedo attack. Wrenn followed through on his dive and sailed right up on the Kates in a shallow high-side turn. The Kates were just spreading out into their final attack formation when Wrenn raced into range of the left *shotai* and fired at the left-outboard Kate using only his four inboard guns. The Kate banked in toward the other Kates in order to clear a field of fire for its observer-gunner. Meanwhile, Wrenn could maintain his position of the Kate's tail only by twisting his airplane into nearly inverted flight. He continued to fire until the Kate began smoking and finally pulled away. As it did, Wrenn smoothly switched his gunsight to the center plane in the same *shotai*. A solid deflection burst set this Kate ablaze just as Wrenn came under fire from Task Force 17. He thought about following through against the lone survivor of this *shotai*, but near misses from friendly guns obliged him to pull away. In the meantime, the damaged first Kate swung sharply away from the fight without launching its torpedo. Wrenn's second target, which was burning when he left it, swung sharply toward the *Juneau*, which was spared a fiery suicide crash when her port battery of 5-inch guns hammered the torpedo plane into the water.

That left five Kates still bearing down on Task Force 17 from northwest of the *Hornet*. The five were blocked from a direct launch against the carrier by the destroyer *Morris*, so they came in high—at 200 to 300 feet—to hurdle the obstruction.

Two of the Kates flew astern of the *Morris*, one flew right over the ship, and two passed ahead of the destroyer. The *Morris's* guns downed the Kate that was passing directly overhead, but the four survivors launched their torpedoes at ranges varying from 800 yards down to 300 yards from the burning aircraft carrier. None of these torpedoes hit the ship, and all four of the Kates evaded clouds of antiaircraft fire.

Only four Vals from the *Zuikaku's* seven-plane third *chutai* survived their early encounter with two Fighting-72 Wildcat divisions. The *chutai* leader, Lt Yutaka Ishimaru, grew cautious at the last moment and circled well to the south of Task Force 17 before leading his Vals into the attack.

Lt Dave Pollock's three-plane Fighting-10 division (short one Wildcat because of an engine malfunction) had been at 10,000 feet and between the two carrier task forces at 0850, when the first news of the incoming strike was broadcast to the CAP. Pollock was given a heading to the southwest and told to climb, but he was called back to orbit the carriers after only four minutes. At 0903, Pollock was again vectored to the southeast to look for bogeys. He was ten miles from the *Hornet* and had climbed to 22,000 feet when Cdr Jack Griffin radioed, "Bogey. Angels seven. Look south." Pollock turned as directed and saw distant smudges in the air—burning airplanes from 10,000 feet down to 7,000 feet. This was evidence of the attack by Red Hessel and Bob Rynd. Pollock asked for permission to get into the fight, received no response, and went ahead on his own.

Pollock's division arrived at 0914, moments after the survivors of Lieutenant Ishimaru's third Val *chutai* had already begun their combat dives. To conserve precious ammunition, Pollock fired only his two outboard guns from 500 yards at a receding Val, the second plane in the string. The burst missed the target. Closing to 350 yards, Pollock fired the two outboard guns again and saw the Val's rear gunner slump in his seat. As he continued to close on the target, Pollock switched on all six .50-caliber wing guns and fired again. A long stream of smoke and flame burst from the Val's belly as it dived away from more punishing blows. An instant later, Pollock had to pull away to avoid the streaming wreckage.

Ens Steve Kona, Pollock's section leader, was unable to release his empty wing tank a moment before Pollock committed to the attack on the diving Vals, so he hauled it along for the ride. He gave his wingman, Ens Lyman Fulton, the attack signal and commenced a high-side run on the third Val in the string. As Kona swung into his dive, the errant wing tank was torn away. Kona and Fulton followed their target all the way to 7,000 feet, where they were chased off by intense friendly antiaircraft fire.

The three survivors, including Lieutenant Ishimaru, dropped their bombs over the *Hornet*, but they scored no hits.

What turned out to be the last and best-executed coordinated attack by Imperial Navy carrier aircraft in the Pacific War was over. The last of the attacking Kates and Vals had been demolished, and the survivors were fleeing the scene, some of them right past the *Hornet*.

The *Hornet* had been struck by three bombs and a burning Val. More than a hundred of her crew had been killed, and many more had been burned or otherwise injured, but the ship was in good shape despite several fires and three or four holes in her flight deck. The fires were containable, the wounds could be healed, and none of her engineering spaces had been touched.

For all that, two aerial torpedoes—launched by the slain LCdr Shigeharu Murata and one of his wingmen—were still bearing down on the great ship.

Chapter 29

As the air battle closed in on his ship, EM1 Samuel Blumer, operator of the *Hornet's* midships crane, left his station to watch the show from the port side of the hangar deck. He arrived just as Lieutenant Commander Murata's Kates were turning toward the ship from the southeast, and he eventually picked out a torpedo bomber that seemed to be heading right at him. When the Kate finally launched its torpedo and banked to the left, Blumer distinctly saw its pilot turn his head and stare at the ship. He also distinctly saw the foaming wake of the oncoming torpedo, so he went back to the crane room to await the inevitable detonation.

On the starboard side of the ship, from a bomb shelter built into the flight-deck catwalk, AMM3 Chuck Beck saw a Kate release its torpedo as it was heading straight at him. Beck began to crawl forward along the catwalk, which had large perforations that protruded upward to assist sailors in keeping their footing. Though Beck's hands and knees ached beyond description, he continued forward as far as he could, until stopped by the LSO platform affixed to the starboard forward corner of the flight deck (used in the event the ship had to back down to recover airplanes). He tucked himself into a ball and waited.

Capt Perry Mason saw two torpedo wakes heading straight for the starboard side of his ship. "Right full rudder," Mason brayed in the hope he could throw the carrier's stern around in time to evade the deadly fish.

The two torpedoes passed from the captain's view beneath the overhang of the flight deck. Several long seconds passed before LCdr Harry Holmshaw, the command duty officer, spoke up from Captain Mason's elbow. "I guess they missed us, sir."

"Well," Mason ventured, "it seems as though there's been enough time."

At that moment, the deck beneath Captain Mason's feet shuddered, and a great geyser of water rose into view.

AMM3 Chuck Beck was bounced up and down like a ping-pong ball between the perforated steel catwalk and the forward emergency LSO platform, his ears ringing from the nearby concussion. Beneath Beck, the entire ship lifted out of the water and jumped to the left.

The first shallow-running aerial torpedo detonated against the *Hornet's* starboard hull in line with the forward engine room. Lights throughout the ship flickered, and fuel oil bunkered in a breached cell beside the engine room poured in atop the engineers and electricians manning the vast engineering compartment.

ARM1 Billy Cottrell, of Bombing-8, was just stepping from the squadron ready room, when he was staggered by the impact of the first torpedo. Someone yelled, "Look out!" and Cottrell reflexively reached up to help several pilots and gunners hold up a spare 5-inch gun barrel that had been jarred from its lashings against the overhead.

Within seconds of the first torpedo blast, the *Hornet* had taken on a list to starboard just under 11 degrees and had lost her primary electrical circuits.

Twenty seconds later, the second shallow-running aerial torpedo struck the starboard hull abreast several magazines filled with antiaircraft rounds and powder. Once again, AMM3 Chuck Beck was violently bounced between the catwalk and the forward LSO platform as the ship twisted up and away from the force of the blast.

♦

Closed off from any view of the action, the sailors manning the engineering spaces and all below-decks compartments had to ride out the twisting shudders of each successive body blow. They had heard the loudspeaker messages announcing that the strike was imminent, and they had heard the guns firing—5-inchers at maximum range, then the 1.1-inch guns, then the 20mm guns, which sort of marked the progress of the Japanese warplanes. They knew the ship had been struck several times, but they had no idea what had hit her or what the damage was. Only the officers and sailors who were topside and had a clear view, or those in damaged compartments, had a sense of the battle or any of its parts.

At 0917, seconds after the torpedoes struck and as the *Hornet* glided to a stop, a fiercely burning Val arrived off the carrier's port quarter. Heavy gunfire ripped the airplane, but its pilot hung in and lofted his bomb at the carrier. The bomb's momentum carried it over the target, and it exploded fifty yards ahead of the ship. The pilot then pulled out over the *Hornet's* starboard bow, reversed course over the *Northampton,* and glided back toward the *Hornet,* which was still slowing to a gentle stop. Still taking hits from every gun in Task Force 17 that could bear, the Val crossed ahead of the *Hornet's* bows, turned in sharply, and with its forward machine guns firing, flew straight into the port side just below the leading edge of the flight deck. Both wings sheared off upon impact, but the fuselage penetrated 120 feet through the forecastle and officers' staterooms and came to rest in the forward elevator shaft, directly over the ship's main supply of aviation gasoline. The fuel supply thrown from the Val's ruptured tanks ignited. As the dying pilot and gunner writhed in the wreck, the fuel spread over the steel deck around the elevator shaft. By the time the last of the machine-gun ammunition aboard the Val finished cooking off, the steel deck was glowing cherry red.

Less than a minute after the Val crashed into the forecastle, the pilot of a torpedoless Kate—almost certainly Lt Goro Washimi—tried his luck from dead ahead, but his shattered airplane fell into the sea off the carrier's port bow.

♦

Though devastating, the combined effects of the multiple bomb blasts and two crashed Vals were by no means mortal. But the first torpedo hit abreast the forward engine room was life-threatening in that it deprived the great ship of electrical power needed to run her great propellers and, worse, essential to maintaining water pressure at the firefighting mains.

A moment after the Val crashed into the forecastle, Captain Mason noticed that his ship was losing way. "Does she respond to helm?" he asked the helmsman.

"No, sir," the helmsman answered. "The rudder is jammed hard right."

It was 0920. The Japanese had departed. The guns of the fleet were silent. The *Hornet* was dead in the water. All power and communications aboard the carrier were out.

On the wreckage of the signal bridge, LCdr Oscar Dodson, the carrier's communications officer, heard a query from one of the screening warships: "Is [the *Hornet*] hurt?" Dodson got on the task force radio net and replied, "Affirmative." A moment later, a bleeding signalman raised his semaphore flags and wig-wagged to the nearest ship, "We are ready to receive messages."

RAdm George Murray looked down from the flag bridge and saw five gray forms emerge from the smokey pall covering the signal bridge. Four of the sailors were carrying two other sailors. A seventh man, a chief signalman, was in the lead, groping for a route to safety. Murray saw that all seven men were wearing the charred remnants of their work clothes, and all the bare skin the admiral could see was glowing red through a layer of what looked like black grease.

"Where are you taking those men?" the admiral called down to the man in the lead.

The chief signalman straightened up to attention, "To the dressing station, sir."

The admiral told him that the access was barred. "Bring then in here, man," he called, pointing to his small flag bridge.

The two sailors with the worst burns were helped to the deck while the two with the least burns ran to fetch a doctor or corpsman. Admiral Murray stood over the chief, who was on his knees over the two recumbent signalmen. "Go below to the dressing station," the admiral ordered the chief.

"Sir, must I? I'd rather . . . "

"Yes, you must."

As the tearful chief left, Admiral Murray knelt beside the two burned bodies. One, the younger, looked up and apparently recognized the task force commander. "Sir," he breathed, "am I being brave enough?"

The admiral nodded, which was all he could do for a choked second, and then answered in a cracked voice, "Yes, son. Just take it easy." The youngster, who was seventeen years old, eventually died on the deck of the flag bridge.

Meanwhile, Lt Robert Noone, the signal officer, refused treatment for his burned and shattered leg until every one of the surviving signalmen had been treated. As he waited, Noone wondered aloud to LCdr Oscar Dodson if the leg injuries would prevent him from qualifying for flight training.

At 0925, there were major fires burning out of control on the signal bridge, flight deck, ready rooms, chiefs' quarters, forward messing compartment, storerooms, Number-1 elevator pit, hangar deck amidships and aft, and along the forecastle deck.

AMM3 Chuck Beck was only just pulling himself together from the torpedo and bad concussions in the catwalk space beneath the forward LSO platform when he heard the *Hornet* Air Group line chief yell, "Fire crew! Fire crew! Get your asses out here!" Beck instantly responded to the call, peeled a hose off its drum, and headed for a fire midships on the flight deck, next to the island—Warrant Officer Sato's Val. As Beck aimed the nozzle, several other firemen arrived to help steady it against the water pressure. "Turn it on," Beck yelled as he braced himself for the onset of the pressure. A sickly *pshshshshoo* emanated from the limp hose. Then nothing. The lack of electrical power throughout the ship had disabled the water mains.

The air group line chief improvised a team to break out large cans of dry fulmite, a fire retardant usually mixed with water in high-pressure hose lines. Other sailors were sent to break out buckets and lines, and they began dipping the buckets into the ocean and painstakingly hauling seawater up to the flight deck. Then, as the line chief and AMM3 Beck threw the dry fulmite into the fire, other sailors threw buckets of water in after it. The results were slow in coming, but the tide was turned as scores of men—officers, sailors, and Marines—converged on the Val to help. For all the effort, however, AMM3 Chuck Beck was not sure whether his hard work helped retard the fire or if the fire around and within the Val simply burned itself out.

Word of the flight-deck improvisation spread to fire-ravaged areas below decks, and there fires were also slowly fought by hand to uncertain standstills. Nevertheless, most of the effective firefighting was performed by destroyers *Morris, Russell,* and *Mustin*. Under the direction of the carrier's air boss, Cdr Marcel Gouin, the three warships gingerly came alongside the carrier, close enough for sailors on their decks to play streams of water on all the fires they could reach.

At length, the *Morris* was ordered alongside to starboard, and she passed three hoses directly to sailors aboard the *Hornet*. That act, incredibly brave because of the danger from submarines and the swell, turned the tide. One of the *Morris's* hoses was used to beat down the persistent main fire on the signal bridge, and the last of the major fires in the forecastle area were contained by the *Hornet* firefighters using the *Morris's* other two hoses.

The *Russell* came alongside next, off the port bow, to help with the forecastle and elevator-pit fires. She was only just getting into position when a large swell pushed her right up against the carrier's side. The shock of the contact released a lever controlling one of the destroyer's depth-charge racks, and a 600-pound depth charge dropped off the fantail. When the captain heard the news, he just started counting. Then, after enough time had passed without the feared detonation, he passed the word to forget about the depth charge; it apparently had been locked on "safe."

Finally, the *Mustin* came alongside the *Hornet's* port quarter so her hoses could be used by the *Hornet* firefighters to battle the blazes in the chiefs' quarters and the storerooms.

All major fires were under control by 1000, though a great deal of work still needed to be done to finally quell several of them. The most persistent fire was in the chiefs' quarters; it was fed by mattresses and upholstered chairs. Though contained by hoses passed from the *Mustin*, this series of smoldering blazes was finally extinguished altogether by seawater supplied by a portable "handy-billy" water pump set up on the carrier's own main deck. Another persistent fire was in the Scouting-8 ready room; it too was fed by upholstered chairs, and it was eventually quenched by a hose from the *Morris* and a 200-man bucket brigade using water and dry fulmite.

While being rocked by the swell, the *Russell* had her starboard anchor knocked off in a particularly violent collision with the carrier, and a good part of her starboard hull and bridge, and every gun director, were dished in by repeated shocks. The *Morris*, a destroyer leader, suffered major damage to her superstructure and antenna system; the damage eventually obliged the commodore of Destroyer Squadron 2 to transfer his flag to the *Mustin*. (Coincidentally, the *Morris* had suffered similar damage conducting a similar task alongside the *Lexington* during the Coral Sea battle.)

The *Hornet* was saved for the moment largely because her gasoline handlers had flooded her aviation-fuel lines prior to the attack with inert carbon-dioxide gas. The potential for disaster was great, and the fear was palpable, for the *Hornet's* crew had witnessed the incineration of the *Wasp* a month earlier. But the huge fireball everyone expected to erupt did not engulf them.

Doctors, dentists, and corpsmen from the medical department—M Division—manning seven medical battle stations throughout the ship swung into action at the instant burning fuel from Sato's Val cascaded onto the signal bridge. While the carnage there at first appeared absolute, survivors were plucked from the flames, and their burns and other injuries were quickly and expertly treated.

The first bomb, which had gutted the forward repair party, also killed a doctor and several of his corpsmen. Thus, in addition to severe casualties among the nearest firefighters, treatment of the wounded in the immediate area of the detonation was severely limited. The Val that drove itself through the forecastle into the forward elevator pit severely wounded Dr. Gerald McAteer and killed or wounded several corpsmen at his medical battle station. Though Dr. McAteer could not participate directly in the treatment of the wounded, he issued a steady stream of directions to his surviving corpsmen and volunteers, who lacked the training to treat many of the more serious injuries.

PhM1 Floyd Arnold, who stopped to help pull a hose to the vicinity of the ready-room fires from the deck below, made his way to the midships area of the hangar deck and began treating several sailors who had burns on exposed areas of their skin, particularly hands and faces. The treatment consisted mainly of cleaning the burned areas with gentian violet and larding on a thick dollop of burn ointment. The wounded were bandaged, tagged, and ordered to casualty clearing stations on the flight deck and fantail, but a number of them undoubtedly ignored the order and returned to work to help save the ship.

After being pulled from the path of burning aviation gasoline spreading across the Scouting-8 ready room, Lt(jg) Ivan Swope was assisted to the flight deck. He was groggy and unable to focus on his plight because of a mild concussion he had suffered when he was thrown from his seat to the steel deck of the ready room. He aimlessly wandered around on the flight deck for a few minutes before the haze in his head cleared enough for him to realize that he had suffered burns on his face, left hand, both legs below the knees, and both feet. Oddly, his pants legs and shoes were not even scorched. He found the tiny dressing station in the after part of the island. There, gentian violet, burn ointment, and gauze bandages were applied to his burns, and he was placed in one of the tiny compartment's six narrow bunks.

Ed Knobel, who had been temporarily blinded by the flash of one of the flight-deck detonations, lay doggo while corpsmen moved to succor the Navy and Marine gunners around him who had caught the full force of the second bomb blast. Knobel spent the time trying to fix in his mind what had been hit and who might have been injured. After a few minutes, he was handed up to the flight deck and stretched out beside other wounded men on the after edge of the after elevator. Unable to see and with ears still ringing, Knobel had to fight against his worst fears taking hold.

Tom Kuykendall, who had barely survived the conflagration that destroyed the forward repair party at the site of the first bomb detonation, reached the flight deck and went right to work helping beat back the flames from what at first seemed like windrows of dead and wounded sailors. Only as Kuykendall confronted the flames did he realize that he had been badly burned himself. Indeed, he was covered with blood. The skin on his face, legs, and arms looked like loose strips of torn cloth. As the pain and shock began taking hold, a doctor grabbed him, helped him lie down on a litter, and injected a dose of morphine. Then litter bearers carried him to the open fantail, where other wounded men had already been assembled. By the time Kuykendall's litter was set down, the pain and shock were virtually unbearable.

Lyle Skinner, who had escaped from the compartment directly aft of Kuykendall's obliterated battle station, nearly went into shock when he reached the hangar deck and saw the vast scene of destruction and suffering. Thankful for his own salvation, Skinner went to work with another watertender, sorting the living from the dead.

Vic Kelber, who had been shot through the cheek and blown from his 1.1-inch gun tub, was ordered to the hangar deck to have his face treated. Though blood was pouring from the hole in his cheek, Kelber made his way below under his own power and reached an emergency operating room adjacent to the burned-out ready rooms. The scene that greeted the Marine was right from the depths of hell. The narrow compartment was packed with sailors—sitting, standing, lying, wounded, dying, and dead. The doctors and corpsmen were working with machine-like precision, totally immersed in their jobs. A Marine sergeant Kelber knew had both legs mangled and was profusely bleeding despite the two tourniquets that had been applied above his wounds. The sergeant nodded a greeting to Kelber, who immediately left. Later, Kelber learned that the sergeant bled to death where he lay. After leaving the operating room, Kelber entered an adjacent compartment that had three empty cots and a dark ball on the deck. A closer look revealed that the ball was in fact a human head. At last, Kelber was ordered to report to the fantail sickbay for treatment. On the way, he passed a body that had been burned totally beyond recognition. On reaching the fantail, Kelber's facial wounds were tightly packed, the free flow of blood finally staunched.

Lt(jg) Earl Zook was the only officer on duty this day in Central Station—the damage-control center located in a vertical steel tube two decks beneath the hangar deck. When the first torpedo detonated seventy feet away from Central Station, the concussion traveling through the confined space buckled Zook's knees, severely jarred his body, and left him confused, without any direct memory of the moment of impact. Within seconds, gasses released by the bomb that had detonated in the forward crew messing compartment leaked into Central Station and further impaired Zook's ability to control the fight to save the *Hornet*.

Cdr Henry Moran, the ship's first lieutenant and damage-control officer, was at a conference of officers in the wardroom when the guns started firing, and he did not reach Central Station until the action had nearly abated. Within a minute, the ship had taken on an 11-degree list to starboard, which Moran began working to correct with a set of valves controlling the flow of seawater into trimming tanks in the hull of the ship. The best Moran could accomplish was a reduction of the list to 7 degrees. As he worked, crewmen who had been manning the compartments adjacent to Central Station entered the crowded space to get away from the effects of a bomb blast. A warrant officer who had been standing directly beneath a ventilation duct was blackened with soot from the blast and had to be treated with salve for flash burns.

Faulty communications throughout the ship prevented the Central Station crew from accomplishing much more than the correction of the list, which they could monitor themselves with the aid of an inclinometer. Thus, the firefighting and other repair efforts were conducted locally, without central control.

After leaving the burning ready rooms, ARM1 Billy Cottrell of Bombing-8 made his way up to the flight deck to see what was going on. By the time he arrived, other air-group enlisted men were breaking out spare .30-caliber airplane machine guns and setting them up on improvised sandbag shelters around the edge of the useless flight deck. Cottrell, who was drawing pay as a Dauntless rear gunner, joined one of the gun crews and waited for the next Japanese strike to appear over his ship. Most of the men streaming up to the flight deck, however, worked at fighting fires or treating the wounded, or did nothing at all but mill around in stunned confusion.

♦

EM1 Samuel Blumer, who had left his post in the hangar-deck crane room to see what was going on, saw F1 Harold Blanco burst out onto the hangar deck from a ladder leading below. "Blanco," Blumer called, "what are you doing up here?" Blanco looked at Blumer and blurted out, "Abandon ship!" At that instant, sailors from below began streaming up to the hangar deck in nearly uncountable numbers. Blumer instantly grasped that something was amiss; it seemed as though the incessantly practiced lessons of the *Hornet's* year afloat had been lost in a universal wave of panic undoubtedly brought on by the loss of viable communications throughout the great ship. Blumer sensed that the refugees from below were on the brink of hysteria, but there was nothing he could do to set things right, so he joined the exodus to the flight deck.

Unbeknown to Blumer, officers and sailors manning many compartments and work areas below the waterline had indeed been ordered by the captain to make their way topside. For example, electrician's mates manning the blind after generator room received the word to abandon their station without having, to that point, a clear idea of the damage that had befallen their ship. EM1 Leroy Butts got all the way up to the hangar deck before he saw any clear evidence of the damage. There, spread out on the steel deck, were wounded sailors. Stunned, Butts wandered over to the twelve-inch hole that had been punched by the first bomb in the forward section of the vast space. Beneath his feet, officers' staterooms had been destroyed in the conflagration that gutted the forward repair party. Farther forward, smoke was still rising out of the forward elevator pit.

While twenty-nine other officers and ratings left the forward engine room because of flooding by bunker oil from a torpedo-breached fuel tank, the ship's chief engineer, Cdr Pat Creehan, stood by his post with a chief machinist, a chief machinist's mate, and EM3 Tom Reese. It was Reese's job to try to get the electrical pumps going in order to clear the deck of the sloshing oil, but there was no way to stem the flow of the thick, gooey fuel from the adjacent tank. After only a few minutes of frenetic, prayerful activity, Creehan had to tell the captain that his was a losing fight. He was ordered to clear out of the compartment.

♦

Once Warrant Officer Sato's Val had stopped burning, AMM3 Chuck Beck got a grappling hook from an emergency locker and went fishing in the smoldering wreckage for souvenirs. He pulled out several instruments, from which he pried metal tags with Japanese characters on them, then got the tail wheel, and finally snagged a large book. The book was of definite interest and, on inspection, appeared to be filled with recognition silhouettes of Allied aircraft and a great many notes. Beck was just shoving the book into the front of his shirt when a voice from the island called down and ordered him to bring it topside. Grudgingly, the plane captain handed the book over to the officer and went back to fishing in the wreckage. His next catch was a charred corpse, Warrant Officer Sato or the Val's gunner. After only a moment's hesitation, Beck dragged the body up the canted flight deck with the intention of dropping it over the side of the ship. He was again stopped by an officer, who asked whether Beck was sure it was not an American body. Beck answered that he was not sure. As the two spoke, a wild-eyed sailor ran up and began plunging a knife into the corpse. The man told Beck, "I want some Jap blood on my knife." When the deranged sailor had had his gruesome revenge, the officer ordered Beck to leave the body where it was and get back to work.

After his ship had been drifting aimlessly for about a half-hour, Cdr Henry Moran, the damage-control officer, decided that there was no point in his staying below in Central Station. He checked with the bridge to see whether there was anything else he could do from that post—there was not—and ordered all hands to clear the compartment and climb more than a hundred feet to the bridge-level deck of the island

Counting engineering personnel from adjacent spaces, more than a hundred officers and men had to evacuate the lower decks through the three-foot-wide escape trunk. One, a chief machinist's mate whose palms had been severely burned, had to drag himself up the entire ladder without assistance, for there was no room for anyone to lend a hand. An officer from a nearby compartment began screaming at the top of his lungs when ship's cooks who had been manning an ammunition-handling room preceded his group with a bit less alacrity than he thought was warranted. The going was tedious because everyone insisted upon wearing his life vest in the confined tube. Lt(jg) Earl Zook, who was third-from-last to leave, was nearly overcome by fumes by the time he reached the exit, which was located in Radar Plot, high up in the island. The next-to-last man asked Commander Moran for the honor of being the last to leave the compartment, but Moran turned him down; it was the senior's duty to be the last man out.

Earl Zook stumbled out of Radar Plot in search of some fresh air and stepped on the corpse of one of the men killed in the signal-bridge conflagration, one of the twins who had died in his brother's arms.

Once Commander Moran was clear of the tube, he walked forward to the bridge to confer with Captain Mason, the exec, and others. The senior group determined that the *Hornet* was in no immediate danger of sinking and that she could be saved, but she might also be lost if more Japanese bombs or torpedoes—including submarine torpedoes—struck her. The senior group decided to evacuate the wounded and nonessential personnel to destroyers and to attempt to take aboard a towing cable from the heavy cruiser *Northampton*, for it was clear that it would take hours of frantic activity for the electrical department to get the *Hornet's* vital electrical power back on line.

Chapter 30

The first Japanese strike was over, but there was still work for the airmen of Fighting-10 and Fighting-72 to do. It was almost as important to shoot down Japanese airplanes leaving the vicinity of Task Force 61 as it had been to shoot them down before the attack, for the day was still young and a crippled friendly carrier needed protection from follow-on strikes in which the first-strike survivors might take part.

Lt Hisayoshi Miyajima, the *Shokaku* escort leader, had only one other Zero with him when he left the vicinity of Task Force 17. On the way out, the Zero pair was met by Fighting-10's Ens Maurice Wickendoll and Ens Whitey Feightner, who had pulled away from an attack against diving Vals when Wickendoll's machine guns had failed to fire. By the time Wickendoll could get his guns operating, the Vals were beyond reach. As the pair of Americans climbed back to 12,000 feet, Miyajima and his wingman, who were also flying at 12,000 feet, looped in to get at the two slower Wildcats. Wickendoll decided to evade the challenge in favor of picking up more speed, so he led his wingman away from the Zeros. At length, the Wildcats reversed course and began a head-on run at the Zeros, but the Japanese broke away and fled.

As Ens Steve Kona, also of Fighting-10, recovered from a long dive in pursuit of attacking Vals, he spotted three Vals as they passed through 3,000 feet to recover from their dives on the *Hornet*. Kona, followed by Ens Lyman Fulton, attacked the first Japanese dive-bomber as it leveled off at 50 feet. A high-side run and recovery produced no discernible results because the body of his Wildcat cut off Kona's view. Kona recovered in time to slip into attack position on the third Val. Again, no results were observed because the body of his Wildcat got in the way. Kona was recovering from this firing run when a Zero attacked from dead astern. Kona and Fulton instantly entered a scissor weave, but ran into a cloud before the Zero pilot could be suckered into committing himself.

After recovering at low altitude following his attack against incoming Kates, Ens George Wrenn of Fighting-72 found a pair of Kates as they ran from antiaircraft fire after releasing their torpedoes. Both Japanese inadvertently turned toward Wrenn, who shot at one in a head-on pass and then turned his guns on the other as it passed him at a right angle. Unfortunately, Wrenn's second firing pass carried him too close to Task Force 16 and he ran afoul of the *South Dakota's* jumpy 5-inch and 40mm gunners. It was all Wrenn could do to escape, and he nearly dragged a wingtip in the water as he ran from range. Wrenn was credited with both of these airplanes as full kills, but both actually survived.

Lt Claude Phillips, the section leader of Lt Red Hessel's Fighting-72 division, got some bullets into a departing Kate, which he claimed as a probable. And Lt(jg) Robert Holland, a member of Lt Ken Bliss's Fighting-72 division, shot at another departing Kate, which he also claimed as a probable.

Finally, Lt(jg) Howard Burnett, a returning Scouting-10 searcher, took on a retiring Kate at low level near Task Force 16. Burnett, who had bagged a Val during the Eastern Solomons battle, went after the Kate with a vengeance. And he did force it into the water, an outcome corroborated by the crew of another Kate. As the downed airplane was sinking and its crew was getting into the water, Burnett and his radioman shot it up and presumably killed both Japanese airmen.

Burnett and his radiomen were the last Americans to see any of the Japanese strike bombers. Of twenty Kates taking part in the attack, five of the first (Murata's) *chutai* rendezvoused and proceeded directly north on a homeward course. Five from the second *chutai* (Washimi's) ended up southwest of Task Force 17. On their way around the *Hornet* force, at least one of the second-*chutai* survivors spotted Task Force 16. Nearly an hour later, at 1020, the radioman aboard this *Shokaku* Kate dispatched a report indicating the last known position of the second American carrier task force.

There was still some fighter action, in which elements of Fighting-72 and Fighting-10 engaged the escort Zeros. Ens James Caldwell, of Fighting-10, was forced to bail out of his Wildcat at 0925 after being overwhelmed during a one-man attack against several *Zuikaku* Zeros. He was seen beneath his parachute canopy, but he was never recovered. Caldwell's section leader, Lt(jg) Jim Billo, shot down a Zero in the same fight.

At about 0928, Fighting-10's Ens Steve Kona and Ens Lyman Fulton were running north to protect the *Enterprise* from a false alarm, when Fulton suddenly turned back toward Task Force 17. Assuming his wingman was responding to a call he had not heard, Kona turned to follow. He made several circuits around Task Force 17 but did not find Fulton again. Nobody did; Fulton was lost without a trace or a clue as to his fate.

Lt Ayao Shirane and five other members of his *Zuikaku* Zero *chutai* were probably the last of the first-strike aircraft to leave Task Force 61. In the course of battling an estimated thirty Wildcats, Shirane and his fellows had shot down and killed Fighting-72's Lt(jg) John Franklin and Lt(jg) Paul Landry, as well as Fighting-10's Ens Jim Caldwell. They might even have shot down Steve Kona's missing wingman, Ens Lyman Fulton. Their own losses came to two Zeros and their pilots.

This fighter-versus-fighter action brought to a close the first Japanese strike of October 26 against Task Force 61.

Summing up, twenty-one *Zuikaku* Vals attempted to attack the *Hornet*. Five were apparently shot down by CAP fighters during the attack but before they could drop their bombs, ship's fire destroyed four others, and two were shot down while retiring—a total of eleven Vals destroyed outright. Several others were crippled or badly damaged. Of the twenty *Zuikaku*

Kates taking part in the torpedo attack, one was shot down and several were crippled by CAP fighters on the way to the *Hornet*, antiaircraft fire downed eight during their torpedo runs or while they were recovering from torpedo launches, and one was destroyed by an SBD crew while retiring. At least three crippled Kates attempted to intentionally crash into ships, of which one succeeded. Three of twelve Zeros were shot down by CAP fighters.

Claims by both sides were, as usual, wildly inflated. Zero pilots claimed eighteen Wildcats and two carrier bombers shot down (actual losses were six Wildcats downed and four pilots killed). Japanese bomber crews claimed a carrier sunk by six bombs and two torpedoes, a heavy cruiser sunk by torpedo, a destroyer sunk in a suicide attack by a Kate, and a destroyer damaged in a suicide attack by a Val. In addition to one actual kill by an SBD crew, American fighter pilots claimed six Zeros, ten Vals, and five Kates shot down, plus twelve Vals and five Kates probably shot down. Many of the kills were real enough, but most of them, and others, were also claimed by gunners aboard Task Force 17 warships, of which a fair number were really downed by ships' fire.

The Japanese losses over and around Task Force 17 were compounded when six Kates, six Vals, and two Zeros later ditched because of battle damage or fuel depletion. In all, then, only seven Zeros, four Vals, and four Kates survived the first strike. In return, the Japanese airmen had killed or maimed several hundred American sailors and Marines, and their bombs, torpedoes, and two crashed aircraft had crippled one of the two operational carriers left to the United States Navy earlier that morning.

Chapter 31

The first of the Air Group 10 morning scouts began returning to the vicinity of Task Force 61 shortly before the arrival of Lieutenant Commander Murata's first strike group. All but one of these aircraft—Lt(jg) Howard Burnett's SBD—stood off well out of the battle arena as the attack on the *Hornet* unfolded, but they flew back in over Task Force 61 as soon as the Japanese survivors departed. When they returned, the scouts and many CAP fighters in need of fuel, ammunition, and repairs found the *Enterprise* and the rest of Task Force 16 sailing southeast at 27 knots in order to take cover beneath a line of rain squalls marching across the ocean in that direction. By 0930, with as many as twenty fuel-hungry bombers and fighters circling expectantly in its vicinity, it was time for the U.S. Navy's last operational carrier deck to begin recovering airplanes.

When Bombing-10's Lt(jg) Hal Buell and his wingman arrived from their fruitless search mission, they saw that the *Hornet* was burning. Buell made a long orbit well away from the carriers to make sure it was safe to proceed. As he did, other search elements appeared and joined on him.

Suddenly, at 0931, the *Enterprise* turned into the wind and signaled all returning planes to land. Buell led the way up the groove, from which he could see that the flight deck was clear; everything had been launched or stowed on the hangar deck. The landing was routine, and Buell's SBD was spotted in the forwardmost position on the flight deck. Behind it, numerous scout and fighter pilots responded to the crisp signals Lt Jim Daniels, the Air Group 10 LSO, signed with his paddles. After jumping from the wing of his Dauntless, Buell walked over to the 40mm gun tub located farthest forward on the starboard side of the ship. It was then that he learned that a follow-on Japanese strike force had been picked up on the *Northampton's* CXAM radar.

Ens Doan Carmody and Lt(jg) Les Ward of Scouting-10 returned from their confrontation with the Japanese carriers, but they could not immediately locate any friendly vessels at the appointed place. Finally, a column of smoke from the *Hornet* appeared on the horizon and served as a grim beacon for the two searchers at the end of an altogether too-adventure-filled mission. It was clear to Carmody that he could not land aboard the *Hornet*, and he did not at first see the *Enterprise*, which had not yet emerged from its concealing rain squall. Fuel was almost gone aboard the two Dauntlesses, and Carmody was just resigning himself to a water landing when the *Enterprise* sailed into view. The two searchers joined up on the gathering behind Hal Buell and made safe landings on the very last of their fuel. Carmody and Ward had been airborne for nearly five boring hours and more than a dozen exciting minutes.

Fighting-10's Lt Bobby Edwards was the first Wildcat pilot to land. Control of his airplane was hampered by a runaway propeller. Then Lt Mac Kilpatrick landed his fighter, whose engine was overheating.

Ens Steve Kona had only about one-fourth of his starting ammunition supply left when the sky was finally clear of Japanese. At length, Kona was joined by another Fighting-10 pilot who had also been shaken loose from his parent formation. The two heard orders from the *Enterprise* to "pancake"—to land as quickly as possible—and they immediately joined the line in the carrier's traffic circle. Kona was certain his fighter would be quickly serviced and relaunched, but he was sent below without an explanation.

Following Steve Kona were three Fighting-72 Wildcats in need of succor: Lt Red Hessel, Lt Bob Rynd, and Lt(jg) Ken Kiekhoefer all had to nurse their shot-up fighters aboard.

Lt Claude Phillips of Fighting-72 knew he needed ammunition for his wing guns, but he did not know the extent of the damage the Wildcat had suffered from a 20mm round fired by a Zero into the fuselage. Phillips saw that the *Hornet* was throwing up a huge pillar of black smoke, so he headed for the *Enterprise,* which looked okay as it sailed into the wind. Phillips passed along the carrier's starboard side with his wheels down. When he attempted to lower flaps, however, he discovered that the 20mm round had holed the vacuum tank through which the flaps were controlled. Only the protection of the armored seat back and self-sealing tanks had saved this Wildcat pilot from a fiery death, for the vulnerable vacuum tank was directly behind the cockpit. Having committed himself to flying up the groove, Phillips watched for the LSO's fine-tuning signals. He got a Come Ahead followed by a Too Fast, followed by a last-instant Wave-off. As Phillips passed right over the LSO platform, he signed that he had no flaps. He came around again, hoping his message had been clear, and was allowed to come ahead and execute a hot landing. In fact, the LSO, Lt Jim Daniels, had disobeyed a direct order to keep damaged airplanes from landing. If Phillips had piled up, many other warplanes might have been lost. As it was, he was the last pilot allowed to land. At 0948, Jim Daniels was ordered to stop bringing airplanes aboard so the flight deck could be respotted.

Lt Ken Bliss of Fighting-72 needed more ammunition. He started back toward the *Hornet* minutes behind his squadronmate, Claude Phillips, but saw for the first time that she was burning, so he also headed toward the *Enterprise*. Before flying into the groove, Bliss took the precaution of clearing his presumably empty machine guns and found that the right outboard gun was still operating; clearly, it had earlier jammed and still had an unknown number of rounds left in its magazine. As Bliss flew up the *Enterprise's* wake, he received a curt Wave-off. He had no idea why the signal was passed, but the rule was that he had to clear out. Presumably, another Japanese strike was inbound. Lacking options, Bliss nudged his Wildcat over toward a cloud bank 2,000 feet up and virtually beside the battleship *South Dakota*. The jumpy *South Dakota* gunners fired a pattern of 5-inch rounds all around the orbiting Wildcat. Bliss radioed the ship to remind its crew that all the midwing monoplanes in the sky were friendlies. The firing abruptly ceased, and Bliss maintained his station around the battleship, ready for anything.

Among the many fighter pilots turned away by the *Enterprise* was Ens Chip Reding, the only survivor of Lt John Leppla's Fighting-10 division, which had been ambushed along with the outbound Torpedo-10 Avengers. Reding had made it back home after the survivors of the first Japanese strike had left, and he joined right up at the end of the traffic circle. When Jim Daniels finally had to shut down landing operations, Reding obligingly flew his shot-up Wildcat to the nearest cloud and hid out. In all, six Fighting-10 and four Fighting-72 Wildcats and two battle-damaged TBFs in need of a safe haven had to be turned away.

Tom Kinkaid radioed the Task Force 17 screen commander, RAdm Howard Good, at 0941 to ask whether the *Enterprise* should land the *Hornet* Air Group aircraft that were still aloft in the area. Good responded to Kinkaid's query with "Affirmative." It was Good's hope, once the fires aboard the carrier had been quelled, to take the powerless ship under tow by the *Northampton*. In order to insure the highly vulnerable towing sequence against interference from an oncoming Japanese strike, Good requested immediate fighter support. The result was disheartening. Only four Wildcats had fuel enough to remain in the vicinity of Task Force 17—Lt Al Emerson's three-plane Fighting-72 division and Lt(jg) Jim Billo's lone Fighting-10 fighter. A request to the *Enterprise* for more fighters brought a negative response; the flagship had only eleven Wildcats from both squadrons aloft over Task Force 16.

At 0949, Kinkaid sent a two-word radio message to South Pacific Area headquarters: "*Hornet* hurt." VAdm Bill Halsey, who must have been dying to be in Kinkaid's place aboard a fighting carrier, responded, "Operate from and in positions from which you can strike quickly and effectively. We must use everything we have to the limit." Kinkaid was doing just that, using his assets to the limit.

♦

The first debriefing report from the scout pilots began reaching the bridge of the *Enterprise* while Tom Kinkaid was exchanging messages along the command chain. It was that of Bombing-10's Lt Vivian Welch and Lt(jg) Bruce McGraw, who had pinpointed RAdm Hiroaki Abe's Vanguard Group. Based on this report, the *Enterprise's* skipper, Capt Osborne Hardison, proposed launching an immediate strike composed of ten available Bombing-10 SBDs that could then fly on to Henderson Field to refuel. While the plan was being discussed and thought through, Task Force 16 came to a southwesterly heading in order to stay within range of the enemy force and the returning friendly strike forces.

Because of limited space on the flight deck, many of the fighters had to be struck below to the hangar deck in order to make room for the arming and fueling of the dive-bombers that might take part in the proposed strike. Nevertheless, as the work progressed, it became possible to land several Wildcats at a time to refuel and rearm. First in, at 0952, was the three-plane Fighting-10 division led by Lt Fritz Faulkner. That left only eight fighters to protect Task Force 16 at a time when the Japanese second strike was bearing down on Task Force 61.

As the *Enterprise's* flight-deck and hangar-deck crews worked feverishly to refuel and respot the mixed bag of Wildcats and Dauntlesses Jim Daniels had guided in, many turned their attention to the first radar contact with the approaching Japanese follow-on strike. Thus, few eyes were on a drama unfolding in the midst of the Task Force 16 circle.

The first American strike aircraft to return to Task Force 61 were the two damaged Avengers that had survived the ambush of the outbound Torpedo-10 strike group. Lt Doc Norton, in the lead TBF, saw that the *Hornet* was burning on the horizon so he continued on to find his own ship, the *Enterprise*. Rather unwisely, in view of the terrible condition of his Avenger, Norton made a pass at the carrier's LSO platform. Instead of a comradely offer to guide the Avenger down, Lt Jim Daniels vigorously waved Norton away. Norton was put off by the rejection, for he had no way of knowing that another Japanese strike group had been picked up on the ship's air-search radar. There being no alternative, Norton raised his Avenger's wheels, remained low and slow, and flew as far from the task force as he dared, given the condition of his airplane.

Doc Norton's wingman, Ens Dick Batten, followed Norton away from the *Enterprise* and landed his virtually fuelless, badly damaged TBF at about 1000 only 200 yards off the destroyer *Porter's* port beam. Despite mounting news of an incoming strike, the *Porter* was ordered to leave the *Enterprise* screen and pick up Batten and his crewmen.

The *Porter* was an 1,850-ton destroyer leader, flagship of Capt Charles Cecil's Destroyer Squadron 5 and thus larger than the *Mahan*-class destroyers under Cecil's command. Though the *Porter* was outfitted with four dual 5-inch gun mounts, she was not of much use in defending the *Enterprise* against Japanese warplanes because none of the 5-inch guns could be raised far enough to provide antiaircraft fire. This, along with the spot in which Dick Batten chose to ditch, was undoubtedly behind the decision to send the *Porter* to the aid of the downed TBF crew.

The sinking TBF was to port when the *Porter* began slowing for the pick-up. To avoid swamping the three aviators in the life raft, the destroyer's skipper, LCdr Dave Roberts, ordered the ship to come dead in the water a short way from the raft and to wait while Batten and his crewmen paddled to the leeward side, which happened to be to starboard. Thus, the attention of Commander Roberts and most of the topside crew was directed toward the airmen as they clambered up the starboard side of the ship.

S2 Ross Pollock's attention was fleetingly diverted from the clambering airmen to a diving fighter to port. A 1.1-inch loader with a clear view all around the ship, Pollock realized that the fighter was friendly and that it was strafing an unseen object in the water off the port side of the ship.

Coincidentally, the Wildcat pilot was also named Pollock—Lt Dave Pollock, of Fighting-10. He had seen a torpedo wake rushing toward the *Porter* on a curving track and had dived in the slim hope of detonating the fish with his machine guns, just as Ens Johnny Cresto had done a month earlier to help save the *Hornet*. The torpedo upon which Lieutenant Pollock could lay his guns was curving toward the destroyer. He fired two long bursts without results, pulled up, and dived again. During those two dives, Lieutenant Pollock became increasingly aware of the fire the *Porter* was putting out in his direction. Since he could not hit the torpedo and was in danger of being downed by the ship he was trying to save, he zoomed from range under the prodding of the friendly guns.

Only as Lieutenant Pollock flew from range did it dawn on Seaman Pollock—a veteran of only three months in the Navy—that the fighter's unseen target might be a torpedo.

As Ensign Batten and his crewmen climbed aboard the *Porter* on the starboard side, Lt(jg) Bill Wood, the officer of the deck, glanced to port and saw a torpedo wake heading right at him from a relative bearing of 270 degrees. At the same instant, S1 Don Beane, a signalman striker manning a lookout station on the port wing of the bridge, also saw the oncoming torpedo. He yelled "Fish!" as loud as he could. The captain and executive officer turned toward Beane.

In Control-II, one deck above the main deck and aft of the bridge, SM2 Al Muccitelli thought he saw three torpedo wakes to port. One was clearly going to pass ahead, and one was clearly going to pass astern. The center wake was heading for the ship. Y2 Francois Ogden, Destroyer Squadron 5's staff yeoman, saw only two torpedoes. When he realized that one would pass ahead and the other would pass astern, he relaxed. A messman who had just brought coffee to the bridge stopped in his tracks beside Ogden and became so agitated that Ogden thought he was going to jump overboard. "Take it easy," Ogden said in his most soothing voice. "They missed us." That said, he finally spotted the torpedo that was heading right at him. Without a word, he dived into the corner farthest from the presumed point of impact.

RM3 R. C. Tannatt was leaning out of the radio shack to watch the rescue when he glanced to port in time to see Dave Pollock's diving Wildcat veer away from the ship. Tannatt clearly saw the a torpedo coming right at him. A sailor on the main deck, just below the radio shack, was leaning against the railing, his back to the oncoming torpedo. Tannatt and a fellow radioman bellowed a warning.

As the torpedo raced toward the *Porter*, Bill Wood dived into the pilot house from the port wing of the bridge and rang up emergency flank speed on the repeater to the engine room. It was 1002.

MM1 Al Anundsen, in the after engine room, swiftly responded to Wood's signal from the bridge. The throttle was thrown forward as the chilling call "Torpedo wake" sounded over the intercom. But it was too late.

Before the destroyer could move, SM2 Al Muccitelli helplessly watched as the torpedo passed from view beneath the *Porter's* whaleboat, almost directly between her two firerooms—dead on the transverse bulkhead between the two compartments. The blast instantly deprived the *Porter* of all her power. Anundsen, one compartment aft of the point of impact, heard what sounded to him like the vastly amplified sharp *CRACK* of two stones being thrown together. The ship went dead still and seemed to settle.

Clad only in a skivvy shirt and shorts, F1 Thomas Anderson was standing in the after fireroom right beside the point of impact and was blown out into the water. A radioman saw Anderson almost as soon as he emerged from the hole in the side of the ship, and he dived into the water to rescue the dazed fireman. Anderson's only apparent injury was an instant reddening of his exposed skin to scalding-hot live steam escaping from ruptured steampipes. The burns would prove fatal within several days.

The sailor below the radio shack did not have time to react to RM3 R. C. Tannatt's shouted warning. The detonation threw him high into the air and twenty feet out from the ship. He was pulling for the stricken warship almost as soon as he plunged into the water. He later told Tannatt that he had found himself looking down on the ship from midair without any idea about how he had gotten there. He was one of the lucky ones. The full force of the blast erupted upward and engulfed the midships repair party, located on the main deck just aft of the bridge. One officer and one sailor were blown overboard, or perhaps vaporized; neither was ever seen again.

Ross Pollock was knocked back against his 1.1-inch gun shield as the entire ship seemed to rise out of the water inside a funnel of smoke, flame, and debris. Shrapnel and flying metal struck all around and within Pollock's gun tub, denting the fixtures but sparing the gun's crew from serious injury.

CWT Robert Baner and WT1 Charles McCarthy were on the starboard side of the after fireroom—away from the blast—when the torpedo detonated. Neither was hurt, though nine other members of the "black gang" were killed in the blast. Baner thought he heard someone shout that the airlock exit was blocked, so he decided to lead McCarthy to the escape hatch on the port side. There was absolutely no light, so Baner ordered McCarthy to hang on to his shirt while he felt his way over the catwalks.

Three more sailors found them on the port side of the fireroom, and Baner ordered them to fall in behind McCarthy while he, Baner, led the way up the escape trunk—a metal tube with a ladder—to the escape hatch. The five men were only halfway up the ladder when they entered a cloud of superheated steam that had become trapped against the overhead. Though Chief Baner could feel the flesh melting from his hands, he reflexively scuttled to the top of the ladder and used his belt knife to cut through a rope securing the hatch. McCarthy and WT2 Chester Schirmer were also scalded as they followed Baner to the top of the ladder. When the hatch flew open, the hot steam dissipated into the air outside.

RM3 R. C. Tannatt was one of the men who had gathered outside the escape hatch to help Chief Baner and the other men to the main deck. He grabbed one of the emerging sailors by a wrist and placed his other hand beneath one of the man's armpits. Only after the man was laid out on the deck did Tannatt notice the victim looked like stewed beef. Indeed, he had been literally cooked to the bone. Only the last two of the five emerged without injury. Baner, McCarthy, and Schirmer had all received fatal doses of the superheated steam.

Lt Harold Wells, the damage-control officer, arrived on the bridge and requested permission to jettison all the ready torpedoes in order to reduce topside weight. Bill Wood, who was the ship's torpedo officer as well as officer of the deck, had to refuse Wells's request on several counts. In the first place, two of the four fish in the forward mount had been triggered by the detonation and had become embedded in the forward stack; they were running hot in their tubes. Also, Wood thought he had seen a submarine periscope feather off the port bow, and he wanted to hold torpedoes in the aft mount in case there occurred an opportunity to launch them at the Japanese submarine.

Nine burned and scalded firemen and watertenders provided a gruesome sight for many members of the topside crew as they were treated by corpsmen on the main deck. Nearly all of the injured were a deep red color, and one had long strips of cooked flesh hanging from his arms and legs.

The carrier battle force had long since passed from sight and sound over the horizon. As the stricken destroyer's entire crew assembled topside, the odd quiet moment brought forth a ponderous creaking from below as bulkheads gave way under the unremitting pressure of the water entering through the gash in the *Porter's* side. The ship settled slowly but remained on an even keel. No one quite knew if she might simply break up, or how much time there would be to abandon her if she did. Once, when the ship settled with a particularly nasty jolt, a group of rattled sailors sitting on the fantail jumped over the side. Nearby, the destroyer USS *Shaw* was circling the cripple in search of a submarine, and she released a spread of eight depth charges as the group of sailors stepped into the water from the *Porter's* fantail. The detonations washed the swimmers back aboard the *Porter,* where they nursed bloody noses and ears inflicted by the pressure of the underwater blasts.

S2 Ross Pollock passed the time carrying on a semaphore conversation with a signalman on the bridge. In due course, the vital matter of where the nearest land lay came up. The crew was forbidden to go below in the event the ship suddenly sank. Pollock was chagrined by this order because he had to leave behind a carefully hoarded stash of candy, cookies, and twenty-dollar bills.

The *Porter's* fate was sealed by the condition of her firerooms, which were dead. Though the crew was operating without a trace of panic and the damage was limited to the area of the initial detonation, the ship could not sail under her own power. The decision, a difficult one, was made to scuttle her rather than risk more precious warships in a towing operation through submarine-infested waters. At 1055, the *Shaw* was ordered to close on the *Porter* and take on survivors.

As soon as the order to abandon ship was passed, Y2 Francois Ogden, the destroyer-squadron yeoman, went to his office to begin disposing of secret documents and codes. There was a delay in getting the safe opened in the dark, and the staff communicator, a young ensign, began needling Ogden to hurry up. Ogden had had earlier run-ins with the abrasive young officer and simply told him to shut up, which sufficed. The codes and documents were tossed into a canvas bag, which Ogden weighted with a typewriter and then threw over the side. Nevertheless, the weighted bag did not sink. Ogden removed his shoes and jumped overboard to cut holes in the tough material with a belt knife. As he climbed back aboard the doomed destroyer, Ogden realized that all the secret materials could have been left in the safe to go down with the ship.

The *Shaw* closed on the *Porter's* undamaged starboard side and began taking the wounded first. The entire evacuation was calm and orderly, entirely without untoward incident. Before leaving the ship, the two bridge signalmen, S1 Don Beane and SM3 Dave Meredith, ran up flags meaning "good luck" on the port and starboard yardarms. Francois Ogden was so rattled that the only possession he took aboard the *Shaw* was a little sign which read, "Smile, damnit, smile!"

As the *Shaw* held her position after taking off the bulk of the survivors, LCdr Dave Roberts headed forward to make sure everyone was off while Bill Wood headed aft to do the same. They and the commodore, Capt Charles Cecil, were the last to leave the ship.

When all the living, and most of the dead, had been removed from the *Porter*, the *Shaw* circled around and fired two torpedoes at point-blank range. Both fish struck the *Porter*, but they failed to detonate. With gunners and loaders from the *Porter* helping out to speed the action, the *Shaw* fired fifty 5-inch rounds into the destroyer. In a short time, the *Porter* rolled over to starboard and sank stern-first.

Lt(jg) Bill Wood was sure he spotted a submarine periscope from his place on the *Shaw's* bridge, but the ship was by then bending on all speed to rejoin Task Force 16, and no effort was made to confront the submerged raider.

The carrier battle force was still over the horizon when a mishap in the engineering department caused the *Shaw* to slink to a halt with black smoke pouring from her stacks. It took a half-hour for the black gang to correct the problem and get her under way again.

The British Broadcasting Corporation announced the loss of the *Porter* less than a day after the event, a distressing bit of news for next-of-kin who would not hear from their loved ones for nearly two weeks.

Ten sailors and one officer were killed at the time of the blast. Three of the nine sailors injured in the blast succumbed to their grievous burns aboard the *Shaw* and one died later aboard the *South Dakota*.

There is some speculation as to the source of the fatal torpedo. On the one hand, American accounts credit the fleet submarine HIJMS *I-21* with the sinking, but Japanese sources emphatically deny that any submarine was anywhere near Task Force 61 on October 26. Rather, all the Imperial Navy submarines assigned to the operation were tethered to a scouting line well to the south of the battle arena. Details from several key eyewitness accounts make a convincing argument that the torpedo might have been jarred loose from its shackles in the bomb bay of Ens Dick Batten's TBF. Dave Pollock's report mentions a circular track taken by the torpedo wake at which Pollock fired, and that testimony is corroborated in at least one other pilot's after-action report. Nevertheless, this scenario does not take into account many eyewitnesses aboard the *Porter* who saw—or thought they saw—multiple torpedo wakes. If it was indeed a friendly aerial torpedo that sealed the *Porter's* fate, then more's the irony, for it was one of only a few of its type that detonated againt the hull of any ship in 1942.

Chapter 32

Task Force 17 was still reeling from the effects of the first Japanese air strike when, at 1005, the heavy cruiser *Northampton* arrived off the *Hornet's* bows, in position to pass over a tow line. The work had not yet begun at 1009 when a single Kate—mistaken by onlookers for a Val—plunged through the bottom of the cloud cover dead ahead of the wounded carrier.

Officers and sailors on the carrier's bridge were certain the carrier bomber was heading straight for them, and many feared a crash that would outdo WO Shigeyuki Sato's spectacular self-sacrifice. Lt(jg) Bob Brown, the destroyer *Russell's* gunnery officer, was on the main deck of his ship, having been forced from his gun director by repeated collisions with the carrier. Brown was both certain that the airplane was going to hit the *Russell* and totally frustrated because he had been caught out of position to direct his guns.

There was almost an audible sigh of relief aboard the carrier and the three destroyers nuzzling at her flank as an object detached itself from the airplane, which recovered and flew away . The object sailed into the water outboard of the destroyer *Morris* sixty yards from the carrier and only twenty-five yards astern the destroyer. It appeared to be a dud bomb. Nevertheless, all the destroyers around the *Hornet* precipitously stood away from the target and prepared to repel another Japanese air strike. The *Northampton* also ran from her vulnerable position ahead of the *Hornet*, further delaying the vital towing operation.

In fact, the attacker was an unarmed *Zuiho* Kate serving as a control plane. It had been stalking Task Force 17 for some time when the pilot decided to do what he could to disrupt and delay the towing operation. At 1009, he entered a shallow glide toward the crippled carrier and dropped a target marker—the so-called bomb seen by hundreds of jumpy American seamen. The ruse worked beautifully, for it indeed disrupted and delayed the towing operation, and in fact set the *Hornet* up for more troubles later in the day.

The second Japanese strike force—nineteen *Shokaku* Vals escorted by five Zeros leading by forty-five minutes seventeen *Zuikaku* Kates escorted by four Zeros—had begun taking off at 0822, its target not yet determined. As it flew on toward Task Force 61, the Japanese commanders became increasingly convinced that the American force was composed of at least two carrier battle groups.

The basis for the supposition was excellent work done by radio monitors aboard the Japanese carriers, who deduced from voice transmissions that there were two fighter-direction teams controlling the American CAP before and during the first strike. At 0927, VAdm Chuichi Nagumo informed all forces afloat and in the air, "There appear to be two carriers, one as yet unknown, estimated south of [the *Hornet* at] 8 [degrees] 35 [minutes] S[outh], 166 [degrees] 45 [minutes] E[ast]."At 0928, RAdm Kakuji Kakuta, aboard the *Junyo*, transmitted, "Enemy force is in two groups of at least ten ships centering on large carriers." Next, at 0937, a *Zuikaku* Kate acting as a contact plane reported, "Another large enemy force, one carrier, one light cruiser, six destroyers, speed twenty knots, position 8 [degrees] 37 [minutes] S, 166 [degrees] 37 [minutes] E."

As a result of the skillful interpretation of American radio traffic by

Japanese monitors, and the 0937 sighting report by the contact Kate, LCdr Mamoru Seki, the *Shokaku hikotaicho* and leader of the second-strike Val contingent, knew where to look for the *Enterprise*.

For their part, the first hard news of Seki's approach by the Americans came at 0930, when the *Northampton's* CXAM radar made its first contact. Within the minute, RAdm Howard Good told RAdm Tom Kinkaid that a large bogey was approaching Task Force 61's widely separated elements from a bearing of 315 degrees—north of northwest—at a distance of seventy-six miles. At 0937—as the contact Kate's radioman was transmitting his position fix on the *Enterprise*—Admiral Good came up on the command net again to say that the incoming bogey was bearing 290 degrees and had closed the distance to thirty-five miles from Task Force 17. Next, at 0945, the *South Dakota,* with Task Force 16, reported that her powerful SC-1 air-search radar had pinpointed "many" bogeys bearing 325 degrees and fifty-five miles out. It was not until 0953 that the *Enterprise's* own CXAM set registered the incoming strike—bearing 340 degrees and forty-five miles away. By then, Lieutenant Commander Seki was able to eyeball the wakes of the Task Force 17 screening vessels.

The sighting of Task Force 17 and the damaged *Hornet* was a bit unsettling to Seki, who believed the second carrier was fifteen miles to the north of the damaged carrier. Since all he could see was the damaged carrier and her screen, he decided to press on to the southeast. There was not much risk in this decision as the Vals and Zeros had plenty of flight time left and at worst could attack the stalled *Hornet* if the second carrier eluded them or was able to retire beyond range.

Seki spotted Task Force 16 off to starboard at exactly 1000. Before doing another thing, the *hikotaicho* broadcast a triumphant sighting report, placing the *Enterprise* twenty miles due east of the *Hornet*. As Seki went to the airwaves, the *South Dakota's* radarmen reported a large bogey closing on Task Force 16 from twenty-five miles, and the *Enterprise's* CXAM registered bogeys north of the ship and circling to the east. A Pacific Fleet radio-intelligence unit aboard the *Enterprise* began producing transcripts of snatches of radio conversations between Seki and his base and among the Japanese aircraft. The gist of these radio messages was ongoing refinement of the sighting report—down to the identity of the *Enterprise*, the fact that she had twenty aircraft on her flight deck, and the identity of the battleship following in her wake as an example of the new *South Dakota* class.

At 1008, Seki ordered, "All forces attack."

The American CAP was ill prepared to defend the *Enterprise* against the *Shokaku* Vals. Initially, only eight Fighting-10 Wildcats, organized into one four-plane division and two separate sections of a second division, were at high enough altitude to repel dive-bombers. Thirteen other Wildcats were lower down, but several of these were disabled in one manner or another. The four Fighting-72 pilots in the lower CAP were not even organized into elements; all were flying on their own, as were two Fighting-10 pilots.

Nevertheless, Cdr Jack Griffin did the best he could with what he had. In one sense, he had too much information, but in another sense he didn't have enough. Since the departure of the Japanese first strike, the *Enterprise's* marginally performing CXAM had been registering numerous bogeys. Early on, Griffin had responded to these threats, which all proved illusory and no doubt compromised his faith in the radar.

At 0959, long after several radars had pinpointed Lieutenant Commander Seki's incoming strike force, Griffin sent LCdr Bill Kane and his wingman to the northwest to take on a bogey. At 1004, Griffin ordered Kane to orbit where he was and advised the Fighting-10 exec that the bogey was north of his (Kane's) position. A minute later, after warning his entire CAP to look north, Griffin ordered Kane to fly back toward Task Force 16 while scouring the sky to the east and northeast. It was during this sequence, at 1004, that the *Porter* was struck by a torpedo, an event that drew the attention of just about every lookout to the surface.

At 1007, Griffin made a fatal assumption based on the fact that Bill Kane had not spotted the oncoming bogey: "Look out," he warned the entire CAP, "four bogeys approaching from the north and northeast. Angels probably low." At 1011—three minutes after Seki ordered his Vals to attack the *Enterprise* and *eleven* minutes after Seki first spotted the ship—the FDO ordered all fighters to orbit three to five miles northeast of the

Enterprise. He then ordered Bill Kane's returning section to turn to course 150 degrees to cut inside the approaching enemy planes. At 1014, he ordered Kane and his wingman, "Look for bogeys northeast. They are astern the *[South Dakota*]."

In one sense, Griffin was right all along. The threat was indeed coming in from the northeast—three radars were telling him that. But he assumed the bogey was composed, all or in part, of low-flying bombers, no doubt torpedo bombers. He never told the low-flying majority of CAP fighters to climb.

For their part, the pilots had no idea what to make of the information Griffin was feeding to them; it was everything he knew, and it did not include any estimates pertaining to the altitude of the Japanese strikers. The CAP pilots were depending on Griffin to tell them about the enemy's altitude, but Griffin had no way of knowing, because by the time the Vals came up on the Task Force 61 radarscopes, they were too close for such a fix to be made. In fact, Griffin must have been keeping Bill Kane hopping all over the sky in the hope that Kane would be able to tell him—Griffin—how high the bogey was, simply by sighting it. That didn't happen, so the CAP was never adjusted to the threat.

High overhead and obscured by scattered clouds at 6,000 feet, the Japanese dive-bombers opened out into a line-astern formation. LCdr Mamoru Seki was in the lead, taking with him six Vals making up the squadron's 3d *Chutai*. Next was the squadron's seven-plane 1st *Chutai*, commanded by Lt Keiichi Arima, a non-pilot veteran flying as observer in his section's lead Val. Last was Lt Shohei Yamada's 2d *Chutai*, five planes strong. Covering the Vals into the dive were five *Shokaku* Zeros commanded by Lt Hideki Shingo.

There was almost nothing except blue sky between the attackers and their priceless target.

Chapter 33

Minutes before the *Shokaku* Vals flew into view, Lt Dave Pollock was ordered to race to a position east of the *Enterprise* battle group and orbit at 12,000 feet. He arrived on station just in time to watch the first Val *chutai* commence its dive from the opposite side of Task Force 16.

As Pollock looked on in helpless frustration, he thought he saw two Wildcats in among the diving Vals. These were flown by Ens Maurice Wickendoll and Ens Whitey Feightner, the second section of LCdr Bill Kane's Fighting-10 division.

Wickendoll's machine guns had failed him in the clutch during the defense of the *Hornet*, and in the interim he had been able to get only his left outboard gun working. Nevertheless, he and Feightner were the only Wildcats to catch the Vals as they entered their dives, so the two pressed an all-but-hopeless attack, catching Lt Shohei Yamada's five-plane rear *chutai* as it pushed over. Following the Vals into the dive, Wickendoll got off four bursts with the one working gun, but the uneven recoil from each of them forced the fighter into a skid from which Wickendoll had to recover before realigning his gunsight. Feightner, on the other hand, split off from his section leader and blasted one of the Vals from its path and sent it on a fiery dive all the way into the water. As Feightner pulled up, Wickendoll grimly followed the rear Val all the way down to 4,000 feet. He killed or disabled the rear gunner, but the Val would not flame. Instead, bullets or shrapnel set the Wildcat's wing tank aflame, and Wickendoll had to pull out to deal with the fire.

Fighting-10's Ens Don Gordon had been turned away from the landing circle as he waited with his wheels down to go aboard the *Enterprise* to rearm and refuel. As Gordon rolled up his wheels and clambered back back up to 10,000 feet, all alone, he saw two Vals go by right in front of him. He fired bursts at both dive-bombers, but missed each time. He met another Val as he continued to climb out of the rising antiaircraft fire. After setting up the best shot he could manage, Gordon squeezed the gun-button knob on his joystick. He felt the heavy recoil of his F4F's six wing guns for only a second, until the last of his ammunition was expended. Gordon watched the diving Val long after it passed his climbing Wildcat and was rewarded for his diligence when the Val suddenly pulled out of its dive at about 4,000 feet, staggered a bit, and exploded in midair. Gordon had no idea if the kill was his or the result of the antiaircraft fire.

Likewise, another loner, Fighting-10's Lt(jg) Bill Blair, managed to make a run at a Val that was passing through 12,000 feet. Blair dived after this dive-bomber and stayed with it down to 9,000 feet, firing all the way. After pulling up, he watched the Val dive all the way into the water, but he was uncertain over whether he had knocked it down or if it had been taken out by antiaircraft fire.

Survivors of Lieutenant Yamada's *chutai* reported that two of its five Vals, possibly including Yamada's, were shot down during the dive. But they were the only two Vals to be destroyed before they could drop their bombs.

For all practical purposes, the fighter response was nil. Thus, the carrier's last lines of defense—her speed, maneuverability, and antiaircraft batteries—became her first lines of defense.

The *Enterprise* sported a new array of modern quadruple 40mm guns in place of all but one of the 1.1-inch gun stations that had performed only marginally at Eastern Solomons. Though the larger-caliber 40mm guns fired at a slower rate than the 1.1-inch guns, they automatically ejected spent magazines, which saved time for the loaders. Also, the 40mm antiaircraft rounds were fused to automatically detonate at 4,000 feet if the round did not connect with a target before that. Thus, unlike the 1.1-inch point-contact rounds they replaced, the 40mm rounds built a curtain of flak at intermediate ranges through which oncoming bombers had to fly. This allowed for more damage even if the gunners were less than perfectly accurate. Unlike the 1.1-inchers, the new guns were controlled automatically from a gun director, but they could also be fired manually. The tracker in the gun director only had to hold his target in a light-reflected cross-shaped reticle. The 40mm battery officer, also manning the gun director, watched the fall of tracer and could adjust vertically or horizontally while the tracker traversed the guns. The system seemed flawless, but the gunners were concerned because practice had pointed out that the guns could fall behind during sudden swerving motions by the ship—exactly the sort of problem that was bound to crop up in combat while the ship was evading incoming Vals and Kates. Still, on balance, the former 1.1-inch gunners found little to complain about when making comparisons.

In addition to the *Enterprise's* many modern antiaircraft guns, the screen incorporated the *South Dakota's* numerous 5-inchers and lighter weapons, and the light antiaircraft cruiser USS *San Juan,* which sported sixteen rapid-fire 5-inch guns in eight mounts and a large array of 1.1-inch and lighter antiaircraft guns. Batteries aboard the heavy cruiser USS *Portland* and the five highly maneuverable destroyers remaining in the *Enterprise* screen were also trained out to meet the oncoming Vals.

When the radarmen reported that the Vals were getting close, Capt Osborne Hardison, the *Enterprise's* new skipper, ordered the ship to begin a tight skidding turn to the left, away from the Vals. While this maneuver was well known to carrier captains, it had not been rehearsed with the screening warships. The result was confusion in the screen, where, in the best of circumstances, the lighter vessels had to race to keep station on the ship at the center of the formation; the carrier's tight turn forced the screening vessels farther out into much wider turns, and the carrier's great speed all but outdistanced the other warships. The net result was an antiaircraft umbrella that was at least a little out of kilter throughout the action.

All the modern marvels in the world are of no use if someone in authority will not allow them to be used. Lt(jg) Art Burke, who had supervised the *Enterprise's* starboard 20mm guns during Eastern Solomons, was back as the gunnery fire-control radar officer in charge of the forward 5-inch radar gun director. The new gear was working perfectly, and Burke's radarmen had acquired an excellent track as the lead Val *chutai* ducked into the 40 percent cloud cover at 15,000 feet during its final approach on the carrier. The fire-control solution was perfect, and the forward 5-inch battery was dead on target. Burke was about to request permission to open fire when the officer in charge of the director pulled it off the oncoming planes. That officer, who had made his negative feelings about the newfangled radar well known to the young radar enthusiasts serving under his command, began sweeping the horizon in search of nonexistent torpedo bombers with the old optical range-finding equipment. By the time it became clear that there were no torpedo bombers, it was too late to reacquire the high targets with the radar and lay on the forward 5-inch guns.

The destroyer *Maury* fired first at 1015—at exactly the same moment lookouts aboard the *Enterprise* first eyeballed the diving Vals. The remaining Task Force 16 5-inch antiaircraft batteries opened fire almost in unison a moment later. Indeed, the *San Juan's* 5-inch guns belched so much smoke at the outset that the pilot of an orbiting Wildcat was certain she had suffered a catastrophic internal explosion. Officers and sailors topside aboard the *Enterprise* and several other vessels were certain that the *South Dakota* had also blown up, so thick was the smoke around her main deck and upper works.

LCdr Orlin Livdahl, the *Enterprise's* gunnery officer, was in Sky Control, high up on the main mast over the bridge, when the attack commenced. He was certain that the amount of gunfire put out by the fleet far surpassed the prodigious volume put up at Eastern Solomons, but he was not sure it would be enough to finish the huge job the fighters had barely started. Livdahl's worst moment came early, when a smoking Val—no doubt piloted by Mamoru Seki—carried its bomb all the way down toward the island and seemed about to crash. At the last moment, the ship heeled over and threw the pilot's aim off (if he was still able to aim). The Val flew straight into the water, the bomb exploded, and debris and water fell across the flight deck and as high as Livdahl's perch in Sky Control.

Pfc George Lanvermeier, who was serving as loader on one of the Marine-manned starboard 20mm guns forward of the island, was lying back on the flight deck, looking straight up, when he saw a bomb detach itself from the underside of the second Val and begin the long fall toward the *Enterprise*. So keenly was Lanvermeier staring that he saw the finned after end of the projectile swing through several brief arcs before settling on its plummeting course. For a heartstopping moment, the Marine was certain the bomb would hit him. It didn't miss by much.

The third plane in the seven-plane lead *shotai* was blown out of the air by the antiaircraft fire, as were the fifth and seventh planes. No bombs had yet struck the *Enterprise*.

The carrier stayed in its radical left turn, which obliged Lt Keiichi Arima's *chutai* to complete its attack from astern. As Arima's Val emerged from the clouds about two minutes behind Seki, LCdr Benny Mott, the *Enterprise's* antiaircraft gunnery officer, yelled through his bullhorn at all who might hear him through the din of continuous fire, "Four o'clock! Four o'clock! Get him."

But they didn't get him. Arima's bomb struck the *Enterprise* at 1017. The 250-kilogram semi-armor-piercing projectile passed through the forward lip of the flight deck twenty feet from the leading edge and just to port of the centerline. It penetrated fifty feet through the forecastle, passed through the outer hull, and exploded in midair in front of the carrier's bows, just above the water. The upward force of the blast blew Lt(jg) Marshall Field, Jr., scion of the Chicago newspaper and department-store family, out of the 1.1-inch gun director and up onto the flight deck, where he lay unconscious with shrapnel in his neck, an arm, and a leg. Bomb fragments pierced the 5-inch radar gun-director compartment in the bow, where one sailor was killed and several were wounded, and the radar-control equipment was destroyed. The blast also blew the forwardmost Dauntless over the side. The airplane carried AMM1 Sam Davis Presley to his death moments after he had jumped into the rear compartment to fire the twin .30-caliber machine guns at the incoming Vals. There was so much noise going on around the 40mm gun tub in which the lost SBD's pilot, Lt(jg) Hal Buell, had taken refuge that Buell, who had weathered innumerable bombing raids while flying with Flight 300 on Guadalcanal, did not hear the bomb that destroyed his Dauntless.

As the ship swung back on course, Mach Bill Fluitt, the carrier's gasoline officer, saw that the fuel tank of a parked SBD had been ruptured by the blast and that leaking aviation gasoline was fueling a spot blaze near the point of impact. Fluitt yelled for volunteers and raced down the exposed flight deck under the guns of incoming Vals to oversee the jettisoning of the burning scout-bomber before its 500-pound bomb cooked off.

Despite the bomb hit, Captain Hardison kept his ship in that tight left turn. A seasoned pilot who well understood the physics involved at both ends of a bomb's course, Hardison thus forced the oncoming Vals to come at the carrier in shallower and shallower dives, which was bound to affect the accuracy of the bomb drops.

The ship had not yet settled down from the first blast when Ens Ross Glasmann, who was in charge of Sky Lookout Forward, high up in the main mast, also became convinced that the next bomb was going to hit him. Just after it passed close by his perch, he saw a hole suddenly appear in the flight deck just ten feet aft of the forward elevator.

The second 250-kilogram bomb, which struck the *Enterprise* within less than a minute of the first, penetrated the flight deck, struck a girder, and broke in two. One half of this bomb blew up right on the hangar deck, while the other half penetrated to the third deck, where it blew up in a warren of officers' staterooms.

The hangar-deck detonation set fire to three SBDs lashed to the overhead and scorched the fabric off the control surfaces of five other SBDs parked on the hangar deck. The concussion killed several sailors and disabled others, but it was of relatively low order and, on the day's scale of terror, was relatively minor. Firefighters moved straight into the damaged sections and overwhelmed nascent conflagrations before they quite took hold.

♦

Repair Party II—one officer and thirty-five enlisted sailors—was located on the third deck just aft of the forward elevator. Nearby, an emergency medical team was manning a battle dressing station. The core of the repair party had been together since the start of the war, had been through Eastern Solomons, knew what could happen if a torpedo or bomb detonated anywhere near its position; they called their station "torpedo junction" because it was located right at the waterline on the level at which most armor-piercing bombs seemed to detonate. The job was nerve-wracking because it involved a long wait without anything to do or see; the men could only listen to the progression of antiaircraft gunfire from the long-range 5-inch batteries to the light 20mm guns, and that only added to the anxiety.

During their long vigil, the Repair Party II sailors had heard loudspeaker announcements about the incoming strikes—the first strike, which hit the *Hornet*, and the second strike, which might hit anywhere. Then there was the chilling announcement, "Stand by for air attack."

At that, all hands lay prone in the narrow steel passageway outside a suite of officers' staterooms. They were well protected, dressed in flashproof jackets with the hoods and cuffs secured and wearing steel helmets with clear pull-down face shields. Everyone had a gasmask near to hand, and a large flashlight. All the firefighting and lifesaving equipment was neatly laid out within reach. As the crescendo of outgoing gunfire rose, each man supported the weight of his torso and abdomen on his forearms and elbows; if there was a hit, the deck would be likely to bounce hard enough to knock the wind out of someone whose chest and abdomen were all the way down. Breathing through open mouths was mandatory to overcome the effects of concussion. All the ship's ventilators had been secured; the air was fouled from body odor and the strong odor of camphor from the denim flashproof jackets.

F3 Ralph Morgan, who was wearing a set of battle phones, heard "They're going after the *Hornet*." He repeated the announcement aloud and relaxed. Experience had shown that the Japanese invariably concentrated their strength on one carrier. No doubt, the message was the result of the dummy attack on the *Hornet* by the *Zuiho* Kate. Though the *Enterprise* antiaircraft batteries were still firing all out, all hands in the repair party relaxed. F3 Morgan first sat up and leaned against a six-inch steel stanchion welded to the deck and the overhead; then he stood up, removed his helmet, and bent his head to take off the earphones.

At that precise instant, the half-bomb that had punched through the hangar deck detonated in the cramped passageway. F3 Morgan was engulfed in a great orange flash and the loudest noise he had ever heard. Then there was total silence. Somewhere in his head, Morgan saw his whole family gathered around a Christmas tree. Then he spluttered as the piercing odor of sulfur dioxide assaulted his sense of smell. He was fully alert, lying on his back, unable to get up. There was the taste of blood in his mouth and a loud ringing in his ears. His nose was bleeding and clogged. He groped for his flashlight and turned it on, but the strong beam penetrated all of about six inches; the area was completely filled with thick, black smoke. Morgan could see and smell fires breaking out, so he wiggled out from beneath a steel ladder that had fallen across his legs and felt his way through the murk. He found a hatchway and crawled through—and by feel and memory alone kept on going through six more compartments, all plunged into total darkness. On the way, he found a gasmask, which relieved him of a great deal of his anxiety. There was light behind the eighth door, and people, all balanced on their forearms and elbows. Morgan tried fervently to explain that there were fires breaking out forward, that help was needed. But no one listened. The ship was still maneuvering and the guns were still firing; everyone seemed to be mesmerized by some inner vision of doom. Finally, there was a lull. Someone yelled an order for firefighters to head forward to fight the fires.

Morgan grabbed a fire hose while someone else turned on the water. As Morgan was clearing the first hatchway, the hose in his hands went stiff and then burst; he had neglected to open the nozzle. He grabbed a fire extinguisher and rushed back to his original station, where he fought down several small blazes. Within minutes, all the small fires in Repair Party II's passageway were doused. By then, dozens of firefighters had converged on the area to douse flames in adjacent staterooms, in which bedding and clothing were feeding the fires.

The confined bomb blast had killed the repair-party officer and killed or mortally wounded nearly every other member of Repair Party II. Fragments that penetrated into the nearby emergency medical compartment killed several corpsmen and wounded most of the others. And three of five sailors in an adjacent ammunition handling room were killed. Power cables to the stricken area were severed, knocking out lighting and communications.

Ralph Morgan's hair, eyebrows, and eyelashes had been burned off in the fireball, and his face and hands were red from burns. After the fires had been doused and the smoke cleared, Morgan saw that the six-inch steel stanchion he had been standing next to had been ripped out of the deck and bent into a **U** shape. There were shrapnel holes everywhere.

On balance, despite the catastrophic loss of life from the blast, the worst blow to the ship's capacity to operate was the jamming of the forward elevator in the "up" position.

At 1020, a 250-kilogram bomb dropped by one of the survivors of Lieutenant Yamada's rear *chutai* detonated right next to the carrier's hull on the starboard side aft. It threw seawater up over gunners manning the starboard catwalks and the 40mm gun tubs aft of the island, ruptured numerous hull-plate welds below the waterline, tore a fifty-foot-long, three-inch-wide gash in the side of the ship, and damaged the main turbine bearing. In addition to other serious damage caused by the severe shock of this detonation, the foremast rotated a half-inch, throwing a complex of antennas mounted on it out of line. A Wildcat on the flight deck bounced laterally over the side, and an SBD was stopped from doing so when its landing gear became entangled in the starboard 20mm gun gallery. The bomber was jettisoned from its perch at the first opportunity. Finally, and perhaps worst, two empty fuel tanks and a full one were opened to the sea. So, to add to her troubles, the *Enterprise* was trailing a broad patch of fuel oil to help guide additional Japanese warplanes up her wake.

The American fighters had done little to stop the Vals before they dove, and only one of them was in position to prevent the bombers and their crews from getting home—Fighting-72's Lt(jg) Dick Hughes, who had picked a target before the Val even dropped its bomb. As the dive-bomber leveled out on the surface, Hughes followed it through a cone of fire put out by one of the screening destroyers. From there, the Val turned sharply, taking it right into the Wildcat's gunsight. Hughes fired, but only one gun actually put out a stream of bullets. The Val's rear gunner responded with his own machine gun and Hughes crossed over the Val's path . . . once . . . twice . . . three times before Hughes was able to walk the single line of .50-caliber bullets into the Val's engine. The Japanese dive-bomber immediately burst into flames and spread itself across the surface of the ocean.

One of the recovering Vals passed right over the destroyer USS *Cushing's* bows, a perfect setup for the forward 20mm gun—if the gun hadn't jammed. Instantly, a signalman standing on the bridge yanked out his .45-caliber pistol and emptied all seven rounds into the departing dive-bomber. At the last second, the Japanese rear gunner thumbed his nose at the destroyer.

Meantime, Cdr Jack Griffin was trying to rally his fighters. At 1017, he radioed, "Hey Rube! Looks like hawks. Close in quick!" But it came to nothing. Except for Dick Hughes, none of the low CAP fighters were in position to take on the recovering Vals, and none did.

Ten of nineteen Vals were shot down during this phase of the attack, three by Wildcats (Feightner, Blair or Gordon, and Hughes), and seven by antiaircraft fire. Several veteran Val pilots and crewmen were killed, including LCdr Mamoru Seki, the *Shokaku hikotaicho*, and Lt Shohei Yamada, a Pearl Harbor veteran.

On the way home, and thereafter, the surviving Val crews reported six bomb hits on an *Enterprise*-class carrier, which is certainly how it might have appeared to them from the air when taking actual hits, near misses, and Seki's spectacular crash into account. Two solid hits and a damage-producing near miss were bad enough.

Matching the ineffectual American fighter response to the attack—indeed, not rising to even that level—the five *Shokaku* fighters commanded by Lt Hideki Shingo escorted the surviving Vals home without having fired a single round at an American airplane. Balancing this, it must be said that at the height of the attack, Shingo led an all-fighter strafing pass against the *South Dakota* in the hope of diverting some of her terrible fire from the diving Vals.

Fifty miles northwest of the *Enterprise*, Shingo and his Zeros attacked a Patrol-24 PBY piloted by Lt(jg) Norman Haber that happened to cross their path while on the way home from an abortive search. The Zeros blasted the PBY, wounding two crewmen and tearing up control surfaces, but the PBY gunners put up an able defense in which two of the Zeros were struck by machine-gun bullets. In spite of the high, nerve-wracking drama of the moment, Haber dutifully counted the Zeros and the Vals they were escorting—five of the former and nine of the latter.

As the dive-bombing attack against the *Enterprise* was winding down, Torpedo-10's Lt Doc Norton was looking for a place to land his TBF, which had been damaged in the ambush of the Air Group 10 strike hours earlier. As soon as he dared, Norton flew toward his ship, tailhook extended to request a deferred forced landing. In reply, he received streams of fire from tense gunners aboard the carrier and several screening warships.

Realizing that there was little hope of getting back aboard the *Enterprise* and feeling that it was urgent that he make a controlled landing while it was still possible, Norton reluctantly elected to ditch as near to a screening vessel as possible. The landing, which was clocked at 1020, was shaky. When Norton was too low to back out, a shudder passed through the Avenger's abused frame, and the damaged right wing looked like it was about to buckle. Then the torpedo bomber settled in. Immediately, Norton and his crewmen deployed their life raft and furiously paddled away from the sinking wreck. But the Avenger did not sink. Its nose disappeared into the water, and then most of the fuselage also sank from sight. What remained was a section of the tail, which looked exactly like a small replica of a submarine conning tower.

Lt Ken Bliss of Fighting-72 was still orbiting his Wildcat over the *South Dakota* when the 5-inch guns that had earlier menaced him opened on what appeared to be a submarine conning tower but which Bliss correctly identified as the tail of a bilged airplane. The destroyers *Smith* and *Conyngham* also fired at the TBF's tail.

Five miles from the battleship, the 5-inch rounds were splashing into the water all around the submerged TBF and its thoroughly shaken crew. Without a word, the three airmen dived overboard and flipped their yellow life raft over to show its muted blue underside. As visions of their lives passed before the three airmen, LCdr Max Stormes saw what was happening and conned his ship, the destroyer USS *Preston*, to a position between the bilged airmen and the nervous gunners. At the same time, Lieutenant Bliss once again admonished the battleship gunners for firing on a friendly airplane. In spite of the *Porter's* fate rescuing Ens Dick Batten's TBF crew less than ten minutes earlier, and even though more Japanese bombers might arrive at any moment, Stormes ordered his vessel stopped so that Doc Norton and his crewmen could be safely brought aboard. As soon as this was done, the *Preston* resumed full speed and caught up with the *Enterprise* screen.

Chapter 34

The second wave of the second Japanese strike force was composed entirely of the sixteen *Zuikaku* Kates led by Lt Shigeichiro Imajuku, one Kate contact plane, and four *Zuikaku* escort fighters led by WO Katsuma Shigemi. There were only twenty-five American fighters in the air, and many of these were low on fuel and had expended all or most of their ammunition. Of the twenty-five, only eleven were at higher altitudes.

At 1030, RAdm Howard Good came up on the command net from aboard the *Northampton:* "*[Hornet]* stopped burning. Request fighter coverage." But there was no way for Cdr Jack Griffin to fulfill the request as a new bogey was bearing down on the *Enterprise* from the northwest. Without even answering the commander of the Task Force 17 screen, Griffin asked the leaders of two of the four high-altitude fighter formations—Fighting-10's LCdr Bill Kane leading Lt(jg) John Eckhardt, and Fighting-10's Lt Dave Pollock leading Fighting-72's Lt(jg) Bob Holland—whether they could see any enemy aircraft off the *Enterprise's* port quarter. For the moment, Griffin had no idea that two other Fighting-10 formations were available at high altitude: Lt Swede Vejtasa's four-plane Fighting-10 division and Lt Fritz Faulkner's Fighting-10 trio.

At 1035, Jack Griffin responded to a CXAM return—incoming bogey to the northwest—by vectoring Dave Pollock and Bob Holland to the northwest and ordering them to orbit just fifteen miles from the *Enterprise*. Bill Kane and John Eckhardt were also vectored out to the northwest, but no limit on distance was set. Though lacking orders, Lt Swede Vejtasa led his entire division to the northwest to render assistance if needed, and Lt Fritz Faulkner, also lacking orders, decided to go low to look for torpedo planes. On the way down, Ens Gordon Barnes's tail-end Wildcat lost contact with Faulkner and his wingman, Ens Phil Long.

When Dave Pollock reported himself on station, the FDO told him to look down to see if he could spot any incoming torpedo bombers. At 1040, in response to a clearer CXAM return to the northwest—and closing—Griffin ordered Pollock to search just above a squall line that was partially screening the *Enterprise* from the bogey. Fearful of giving up his altitude advantage, Pollock opted to remain at 12,000 feet.

At 1035, Lieutenant Imajuku's *Zuikaku* Kate squadron was closing on Task Force 61 at just over 13,000 feet. Imajuku had been able to make out the burning *Hornet* and her escorts, but the Kate leader knew there were two American carriers, so he decided to lengthen his track in the hope of finding the other. Two minutes later, while still above the squall line that separated the two American carrier task forces, Imajuku spotted the wakes of the Task Force 16 warships. Within a minute, the sharp-eyed torpedo pilots and their observers had identified the *Enterprise*, a *South Dakota*-class battleship, two cruisers, and eight destroyers—two destroyers too many, but close enough under the circumstances.

With the enemy in sight and firmly fixed, Lieutenant Imajuku pondered the correct course of action.

As Jack Griffin watched the bogey's approach, he suddenly realized that the *Enterprise* was minutes away from undergoing a torpedo attack. At 1044, the senior FDO went to the radio again with news that the bogey was still coming in from 330 degrees and had closed to fifteen miles. "Look out for [torpedo planes]," Griffin warned. "Look out for [torpedo planes]. [Torpedo planes] bear about 330 degrees from base."

As Griffin was speaking, many eyes in Task Force 16 were drawn to a lone airplane as it broke through the base of the clouds. This was Ens Gordon Barnes's Fighting-10 Wildcat, which Barnes had detached from Lt Fritz Faulkner's division when its fuel ran out. As soon as Barnes had completed a neat water landing well to the *South Dakota's* port quarter, LCdr Gelzer Sims ordered his ship, the destroyer USS *Maury*, to leave the screen in order to pick up the bilged pilot.

Meanwhile, Jack Griffin had a moment of doubt about the identity of the incoming aircraft. He warned Dave Pollock that they might be friendly. Pollock responded that he could see nothing. In the next instant, Pollock sighted Kates to the northwest and only fifteen miles out.

Only moments after assaying the composition of the enemy task force ahead, Lieutenant Imajuku opted to lead his *chutai* of eight Kates straight in against the carrier while splitting Lt Masayuki Yusuhara's eight-plane *chutai* wide to port in order to set up a hammer-and-anvil approach. For most of the way in, the Kates would be screened by the squall.

Upon sightng Kates below, and with Bob Holland's ammunitionless Fighting-72 F4F in tow, Dave Pollock started an overhead firing run on an airplane on the port side of the Japanese formation. As he dove, Pollock glanced to starboard and saw two more Wildcats boring in on the Kates from that flank. Then, at nearly the last moment, as Pollock was coming up on the tail of his target, Holland reported that the enemy airplane was a Zero. Though he might have enjoyed an easy kill, a Zero was not, at that moment, worth what might have been the last of Pollock's ammunition. The pair pulled up and banked away in search of a torpedo bomber.

Ens Hank Leder was the first of Swede Vejtasa's Fighting-10 quartet to spot the Kates: "Tally-ho. Nine o'clock down," Leder sang out on the fighter net, and an instant later Lt Stan Ruehlow led the sharp-eyed ensign down from 13,000 feet. Unfortunately, their targets were two Zeros that had gotten ahead of the Japanese formation, perhaps in an intentional bid to cut

Ruehlow and Leder off from the Kates. If so, it worked, for the two never got near the torpedo planes.

Swede Vejtasa, leading Lt Tex Harris, did much better. Reacting to what he thought were eleven dark green Kates trooping beneath his Wildcat in column formation, Vejtasa led Harris in a steep dive to intercept the Kates before they dashed beneath the squall. The Kates—Lieutenant Yusuhara's *chutai*—were themselves descending at a high rate of speed and were nearly out of range when the Wildcats got to their altitude. But Vejtasa and Harris were closing on them at nearly 350 knots, as fast as a Wildcat could go and remain controllable. Quickly, Vejtasa moved up on the rear *shotai,* two planes strong. He fired at the leader, and Harris fired at the last Kate in the string. Then they both fired on the trailing Kate, which burst into flames and fell away. One Kate down and fifteen to go.

As Vejtasa pulled up, he saw a pair of Wildcats take on the rear Kate in the lead *shotai* just before the *shotai* reached the wall of white clouds. It was Dave Pollock and Bob Holland.

Passing through 4,000 feet, Pollock lunged at the Kate and closed just in time to fire on it before it entered the squall. The last of Pollock's bullets caused a plume of smoke to erupt from the Kate just as the bomber was lost from sight in the cloud. Two down, maybe

Returning his attention from Pollock and Holland to the Kates, Swede Vejtasa was surprised when the Japanese flew directly into the wall of cloud rather than beneath it. Nevertheless, he followed the three-plane second *shotai* of Lieutenant Yusuhara's left *chutai* into the squall. Shortly, he caught up with the center Kate, fired two quick bursts at it, and moved his gunsight ahead to the *shotai* leader. A solid burst seemed to tear the rudder from this airplane, so Vejtasa dropped back to fire a long burst at the number-three Kate in the same *shotai*. Certain he had fatally damaged this Kate as well—for a total of three kills for three tries—Vejtasa surged ahead. Though each of the three Kates probably suffered some damage from Vejtasa's guns, all three proceeded toward the *Enterprise*.

In a matter of moments, Swede Vejtasa made out a lone Kate slightly above his Wildcat. This was probably the Kate already damaged by Lt Dave Pollock as it entered the cloud. As the damaged Kate descended rapidly toward the surface—still under its pilot's control and undoubtedly capable of pressing its attack—Vejtasa climbed into a low-side firing pass, which might have caused some more damage. Vejtasa recovered from the climbing pass and followed the crippled Kate as it descended nearly to the surface and cleared the squall.

At best so far, Vejtasa and Harris had destroyed one Kate (confirmed) and damaged another; Pollock and Vejtasa had severely damaged or crippled another Kate in two separate attacks; and Vejtasa had damaged as many as three Kates. Bottom line: Six of Yusuhara's Kates were still bent on attacking the *Enterprise*, although the cohesion of the force had been compromised, albeit more by the exigencies of the high-speed descent through the squall than by the efforts of the defending Wildcats.

During most of its approach, Lieutenant Imajuku's right *chutai* was not attacked by any of the Wildcats over or around Task Force 16. Unlike Yusuhara, Imajuku led his Kates beneath the squall at wave-top height and aimed his nose at the *Enterprise* while still miles away. As the Kates closed on the carrier, they spread out into a loose *shotai* formation and came from a westerly heading to a southwesterly heading in order to stay on the *Enterprise's* starboard side through the ship's sharp turn

As the Kates settled on their final course, several Wildcats marking time because of low ammunition or fuel states were able to reach them. The Kates were only ten feet above the waves when Imajuku chugged past Ens George Wrenn's Fighting-72 Wildcat. Wrenn immediately turned onto his tail. Next, Imajuku found himself approaching the destroyer *Maury*, which minutes earlier had dropped out of the Task Force 16 screen to pick up Ens Gordon Barnes from his ditched Wildcat.

There was no way for Imajuku to avoid the *Maury* or George Wrenn, so he remained on course. The *Maury* turned from its path toward Ensign Barnes and opened fire with its 20mm cannon, which sheared off Imajuku's left wing. The Kate rolled to the right, dropped the right wingtip into the water, and cartwheeled to destruction. Wrenn, the destroyer's 20mm gunners, and even one of the *Enterprise's* 5-inch guns were each given credit for a full kill apiece. Fighting-10's Ens Jim Dowden, who also turned in behind one of Imajuku's Kates, was credited with a probable. In a sense, the downing of Lieutenant Imajuku's Kate cost Gordon Barnes his life, for the *Maury* was unable to relocate him, and he was never seen again.

As Lieutenant Imajuku went down to his death, the number-two Kate in his *shotai* launched a torpedo from abaft the *Enterprise's* starboard beam and recovered right down the starboard side of the ship from ahead to astern. Every gun that could bear depressed to follow the attacker, but none could reach it. Many of the gunners thought they saw the rear gunner raise his hand and offer a middle-finger salute as the plane flew from sight. Even if it had been hit, its job was done; its torpedo had been launched and was following the Kate toward the carrier. The Kate got clean away, but its torpedo missed.

The last plane in the lead *shotai* pulled away a bit in order to set up a better shot. It flew parallel to the *Maury's* starboard side and very close in and then settled on a course parallel to the *Enterprise,* straining to get ahead of the carrier. For the moment, this Kate was not a threat.

The second *shotai* of Imajuku's *chutai* was composed of three Kates, which dropped their torpedoes in unison from off the carrier's starboard side and recovered right up the port side of the target. They all crossed ahead of the *Enterprise* and came out in full view of the *South Dakota.*

When Captain Hardison counted the three torpedo wakes coming in forward of his starboard beam—along parallel tracks, a small blessing—he wrenched the huge ship into a hard right turn to comb their wakes. Pfc George Lanvermeier, manning a starboard 20mm gun, saw only two fish pass from view beneath his position on the catwalk, but neither of them—nor the third torpedo—struck the vessel's side.

The last of Imajuku's Kates, a two-plane *shotai,* were unable to get into position to attack the *Enterprise,* so they turned in sharply to their left and lined up to attack the *South Dakota* from astern. As the great ship followed the *Enterprise* through her turn, the Kates wound up in launch position off her starboard side. The number-two Kate launched its torpedo and pulled away, but the *shotai* leader bored in despite flames that were wreathing his cockpit. At 1048, with his control of the burning airplane lapsing, the pilot released the torpedo. The projectile's trajectory carried it over the main deck, and it landed harmlessly in the water twenty yards to port. The burning Kate crashed 200 yards off the battleship's port beam.

♦

At about this time, the Kate from Lieutenant Yusuhara's *chutai* that had been tagged by Lt Dave Pollock and then by Swede Vejtasa flew out of the squall, well ahead of the rest of its *chutai*. As Vejtasa followed this Kate into the clear, he decided that it was too high and out of position to line up on any target in the task force, so he pulled up in order to avoid the sheets of friendly antiaircraft fire that suddenly threatened his Wildcat. As he did, the Kate burst into flames, either from accumulated hits from Pollack's and Vejtasa's guns or from the antiaircraft fire.

What happened next took everyone by surprise. The flaming Kate deliberately turned toward the destroyer USS *Smith* and crashed into the shield of her Number-2 gun mount. The *Smith* immediately lost speed and turned sharply to starboard, forcing the *Enterprise* to veer sharply from her own track in order to avoid a collision.

Of Imajuku's eight, only one armed Kate remained, the one from the lead *shotai* whose pilot had opted to try to race ahead of the *Enterprise*. Flying away to starboard of the task force, the pilot of the lone Kate finally swung in from dead ahead of the carrier and launched his torpedo just as the *Smith* turned in toward the *Enterprise*.

Captain Hardison had just straightened the *Enterprise* following the tight turn required to prevent a collision with the *Smith* when lookouts announced the approach of another torpedo, also from the starboard bow and by then only 800 yards away. Once again, Hardison ordered his helmsman to bring the rudder all the way over to the right. The great ship swung toward the oncoming torpedo and once again slid by the danger, this time with a hundred feet to spare. The Kate that dropped that fish was shot down close aboard the *Enterprise* as it followed through its release. Credited with the kill was the quad-1.1-inch forecastle mount commanded by a wounded but game Lt(jg) Marshall Field, Jr.

Unbelievably, the Kate's pilot and gunner were spotted as they climbed from shot-up wreckage. The *Enterprise* passed so close that 20mm gunners on the catwalk could distinctly see their upturned faces. LCdr Benny Mott, the carrier's antiaircraft gunnery officer, called attention to the rare sight through his bullhorn and then was horrifed as several of his gunners took his simple observation as permission to open fire. The two Japanese airmen were ripped to shreds.

Of Imajuku's eight-plane *chutai*, only Imajuku failed to launch his torpedo. Two others were shot down by antiaircraft fire after they launched, and the other five made it out of the Task Force 16 screen. But none scored a hit on either of their targets, the *Enterprise* and the *South Dakota.*

While Imajuku's Kates bored in from starboard, the five survivors of Lt Masayuki Yusuhara's *chutai* were still bearing down on the *Enterprise*. All were nearly indiscernable against the dark backdrop of the squall they had used to cover their final approach.

The five came straight up the *Enterprise's* wake to evade the worst of the antiaircraft gunfire and jockey for better than a going-away shot. Suddenly, as the carrier swung out to evade the last torpedo to be launched from starboard, Yusuhara's Kates swung wide to port to set up their launches against the carrier's port side. But Captain Hardison showed them his stern again, forcing them to maneuver once more as they closed on the carrier.

At length, one of the Kate pilots tired of the game and followed the carrier from dead astern while his fellows continued to maneuver. Among many other guns blazing away from the *Enterprise's* stern were the dual-.30-caliber machine guns aboard two of five or six SBDs parked near the stern edge of the flight deck. The gunners were the *Enterprise* and Air Group 10 LSOs, Lt Robin Lindsey and Lt Jim Daniels. They or other lucky gunners apparently wounded or killed the pilot of the oncoming Kate, for the airplane suddenly pulled up sharply, loosed its torpedo, rolled over, and crashed in flames close astern the heavy cruiser *Portland.*

In quick succession, the four remaining Kate pilots took the best shot they could get—from off the carrier's port quarter. All four Kates escaped through the Task Force 16 screen, heading south when last seen. One of their torpedoes missed the *Enterprise* following a long chase up the carrier's wake, and the other three never came close. Rather, all three clanged into the starboard side of the heavy cruiser *Portland* as she tried to recover from a momentary steering malfunction. Fortunately for the crew of the relatively thin-skinned cruiser, none of the torpedoes detonated. Rare among Japanese torpedoes of every kind, all three were duds.

All firing from Task Force 16 ceased at 1052. There were no more targets in range.

Though they had successfully weathered the fire from Task Force 16's numerous guns, the retiring Kates—numbering nine in all—were not quite out of danger. Two of the survivors from Lieutenant Imajuku's *chutai*, retiring on the surface, ran right into three Fighting-10 Wildcats.

Ens Don Gordon, who had been joined minutes earlier by Ens Chip Reding, the only survivor of Lt Johnny Leppla's Fighting-10 escort division, saw a Fighting-72 Wildcat make a mock firing pass at one of a pair of the recovering Kates, and he decided to do the same despite the knowledge that he had no ammunition left aboard his Wildcat. Hoping against hope that his guns would resume firing, Gordon bored in on the Kate from dead ahead. The Japanese pilot was looking away when Gordon's attack began, and when he turned to face ahead again, he naturally flinched when he saw Gordon's Wildcat coming straight at him. The Kate's left wing dropped. As the wingtip bit into the surface, not ten feet below, the entire torpedo bomber cartwheeled into the water, where it was consumed in a violent explosion.

Swede Vejtasa was circling around the friendly antiaircraft curtain when he spotted the same two outbound Kates as they flew close to the water. Though he knew he was almost out of ammunition, Vejtasa selected the nearer Kate—which was being chased fruitlessly by Ens Whitey Feightner—and dived on it. As Vejtasa fired his last bullets, the Kate violently skidded to evade. It began burning but would not fall until it had flown five miles farther. This was Swede Vejtasa's seventh confirmed kill of the day. Counting three Zeros downed at Coral Sea, when he had been flying an SBD, but not counting the Kate that dived into the destroyer *Smith*—scored a probable—Vejtasa was reckoned a double ace.

The four Zeros that had escorted the *Zuikaku* Kates accomplished little. They engaged in a brief, indecisive fight with Lt Stan Ruehlow and Ens Hank Leder (of Vejtasa's Fighting-10 division) that only served to tie up Ruehlow and Leder while the Kates passed. During the brief action, the *shotai* leader, WO Katsuma Shigemi, became separated from the others. He flew on to make a successful landing at Buin while the others returned safely to the *Zuikaku*. The four claimed seven of ten fighters they thought they engaged, but they actually engaged no more than four Wildcats (counting the aborted attack by Dave Pollock and Bob Holland), and they didn't even get a bullet into anyone.

The attack by the *Zuikaku* Kates was a failure, except for the suicidal crash of the burning Kate into the destroyer *Smith*.

Chapter 35

LCdr Hunter Wood's destroyer *Smith* commenced firing all guns at 1015 as Task Force 16 came under attack by steeply gliding Vals. Five minutes later, after the *Enterprise* was struck on the forward edge of her flight deck, the survivors of the second group of Japanese dive-bombers left the area and Wood ordered powder and shell brought up from the magazines to replenish the ready ammunition boxes. It was known that another attack group, presumably torpedo bombers, was on the way in.

When Lieutenant Imajuku's torpedo attack commenced, the *Smith* opened fire with 20mm and 5-inch batteries as soon as targets were visible. At 1048, Ens Herb Damon, the *Smith's* machine-gun officer, saw a burning Kate closing on the starboard side of the ship. The Kate was so close that Damon could hear the crackling noise of the flames that were enveloping the fuselage and could clearly see the pilot and rear gunner. The Kate briefly paralleled the *Smith's* course twenty yards to starboard and fifty feet off the water, then it abruptly swung left, toward the destroyer.

The *Smith's* exec, LCdr Bob Theobold, was preparing to return to the secondary conn from the bridge following his examination of a false sonar contact, when he happened to glance forward in time to see the Kate dive on the *Smith* from slightly abaft the starboard beam. The burning torpedo bomber hit the shield of Number-2 5-inch gun and crashed into the forecastle deck on the port side, abreast Number-1 5-inch gun.

Observers throughout the task force and topside aboard the stricken destroyer saw a bright flash as the entire forward part of the ship was enveloped in a sheet of flame and a pillar of smoke undoubtedly caused by the Kate's bursting gasoline tanks. Most of the wrecked Kate tumbled over the side and sank astern the swiftly passing vessel.

BM1 Lee English, a member of the after damage-control party, was on the main deck between the aft torpedo tubes when the Kate struck. He felt the shock of the impact and looked up in time to see smoke and debris passing over the main mast. Cursing under his breath, English ran to the starboard rail and peered forward. The entire forward section of the ship was engulfed in smoke and flame. Streaming out from the smoke was a ragged line of sailors. Many of the survivors of the forward gun crews were grotesquely burned, with strips of flesh hanging from their bodies, hair burned off their scalps, and clothing still smoldering. English saw that a cord dangling from the earphones on one survivor was slowly burning.

MoMM2 Pat Cosgrove, who was manning a 20mm gun on the well deck, abaft the bridge, reflexively ducked as the first sheet of burning aviation gasoline passed right over his head. When Cosgrove stood tall again, he immediately saw that another sailor was leaning back over the rail. Cosgrove asked the man how he was, but he received no response. Slowly, the other man leaned overboard and fell into the water. At that moment, an officer standing near Cosgrove screamed "Abandon ship!" and led a dozen panicked sailors into the water. Horrified, Cosgrove nevertheless remained aboard the *Smith* and watched as the next destroyer in the screen passed right over the swimmers, none of whom was saved.

Ens Herb Damon was scared witless by the clear view he had of the Kate's intentional dive on the *Smith*, but he stayed at his post while, all around him, sailors abandoned their battle stations. Within a few seconds, Damon realized that he was alone. Though he felt he had his fear under control, Damon angrily tried to pull apart the cord of his headset rather than simply remove his earphones. Then, cursing the human race, he grabbed the nearest machine gun and began hammering away at every airplane—friend or foe, it did not matter which—that flew into his sights.

BM1 Lee English looked aft from his position beside the aft torpedo mounts in time to see a knife-wielding sailor preparing to cut loose a pair of life rafts. English ordered the sailor to get down and leave the rafts alone. He looked up from the panicked man in time to see another sailor standing on the propeller guards, getting set to jump. English cursed at the sailor and pointed out that the ship was still making better than 30 knots.

At 1049, the intense heat sweeping from the forecastle back along the ship forced Lieutenant Commander Wood to order the bridge and gun director cleared. The captain made his way back to the secondary conn with CQM Frank Riduka, who had been at the helm when the Kate struck the ship. Communications with the steering-engine room had by then been disrupted by the damage and excitement, so Chief Riduka proceeded to that compartment, where he took the conn and controlled the ship until, after several unsuccessful attempts, control could be shifted to the secondary conn. As soon as that was accomplished, Chief Riduka was able to guide the ship by means of phoned directions from Lieutenant Commander Wood. With Wood guiding him, Riduka nudged the stricken warship beside the *South Dakota's* wake, the spume from which helped smother several of the smaller forecastle fires. Shortly thereafter, Wood guided Riduka to the *Smith's* former position in the screen around the *Enterprise* and together they maintained that position through numerous tight maneuvers.

While Chief Quartermaster Riduka and Lieutenant Commander Wood were fighting to regain control of the ship, LCdr Bob Theobold had run forward to direct the fire-fighting effort. The forward repair party was already leading out hoses, and the destroyer's torpedo, engineering, and damage-control officers arrived on Theobold's heels with reinforcements to help quell the intense flames that were sweeping back from the bows. As the repair parties began dumping accessible ready ammunition over the sides to keep it from cooking off in the advancing flames, Theobold dispatched one sailor down through the mess-hall hatch to check the status of a key fire main and to ascertain the situation in the forwardmost part of the hull. Then Theobold struck out alone to assess damage in the wardroom spaces, which were located on the main deck.

The exec found that the entire forward deck was burning, and the entire upper deck forward of Number-1 stack was made uninhabitable by flames, smoke, and intense heat. The wardroom was filling with smoke. Though no flames were yet visible, the ship's surgeon had to shift his main battle-dressing station from there to the sickbay. Theobold continued forward and found that the next compartment was just beginning to burn. He then returned to the forward repair party, where he learned that the forward fire main was unaffected by the crash and fires.

A second large detonation—probably the warhead of the Kate's torpedo—rocked the ship at 1051. Sparks and burning debris from the center of the blast showered the upper works and started several new fires among the flag bags and on the bridge. These small blazes were immediately extinguished by alert fire-fighting teams. Several smaller explosions—ready ammunition cooking off around Number-1 5-inch gun—were also felt and heard.

About then, Bob Theobold grabbed a carbon-dioxide fire extinguisher and returned to the smoke-filled wardroom just as a powder case that had fallen into the space from Number-2 5-inch gun ignited. Flames drove the exec back to the main deck, where he turned on the fire extinguisher in his hands and blindly tossed it into the compartment. At that moment, 1154, the leading hose team caught up with Theobold and turned the stream on the advancing flames. The fires never got beyond that point.

The *Smith's* remaining guns ceased firing at 1054.

When Herb Damon came to his senses and realized that the Japanese were gone and the sky was clear of targets, he let go of his machine gun and looked around to see that several sailors were preparing to cut loose several life rafts already manned by other sailors. Damon was instantly gripped by the shared sense that the ship might blow up at the next instant. Still, he tried to dissuade the nearest sailors from abandoning ship. His intense anger, which had not nearly been quenched by the cathartic release of bullets at every warplane in sight, took the form of curses at the sailors about to leave the ship. Damon called them fools and cowards and managed to dissuade a few. But others left the ship and were not seen again.

BM1 Lee English, who had run forward with most of the after repair party, was leading a hose team up the starboard side of the forecastle deck at 1058 when the captain ordered the forward magazine flooded to prevent a fatal detonation. The pressure to all fire-fighting hoses immediately dropped as seawater was diverted to the magazine.

At 1059, a minute after the magazine was flooded, smoke and flame being sucked down to the forward fire room by forced-draft blowers resulted in the securing and abandonment of that space by the black gang.

BM1 Lee English's hose team reached the Number-1 5-inch crew shelter and put out the gasoline fires there, but residual fires threatened to set off ready ammunition and powder in the hoists. English shot a stream of water down the hoist and then dogged down the cover. The shells and powder cans were still intact in the mount's stowage racks but were very hot. English turned to Lt George McDaniel, the ship's engineering officer, and said, "Let's get this stuff out of here." He handed McDaniel the hose nozzle and asked him to cool ammunition and powder while he and MM1 Red Cottrell threw it over the sides. English had earlier taken off his work gloves to help load 20mm ammunition clips and had forgotten to put them back on when he ran forward to help fight the fires. Thus, his hands were burned by the first round Cottrell passed to him as he stood at the mount hatch, six feet from the rail. English got the first two shells safely over the side, but the third was too hot to hold on to, and he dropped it on the main deck halfway to the rail. There was nothing to do then but gingerly kick the volatile refuse overboard. English held on to all the rest of the hot shells to avoid the trauma of dropping another one. The powder cases were not as hot, and all were dumped into the water.

Though the firefighting crews were making steady progress, the four torpedoes in the forward mount were jettisoned as a precaution at 1112. The forward fire room was reoccupied; the boilers there were relighted at 1140 and put on line again at 1145.

The scene around the smoldering gun mounts was ghastly. Bodies lay everywhere, dismembered and burned in the explosion and flames. Several were charred beyond recognition, and a few looked to Lee English like well-browned roast turkeys. English only saw one dead man who was not burned; he was stretched out on the forecastle, his intestines and blood trailing back to the gun shield. As soon as order was restored, officers ordered dogtags removed from the charred corpses around the forward guns. BM1 English was rolling over one body to get at the dogtag when the man's charred arm came off in his hands. Herb Damon, who had come forward to help, wordlessly watched as sailors removed dogtags from bare bones from which the flesh had sloughed off. The living then rolled the diminished, disintegrating, charred corpses right into the water.

All fires aboard the *Smith* were declared secure at 1235. Losses amounted to two officers and twenty-six men killed in action, two officers and twenty-seven men missing in action, and twelve men wounded in action. Major awards to the *Smith's* crew were nine Navy Crosses, thirteen Silver Stars, and two Bronze Stars.

Later, while inspecting the charred remains of the Kate, *Smith* crewmen recovered a document from the cockpit that turned out to contain the latest Imperial Navy aircraft codes. It was an extremely important find.

Chapter 36

Following the American air strikes against his battle formations and the launching of the first follow-on strikes, VAdm Chuichi Nagumo turned his Carrier Group of three carriers and their screens to the northwest, directly away from Task Force 61. Of the three flight decks directly under Nagumo's control, only the *Zuikaku's* could support flight operations. Moreover, Nagumo's flagship, the *Shokaku,* had suffered the loss of most of her communications assets, and the fleet communications duty eventually had to be handed off to the destroyer HIJMS *Arashi.*

As Nagumo steamed away from Task Force 61, VAdm Nobutake Kondo's Advance Force—Kondo's own Main Body of five cruisers and six destroyers, VAdm Takeo Kurita's Support Group of two battleships and two destroyers, and RAdm Kakuji Kakuta's Air Group of the fleet carrier *Junyo* and two destroyers—initially turned in the same direction to try to join up with Nagumo.

The *Junyo* had launched the first of two planned strikes—seventeen Vals commanded by Lt Masao Yamaguchi escorted by a dozen Zeros commanded by the *Junyo hikotaicho,* Lt Yoshio Shiga—at 0905 from a distance of 280 miles. As soon as the Vals and their escorts were away, the *Junyo* launched four CAP fighters and prepared to launch seven Kates under Lt Yoshiaki Iirkiin (the *Hiyo's* torpedo *hikotaicho*). As the Kates were being readied, however, lookouts aboard the battleship *Haruna* reported that ten large unidentified airplanes were making their way toward the *Junyo,* so the Kates and several Zeros were launched simply to clear the carrier's decks of volatiles. When the sighting report turned out to be an optical illusion, the Kates and Zeros had to be recovered, refueled, and respotted. As a result, for the time being, their final launch was scrubbed as Kondo's entire battle force turned southeast again at 0945 on the strength of a report that at least two crippled American carriers lay in that direction. It was Kondo's hope to directly engage the carriers and their escorts with his formidable surface battle forces. At 1045, RAdm Kakuji Kakuta's Air Group—the *Junyo* and her escorts—reversed course yet again in order to catch up with Nagumo.

Though two of their flight decks were down, the Japanese were in far better shape than the Americans. The *Junyo* had not been found by any American search or strike aircraft, her Val squadron and escorts were boring in against two damaged carriers that had been virtually stripped of their fighter protection, and the *Zuikaku* could be turned back toward Task Force 61 if the use of her undamaged flight deck became necessary. And those were just the options the Japanese commanders knew about. They did not yet know that the *Hornet* was dead in the water, a fantastic target if she could be found by the *Junyo* Vals.

For many American and Japanese morning strikers, the battle did not end over the decks of enemy ships. As had occurred during the outbound legs, retiring Japanese and American aircrews often met each other as they headed for their respective homes.

Possibly the first returning strikers to find enemy aircraft flying reciprocal headings were Fighting-72's Ens Phil Souza and his severely wounded wingman, Lt(jg) Willie Roberts. The two had been among the first *Hornet* pilots to turn for home, on account of battle damage and Roberts's heavy bleeding. Because they did not have navigational aids, Souza merely took a reciprocal heading at 2,000 feet and hoped for the best. At about 1000, after forty-five uneventful minutes, Souza spotted five aircraft coming toward him. These proved to be *Shokaku* Vals led by Lt(jg) Takeo Suzuki on their way home from attacking the *Hornet.* Without much effort or hope of scoring, Souza executed a quick firing pass that appeared to draw smoke from one of the Vals. Indeed, it killed the Val's rear gunner but did no fatal damage to the airplane. Farther on, Souza and Roberts joined up with LCdr Mike Sanchez, the Fighting-72 skipper, and they soon spotted Task Force 17 in the distance. "Blue One," Sanchez radioed, "we are coming in."

On their way back home, three Fighting-72 Wildcats that had escorted the Torpedo-6 aircraft to the enemy battle group ran into a flight of Vals, quite possibly the survivors of the *Zuikaku* squadron. Undertaking a quick firing pass, Lt(jg) Bob Sorenson claimed a kill and Ens Roy Dalton claimed a probable. If the Vals were indeed from the *Zuikaku,* then one of the American fighter pilots killed the observer aboard the plane flown by the squadron commander, Lt Yutaka Ishimaru. Sometime later, Ishimaru ditched his damaged airplane beside a destroyer. He was rescued, but he succumbed to bullet wounds later that day.

At about 1045, a flight of six *Hornet* SBDs and several Fighting-72 Wildcats from the second strike force came up on the *Hornet,* where visible battle damage caused them to circle uncertainly. In minutes, Lt Warren Ford noticed that a lone airplane was also circling the task force, so he went to investigate. It turned out to be a Val—probably a *Shokaku* contact plane. Ford attacked and left the Val battling an intense fuel fire in the left wing root. The crew bailed out of the stricken Val and lived to be picked up the next day by an Imperial Navy destroyer.

Three Scouting-8 Dauntlesses bypassed Task Force 17 when they saw that the *Hornet* was damaged. They found Task Force 16 in due course, thanks to the frightful pyrotechnics display the friendly warships were putting up in the face of the second wave of Kate torpedo planes. At 1045, a pair of low-flying *Zuikaku* Kates emerged from the firestorm, making almost straight for the three Dauntlesses. Lt Ed Stebbins and Lt(jg) Phil Rusk turned to intercept one of the Kates, and Lt(jg) Albert Wood was able to get right on the tail of the other. Wood dueled the Japanese rear gunner with his cowl-mounted .50-caliber machine guns, but when one of the guns jammed he broke contact. Nevertheless, the Kate erupted in flames and crashed. The other two Dauntless pilots were unable to catch the other Kate.

A pair of Bombing-8 Dauntlesses piloted by Lt(jg) Ralph Hovind and Lt(jg) William Carter encountered several retiring second-strike *Shokaku* Vals while flying from the damaged *Hornet* to the *Enterprise*. The two made a quick firing pass that might have caused some damage. Other *Hornet* Air Group Dauntless pilots in the same area apparently decided to adopt a live-and-let-live outlook, for none made a move on the many Japanese bombers transiting the area between Task Force 16 and Task Force 17.

Neither were the Japanese bomber crews moved to undertake aggressive action against the returning American bombers. And only one incident involving fighters was recorded: Lt(jg) Humphrey Tallman, piloting the last Torpedo-6 TBF to make its way home, was attacked at 10,000 feet by several of Lt Ayao Shirane's first-strike *Zuikaku* escort Zeros. The Zeros wounded Tallman's radioman but did not follow up as Tallman dived away.

Finally, as Scouting 8's Lt(jg) Joe Auman neared Task Force 17 alone at 500 feet, he spotted a Kate flying toward him. Auman dived to fire his cowl guns at the Kate and then reversed course and flew up alongside to give his radioman-gunner, ARM3 Samuel McLean, a shot. The Japanese gunner returned this fire with his single 7.7mm machine gun, and the bullets riddled the SBD's previously damaged right wing. At the precise moment Auman turned to evade this fire, McLean sharply pivoted his guns to get the Kate, but he wound up putting a solid burst into the SBD's tail, disabling the rudder. Thoroughly chastened, Auman headed for the nearest cloud to sit things out. It is likely that the Kate was a *Zuiho* contact plane that had been shadowing Task Force 17 for several hours. At 1106, moments after Auman flew off, lookouts in Task Force 17 spotted a burning airplane at an estimated distance of nine miles, on a bearing that matched the position of Auman's engagement.

At 1100, just five minutes after the last *Zuikaku* second-strike Kates flew from the area, the *Enterprise* was making 27 knots into the wind, streaming a great plume of black smoke through holes in her flight deck. Although badly damaged, she appeared in no danger of sinking. The greatest danger was from fires that could spread to volatile fuel- and ammunition-storage areas, from undetected submarines thought to be lurking in the area, or from an accident closing down her flight deck.

Dozens of American strike aircraft were due to arrive back at Task Force 61 any time—many had already arrived and were marking time over the horizon—and fuel-depleted CAP fighters were forming in the landing circle. Nevertheless, Cdr John Crommelin, the carrier's air boss, decided to shut down the flight deck until the damage-control parties had fought the potentially explosive blazes to a standstill.

The worst fires were forward, on two decks of living areas directly over magazines packed with 5-inch projectiles and powder cans. As was the case aboard the *Hornet,* where living areas were also ablaze, the fires were being fed by mattresses, clothing, upholstered furniture, and similarly flammable materials. In addition, fires on the hangar deck were being fed by aviation gasoline from ruptured fuel tanks aboard shattered warplanes, and this firefighting problem was further exacerbated by burning fuel leaking into the Number-1 (forward) elevator pit.

Though the hangar deck was burning at its forward end, plane handlers began bringing down fighters and bombers by way of the midships and after elevators; the flight deck had to be cleared if the returning strike planes and remaining CAP fighters were to be safely landed. It was a calculated risk, but there was absolutely no sense in avoiding it; if the ship blew up, all would be lost anyway, and if the ship did not blow up, much could be gained by jumping the gun a bit.

At 1055, one of the departing Kates got off a broadcast pinpointing the positions of both American carriers for the incoming *Junyo* strike waves. At 1101, the *South Dakota's* powerful gunnery radar picked up the *Junyo* Val formation forty-five miles out to the northwest.

At 1110, the *South Dakota's* trigger-happy antiaircraft gunners opened fired on six returning Dauntlesses that were trying to find a way into the *Enterprise* landing circle. All of the SBDs escaped without damage.

At 1115, Cdr John Crommelin, the *Enterprise* air boss, reopened the newly cleared flight deck in the hope of recovering the *Hornet* and *Enterprise* Wildcats, Dauntlesses, and Avengers with the most serious battle damage or most critical fuel shortages. All the American fighters that could still fly and fight were given a general heading and ordered to altitude to try to blunt the coming attack.

But there were no American fighters available for such a mission. Worse, the *Enterprise* FDOs had no means of controlling another air battle. The violent jolts of the bomb hits had thrown the CXAM antenna out of line, and at 1058 the carrier's entire radar complex went down when the radar antenna's drive motor stopped functioning. The ship's radar officer, Lt Brad Williams, bravely climbed the mast with a toolbox in hand and lashed himself to the radar dish to free both hands for work. He was frantically attempting to repair the antenna and its hobbled drive motor when news of the incoming strike arrived from the *South Dakota*. There was no way Williams was going to get the job done in time.

Two hundred feet below Lieutenant Williams's perch, Lt Jim Daniels stood out on his tiny LSO platform and held his paddles straight out from his shoulders as the first returning fighter swung into the groove directly astern the carrier. At that moment, news arrived that the midships elevator was temporarily stuck in the down position. Williams shrugged off the bad news; there was room enough for at least the first few returning warplanes. Out behind the carrier, the first fighter was on its final approach. Behind it, a mixed bag of broken airplanes flown by desperate men were wobbling into the landing circle. In short order, Daniels guided LCdr Mike Sanchez and two other Fighting-72 escorts aboard. Then three more fighters came aboard. Next up was Fighting-72's Phil Souza.

Souza had arrived over Task Force 17 at 1029 in the company of Lt(jg) Willie Roberts, whose Wildcat was leaking fuel from many bullet holes in its gas tanks. As the two Wildcats prepared to make an emergency approach on the *Hornet*, gunners aboard the light antiaircraft cruiser *Juneau* reflexively opened fire on them. Souza screamed into his microphone, "For Christ's sake, we're trying to get back in with damaged airplanes! Cease firing!" At that moment, Willie Roberts's battered Wildcat ran out of fuel. Roberts made a water landing several miles short of the friendly task force. He got out and deployed a dye marker, but he soon slipped beneath the waves as Phil Souza attempted to get a destroyer to break formation to pick up his friend.

Now nearly out of gas himself, and flying a rickety, bullet-riddled wreck of an F4F, Souza passed the "Prep Charlie" emergency signal to Jim Daniels and rocketed toward the *Enterprise's* ramp. When Souza was in the groove, he took his final adjustment signals from Daniels, received his Cut, and fell heavily to the deck. Plane handlers released the Wildcat's tail hook, and Lt Robin Lindsey, the *Enterprise* LSO, told Daniels the barrier was clear, but the *Junyo* strike was nearly upon the carrier, and John Crommelin ordered Jim Daniels to secure. Souza and the plane handlers abandoned Souza's airplane and ran for cover. As they did, someone ordered the CXAM turned on. Brad Williams had just fixed the drive motor, but he was still lashed to the radar assembly, and he began rotating as soon as the motor was turned on.

The warplanes circling the *Enterprise*—all of them nursing low fuel supplies and many of them exhibiting varying degrees of battle damage—scattered to avoid the friendly fire that was about to erupt.

Setting up on the *Junyo* strike force and following it in toward the *Enterprise* had been another exercise in frustration for Cdr Jack Griffin, the fighter pilots who were still aloft, and the senior officers in Task Force 16. They caught only a few breaks.

Lt Yoshio Shiga, the *Junyo hikotaicho,* had spotted the *Hornet* at 1040, but he had turned his nose up at the cripple and opted to fly on in search of an undamaged American carrier. The sky was overcast, which did not help Shiga's quest, and he was thinking of returning to Task Force 17 to attack a "battleship" he had seen towing the damaged carrier—actually it was the heavy cruiser *Northampton*—but at the last minute news arrived from Nagumo that an enemy carrier was located thirty miles southeast of the cripple.

It was not until 1101 that anyone in Task Force 16 officially knew that the *Junyo* strike was in the area. The initial report from the *South Dakota* settled that issue for some, but it never reached the *Enterprise's* FDOs, so no action was taken to deploy the fighters. The *Portland* reported bogeys at 1110, only twenty-five miles out, but Tom Kinkaid interceded to say they were friendly aircraft. The *South Dakota* emphasized the call when her radar-directed 5-inch antiaircraft guns opened fire on bogeys—American aircraft whose crews tartly demanded a ceasefire.

The *Enterprise's* CXAM went back on line at 1115—following a brief respite in which Lt Brad Williams freed himself—and its operator immediately reported that a large bogey was only twenty miles out and closing. Commander Griffin instantly advised the CAP—whatever that might be—that bogeys were coming in from the north. And then he added, rather diffidently, "They may not be friendly." A moment later, Griffin transmitted, "All planes in the air, prepare to repel attack."

At 1119, the *South Dakota's* formidable antiaircraft array once again opened fire, this time at friendly aircraft astern. But thanks to an observant lookout studying a break in the overcast, Jack Griffin countered the cries for a ceasefire from the friendlies with a firm, "Bandits above clouds. All planes in air, stand by to repel attack approaching from north. Above clouds. Above clouds."

In gun positions ringing the *Enterprise's* flight deck, tense gunners and pointers peered into the murky sky and tried to divine the location of the incoming strike. In the bomb-damaged forecastle 1.1-inch gun director, Lt(jg) Marshall Field, Jr., continued to shrug off the numerous shrapnel wounds he had suffered during the first strike. Like everyone else aboard the damaged carrier, Field well knew that the ship might evade destruction, but only by the slimmest of margins. When Lt(jg) Ken Kiekhoefer, of Fighting-72, heard about the incoming strike, he purposefully strode out onto the flight deck with a group of fellow pilots, ready to do battle with the best weapons they had at their disposal, their .45-caliber automatic pistols.

The *Junyo* pilots were having problems of their own. The cloud cover was down to 500 feet along the line of approach, and the *Enterprise* herself was partially obscured by a passing rain squall. Unable to dive from great height, the two Val *chutai* split up to find whatever targets they could; the flight leaders were by then willing to launch attacks against any surface target.

At 1121, the squall line passed, the cloud ceiling abruptly rose to 1,500 feet, and the *Enterprise* appeared in the sights of Lt Yoshio Shiga, in his lead Zero, and Lt Naohiko Miura, the leader of the eight-plane second Val *chutai*. But Lt Masao Yamaguchi and his nine-plane lead *chutai* had run afoul of clouds again and thus entirely missed an opening on the carrier.

After signaling his fighters to drop their external fuel tanks, Lieutenant

Shiga set Miura's *chutai* on course for the *Enterprise* and then pulled up with the rest of his fighters to let the Val crews do their job. By then, however, the Vals were all committed to a shallow 45-degree glide attack—and the lifting cloud cover had revealed their positions to American gunners as much as it had revealed the American warships to them. The carrier's 5-inch batteries opened fire, but the Vals were too low for effective radar control, and the automatic fuses were set for many thousands of feet higher than the Vals were flying. On the other hand, the shallow-diving Vals were perfect targets for the *Enterprise's* 40mm and 20mm guns, as well as every gun that could bear from aboard all the screening warships. Among the ships that opened fire was the battered destroyer *Smith*.

Lieutenant Miura and both his wingmen were shot down in a matter of seconds; of the three, only the number-three pilot got his bomb away, but it missed. Next up was WO Masataka Honmura, leader of Miura's second *shotai*, whose 250-kilogram bomb struck the carrier on the port bow twenty-five feet underwater. Fortunately, the delay-fused bomb did not penetrate the hull, nor did it detonate for several seconds. Thus it caused only minor damage to the carrier's hull about fifteen feet below the waterline and knocked out the motors controlling the Number-1 elevator. The four Vals behind Honmura all missed, and Honmura led them away at low level.

Meanwhile, on the flight deck, Ens Phil Souza's hastily abandoned Fighting-72 Wildcat caused a few wild moments. The fighter bounced once as the carrier twisted and turned beneath the Vals and then it was jarred loose from its wheel chocks. The landing gear collapsed, and the Wildcat slid forward along the deck toward the starboard 5-inch gun gallery until plane handlers diverted it straight over the side. Souza lamented that he never had a chance to retrieve his expensive sunglasses from their place atop the gunsight.

As soon as the shooting over the *Enterprise* stopped, Fighting-72's Ens George Wrenn flew up the groove in a fighter he knew was about out of fuel. The carrier was still twisting to evade potential attackers, but Lt Jim Daniels had not left the LSO platform, so he guided Wrenn aboard even though the ship was not on a steady course into the wind. Wrenn made it, and a plane handler ventured from cover to lift the Wildcat's tail hook free from the arresting wire. No one came out to chock the wheels, so Wrenn stood on the brakes and rode out the wild ride in the cockpit.

♦

There was a brief lull over Task Force 16 while Lieutenant Yamaguchi's Val *chutai* groped through the clouds and came into the clear only 1,000 feet above the Task Force 16 screen. It was nearly 1129, and the screen had spread out quite far while trying to keep station on the turning, twisting *Enterprise*.

Visibility over Task Force 16 was poor, but the slightly dispersed nine-plane Val *chutai* emerged from the clouds in sight of the *South Dakota*, an obvious target in lieu of the unreachable carrier. As the Vals turned toward the battleship, their formation came unglued, and soon it was pretty much every plane for itself.

At the last possible moment, a power failure left the *Enterprise's* forward 5-inch gun director inoperable, even as it was tracking Lieutenant Yamaguchi's Vals. Thus, the radar-director officer, Lt(jg) Jim Kraker, was left with nothing to do except watch; it would be his first actual view of an air strike, though he had been through Eastern Solomons and had directed his 5-inchers only minutes earlier. The first and biggest thing Kraker saw was the *South Dakota*, which was steaming close in to the carrier's starboard beam when she opened fire with everything she had. The great fast battleship was instantly wreathed in billows of yellowish smoke. Aghast, Kraker turned to the battery officer, Lt Joe Roper, and yelled in his ear, "Oh, God, Joe, the *South Dakota* is burning from stem to stern!" Roper could not see the battleship from where he was sitting, so he slowly lifted himself from his seat and peered over the side of the roofless director station. "Hell no," he countered in his good-ole-boy drawl, "That's muzzle blast!"

No sooner said than the fourth Val in the string planted its 250-kilogram bomb directly atop the battleship's Number-1 main turret. There was a large explosion and a great deal of smoke. Lieutenant Roper watched for a second, deep in thought, and drawled to Kraker, "Look. The sonsabitches can' even sink 'er." In fact, the turret's crew was unaware that the bomb had detonated right over their heads.

What neither Kraker nor Roper could see were the bomb fragments that peppered the battleship's bridge and laid open the throat of her skipper, Capt Thomas Gatch, as he stood erect on the walkway in front of the armored bridge. Only the quick thinking of the helmsman saved the captain; the sailor closed off the open artery with his fingertips until corpsmen arrived. In that moment, control of the battleship passed to Battle-II, but the phone lines also went dead, so the great ship was running out of control. For a heartstopping moment, she veered directly toward the *Enterprise*, but then she veered away. Fifty battleship officers and sailors were injured by fragments or the concussion, and one sailor was killed.

Only four Vals, led by Lieutenant Yamaguchi, were in position to attack the *South Dakota*. At 1132, the five remaining *Junyo* Vals, led by Lt(jg) Shunko Kato, picked on the light antiaircraft cruiser *San Juan* just as she was turning at maximum speed with full right rudder.

GM2 Jim O'Neill, a 20mm gunner, saw a silver streak low in the sky and then made out the entire string of Vals. He got a good burst into the second silver streak just as a bomb detonated in the water a hundred yards off the port beam.

Almost instantaneously, a second bomb struck the water twenty-five yards away, just to starboard and well forward. And a second later, the third bomb detonated only fifteen yards off the port beam and threw up enough water to drench everyone on that side of the ship. The concussion lifted Jim O'Neill from the deck, but he was saved from a nasty tumble by the harness with which he was attached to his gun. The blast knocked down everyone who was not strapped in and severely jolted everyone who was.

The fourth bomb struck the *San Juan* a glancing blow on the starboard side level with the second deck. It was a delay-fused bomb, so it did not go off until it was in the water. At almost the same instant, the fifth bomb, a 250-kilogram semi-armor-piercing projectile, plummeted through the *San Juan's* fantail deck. Its shallow trajectory carried it forward through the chiefs' quarters and a storeroom. Then it emerged through the bottom of the ship and exploded beneath her keel. The entire stern of the ship was lifted out of the water and wrenched sideways. Sailors who were just recovering from the near miss tumbled to the steel decks again. The smoke generator, located on the fantail, was jarred into action; a great plume of black smoke trailed from the ship, and everyone aboard it and the other screening vessels was certain that the *San Juan* was burning. As it was, the rudder was jammed hard right and the cruiser veered sharply clockwise, away from her position in the screen. She nearly ran down several smaller vessels as they raced to get out of her path.

Thirteen men aboard the *San Juan* were injured. and it was ten minutes before steering control could be regained. As it turned out, the rudder suffered no material damage; concussion from one of the bombs had merely jarred loose the circuit breakers in the steering-control system.

The *Junyo* Vals that survived their dives on the *Enterprise, South Dakota,* and *San Juan* did not get away free, even though the CAP and sundry other fighters were out of position when the attack began.

Lt Ken Bliss spotted a Val as it fled the scene, and he gave chase even though his Wildcat was riddled. To evade Bliss, the Val pilot swooped all the way to the surface and stayed there, running at full power. Bliss followed at a very close distance, but he withheld fire until he was sure of scoring; he had no idea how much ammunition he had left and was sure that only his right outboard gun was operable. The Val had been badly damaged by antiaircraft fire, and the rear gunner never fired; perhaps he had been killed. At last, Bliss felt he had to fire a burst. As expected, only the one gun worked, and its heavy lopsided recoil caused the Wildcat's nose to kick strongly to the right. Bliss fired several bursts, violently correcting each time, but he was unable to down the fleeing Val before he exhausted his ammunition.

Lt John Eckhardt, also of Fighting-72, was the only other CAP pilot to engage a departing Val. Hitherto frustrated by orders from the FDOs that had caused him to miss three earlier opportunities, Eckhardt latched onto a Val and followed it out, pounding away with all his guns until it crashed.

Lt Jock Sutherland's Fighting-72 escort division had only just returned to the vicinity of Task Force 61 when the quartet spotted many of the fleeing *Junyo* Vals on a reciprocal course. In running fights that lasted many minutes, Sutherland claimed two Vals, and Lt(jg) Dave Freeman and Lt(jg) Al Dietrich claimed one apiece.

Another returning Fighting-72 escort pilot, Lt(jg) Henry Carey, went after one of Lieutenant Miura's Vals as it fled from its attack on the *Enterprise,* even though he had to fly through the *South Dakota's* antiaircraft umbrella to do so. Carey briefly dueled the Val's gunner and then closed in to chop the Val into the waves. As Carey was recovering, three of

Lieutenant Shiga's Zeros jumped him, and a 20mm round passed through the Wildcat's main fuel tank before detonating beside the fuselage and sending shrapnel into Carey's armored seatback. Carey gamely turned into the Zeros, winged one, and managed to get away.

Lt Warren Ford's three-plane Fighting-72 escort division was orbiting outside the Task Force 16 screen, at 300 feet, and was taking fire from the *South Dakota,* when Ford saw a Val pull out low at high speed. Ford followed the Val, and his two wingmen followed him, but he was distracted by a melee overhead involving a pair of Zeros beating up on a lone Wildcat—possibly Lt(jg) Henry Carey's. Ford, whose only remaining fuel was in the Wildcat's drop tank, pulled up to assist the lone Wildcat, but he was afraid of running out of fuel and did not apply maximum throttle. The Zero pilots must have sensed Ford's vulnerability, for they gave up on the other Wildcat and dived away to engage Ford's. Ford attempted to set up a head-on shot at the diving lead Zero, but the Wildcat stalled and fell away. The oncoming Zeros fired at Ford and then set him up between simultaneous firing runs from ahead and astern. At length, a 20mm cannon round slammed into Ford's armored seatback and knocked free several bolts, which buzzed around inside the cockpit. That was enough for Ford, who went into the steepest dive he could manage. After entering a cloud, Ford emerged among a flight of TBFs.

One of Ford's wingmen, Lt(jg) Al Fairbanks, teamed up with Fighting-10's Lt(jg) Jim Billo to go after a departing Val from Lieutenant Miura's *chutai*. The pair shared this easy kill and then came up on one of Lieutenant Yamaguchi's Vals as they turned back toward Task Force 16. In very short order, Fairbanks sent this Val into the waves.

The third member of Ford's division, Lt(jg) Morill Cook, was never seen again after Ford broke away to assist the F4F overhead. Several Fighting-10 pilots saw a Wildcat pilot bail out from about 7,000 feet and land in the water, but this pilot was never picked up. Likewise, Fighting-10's Ens Jerry Davis must have run afoul of Lieutenant Shiga's Zeros, or possibly friendly antiaircraft fire. A number of pilots saw a man afloat in one of the new life rafts the Air Group 10 pilots were taking into combat for the first time, but their efforts to get a ship to pick him up came to nought. When Davis failed to return from the morning action, it was assumed that he was the man in the raft.

Many Bombing-8 and Scouting-8 SBDs returning from the strike arrived in time to get their licks in against the retiring *Junyo* Vals. Lt(jg) Tom Wood claimed two, and ARM3 William Berthold and ARM3 Wilson Lineaweaver were given joint credit for another. Lt Ed Stebbins, of Scouting-8, led his two wingmen in a wave-top tail chase against a *shotai* from Lieutenant Yamaguchi's *chutai*. Following a long, slow closure, Stebbins was just about to fire his cowl guns at the rear Val when that airplane dipped a wing into the water and cartwheeled to destruction.

Torpedo-6's Lt(jg) Rufus Clark, a fighter pilot shanghaied into bomber duty, was seen by others to go after the departing *Junyo* strikers, but he and his crew were never seen again. Fellow pilots saw a TBF fly into friendly antiaircraft fire, but no one saw it emerge. Friendly fire nearly claimed Lt(jg) Stan Holm's Scouting-8 SBD, but this time the culprits were the gunners aboard all three Scouting-10 SBDs led by Lt(jg) Glenn Estes. And Lt(jg) Joe Auman briefly encountered a Zero, but he escaped with even more holes in his thoroughly riddled Bombing-8 Dauntless.

Finally, at 1135, LCdr Jimmy Flatley's four-plane Fighting-10 escort division was at 4,000 feet, covering several SBDs lower down, when Flatley spotted Zeros overhead. The Fighting-10 skipper called his wingman and second section: "Let's line abreast. Keep sharp lookout. If you see anything, start weaving." He added to his section leader, "Stay in line abreast and keep your eyes open." Moments later, Lieutenant Shiga, who had become separated from all the other Zeros, began a solitary dive on Flatley's division,

Flatley's division was low on fuel and ammunition—so much so that the aggressive squadron commander was reluctant to attack even one Zero operating alone. Nevertheless, Flatley's two sections went into the weaving tactic American fighters had been employing since Midway. Shiga made several runs on one pair or another of the Wildcats, but he was chased away each time when the other pair turned into him. In due course, the outnumbered Shiga gave up and flew on home.

The last action involving this *Junyo* strike force came at noon, when a pair of Zeros ganged up on Lt(jg) Norm Haber's bullet-riddled Patrol-24 PBY, which five *Shokaku* Zeros had attacked during their flight home from Task Force 16. The PBY was at 1,000 feet and on a track to Espiritu Santo when Haber spotted the *Junyo* Zeros diving at him from ahead and starboard. The Zeros had the Catalina dead to rights, but they executed a few desultory runs and departed. The pair claimed a bomber downed, but if they opened fire at all, they missed the PBY altogether.

In all, eight of Lieutenant Yamaguchi's seventeen Vals were lost over and around Task Force 16. Lieutenant Miura and every member of his *shotai* perished over the *Enterprise,* the victims of the carrier's own guns. A fourth member of Miura's *chutai* was definitely shot down by Lt(jg) Jim Billo and Lt(jg) Al Fairbanks. Of Yamaguchi's *chutai,* the Val that dipped its wing in the water just as Lt Ed Stebbins was about to fire was probably the trailer in Lt(jg) Shunko Kato's *shotai.* It is doubtful that American antiaircraft fire destroyed any of Yamaguchi's Vals, but Yamaguchi's and the other two aircraft in his *shotai* failed to return, so three of the many Val claims by Wildcat and Dauntless pilots and gunners were arguably merited.

The departing *Junyo* strikers were the last Japanese to find and attack Task Force 16. As they left, the first of the circling American fighters, dive-bombers, and torpedo bombers made a beeline for *Enterprise's* flight deck. In a way, what followed was the most important contribution America's last marginally operational fleet carrier made that day.

Chapter 37

RAdm Tom Kinkaid's first order of business, as the *Junyo* strikers withdrew from Task Force 16, was to decide if he should continue the battle or save the *Enterprise* to fight another day. He had already heard that the *Hornet* was in serious condition and might not survive, and it was abundantly clear that the *Enterprise* could not carry out the sort of smooth, efficient air operations that would be required if she stayed the course. Moreover, Kinkaid felt that one or two undamaged Japanese carriers remained on the prowl. At 1135, doubtful that the *Enterprise* could survive another Japanese strike, and realizing that Task Force 16 would have no effective CAP for some time, Kinkaid reluctantly informed Task Force 17's RAdm George Murray that no fighters could be provided to support the *Hornet* towing operation and that, indeed, it was time to get the *Enterprise* safely out of range of Japanese carrier aircraft. Specifically, Kinkaid told Murray, with a copy to Halsey, "I am proceeding southeastward toward [Efate]. When ready, proceed in the same direction."

Minutes later, Kinkaid's decision was supported somewhat at SoPac headquarters in a message from RAdm Howard Good, the Task Force 17 screen commander, who had transferred his staff to the unencumbered *Pensacola* a little earlier: "*Hornet* attacked by [Japanese] carrier planes at [1011]. . . . Several bomb hits, one or more torpedo hits. Now dead in the water and burning somewhat. *Northampton* preparing take in tow. Have lost touch with Kinkaid."

And at 1155, Kinkaid sent a final message to Good: "If Murray safe, direct him to take charge salvaging operations. Have been under continuous air attack. Otherwise you take charge."

By the time Kinkaid sent his final message to Good, the *Enterprise* was fully engaged in recovering the seventy-three fighters and bombers of the *Hornet* Air Group and Air Group 10 that were orbiting above Task Force 16. All of these airplanes were low on fuel, many were damaged, and every one of them was priceless.

As if to underscore the urgent need to recover the aircraft, a Fighting-10 Wildcat had ran out of fuel over Task Force 16 at 1130. Its pilot performed a neat water landing near the destroyer *Preston*, and he was taken aboard in minutes.

At 1139, the *Enterprise* was steaming into the wind. The fires belowdecks were under control, and the ship's repair crews had done everything they could to patch the flight deck, but serious problems remained. The Number-1 elevator, forward, was stuck in the up position, and as many as twenty F4Fs and SBDs were parked forward with no immediate prospect of being lowered via the midships or after elevators, which both needed to be up in order for aircraft to be landed.

Lt Jim Daniels assumed his stance on the tiny steel LSO platform at the aft port corner of the flight deck, flexed his paddles, and focused his attention on the ship's wake. As he did, the air-department signalman hoisted flags to indicate that flight recovery operations were resuming. Daniels had to be choosy about whom he let aboard initially; the battle-damaged, fuel-starved fighters would be given first priority, then battle-damaged, fuel-starved dive-bombers. The torpedo bombers had more fuel aboard and would thus be waved off if they muscled into the traffic circle. First on the list were the *Enterprise* and *Hornet* CAP fighters, many of which were running on fumes.

All around the carrier, damaged and fuel-depleted *Hornet* and *Enterprise* fighters, dive-bombers, and torpedo bombers vied for position in the constantly expanding landing traffic circle. The ship was steaming at full speed into the wind. Since most of the returning fighters and bombers were signaling one sort of emergency or another, Daniels was determined to take them aboard without much let-up between landings; he would stop only when he ran out of room, but he would not pause in what appeared to be an endless series of life-and-death decisions. The Air Group 10 LSO's only criterion in turning away incoming aircraft would be their apparent ability to get aboard without crashing and, thus, closing down the flight deck to other planes. The fate of U.S. carrier air operations in the Pacific for the next several months literally hung upon Jim Daniels's decision-making powers.

The screen was warned that many warplanes would be ditching, a situation made more onerous by the apparent presence of lurking Japanese submarines and the searing memory of the *Porter's* fate during just such a water rescue.

When a number of the *Hornet* pilots saw the endless traffic pattern around the *Enterprise*, they chanced flying on to their own ship in the hope she would be able to recover their airplanes. At one point, the *Hornet* air-department signalman flashed "Go to *Enterprise*" with his Aldis lantern. The warplanes turned away, but so did light antiaircraft cruiser *Juneau*, whose captain thought the signal was meant for her.

Between 1140 and noon, Daniels brought six Fighting-10 CAP fighters and several Fighting-72 CAP fighters to safe landings, but four Fighting-10 Wildcats—including LCdr Bill Kane and Lt(jg) Jim Billo—landed in the water. The pilots were all picked up by destroyers.

After taking a wave-off from the *Enterprise* while attempting a no-flaps landing, Lt Ken Bliss guided his fuel-starved Fighting-72 Wildcat toward the destroyer *Mahan* and made an approach close by the ship's starboard side at an altitude calculated to bring him down about 200 yards ahead of her. As he passed the bridge, Bliss gave the standard emergency arm signal to let the captain know that he was in trouble and needed help. Then he made a normal wheels-up water landing. The tired Wildcat slowed without coming to an overly abrupt stop and then the nose cowling dug in and all forward motion ceased. As the tail swung up through 45 degrees, Bliss climbed out onto the canted wing and reached for the rubber-raft stowage compartment just behind the cockpit. The space was open and empty. (The raft had been blown free hours before, fooling the pilot of a pursuing Zero into believing that Bliss had bailed out.) With that, the F4F sank from beneath Bliss's feet.

Bliss began pulling for the *Mahan* with long, strong strokes and was about abreast of the bows and less than twenty feet away when he saw a big, strong-looking sailor just forward of the bridge swing a heaving line far out over the side. Bliss swam right to the life ring at the end of the line and then to a cargo net that had been rigged over the side. When Bliss was led to the bridge to pay his respects to the destroyer's captain, the senior officer asked why he had been waving his arm and then listened with great interest as Bliss explained the procedure for hailing a ship from an airplane in trouble. A bit shaken by the need to explain his action, Bliss was nearly decked by the captain's bland announcement that he was glad Bliss had come aboard on the first try, because he would not have been given a second chance in these submarine-infested waters.

Beginning at noon, Daniels brought in most of the Fighting-10 escorts, then several more CAP fighters. Taking an enormous risk and relying heavily upon the skill of the fighter pilots, Daniels continued to bring in Wildcats even as the midships elevator was lowered away to get several fighters off the crowded flight deck. It is amazing, given all the stress and tension, that no one jumped the barrier while the elevator was down. A single accident could have destroyed the ship.

Mixed in with the last of the escort fighters were the first Dauntlesses, including the worst damaged. Lt(jg) Joe Auman, whose gunner had inadvertently shot the rudder off their Dauntless, made it aboard on the first try, though the airplane had a marked tendency during the final approach to sideslip to the left. The harried plane handlers took one look at the riddled dive-bomber and pushed it straight over the side as soon as Auman and the gunner jumped to the flight deck. Auman's was one of many such sacrificed warbirds; the air department had decreed that it wanted to keep only those airplanes that were fit to fly or required only minimal repairs.

The problem with taking the SBDs aboard was that they did not have folding wings; as a result, they took up considerably more deck space than Wildcats or even Avengers, whose wings could be folded. Nevertheless, in they came, one after another, practically nose-to-tail—*Hornet* and *Enterprise* warplanes, fighters and dive-bombers, all mixed together. Frantic though they were, the plane handlers and flight-deck crewmen worked with cool precision, never faltering and never causing Jim Daniels to falter.

There was a flurry of excitement beginning at 1205, when the carrier's restored CXAM radar registered a bogey. Cdr Jack Griffin knew that there were no Wildcats available to intercept, so he went to the search frequency to try to get a few aggressive SBD pilots to break off for a look. There were no takers, so Griffin asked whether any TBFs would go take a look. Five or six Avengers broke away and flew out on Griffin's 030-degree vector. About twenty miles out they spotted a PBY—Lt(jg) Norm Haber's oft-abused Patrol-24 search plane, making its way home to Espiritu Santo.

Meanwhile, aboard the *Enterprise*, sooner than anyone wished, the three flight-deck barriers, which could stop runaway planes from crashing into parked planes, had to be folded down in order to provide parking space. At that juncture, an exhausted and drained Jim Daniels turned the paddles over to Lt Robin Lindsey. There were still about thirty carrier bombers and several fighters over Task Force 16, and not nearly enough deck space for all of them.

In short order, the number of available landing wires diminished as airplanes were parked closer and closer to the aft end of the flight deck. Each succeeding recovery required greater and greater skill, courage, and patience on the part of every man involved, from pilot to LSO to plane handler.

Then only two arresting wires remained in operation. Someone on the bridge yelled down to Lindsey, "That's all. Knock it off, brother." Cdr John Crommelin, the air boss, ordered the duty signalman to run up the red flag, indicating that landing operations were terminated. But the ship also kept running straight into the wind at full speed, an indication to Rob Lindsey that he could keep bringing them in if he dared.

Lindsey was determined to bring in his brother pilots, but he knew that he would need a lot of luck if he was to succeed in this endeavor. Under these crowded conditions, a flight-deck crash by a damaged plane flown by a nervous, frantic, possibly injured pilot was all but inevitable.

Jim Daniels raised the stakes and cut some of the tension when he offered Lindsey a dime for every additional plane he could guide aboard.

The officers manning Air Operations were furious with Lindsey and recommended that Crommelin come down hard on the headstrong LSO, who appeared to them to be endangering the *Enterprise* and the lives of everyone aboard. But Crommelin was on Lindsey's side. In a a dead-calm tone, he said, "Leave the kid alone; he's hot." More importantly, Captain Hardison let Lindsey go on, too.

Lt Fred Bates, the Bombing-8 flight officer, was one of the *Hornet* pilots who had thought there was a chance that the *Hornet* might take him aboard, but he never got the opportunity to find out. Two approaches were met by a hail of gunfire from the Task Force 17 screen, so Bates cautiously approached the *Enterprise*. By the time his turn came to fly up the carrier's wake, he was in a do-or-die situation; he did not have enough fuel to go around again. Bates had half-convinced himself that he would land no matter what the LSO had to say about it. But the test of wills never came; Rob Lindsey gave him the Cut. Bates's hook snagged on the Number-1 wire.

Lindsey brought in five Dauntlesses and three Wildcats, and the Number-1 landing wire was still unfouled. Lt(jg) Russ Reiserer was in the groove, and the heroic Swede Vejtasa was right behind. It was by no means clear that either Wildcat pilot would make it, but Reiserer's airplane settled in on the remaining wire, and plane handlers swarmed over it to clear the hook. Reiserer taxied forward a few feet and then stopped. As Reiserer's wheels were being chocked, Swede Vejtasa flew up the groove, snagged the wire, and thumped to the deck. The plane handlers cleared the tailhook and signaled Vejtasa to shut down his engine on the spot. It was 1222. The forty-seventh and last airplane to be given the Cut since 1139 was safely aboard. Of all the Wildcats and Dauntlesses that had been overhead at 1139, only five fuel-depleted Wildcats had had to land in the water, and all their pilots had been rescued.

At 1235, as Jim Daniels handed Rob Lindsey ten dimes and went below to refresh himself, the *Enterprise* and her escorts changed course to the southeast and settled on a 27-knot speed. The *Hornet* Air Group and Air Group 10 TBFs still overhead were on their own. As they obligingly continued to circle and wait, every available plane handler was put to work striking aircraft below, jettisoning the worst cripples over the side, and respotting the flight deck so rearmed and refueled airplanes could be safely launched to protect the task force or at least make room. Pilots and aircrewmen from both air groups crowded into the ready rooms or found relief in the heads, their staterooms, or the gedunk (soda fountain, where ice cream was being served).

At 1238, Lt(jg) Humphrey Tallman's battle-damaged Torpedo-6 TBF ran out of time; the last drops of fuel were consumed, and Tallman ditched. As he and his crewmen left the sinking bomber, the *Preston* slid up beside them and took all three aboard to join up with several bilged fighter pilots.

Cdr Walt Rodee, the *Hornet* Air Group commander, was well fixed for fuel; his command TBF had extra tanks built in. Realizing that he was at least temporarily out of a job, and confident that he had plenty of fuel, Rodee graciously exited the area in the direction of Espiritu Santo, where he safely landed around 1500.

Beginning at 1251, the *Enterprise* launched twenty-five rearmed and refueled Wildcats, a mixed bag of Fighting-10 and Fighting-72 machines handed out indiscriminately to pilots from both squadrons and formed into ad hoc divisions in the order in which they took off. The launch ended at 1305, and then the flight-deck crew swarmed over the remaining airplanes to lower them away or simply push them forward to make room for the Avengers. Once again, beginning at 1318, Rob Lindsey did the honors.

Lt(jg) Jerry Rapp, a Torpedo-10 pilot flying a Torpedo-6 Avenger, noticed that he had arrived at a critical fuel state as he circled well away from the main landing pattern, so he joined the traffic circle and eventually found himself next in line to go aboard. Rapp was passing down the carrier's starboard side when he received a Roger signal from Rob Lindsey; it was okay to keep coming. He then proceeded upwind, lowered his wheels and flaps, and turned into his downwind leg. Everything was looking great going in, but Rapp saw a great deal of activity on the fantail around the Avenger that had just landed. He received another Roger, followed by a Wave-off, followed by a Bye-bye.

Rapp figured that he had only 25 gallons of fuel aboard, and no place to land. He dodged around the task force for a few minutes in search of a flat stretch of clear ocean near a destroyer. He found what he was looking for with only 15 gallons of fuel remaining. He alerted the destroyer crew of his intention to ditch and flew upwind, turned back into the wind, and began letting down. Above all, Rapp wanted to get down with his engine still turning over, so he could better control the airplane. He got his wish, but barely. The landing about a thousand yards ahead of the destroyer was uneventful, the Avenger remained afloat, and Rapp and his crewmen waited on the wing as the destroyer made a beeline in their direction.

As the warship was slowing, a man on the bridge raised a bullhorn and asked if there was any live ordnance aboard the Avenger. When Rapp candidly admitted that there were two 500-pound bombs hung up in the bomb bay, the destroyer neatly sidestepped while a second, perhaps unapprised, destroyer came up in its wake and slowed.

By that time, the airplane had begun to sink and the airmen had climbed into their rubber life raft. As the second destroyer, the *Cushing*, crawled gingerly forward, someone yelled for the airmen to grab hold of a cargo net that had been rigged over the side. All hands aboard the life raft made quick grabs and hung on for dear life. The destroyer never came to a complete stop—a legacy of the *Porter* tragedy—and the life raft was dragged along. At length, Rapp and his crewmen inflated their life vests and stepped out of the tossing raft. By that time, the *Cushing* was making about 15 knots. A large group of sailors that had gathered at the top of the cargo net reached over and heaved the three bilged aviators to the deck.

Rapp's airplane was one of five Torpedo-6 Avengers to make water landings, and he and his crewmen were three of about twenty pilots and aircrewmen from all squadrons rescued by the *Cushing*.

At 1322, Cdr Dick Gaines, the Air Group 10 commander, was the tenth and last Avenger pilot to land aboard the *Enterprise*. By then, eight other torpedo bombers had ditched, though all the crews were rescued. In all, since recovery operations began at 1139, Jim Daniels and Rob Lindsey had guided fifty-seven of seventy-three carrier planes to safe landings.

There was still one bird unaccounted for, a Torpedo-10 TBF piloted by Lt(jg) George Welles. The day before, Welles's TBF had suffered damage to a wing, and the repairs had not been completed until well after the Air Group 10 strike force had departed on the morning of October 26. Given the option of remaining aboard, Welles and his crew gamely volunteered to try to catch up with the rest of the strikers. That had not happened, but Welles had nonetheless pressed on, and he had spotted ships' wakes at about 1100 and 300 miles from home. At 1105, after counting ships—no carriers—and transmitting a sighting report that was never received, Welles's TBF was attacked by three *Shokaku* Zeros. It was run or die, so Welles jettisoned his torpedo and dived toward home to pick up speed. As the TBF was fleeing, a 20mm cannon shell knocked out the .50-caliber turret, and a 7.7mm bullet struck the pilot's headrest and grazed Welles's scalp. Withal, Welles was able to duck into a cloud and lose his pursuers.

In due course, Welles turned for home and arrived over Task Force 16 at about 1400, just as a bogey alert was being sounded and several ready fighters were being launched. Welles had not the fuel to wait for the flight deck to be respotted, so he set his airplane down in the water. He and his crewmen were picked up by the *Maury* at 1403.

When the bogey turned out to be a phantom, Tom Kinkaid ordered Task Force 16 to turn southeast again at 23 knots. The flight deck was again respotted, this time to get thirteen refueled SBDs into the air for a flight to Espiritu Santo. The SBDs, a mixed flight of *Hornet* Air Group and Air Group 10 aircraft, were launched beginning at 1507, and all arrived safely around sunset.

After the SBDs were launched, eighteen CAP fighters were recovered and twelve replacements were launched. Counting the CAP fighters, Air Group 10 now numbered ten TBFs, thirty-three SBDs, and forty-one F4Fs—eighty-four warplanes in all from both air groups. And one TBF and thirteen SBDs were safely ashore at Epiritu Santo. More important, more than enough pilots and crewmen were alive and able to fly these airplanes, and several dozen other carrier aviators had been rescued from ditched aircraft.

That evening, after recovering her last CAP of the day, the *Enterprise* turned away from the oncoming Japanese surface forces and withdrew swiftly outside the range of any possible Japanese follow-on air strikes and beyond the line of Japanese submarines that were feared to be infesting the battle area. The *Hornet* was left to her fate, totally in the care of her screen, which had been diminished by the mistaken departure of the formidable light antiaircraft cruiser *Juneau* and the dispatch of the heavy cruiser *Northampton* to rig a tow for the powerless carrier.

Chapter 38

The main Japanese carrier force was also withdrawing. American scouts and strikers had left the *Zuiho* and *Shokaku* damaged and unable to conduct flight operations, and so VAdm Chuichi Nagumo had ordered them to sail away from Task Force 61 at high speed. At 1000, the *Zuikaku* had begun recovering CAP fighters from all three ships, and at 1025 she stopped recovering fighters long enough to launch six of her own and *Zuiho's* Zeros to replace them, then resumed the recovery of the CAP fighters. During the latter operation, a returning CAP Zero made a bad landing, bounced off the flight deck, and sank with its pilot still aboard.

RAdm Hiroaki Abe's Vanguard Group, fifty miles astern Nagumo's Carrier Group, initially followed Nagumo to the northwest, but VAdm Nobutake Kondo ordered Abe to reverse course to help chase down the American cripples. Abe did so, but he dispatched the damaged heavy cruiser *Chikuma* to Truk in the company of two destroyers.

At 1105, three *Shokaku* Zeros intercepted Lt(jg) George Welles's lone Torpedo-10 TBF and chased it away before the American crew spotted

Nagumo's carriers. Welles's was the last American striker to see Japanese warships on October 26.

As all this was going on, the *Junyo* and her escorts were closing on Nagumo, and Nagumo was making plans to use her and the undamaged *Zuikaku* to get more strikes away against the American carriers. The return of various elements of early strike groups gave Nagumo the means to mount follow-on attacks, but the loss of most of his senior air commanders and the resulting confusion of tales by younger, less experienced pilots and observers misled the debriefers into forming a picture that incorporated three American carrier task forces, including one crippled carrier and two untouched carrier battle groups deployed to the east and northeast of the cripple. As a result, Nagumo explicitly ordered the prospective leaders of the follow-on strikes to search for targets well away from Task Force 16's southeasterly track. Furthermore, Nagumo ordered his fliers to pass up the cripple in order to set their bombs and torpedoes against the two unscathed carriers.

Nagumo had no choice but to rearm and refuel returning strikers to make up the follow-on strike groups. And he had to rush the process to be sure there was enough daylight left to finish the job, as well as take into account his own need to withdraw his cripples from striking range of the two unscathed American carriers he thought were out there.

There were precious few resources left to Nagumo for the follow-on strike. Only ten Vals, nine Kates, and fourteen Zeros made it back from the first attack wave; many had sustained battle damage, and many of their pilots and crewmen had been injured or killed. Five *Zuiho* Kates employed for the morning search also made it back.

The *Zuikaku* began recovery operations at 1140, but she advised the aircraft in her landing pattern to look for the *Junyo* if they needed to get down quickly. The *Shokaku's* transmitter had been knocked out by American bombs, so the returning *Shokaku* strikers wasted time and fuel lining up to get aboard her.

In stark contrast to the efficient recovery of nearly two complete air groups by the *Enterprise*, it took the *Zuikaku* fifty minutes to bring aboard ten Zeros, eight Kates, and just one Val. During the same interval, the

Junyo recovered six of her own CAP Zeros, four *Zuikaku* Vals, two *Zuikaku* Zeros, and just one *Shokaku* Kate. While this process was so slowly unfolding, one *Shokaku* Zero, one *Zuikaku* Zero, six *Zuikaku* Vals, and five *Shokaku* Kates had to ditch. Among the pilots of the ditched Vals was Lt Sadamu Takahashi, now nominally the *Zuikaku hikotaicho*.

The *Junyo* had drawn steadily closer to the Carrier Group during the recovery operations, so Admiral Nagumo dispatched the *Zuikaku* to join her. Several screening vessels were also detached.

As the *Zuikaku* departed, Capt Masafumi Arima, the *Shokaku's* very capable commanding officer, implored Admiral Nagumo to allow his ship to accompany the others in order to act as bait for American follow-on strikes. Arima reasoned that the Americans would go for the sure kill while leaving the unscathed *Zuikaku* and *Junyo* free to launch even more strikes. It was wishful thinking, and Nagumo firmly declined. Prevented from transferrng to the *Zuikaku* in the rush of her departure, Nagumo retired with the two cripples, leaving the last part of the battle in the hands of RAdm Kakuji Kakuta.

At 1300, Adm Isoroku Yamamoto took to the airwaves from the command center of the battleship HIJMS *Yamato*, which was anchored in Truk Lagoon. The commander-in-chief of the Combined Fleet implored his fighting ships to pursue the enemy carriers and destroy them. Closer to the action, Kondo and Abe raced after the Americans with their mighty surface forces, and the *Zuikaku* and *Junyo* air departments pulled out all the stops to cobble together follow-on air strikes with their few remaining aircraft.

Following an hours-long delay, the *Junyo* got her second strike away beginning at 1306. The force was composed of seven Kates led by Lt Yoshiaki Irikiin and escorted by a mixed force of five *Junyo* Zeros, two *Zuikaku* Zeros, and one *Zuiho* Zero led by the *Zuikaku's* Lt Ayao Shirane. These strikers were formed up by 1313 and headed out on 120 degrees with orders to search to a distance of 260 miles. At about the same time, the *Zuikaku* launched her third strike of the day from a position about fifty miles to the north, with Lt(jg) Ichiro Tanaka leading five *Zuiho* and two *Zuikaku* Kates (of which six were each armed with a single 800-kilogram "land" bomb); one *Shokaku* Val and one *Zuikaku* Val; and two *Shokaku* and three *Zuikaku* Zeros.

Beginning at 1320, as soon as the strikers were off, the *Zuikaku* and *Junyo* resumed recovery operations. The *Junyo* recovered eight of her own Zeros led by Lt Yoshio Shiga, six *Junyo* Vals led by Lt(jg) Shunko Kato, and a stray first-strike *Zuikaku* Zero. The *Zuikaku* recovered seven *Shokaku* Vals led by Lt Keiichi Arima, six of her own Kates led by Lt Masayuki Yusuhara, one of the *Shokaku's* morning-search Kates, one of her own first-strike Zeros, and four *Junyo* Zeros. By the time this recovery operation ended at 1400, four more Vals, another Kate, and two Zeros had had to ditch.

The senior Val pilot taken aboard the *Junyo* was Lt(jg) Shunko Kato, who was also the youngest officer assigned to the ship's air group. Though Kato was completely wrung out and could not deliver a coherent report of the attack on the *Enterprise* to the *Junyo's* captain, he was nevertheless informed that he would have to take part in an improvised follow-on strike. The youngster shocked everyone when he cried out in disbelief, "Again? Am I to fly *again* today?" But the prospective strike commander, Lt Yoshio Shiga, jumped in and forcefully reminded Kato, "This is war! There can be no rest against the enemy. . . . We have to choice. . . . We go!" That brought the stricken Kato around: "I will go," he declared. And so he did.

At 1535, Shiga led Kato's four Kates and six of his own Zeros off the *Junyo* flight deck—the last Japanese strike of the day.

Chapter 39

Following a pensive wait and word that the *Enterprise* was the target of the first Japanese follow-on strikes, the *Northampton* again approached the *Hornet* and arrived in position to pass up the tow at 1234. It was decided that the tow line would be passed from the cruiser to the carrier and made fast to the *Hornet's* port anchor chain. Before the towing operation could commence, the port anchor had to be detached from the chain, after which a heaving line was thrown from the cruiser and 1¾-inch steel wire was hauled up by hand, there being no power aboard the *Hornet* to run the winches. The cable was attached with a shackle to the port anchor chain, 60 fathoms—360 feet—of cable were veered, the *Northampton* began taking up the slack at 1330, and speed was gradually built up to just under four knots. The course was due east, toward Tongatabu and away from Japanese submarines.

So far, so good.

Then the *Northampton* inadvertently tugged too hard, and the steel hook at her end of the cable parted. The *Northampton* end of the cable fell into the water. Since the break was not aboard the powerless *Hornet*, the entire length had to be jettisoned because there were no winches to haul it aboard the carrier.

The only cable that could begin to do the job was a 200-fathom length of two-inch steel cable stowed at the bottom of the *Hornet's* midships elevator pit. The greased cable weighed many tons and had to be moved nearly eight hundred feet from its stowage space to the forecastle. There being no power winches operating aboard the carrier, the vast reservoir of manpower that was available was pressed into service. Hundreds of sailors eagerly—thankfully—responded to the call.

One end of the great cable was secured to the starboard anchor chain, and the other end was passed to the *Northampton*, which gingerly reeled it in to take up the slack and then began easing ahead. The *Hornet* began to move at about 1445, and the tandem ships soon built their speed back up to nearly four knots.

Everything looked good between the *Hornet* and the *Northampton*, but there was trouble brewing to the north. At 1345, the *Northampton's* CXAM radar had registered a large bogey bearing 310 degrees and 103 miles distant. This was Lt Yoshiaki Irikiin's second *Junyo* strike force of seven Kates and eight Zeros, which, as ordered, was looking for undamaged American carriers to the north of the *Hornet's* last reported position. At 1400, the *Northampton's* skillful radar operators picked up a second large bogey, also bearing 310 degrees and 110 miles distant. This was Lt(jg) Ichiro Tanaka's third *Zuikaku* strike group of seven bomb-armed Kates, two Vals, and five Zeros drawn from the remnants of various carrier squadrons. Like Irikiin, Tanaka was following express orders to search for undamaged American carriers north of the *Hornet*.

There was nothing anyone in Task Force 17 could do about the bogeys, except watch and wait, so everyone who had a job did it.

Several important details and decisions had been worked out during the long interval between the *Northampton's* arrival on towing station and the rigging out of the second cable.

First, at about 1300, RAdm George Murray decided with great reluctance that he would have to transfer his flag from the *Hornet* to the heavy cruiser *Pensacola*. Together with his staff, the former captain of the *Enterprise* transferred to one of the screen destroyers at 1335, and then on to his new flagship. Sailors who greeted him as he arrived aboard the *Pensacola* thought he looked tired and despondent. RAdm Howard Good and his staff followed Murray to the *Pensacola* from the encumbered *Northampton*.

Next, all of the *Hornet's* serious casualties—about seventy-five men—were brought to the flight deck for transfer to one of the screen destroyers. While the casualties were waiting, cooks and bakers passed through the crowd with vanilla ice cream and fresh doughnuts. Lt(jg) Ivan Swope, who had been painfully burned in the Scouting-8 ready room, received a dish of the ice cream laced with bourbon from two of his fellow SBD pilots, and it really hit the spot.

AMM3 Lamar Cotton had been wounded by shrapnel from one of the torpedoes as he was working in the propeller shop during the raids. Only a few tiny fragments had entered his lower left leg, and they did not even hurt much, but the blood soon filled his left shoe. The leg was bandaged and he was placed on the fantail to await evacuation. During the wait, he was visited by his brother, CY Ralph Cotton, of Bombing-8. Ralph remained until Lamar was lifted away by high-line to the destroyer *Mustin* on a wire litter.

The burn cases were the hardest to transport and deal with. They came from all parts of the carrier, but most of them were survivors of the two fiery crashes by Japanese warplanes. The survivors of WO Shigeyuki Sato's death crash had all been brought to the after end of the flight deck and laid out in rows for treatment by the corpsmen. After they had spent a brief time in the sun, someone thought to build a shelter to protect them. The unavoidable bumpy move between ships certainly exacerbated their pain. Some, who might have succumbed anyway, met their deaths sooner as a result.

EM1 Tom Kuykendall, who had been grievously burned as a member of the bomb-gutted forward repair party, was among those transferred to the *Mustin* in a wire litter. The destroyer sailors had a difficult time getting him below to the sickbay through the ship's narrow hatches and passageways, but he hurt so much already that he barely noticed the added discomfort. The last thing Kuykendall was aware of that day was the ship's doctor working over him.

On the other hand, Pfc Vic Kelber, whose facial wounds had been securely bandaged aboard the *Hornet* and who arrived aboard the *Russell* by high line in a bosun's chair, was not treated at all that day by the destroyer's overworked corpsmen. S1 Ed Knobel, who had been temporarily blinded by one of the torpedo blasts, was also transferred by high line. Since he, like Kelber, had no apparent life-threatening injuries, he was dumped in an out-of-the-way corner in the destroyer's machine shop

As soon as the casualty-evacuation operation was completed, the evacuation of all ambulatory wounded and all personnel not essential to running or salvaging the ship began. The word was put out that the partial evacuation of able-bodied officers and men was by no means an indication that the ship was in danger of sinking; rather, the men were told, the danger lay in Japanese submarine attacks and follow-on air strikes against their virtually defenseless ship.

When the destroyer *Russell* came alongside, sailors on the flight deck dropped cargo nets to her main deck, and the squadron personnel, who were first to go, climbed with great alacrity from their ship directly to the other—all without getting their feet wet. For the second time that day, the *Russell's* upper works were severely damaged as she sideswiped the higher side of the carrier.

In all, about 800 air group, flag, and other nonessential personnel transferred to the destroyers. The operation was completed about 1440. The *Russell* was the last rescue ship to cast off. Shortly after she was clear of the *Hornet*, radar operators posted the ominous news that one of the large bogeys being tracked to the north had turned directly toward Task Force 17. This was Lieutenant Irikiin's Kates and Zeros, whose leader had given up hope of finding new prey and had decided to finish off the cripple with torpedoes. As before, all anyone could do was watch Irikiin's progress on the radarscopes and await the blow.

The *Hornet's* only serious hope of salvation lay in restoring power and moving from the battle arena on her own. Thus began an heroic effort by her engineers and electricians to restart the engines and provide power for essential systems.

EM1 Samuel Blumer was one of seven electrician's mates ordered to the auxiliary generator room. Next-to-last in the single column at the start of the hot, smokey trek along dark lantern-lighted passageways, Blumer found himself in last place by the time he reached the auxiliary generator room. Once there, the six remaining electrician's mates disconnected the lines from the controls and hooked them directly into the power source. Eight more electrician's mates arrived before the job was half finished, and that resulted in the ability to work in teams so that relays could leave the hot, airless space for some fresh air topside. The work was going very well there and in the fire room, where the black gang was trying to get up steam to run the electric generators.

ChElec David Sword rounded up a bunch of his electrician's mates and organized them to bypass water- and fuel-filled engineering spaces with jumper cables from the after emergency diesel-generator room. The problem with Sword's plan was that numerous watertight doors had to be left open to allow for the passage of the cable through scores of compartments and along numerous passageways. The threat to watertight integrity was overlooked in the face of the greater threat posed by the ship's total lack of viable motion-generating power sources. The work began in the bowels of the ship, on the seventh deck. The cable was manhandled up to the third deck, then forward past the galley, and then back down to the seventh deck to one of the after fire rooms. Each length of cable had to be connected to the next length with U-bolts, and each connection had to be carefully wrapped in protective rubber sheets to prevent the electrocution of anyone nearby in the steel passageways when the juice was turned on.

When an engineering officer called for volunteers to reman the fire and engine rooms, WT1 Lyle Skinner was one of the first to sign on. He was sent to one of the fire rooms and began working on a system to shunt all the available power to the undamaged after engine room—assuming a useable supply of power could be restored in the ship. The boilers had to be fueled by means of a hand pump, which was worse than exhausting in the hot, airless space. Still, the firemen and watertenders did get a fire going in one of the boilers, and they eventually got pressure up to 150 pounds.

EM1 Samuel Blumer was taking a break from his work in the auxiliary generator room when a machinist's mate he knew asked him for help in the steering-engine room. The ship's rudder had been hard to port when the ship lost power, and the hydraulic ram piping had to be opened to relieve pressure in the hope the rudder could be brought back to zero degrees, a maneuver that would greatly affect the success of the towing operation. The first effort failed, and the ram piping had to be reconnected. Then Blumer and the machinist's mate begged some emergency power from the diesel-generator room. Meanwhile, a volunteer crawled to the very bottom of the *Hornet's* hull and all the way astern—including seventy feet through a dark, water-filled tunnel—to free the rudder. Power from the briefly redirected diesel motor did the trick. The *Hornet* could at least be towed straight ahead.

While the electrician's and machinist's mates were working on getting up some power, Cdr Henry Moran, the ship's first lieutenant and damage-control officer, conducted a thorough investigation of all the major damage, particularly the hull damage that had caused the list he had mostly straightened earlier. Moran had no trouble convincing himself that the damage was not life-threatening and that the ship was seaworthy. Nevertheless, the damage was too extensive to be repaired anywhere outside of a major navy yard.

Lieutenant Irikiin and his fellow airmen spotted the *Hornet* at 1513 and immediately began setting up their attack aganst the virtually stationary target. Shortly, word arrived aboard *Hornet* by means of battery-powered radio sets and flag signals from the screen that unidentified aircraft were approaching. Admiral Murray radioed the *Enterprise* from the *Pensacola* to request air cover, but Tom Kinkaid had to turn him down.

When the air-raid warning was sounded, firemen and watertenders manning the *Hornet's* only operating fire room were ordered to bank the fire and evacuate. Most of the black gang reluctantly climbed toward the hangar deck, but several fanned out on the lower decks to evade possible injury from falling bombs.

During the lull between the warning and the strike, EM1 Samuel Blumer, who had remained on duty in the steering-engine room following the release of the locked rudder, climbed up to the hangar deck for a breath of fresh, cool air. When he arrived, the ship's chaplain was officiating at the burial of a number of dead shipmates. Blumer was sickened but not particularly surprised to see large fish, presumably sharks, attacking the bodies as quickly as they were tilted from boards into the water aft of the fantail. The ongoing service was interrupted by the air-raid alarm.

At 1520, the seven torpedo-armed *Junyo* Kates weaved in from starboard at 6,000 feet and commenced their attack on the carrier. Several of the Kates used the destroyer *Russell* to cover the last part of their approache; the *Hornet* pilots and aircrewmen on the destroyer's main deck were certain they were going to be rammed, but each Kate pulled up and over at the last instant despite the heavy fire the *Russell's* guns were putting out. The rear gunner of one of the Kates strafed the *Russell's* full deckload of *Hornet* Air Group pilots and crewmen, killing and injuring several evacuees and destroyermen. Another Kate gunner strafed the *Pensacola,* now the Task Force 17 flagship, killing three sailors and wounding sixteen others.

At the last second, the *Northampton* severed her end of the towing cable and turned sharply to port, narrowly evading a torpedo dropped by one of the Kates.

The *Hornet* and the screen warships put up all the antiaircraft gunfire they could manage, but it was not enough. The accidental dispatch of the light antiaircraft cruiser *Juneau*—and her sixteen 5-inch rapid-fire antiaircraft guns—to Task Force 16 a few hours earlier was about to be revealed as a fatal blunder.

The carrier's antiaircraft batteries were fully manned, but they were severely hobbled by the lack of electrical power, both for training the guns and for operating ammunition and powder hoists. FC3 Richard Cartwright, who had been helping to run the ship's central fire-control system until power was lost, was helping to operate a handy-billy portable pump to bring up water to cool a pair of quad-1.1-inch gun mounts. As Cartwright ran the pump, other volunteers helped the gunners train the guns by hand, and many others manned an ammunition-passing line from the magazines. All training and traversing had to be done by hand, which badly slowed the aiming.

EM3 Tom Reese watched the Kates from his place midway back on the starboard side of the hangar deck. The lead *shotai* popped up over the

Russell and fanned out. One Kate went forward, one went aft, and one came straight on. When Reese saw the one coming straight on drop its torpedo, he grabbed a lifeline and held on for dear life.

At 1523, Lieutenant Irikiin's aerial torpedo detonated on the *Hornet's* starboard hull athwart the midships elevator, just aft of and above one of the earlier torpedo hits. A torrent of seawater rose sixty feet in front of Tom Reese's place on the starboard hangar deck, and most of it seemed to fall on Reese, who was desperately clinging to a lifeline. When the water subsided, Reese turned and saw the ship's engineering officer, Cdr Pat Creehan, leaning dazedly against a stanchion, covered from head to foot in thick fuel oil. He had been blown up the last few feet of an escape trunk by the force of the blast.

As Lieutenant Irikiin followed through on his release and began his recovery, his Kate was struck by antiaircraft fire. It veered sharply to starboard and smacked into the waves directly ahead of the *Northampton*. Though the Japanese claimed three hits total, all the remaining Kates failed to score. One other was shot down off the *Hornet's* port side, and two of the escort Zeros went astray during the return flight, never to be seen again.

Survivors on the *Hornet's* third deck reported a "sickly green flash" when Irikiin's torpedo warhead detonated, and they were able to determine that the blast had ruptured the forward bulkhead of the forward engine room and damaged equipment in the after engine room and after generator room. Electrical cables were severed and a fire broke out, though it was quickly extinguished by a nearby repair party. The after engine room and fourth deck near the explosion began flooding immediately, and the great ship slowly began rolling into a list that would eventually reach over 14 degrees.

That was nearly enough for Capt Perry Mason and his senior staff. The prodigious efforts of many hours had been wiped out in an instant. The only towing cable capable of moving the ship hung limply from her forecastle, utterly irrecoverable. The electrical system, so laboriously built up by the tireless electrician's mates, was again a shambles. The engineering plant was damaged anew, and there was no viable potential major source of power left aboard the ship. New fires had broken out, the ship was again filling with water, and there was no power aboard to pump it out.

♦

As the dust from the new torpedo hit settled, EM3 Tom Reese heard shouts for help as he stood in a daze on the hangar deck right above the point of impact. He looked down two nearby ladders and saw a dazed, bloody man clinging to each of them. Reese slid down one ladder, grabbed one of the men by his belt, and pulled him up to the hangar deck. Then he did the same for the other blast survivor.

WT1 Lyle Skinner was pulling himself up the steeply inclined hangar deck by means of a lifeline when he heard a plea for help rise out of the midships elevator pit. Earlier, Skinner had seen sailors take cover from bombs on the lowest decks. One of them had apparently found a good spot in which to evade bombs, but he had run afoul of the torpedo. Tom Reese also heard the plaints and joined Skinner at the edge of the dark pit. Putting two and two together, Skinner, Reese, and others who joined them speculated that the cries were actually coming from the upper portion of the already flooded forward engine room. If that was the case, all agreed, the crier was a dead man, for the ship was rolling despite her list, and each dip to starboard brought in a great rush of seawater.

The onlookers remained at the lip of the elevator pit. WT1 Skinner secretly hoped that the next rush of water would still the pathetic screams, but it did not. Skinner finally knew at the core of his soul that he would hear those screams every dark night of his life if he failed to at least try to save the trapped shipmate. There were lifelines all around. Skinner secured one to the guard rail around the elevator pit and tied the other end firmly around his waist. Then he lowered himself into the black pit, climbed over a low bulkhead, and felt his way toward the wounded starboard side of the ship, clearly the direction from which the cries were emanating. It was absolutely black in the confined spaces, and Skinner's eyes had barely enough light to see. But he could see a large jagged hole at the top of one of the fuel-oil tanks and, atop the hole in the far side of the tank, the two eyes of an oil-covered man who was suspended by his clothing from the torn metal. The sailor was as frightened as a man can be. There was nothing Skinner could do without another line. He felt silly telling the man to "remain calm" while he went to fetch another line, but he said the words. Strangely, the trapped sailor seemed to calm down immediately.

Skinner retraced his steps, pulled himself to the hangar deck, got the other line, and went back to the wide-eyed victim. The great fear now was that the man's clothing might give way as he tried to secure the thrown line around his waist. If that happened, he was a dead man. But it did not happen; Skinner threw the line, and the trapped man tied it around his waist without mishap. Then Skinner gently pulled up the slack, braced himself to take the man's weight, and pulled him free. Skinner quickly pulled the sailor across the top of the fuel oil and then hand-over-hand to the top of the tank. They were as good as safe, though the rescued man had a great deal of difficulty scaling the little bulkhead to get into the elevator pit; he had put all his strength into the screaming that had drawn Skinner, and he had nothing left. Once over the bulkhead, Skinner and the sailor were hauled up to the hangar deck by Tom Reese and a number of curious, helpful passersby.

Moments after Lieutenant Irikiin's torpedo hit, Captain Mason ordered all hands except several key officers and gunnery-control personnel to evacuate the island. Next, orders were passed throughout the ship for all hands to *prepare* to abandon ship—but not to cast loose any rafts or go over the side. This carefully worded order was garbled along the way, and about a hundred officers and sailors took to the lifelines after freeing several nests of rafts.

One of the men to leave the ship at this time was PhM1 Floyd Arnold. He joined the small rush to leave the hangar deck and swung overboard by means of one of the many ropes by then hanging off the fantail. Arnold dropped into the water and swam about twenty-five yards to a life raft already occupied by the ship's chaplain and three other men.

At the order to prepare to abandon the *Hornet*, LCdr Oscar Dodson, the communications officer, rounded up three communicators and led them below to the coding room to gather up all the codes, secret messages, and confidential communications materials stored there. The trip was dark and dangerous, and Dodson was particularly consternated when he saw Warrant Officer Sato's unexploded 250-kilogram bomb secured to a bulkhead only ten feet from his objective. Dodson turned back to the flight deck and sought the advice of an ordnanceman, who told him, "Go right up to the bomb and check it. If it's not smoking and not ticking, then it's probably a dud and will not suddenly explode." Thus reassured, the communicators went back to the coding room and filled weighted canvas pouches with the materials they felt they had to destroy. The heavy list nearly bilged the effort; there were ten heavy bags to be moved, and the deck was slippery from oils and slimy fulmite.

TM1 Jim Goldner left his station at the *Mustin's* torpedo director to help haul swimmers aboard his ship. When Goldner saw one man begin to flounder some distance from the destroyer, he stripped down to his shorts and dived into the water to assist him to the side of the ship. Though anxious about being in the water without a life jacket or life belt, Goldner repeatedly swam out to tired swimmers with buoys and lines and returned time and again to assist other tired *Hornet* swimmers toward the nets rigged out over the destroyer's side. Suddenly, the *Mustin's* general-quarters alarm sounded. Before Goldner could climb back aboard, the ship began moving slowly through the swimmers in a bid to pick up some maneuvering room. Another air strike was coming in.

Lt(jg) Ichiro Tanaka's little mixed force of Kates, Vals, and Zeros had followed Lieutenant Irikiin's Kates and Zeros to the search area north of the *Hornet* and of course had found nothing after splitting up into three sections. At length, the pair of Vals headed south to attack the *Hornet,* and they arrived over the target without fanfare at 1541. Attacking against no antiaircraft opposition, one of the pilots missed altogether, while the other scored a near miss that rolled the battered vessel to a 20-degree list.

When the two Vals arrived, WT1 Lyle Skinner was climbing the slippery deck toward the high port side of the ship, gently pushing the exhausted man he had just rescued in front of him. The two never even paused to brace themselves against possible bomb detonations; they seemed to know they would survive.

By then, sailors were leaving the ship again, mainly by way of the fantail. EM1 Samuel Blumer was only halfway down a fantail rope when he heard someone overhead yell "Let go!" Blumer dropped into the water and was nearly brained by a nest of life rafts that had been cut away directly over his head. He swam to the nearest raft and pulled himself in along with another sailor. The two grabbed paddles and pulled away from the ship as quickly as they could. The first antiaircraft guns had commenced firing again.

As the Vals withdrew, all gunnery personnel were ordered to abandon their stations and prepare to abandon ship. Until that moment, all guns had been fully manned and had fired at the departing Vals, albeit without scoring any hits.

During the brief post-attack rush to abandon ship, EM1 Leroy Butts, who had spent the afternoon helping to rig the jumper cable from the diesel-engine room to the after fire room, left by way of a line that, unbeknown to him, had been used earlier by the fire-fighting bucket brigades. When the sailor on the line ahead of Butts jumped from about halfway up the rope, Butts lost his firm grip on the oily line and went down like a shot. When he reached the bottom, he jammed a foot in the unseen bucket. While Butts was trying to free his foot, another sailor lost control at the top of the line and fell on top of him.

All hope was gone. Captain Mason ordered his crew to abandon ship at 1543. Two minutes later, Lt(jg) Ichiro Tanaka's six *Junyo*-launched *Shokaku* and *Zuikaku* Kates, equipped with one 800-kilogram "land" bomb apiece, arrived overhead at 8,000 feet in a perfect stepped-up vee formation. Two of the *Hornet's* own 1.1-inch mounts, not yet secured, and one of the sandbagged .30-caliber flight-deck machine guns manned by a radioman on his way down to the hangar deck fired at the approaching bombers along with a moderate number of guns aboard the screening warships.

When the destroyer *Russell's* gunnery officer, Lt(jg) Bob Brown, saw the Kates overhead, he also saw that his ship's forward 5-inch gun was pointed directly at the *Hornet's* side. Brown was frankly afraid to order his batteries into action against the Kates when there was a chance that a round from the forward gun would hit the ship he was trying to protect. It took a precious minute for Brown to learn that the gun had a shell casing jammed in its breech and could not fire. Only then did the *Russell* add her voice to the antiaircraft barrage.

The precipitous approach of the Kates caught the *Pensacola's* gunners completely by surprise. Most were at ease, eating or making head calls.

When one 5-inch loader who had fallen asleep on his feet was jarred awake by his gun captain, the man looked up at the level bombers, muttered, "Aw, they can't hit anything," and promptly fell asleep again.

EM3 Tom Reese, who had gone over the side in the latest premature rush from the hangar deck, was floating on his back when he saw the six silvery enemy warplanes slip behind a cloud directly over the ship.

Packed into a tight formation, the Kates proceeded through the cloud to the carrier's port quarter, where all the bombardiers dropped their bombs on command from the flight leader. One of the bombs struck the after flight deck and detonated with great fury while causing very little damage. The other five narrowly missed the ship to leeward, away from where most of the ship's company and swimmers had gathered.

Lt(jg) Earl Zook, who had assumed a fetal position at his abandon-ship station on the port side of the hangar deck, was nearly done in when an airplane lashed to the overhead was jarred loose by the near-misses. It fell right next to Zook, who decided it was time to leave the ship.

As soon as the Kates turned away, Captain Mason passed the inevitable order: "Abandon ship." At 1550, the captain and his staff left the bridge and proceeded to the flight deck.

Chapter 40

FC3 Richard Cartwright, who was helping to man the *Hornet's* 1.1-inch gun battery, heard the battery officer call down from the powerless gun director, "Okay, boys, let's go." Cartwright climbed down to the hangar deck from the starboard catwalk and there was shocked to find that he had to crawl on his hands and knees to get across to the large crowd on the port catwalk. He grabbed a thick knotted hawser that was dangling over the side and slid down to the armored torpedo belt, which the ship's heavy list had brought above the surface. There he waited for the chop to carry him away from the ship, but his timing was off and the next incoming wave slapped him back into the ship. A bit stunned, Cartwright pulled away with all his strength and headed for a pair of nearby destroyers. Fuel mixed with salt water kept getting in the fire controlman's mouth and nose, and the chop of the waves had a nauseating effect. To make matters worse, the nearer destroyer slid off at slow speed just as Cartwright was about to hail the sailors on her deck. It was only a matter of moments before a second destroyer—the *Mustin*—slowly arrived on station. A life ring was heaved over the side, and Cartwright used the last of his strength to shoot

forward the last few yards and wrap his arms around it. He was reeled in like a prize game fish but still had a bad time getting his weakened body up a rope dangling over the destroyer's low side. Once on deck, he collapsed against a bulkhead and puked up oil and sea water until he had nothing left inside. Soon, he was sent below, where he was treated to a shower and clean clothes.

LCdr Oscar Dodson was wrestling heavy bags of classified materials up the slippery canted flight deck when the abandon-ship order was passed. By the time he and three helpers reached the edge of the flight deck, the water was filled with swimmers, making it impossible to throw the heavy sacks overboard. It took about a half hour of waiting for little lulls to jettison all ten bags. When done, Dodson climbed back up to the flight deck and reported to Captain Mason. As soon as the skipper saw the communicator emerge at the top of the ladder, he called, "Damn it, Dodson, what are you doing still aboard? Get off the ship so I can!" Dodson reported that the codes and ciphers in his care were "secure" and wished the captain good luck. But Dodson was not quite ready to leave. A lifelong collector of ancient and rare coins, the communicator still had hopes of rescuing his priceless collection. The leather briefcase in which the coins were stored had been roasted on the signal bridge, but the coins had come through unscathed, and Dodson had stowed them in a corner of the bridge. That was his objective when he left Captain Mason. The briefcase was where he had left it, the collection intact. He carried it to the hangar deck, his mind racing for a solution to an obvious problem: How in the world could he swim with the bulky, heavy briefcase in tow? He couldn't, and he knew it, so he removed his shoes, which he placed in line with countless others, and set beside them a fortune that included a small part of the wealth of Rome, of the Kingdom of Lydia, of Athens, of Macedon, and of Carthage. Then Dodson climbed down to the water and swam for his life. In time, he was rescued by the destroyer *Morris*.

The *Hornet's* first lieutenant, Cdr Henry Moran, was one of the last to leave. After waiting for a time with Captain Mason, he made a trip to his stateroom to collect a framed painted miniature of his wife and son. This he placed in his shirt as he climbed back to the hangar deck. Moran went over the side by rope and quickly swam to the *Russell*, which was holding steady nearly alongside the carrier. On the way, he saw that the carrier's supply officer, Cdr R. H. Sullivan, was angling in from another direction. "Are you enjoying your swim, Sully?" he called as he reached the destroyer's side just ahead of his colleague. The two out-of-work department heads climbed aboard together and joined the crowd of wet, oil-covered refugees.

EM3 Tom Reese, who had gone over the side following the fateful torpedo attack, had long since made his way to a large life raft. When the bulk of the carrier's crew began streaming into the water, Reese helped at least fifteen shipmates to climb aboard or grip handholds around the edge. One sailor had swallowed more than his share of oil-fouled seawater, and he had to be hauled bodily aboard to recuperate. At about that point, several of the men aboard and around the raft became hysterical. Reese had been in the water for a while and had become resigned to his plight; he was past the point of panic, so he leaned heavily on several fellow electrician's mates in the group and got them organized to paddle the overfilled raft toward the *Mustin*, which was hundreds of yards away. That seemed to calm everyone down, and all hands pitched in. On the way, another electrician's mate swam past the raft with a strong, purposeful stroke. "Hey," Reese called, "where do you think you're going?" "Why," the man called back over his shoulder, "to San Francisco!"—as if that were the obvious answer.

WT1 Lyle Skinner and the man he had rescued from the damaged starboard fuel tank entered the water together and swam toward a crowded life raft about fifty yards from the side of the ship. As they approached, the two were violently cursed by the occupants of the raft, who threatened to harm them if they got too close. This threat of violence seemed absurd, but there was no way Skinner was going to test it. The two veered away and looked for another raft, but they could not find one nearby. They idled away the time, floating on their backs, taking intermittent peeks to check on the progress of a pair of destroyers in among the swimmers. At last, the *Mustin* approached to within hailing distance, and Skinner and his comrade were pulled aboard. As soon as Skinner was safely on deck, a sailor in dry clothes handed him a lighted cigarette. Later in the afternoon, one of the destroyermen offered Skinner his bunk. Skinner, who was black with oil, was reluctant to take him up on the offer, but the man insisted.

PhM1 Floyd Arnold, who had been afloat in a life raft with the *Hornet's* chaplain since mistakenly abandoning ship early in the afternoon, was finally lifted from the sea by the destroyer USS *Anderson*. It took Arnold three tries to stand up just to get aboard the destroyer because his knees had locked after many hours aboard the cramped raft. Once aboard, he found he could not walk, so he crawled to the bridge and pulled himself up a ladder to report his identity. Next, Arnold slid back down the ladder and made his way aft, where he promptly fell into an exhausted sleep. He had not had a bite of food or a sip of water all day.

Many of the *Hornet's* Marines went over the side in a group and were picked up in a group by the *Mustin*. There, the detachment executive officer, 1stLt Leo Dulacki, requested permission to have his troops spell the destroyer's exhausted gunners on the antiaircraft guns. The destroyer's gunnery officer cheerfully obliged, though a number of Marines soon regretted the favor. Unused to the heavy pitch of the small ship's topside gunnery positions, Marines were soon puking up the sandwiches and coffee the ship's cooks had so thoughtfully provided as fair compensation.

TM1 Jim Goldner had been left in the water following the rescue of *Hornet* sailors when his ship, the *Mustin*, had gotten under way before the horizontal bombing attack. Goldner found a place aboard a life raft and helped other swimmers out of the oily water. But too many swimmers were approaching, and Goldner finally had to tell those who seemed fit to get back into the water to give weaker survivors a place. All the while, but only half-believing it himself, Goldner assured everyone that the *Mustin* would be back to rescue them. At long last, Goldner's ship did come in. A whaleboat was lowered, and it came straight to Goldner's raft, which had two dozen tired, filthy men clinging to it. The torpedoman's reward was a hot shower and a fresh change of clothes—his own clothes.

EM1 Samuel Blumer wound up aboard the *Anderson*. He was given dry socks, a shirt, and trousers by one of the destroyermen before being sent to the after deckhouse to join his shipmates.

One of the last members of the *Hornet's* crew to be rescued was Lt(jg) Earl Zook. A recent Annapolis graduate, Zook got the silly notion into his head that he would like to spend some time aboard a cruiser. Thus, he passed up an early opportunity to board a destroyer and swam on toward the larger warship. It took a very long time for the young officer to realize that he was in over his head—thousands of fathoms, at least—so he finally pulled for a life raft. When he got there, he saw three very grim-faced occupants, and he called out, "Anyone need a fourth for bridge?" The three smiled faintly and moved to make room for the overly chipper jaygee. They were a little stunned to see that Zook still had on his shoes and, of all things, his heavy .45-caliber pistol. Zook and the others were soon rescued by the *Anderson*.

After completing a tour of the silent vessel with his navigator and tactical officer, Capt Perry Mason came up to an abandon-ship station. Beckoning out toward the waves, the *Hornet's* last captain said, "If you please, gentlemen." The two understood perfectly; they selected lines and swung out over the water. Captain Mason followed. No living men remained aboard the ship, but 118 dead shipmates had been left behind. It was 1627.

The ship was listing so badly that the three officers were obliged to stop on the ledge of anti-torpedo armor. There, Captain Mason paused to smoke a cigarette and, no doubt, ruminate about the terrible day he was having. He no sooner lit up, however, than he realized that he was surrounded by a sea of volatile fuel oil, so he immediately crushed out the burning tip on the steel hull of his ship. The two junior officers were sure the captain was simply adjusting to the need to finally give her up. They were about to go when they heard voices from around the curve of the hull. The three climbed along the armored ledge and found twenty sailors working up the courage to enter the water. At once, it dawned on the two junior officers that Captain Mason had no intention of entering the water ahead of these stay-behinds. Indeed. The captain ordered the sailors into the water and coaxed several who were too afraid of sharks to proceed. It took a direct order to get the last two sailors overboard. Then, and only after his two officer companions had gone in, did Captain Mason slip into the water, where he helped the weak swimmers with gentle prodding and words of encouragement.

At length, a motor whaleboat approached the knot of swimmers. Someone called out that Admiral Mason—for his elevation to flag rank had been approved—should be taken aboard first. Mason loudly protested, but the two sailors manning the whaleboat leaned over the older man and dragged him aboard by the collar of his shirt and the seat of his pants. Then, after one more stop to help bilged *Hornet* sailors aboard, the whaleboat made for the *Mustin*.

Chapter 41

The last air strike of the day—Lt Yoshio Shiga's six Zeros escorting Lt(jg) Shunko Kato's four *Junyo*-launched Vals—found the *Hornet* at 1650, and Kato led the Vals down at 1720. Though there was absolutely no fire from the carrier to throw off their aim, the exhausted pilots, each on his second long combat hop of the day, managed only one hit for four 250-kilogram bombs. That missile was clearly seen by hundreds of former *Hornet* sailors to explode on the empty hangar deck forward of the island. Fires burned out of control around the point of impact for about fifteen minutes and then abated. All of the strikers landed safely aboard the *Junyo* after dark and claimed four hits for four bombs.

As soon as Capt Perry Mason arrived aboard the *Mustin* he was greeted by her captain, LCdr Wallis Peterson, who offered the fuel-begrimed near admiral his stateroom, a shower, and a fresh uniform. Mason gratefully accepted and was given over to the care of one of the destroyer's junior officers. As Mason was dressing after his shower, he began dictating his after-action report to the young destroyer officer. At length, he began going on about his plans to put a salvage party back aboard his crippled carrier in the morning. The younger officer put down his pen and stared at Mason with a pained expression on the face.

"Yes," Mason snapped, "what is it?"

"Sir, excuse me, but didn't you know the Flag had ordered us to sink the *Hornet* tonight?"

The final puny Val strike had been the last straw. Though the *Hornet* might still have been salvageable, it seemed certain that Japanese submarines were stalking the area (there never were any Japanese submarines near Task Force 61), and that they would certainly be joined by others of their kind. Japanese surface forces could well be on the way, too; they had last been seen during the afternoon by retiring American warplanes as they sailed steadily toward Task Force 61. The damaged American flight deck could not be allowed to fall into Japanese hands. Moreover, though the Japanese afternoon air strikes were weak, there was no doubt but that there was at least one Japanese flight deck in operation. Saving *Hornet* would mean conducting a slow recovery operation in submarine-infested waters beyond the effective range of friendly ground-based or carrier-based air cover. In the final analysis, the *Hornet* was not worth the possible cost in additional precious American warships.

With great emotion, RAdm George Murray had sealed the *Hornet's* fate with a message from the bridge of his new flagship, the heavy cruiser *Pensacola*: Destroyer *Mustin* was to administer the coup de grace with torpedoes. Murray turned Task Force 17 east at 1740, leaving the *Mustin* and *Anderson* to do the dirty work.

As the *Mustin* came on station one mile off the carrier's starboard beam, TM1 Jim Goldner, who had spent most of the afternoon with *Hornet* survivors in the water, made his way to the ship's torpedo director. It would be his job to line up the sights for the *Mustin's* two quadruple torpedo mounts. When Goldner was set, at 1803, the *Mustin* launched all eight of her ready fish in slow succession. As had occurred during the scuttling of the *Wasp* in these waters a month earlier, the results were humiliating: Two of the torpedoes ran erratically and never came near the stationary target; three fish ran true but did not detonate; the other three hit the *Hornet* and did detonate. Nevertheless, the *Hornet* was made of very stout stuff, and she did not sink.

At 1920, the *Anderson* took up station off the carrier and loosed all eight of her torpedoes. One veered sharply to the right, one detonated prematurely, and six struck the carrier. Though the damage to the carrier's hull was enormous, she still would not sink.

The *Mustin* and *Anderson,* both filled to brimming with *Hornet* survivors, began pumping 5-inch rounds into the carrier's vulnerable hull, trying to penetrate weak spots in the magazines and fuel tanks in order to blow her out of the water. Though there was a great deal lacking in the design of the *Hornet's* back-up power system and anti-torpedo belt, there was nothing basically wrong with her construction. She remained afloat, though the many 5-inch rounds did indeed start raging fires throughout the hulk.

The Japanese Vanguard Group of two battleships, four cruisers, and seven destroyers was only sixty miles from the *Hornet's* position as the *Mustin* began firing her torpedoes, and it was coming on fast. Cruiser-launched scout planes buzzed over the burning carrier just after sundown and lighted her with parachute flares. The Japanese reconnaissance pilots reported the departure of the bulk of Task Force 17 and informed the Vanguard Group commander, RAdm Hiroaki Abe, that a pair of destroyers was shelling the burning carrier.

At 2005, Abe heard direct from Adm Isoroku Yamamoto. The message was essentially a victory exhortation:

> The largest part of the enemy forces north of Santa Cruz has been destroyed. It is quite likely that units composed of capital ships will attempt to rescue survivors.
>
> The Combined Fleet will attempt to destroy these forces.
>
> The [Guadalcanal] Support Force will destroy the enemy forces in a night, or as circumstances dictate in a dawn engagement.

By the time *Mustin* and *Anderson* had expended a total of 430 5-inch rounds, lookouts aboard the Japanese destroyers *Makigumo* and *Akigumo* could see the glow of the *Hornet's* fires over the dark horizon. The

American destroyers rushed away at 2040, virtually the last moment, with a division of Japanese destroyers in hot but ultimately vain pursuit.

The main body of Abe's battle force arrived at the *Hornet's* location at 2220, and Abe sent a message of his find to his chief, VAdm Nobutake Kondo. Then Abe's staff went straight to work trying to figure out a way to get the burning prize under tow. Before Abe could act, an acknowledgement message from Kondo included orders to sink her.

As RAdm Kakuji Kakuta watched the red glow of the *Hornet's* pyre from the bridge of the *Junyo,* just over the horizon, the *Makigumo* and *Akigumo* closed on the hulk, which was glowing cherry-red in spots, and each fired two of Japan's superb, reliable 24-inch Long Lance torpedoes at her. All four Long Lances struck the carrier and detonated.

USS *Hornet,* the eighth and newest of America's fleet carriers, slipped beneath the waves at 0135, October 27, 1942, and plunged 2,700 fathoms to her final resting place.

As soon as the carrier was gone, Abe departed the scene in order to find and reengage the American survivors, but the plan was scrapped when news arrived that a Patrol-91 PBY out of Espiritu Santo near-missed one of the *Zuikaku's* escorts at 0100, killing two and wounding nearly fifty sailors aboard the antiaircraft destroyer HIJMS *Teruzuki.* Then, at 0130, a Patrol-51 PBY launched a torpedo attack against the *Junyo.* The pilot claimed a hit, and SoPac intelligence thought he had damaged the *Zuikaku.* No hit was actually scored, but the Japanese commanders were spooked, and Admiral Kondo called off the pursuit in favor of escorting the precious carriers to safety. As far as he knew, several unimpaired American carriers remained on the prowl.

The PBY attacks were the last shots of the Battle of the Santa Cruz Islands. The remnants of Task Force 61 continued on toward Noumea. And, at 1000, October 27, after learning of the utter failure of the Imperial Army assault on Guadalcanal, all the Japanese warships shaped courses for Truk. Before they departed the area, ships from Admiral Abe's Vanguard Group picked up two Japanese pilots and a crewman, and several Imperial Navy destroyers bagged the four survivors of the Torpedo-10 ambush—Fighting-10's Ens Al Mead and Ens Dusty Rhodes, and Torpedo-10's AMM3

Murray Glasser and ARM1 Tom Nelson. LCdr Gus Widhelm and his radioman gunner were picked up by a PBY on October 29, the last participants from either side to be rescued.

In all, American aircrew losses were low, and Japanese aircrew losses were staggering, especially among group, squadron, and section leaders. Of 203 aircraft available aboard four Japanese carriers at dawn on October 26 (fifty-seven Kates, sixty-three Vals, eighty-two Zeros, and one scout), sixty-seven were shot down (twenty-two Kates, thirty Vals, and fifteen Zeros), and twenty-eight were lost in crashes and ditchings (seven Kates, eleven Vals, nine Zeros, and the scout), and four were destroyed by bombs aboard ship (one Kate and three Zeros). Thus, 99 of 203 combat aircraft were lost.

Of the airmen manning the Japanese warplanes, sixteen fighter pilots, twenty-two Kate pilots, forty-five Kate crewmen, thirty Val pilots, and thirty-two Val crewmen lost their lives—145 in all. Of these, twenty-three were section, flight, squadron, or group commanders.

Of 175 American aircraft available aboard the two carriers (twenty-nine TBFs, seventy-two SBDs, and seventy-four F4Fs), three TBFs, two SBDs, and thirteen F4Fs were shot down, a total of eighteen. Another sixteen TBFs, eight SBDs, and ten F4Fs were lost when they crashed or ditched, a total of thirty-four. And eighteen SBDs and ten F4Fs were lost aboard ships or jettisoned, a total of twenty-eight. Thus, the Americans lost 80 of 175 aircraft, a hard but not insuperable loss.

Perhaps equally important, the Americans suffered fewer pilot and crew losses than the Japanese. Three TBF pilots and five crewmen were killed and two were captured, one SBD pilot and one crewman were killed, and twelve fighter pilots were killed and two were captured, a grand total of eighteen pilots and eight crewmen killed or captured. Of these, just four fighter section or division leaders and one torpedo squadron commander were lost.

Epilogue

Though technically a Japanese victory, the Battle of the Santa Cruz Islands—the fourth carrier-versus-carrier battle in history—was Japan's last serious attempt to win the Pacific War by means of a carrier confrontation. Only one other carrier battle occurred in the Pacific War, in June 1944, in the Philippine Sea. By then, however, the U.S. Navy's Fast Carrier Task Force was operational, and Japan's dwindling fleet of carriers was outnumbered and completely outclassed. Though hundreds of Japanese naval aviators perished in the great Marianas Turkey Shoot of June 19–20, 1944, it was during the first four carrier battles—in the six-month period from early May through late October 1942—that the fate of Japan's small, elite naval air arm was sealed. It was at Eastern Solomons and Santa Cruz that Japan's last best carrier air groups were ground to dust. After their technical victory at Santa Cruz, the Japanese were never able to use their carriers as a strategically decisive weapon.

Of the Japanese carriers that participated in the Santa Cruz battle, only the *Junyo* survived the war; she was surrendered to U.S. forces on September 2, 1945. The *Shokaku* was sunk by a U.S. submarine on June

19, 1944, in the Battle of the Philippine Sea, and the *Zuikaku* and *Zuiho* were sunk in battle off Cape Engaño on October 25, 1944.

The *Saratoga*, which was damaged in Torpedo Junction in late August, was repaired and returned to duty in November 1942. She survived the war, as did the *Enterprise*, the last of the *Yorktown*-class carriers. Indeed, the severe damage *Enterprise* sustained at Santa Cruz was largely repaired in time for her to fulfill a vital support mission a little more than two weeks later, when a Japanese surface force built around two battleships fought what was arguably the decisive surface engagement of the Pacific War.

After Santa Cruz and the series of air and surface engagements known as the Naval Battle of Guadalcanal, the Imperial Navy's Combined Fleet never again attempted a meaningful strategic showdown with the U.S. Pacific Fleet. Though several subsequent surface actions in the Solomons were clearly Japanese victories, their results were short lived. After November 1942, Japan could not again muster the staying power—or the willpower—to wage a strategic war with her navy. Once the veteran carrier air groups had been shredded at Eastern Solomons and Santa Cruz, Japanese carriers ceased to be a strategic weapon.

The Santa Cruz clash was deemed a Japanese victory because U.S. naval forces had withdrawn from the battlefield. That is how victory and defeat are strictly determined. But on the broader strategic level, the U.S. Navy won at Santa Cruz, because it was able to achieve its strategic goal of holding the line and buying time, and Japan was unable to achieve its strategic goal of defeating the U.S. Pacific Fleet in a final, decisive, all-or-nothing battle. The technical victory cost Japan any serious hope she had of winning the Pacific naval war.

On November 2, 1942, the damaged *Shokaku* and *Zuiho* were ordered to Japan for repairs. Much to everyone's surprise, the undamaged *Zuikaku* was also ordered home on November 4. That left only the inadequate *Junyo* on duty on the Pacific War's most active front—and she was never used offensively during the remainder of her tour in the region. The Imperial Navy's diminished carrier fleet had no role to play, and was never a factor, in the full year of fighting that remained in the decisive Solomons Campaign.

Santa Cruz was a Japanese victory. That victory cost Japan her last best hope to win the war.

Order of Battle

October 25–26, 1942

SOUTH PACIFIC FORCE

VAdm William F. Halsey, Jr.

TASK FORCE 61

RAdm Thomas C. Kinkaid

Task Force 16	RAdm Thomas C. Kinkaid
Enterprise (CV) (FF)	Capt Osborne B. Hardison
Air Group 10	Cdr Richard K. Gaines
VF-10	LCdr James H. Flatley, Jr.
VB-10	LCdr James A. Thomas
VS-10	LCdr James R. Lee
VT-10	LCdr John A. Collett

Task Force 16 Screen	RAdm Mahlon S. Tisdale
South Dakota (BB)	
Cruiser Division 4	
Portland (CA) (F)	
San Juan (CLAA)	
Destroyer Squadron 5	
Porter (DD)	
Mahan (DD)	
Destroyer Division 10	
Cushing (DD)	
Preston (DD)	
Smith (DD)	
Maury (DD)	
Conyngham (DD)	
Shaw (DD)	
Task Force 17	RAdm George D. Murray
Hornet (CV) (F)	Capt Charles P. Mason
Hornet Air Group	Cdr Walter F. Rodee
VF-72	LCdr Henry G. Sanchez
VB-8	Lt James W. Vose
VS-8	LCdr William J. Widhelm
VT-6	Lt Edwin B. Parker, Jr.
Task Force 17 Screen	RAdm Howard H. Good
Cruiser Division 5	
Northampton (CA) (F)	
Pensacola (CA)	
San Diego (CLAA)	
Juneau (CLAA)	
Destroyer Squadron 2	
Morris (DD)	
Anderson (DD)	
Hughes (DD)	
Mustin (DD)	

Russell (DD)
Barton (DD)

TASK FORCE 63

(Land-based Aircraft)
RAdm Aubrey W. Fitch

COMBINED FLEET

Adm Isoroku Yamamoto
(at Truk)

GUADALCANAL SUPPORT FORCE

VAdm Nobutake Kondo
(CinC 2nd Fleet)

Advance Force VAdm Nobutake Kondo

Main Body
Cruiser Division 4
Atago (CA) (FF)
Takao (CA)
Cruiser Division 5
Myoko (CA) (F)
Maya (CA)
Destroyer Division 2
Isuzu (CL) (F)
Naganami (DD)
Makinami (DD)
Umikaze (DD)
Kawakaze (DD)
Takanami (DD)
Suzukaze (DD)

Air Group	RAdm Kakuji Kakuta
Carrier Division 2	
Junyo (CV) (F)	
Air Group	Lt Yoshio Shiga
Fighter Squadron	Lt Yoshio Shiga
Bomber Squadron	Lt Masao Yamaguchi
Attack Squadron	Lt Yoshiaki Irikiin
Kuroshio (DD)	
Hayashio (DD)	
Support Group	VAdm Takeo Kurita
Battleship Division 3	
Kongo (BB) (F)	
Haruna (BB)	
Oyashio (DD)	
Kagero (DD)	

STRIKING FORCE

VAdm Chuichi Nagumo
(CinC 3rd Fleet)

Carrier Group	
Carrier Division 1	
Shokaku (CV) (F)	
Air Group	LCdr Mamoru Seki
Fighter Squadron	Lt Hideki Shingo
Bomber Squadron	LCdr Mamoru Seki
Attack Squadron	LCdr Shigeharu Murata
Zuikaku (CV)	
Air Group	Lt Sadumu Takahashi
Fighter Squadron	Lt Ayao Shirane
Bomber Squadron	Lt Sadumu Takahashi
Attack Squadron	Lt Shigeichiro Imajuku

Zuiho (CVL)	
Air Group	Lt Masao Sato
Fighter Squadron	Lt Masao Sato
Attack Squadron	Lt(jg) Ichiro Tanaka
Carrier Group Screen	
Kumano (CA)	
Amatsukaze (DD)	
Hatsukaze (DD)	
Tokitsukaze (DD)	
Yukikaze (DD)	
Arashi (DD)	
Maikaze (DD)	
Teruzuki (DD)	
Hamakaze (DD)	
Vanguard Group	RAdm Hiroake Abe
Battleship Division 11	
Hiei (BB) (F)	
Kirishima (BB)	
Cruiser Division 8	
Tone (CA) (F)	
Chikuma (CA)	
Cruiser Division 7	
Suzuya (CA)	
Destroyer Division 10	
Nagara (CL) (F)	
Kazagumo (DD)	
Makigumo (DD)	
Yugumo (DD)	
Akigumo (DD)	
Tanikaze (DD)	
Urakaze (DD)	
Isokaze (DD)	

Supply Group
Nowaki (DD)
Kokuyo Maru
Toho Maru
Toei Maru
Kyokuto Maru

OUTER SOUTH SEAS FORCE

VAdm Gunichi Mikawa
(CinC 8th Fleet, at Shortland Islands)

Assault Unit
Akatsuki (DD)
Ikazuchi (DD)
Shiratsuya (DD)

Bombardment Unit — RAdm Tomatsu Takama
Destroyer Division 4
Yura (CL) (F)
Yudachi (DD)
Akizuki (DD)
Murasame (DD)
Harusame (DD)
Samidare (DD)

ADVANCE EXPEDITIONARY FORCE

VAdm Teruhisa Komatsu
(CinC 6th Fleet, at Truk)

Submarine Force
I-4, I-5, I-7, I-9, I-15, I-21, I-22, I-24, I-174, I-175, I-176

Bibliography

BOOKS

Belote, James H., and William M. Belote. *Titans of the Seas: The Development and Operations of Japanese and American Carrier Task Forces During World War II*. New York: Harper & Row, 1975.

Burns, Eugene. *Then There Was One: The U.S.S. Enterprise and the First Year of the War*. New York: Harcourt, Brace and Company, 1943.

Dull, Paul S. *A Battle History of the Imperial Japanese Navy, 1941–1945*. Annapolis: Naval Institute Press, 1978.

Griffin, Alexander R. *A Ship to Remember: The Saga of the Hornet*. New York: Howell, Soskin Publishers, 1943.

Hammel, Eric. *Aces Against Japan*, vol. 1, *The American Aces Speak*. Novato, Calif.: Presidio Press, 1992.

———. *Aces Against Japan II*, vol. 3, *The American Aces Speak*. Pacifica, Calif.: Pacifica Press, 1996.

———. *Aces at War*, vol. 4, *The American Aces Speak*. Pacifica, Calif.: Pacifica Press, 1997.

————. *Aces in Combat,* vol. 5, *The American Aces Speak.* Pacifica, Calif.: Pacifica Press, 1998.

————. *Air War Pacific Chronology: America's Air War Against Japan in East Asia and the Pacific, 1941–1945.* Pacifica, Calif.: Pacifica Press, 1998.

————. *Carrier Clash: The Invasion of Guadalcanal and the Battle of the Eastern Solomons, August 1942.* Pacifica, Calif.: Pacifica Press, 1997.

————. *Guadalcanal: Starvation Island.* Pacifica, Calif.: Pacifica Press, 1994.

————. *Guadalcanal: The Carrier Battles.* New York: Crown Publishers, 1987.

Johnston, Stanley. *The Grim Reapers*. New York: E. P. Dutton & Co., Inc., 1943.

Knott, Richard C. *Black Cat Raiders of WWII.* Baltimore: Nautical & Aviation Publishing Company of America, 1981.

Lundstrom, John B. *The First Team and the Guadalcanal Campaign.* Annapolis: Naval Institute Press, 1994.

————. *The First Team: Pacific Naval Air Combat from Pearl Harbor to Midway*. Annapolis: Naval Institute Press, 1984.

Miller, Thomas G., Jr. *The Cactus Air Force*. New York: Harper & Row, 1969.

Morison, RAdm Samuel Eliot. *History of United States Naval Operations in World War II,* vol. 5, *The Struggle for Guadalcanal*. Boston: The Atlantic Monthly & Little, Brown & Co., 1962.

Okumiya, Masatake, and Jiro Horikoshi. *Zero!: The Inside Story of Japan's Air War in the Pacific*. New York: E. P. Dutton & Co., 1956.

Olynyk, Dr. Frank J. *USN Credits for Destruction of Enemy Aircraft in Air-to-Air Combat: World War II*. Aurora, Ohio: Frank J. Olynyk, 1982.

Potter, E. B. *Nimitz*. Annapolis: Naval Institute Press, 1976.

Roscoe, Theodore. *United States Destroyer Operations in World War II*. Annapolis: Naval Institute Press, 1953.

Stafford, Cdr Edward P. *The Big E: The Story of the USS Enterprise*. New York: Random House, 1962.

Stover, E. T. and Clark G. Reynolds. *The Saga of Smokey Stover*. Charleston: Trad Street Press, 1978.

Tillman, Barrett. *The Dauntless Dive Bomber of World War II*. Annapolis: Naval Institute Press, 1976.

————. *The Wildcat in WWII*. Baltimore: Nautical & Aviation Publishing Company of America, 1983.

Toland, John. *The Rising Sun: The Decline and Fall of the Japanese Empire*. New York: Random House, 1970.

Wolfert, Ira. *Torpedo 8*. Boston: Houghton Mifflin Company, 1943.

PERIODICALS

Blee, Capt Ben W. "Whodunnit?" *U.S. Naval Institute Proceedings* (July 1983).

Editors. "Capt Robin M. Lindsey, USN (Ret): The Last Cut for an LSO." *The Hook* (Summer 1984).

Mason, RAdm Charles P., with Don Eddy. "How We Lost a Gallant Lady." *America* (November 1943).

Poulos, George. "Recollections of a VP Pilot." *Naval Aviation News* (September 1982).

Tanaka, VAdm Raizo. "Japan's Losing Struggle for Guadalcanal," Parts I and II. *U.S. Naval Institute Proceedings* (1956).

Toyama, Saburo. "Lessons From the Past." *U.S. Naval Institute Proceedings* (September 1982).

UNPUBLISHED

Norton, Mdn Douglas M. "The Battle of Santa Cruz." Research paper submitted to the faculty of the U.S. Naval Academy.

Index

Abe, VAdm Hiroaki 197, 225–226 357, 379–380
Agnew, Cdr Dwight, 99–100
Aircraft descriptions
Aichi D3A Val carrier bomber, 119
Consolidated PBY Catalina amphibian patrol bomber, 120–121
Curtiss SOC Seagull scout-observation plane, 120
Douglas SBD Dauntless dive-bomber, 117
Grumman F4F Wildcat fighter, 115–117
Grumman TBF Avenger torpedo bomber, 117–118
Kawanishi H6K Mavis long-range patrol bomber, 121
Kawanishi H8K Emily long-range patrol bomber, 121
Mitsubishi A6M Zero fighter, 118–119
Mitsubishi G4M Betty medium bomber, 121–122
Najajima A6M2-N Rufe floatplane fighter, 121
Nakajima B5N Kate torpedo bomber, 119–120
Alexandria, Egypt, 88
Anderson, F1 Thomas M., Jr., 292
Ansley, ARM1 Harry C., 186, 191
Anundsen, MM1 Alfred W., 291
Arima, Capt Masafumi, 222, 357
Arima, Lt Keichi, 301, 306, 358
Arnold, PhM1 Floyd, 275, 368, 374–375
Arnold, Gen Henry H. (Hap), 81–82
Auman, Lt(jg) Forrester C. (Joe), 221–224, 333, 343, 348
Australian Army, 20
Aviation Cadet Act of 1935, 126

Baner, CWT Robert E., 292–293

Barnes, Ens Gordon F., 315–316, 318–319
Barrett, Lt(jg) J. Clark, 227
Bates, Lt Fred L., 219, 222, 224, 350
Batten, Lt(jg) Richard K., 205, 208, 290–291, 296, 313
Bauer, LtCol Harold W. (Joe, Coach), 72–74, 78–79, 99, 102
Baumgartner, ARM3 Nick, Jr., 190
Beane, S1 Donald W., 291, 295
Beck, AMM3 Charles M., 251–252, 268–269, 272–273, 279
Bell, LCdr Frederick J., 4
Berthold, ARM3 William, 343
Billo, Lt(jg) James D., 283, 288, 342, 344, 347
Blair, Lt(jg) William K., 164–165, 303, 311
Blanco, F1 Harold J., 278
Bliss, Lt Louis K. (Ken), 240, 245, 256, 258, 282, 287–288, 312, 341, 347–348
Bloody Ridge, Guadalcanal, 24, 62, 69, 83, 94
  First Battle, 21, 23
  Second Battle, 96–97, 105
Blumer, EM1 Samuel, Jr., 268, 362, 278, 363–365, 369, 375
Bodell, Lt(jg) Joseph, 36
Bougainville Island, 51–52, 55, 150
Bower, Lt John C., 215, 230
British Broadcasting Corporation (BBC), 295
Brown, Lt(jg) Robert G., 297, 370
Buell, Lt(jg) Harold L., 154, 285–286, 307
Buie, 1stLt John H., 169
Buin Airfield, Bougainville, 53, 55–56, 65, 77–79, 149, 322
Buin Anchorage, Bougainville, 56
Buka Airfield, 101
Buka Passage, 55, 63
Burke, Lt(jg) Arthur T., 305
Burnett, Lt(jg) Howard R., 188–189, 282–283, 285
Butts, EM1 Leroy E., Jr., 278, 370

Cactus Air Force, 8, 12, 15, 18–23, 43, 49–53, 56, 59–60, 63–70, 72, 74, 76–77, 80, 98, 101–103, 174, 180
  Fighter Command, 72, 102
Caldwell, Ens James E., Jr., 283
Caldwell, Lt Turner F., 8
Canton Island, 82
Cape Astrolabe, Santa Isabel, 104
Cape Engaño, Philippine Islands, 384
Cape Esperance,Guadalcanal, 8, 52, 57–58, 65, 67, 74, 77, 84, 98
Cape Esperance Battle, 59, 88
Carey, Lt(jg) Henry A., Jr., 57, 341–342
Carmody, Lt(jg) Martin D. (Doan), 189–190, 191, 194, 201, 286
Carrier air operations, 132–141
Carrier gunnery defenses, 249–251
Carroum, Ens Jefferson J., 169–173
Carter, Lt(jg) William D., 333
Cartwright, FC3 Richard K., 365, 372–373
Cecil, Capt Charles P., 290, 295
China Incident, 130
Clark, Lt(jg) Rufus C., 343
Clute, Lt(jg) George S., 177
Coastwatchers, 51
Coffin, Lt Albert P. (Scoofer), 173
Collett, LCdr John A., 198, 202–203, 224
Conger, 1stLt Jack E., 101
Cook, Lt(jg) Morrill I, Jr., 342

Coral Sea, 53
Coral Sea Battle, 88, 114, 128, 148, 165, 193, 201, 232, 248, 274, 322
Corpus Christi Naval Air Station, Texas, 127
Cosgrove, MoMM2 Pat, 325
Cotton, AMM3 Daniel L. (Lamar), 361
Cotton, CY Ralph L., 263, 361
Cottrell, ARM1 Billy R., 269, 277
Creehan, Cdr Edward P. (Pat), 278, 366
Cresto, Ens John, 22; Lt(jg),56, 290
Crommelin, Cdr John G., Jr., 174–175, 192, 196, 334, 336, 349–350
Cumberledge, LCdr Arthur A., 54
CXAM radar, 232–237, 239,245–246

Dalton, Ens Roy B., 215, 332
Damon, Ens Herbert S., 324–329
Daniels,Lt James G., III, 286–289, 321, 335–336, 338, 346–350, 352
Davis, Capt Arthur C., 152
Davis, Ens Gerald V., 264, 342
Davis, Maj Leonard K. (Duke), 72–73, 76, 78, 99, 102
Davis, Lt Ray, 65, 104
Dickey, Cdr Fred C., 29, 37-38, 40–41
Dietrich, Lt(jg) Alfred E., 341
Dodson, LCdr Oscar H., 252, 262, 271, 368–369, 373
Doolittle, LtCol James, 149
Doolittle Raid. *See* Tokyo Raid
Dowden, Ens James H., 318
Drury, 1stLt Frank C., 79
Dulacki, 1stLt Leo J., 375

Eastern Solomons Battle, 3, 6–7, 9–10, 15–16, 17, 36, 116, 128, 148–151, 153, 165, 193, 232, 238–239, 248, 282, 305, 383–384
Eastern Solomon Islands, 146
Eckhardt, Lt(jg) John C., Jr., 314–315, 341
Edmundson, Maj James V., 104
Edson's Ridge Battle. *See* Bloody Ridge, First Battle
Edwards, Lt(jg) J. L., 33–34
Edwards, Lt Thomas E., Jr. (Bobby), 286
Efate Island, New Hebrides Islands, 79, 345
El Alamein, Egypt, 88
Eldridge, LCdr John, Jr., 52, 103–104
Emerson, Lt Alberto C., 240, 245, 288
Emmons, MajGen Delos, 81–82
English, BM1 Oscar L. (Lee), 325–326, 328-329
Enloe, Lt(jg) George A., 158
Ervin, Lt(jg) Henry N. (Skip), 227
Espiritu Santo, Island, New Hebrides, 12, 18, 24-25, 43, 63, 83, 86, 158–159, 162, 210, 212, 343, 351, 353, 380
Estes, Lt(jg) George G. (Glenn), 227, 343
Eta Jima Naval Academy, 128–129

Fairbanks, Lt(jg) Henry A. (Al), 342, 344
Faisi, Shortland Islands, 56
Fara Island, Solomon Islands, 104
Faulkner, Lt Frederck L. (Fritz), 171, 241, 261, 315–316
Feightner, Ens Edward L. (Whitey), 173, 262, 281, 302–303, 311, 322
Ferguson, ARM3 George E., 220
Field, Lt(jg) Marshall, Jr., 306, 320, 337

Fighter-1 Airstrip, Guadalcanal,51–52, 61, 64, 74–75, 79, 80, 98-99, 103
Fink, Ens Christian, 9
Fisher, Lt(jg) Clayton E., 219–220
Fitch, RAdm Aubrey W., 83, 161–163
Flatley, LCdr James H., Jr., 198, 201, 207–208, 224–225, 227, 343
Fleming, Lt Allan F., 235, 237, 240, 245–246
Fletcher, VAdm Frank Jack, 7, 9–10, 12-13
Florida Island, Solomon Islands 74, 103
Fluitt, Mach William E., 307
Ford, Lt Warren W., 199, 226, 332, 342
Formanek, Lt(jg) George, Jr., 245, 258
Foss, Capt Joseph J., 61, 78, 99, 101
Franklin, Lt(jg) John R., 242–243, 245, 283
Freeman, Lt(jg) David B., 341
Fulton, Ens Lyman J., 266, 283

Gaines, Cdr Richard K., 169, 172, 198, 200–201, 352
Gallagher, Lt(jg) Thomas J., Jr., 240–242, 244–261
Garlow, ARM1 Clarence H., 193–195
Gatch, Capt Thomas L., 339–340
Gee, Lt(jg) Roy P., 224
Geiger, BriGen Roy S., 63–64, 66, 68, 71, 92
Germany
  Third Reich, 88
  Wehrmacht, 88
Ghormley, VAdm Robert L., 7, 15, 20, 52, 57, 74, 81–83, 86–90, 150
Gilbert Islands, 157
Gilbert Islands Raid, 193
Gizo Island, Solomon Islands, 102
Glasmann, Ens Ross C., Jr., 307
Glasser, AMM3 Murray, 204–205, 230, 381
Goldner, TM1 James A., 369, 375, 378
Good, RAdm Howard H., 235, 288, 299, 314, 345–346, 361
Gordon, Ens Donald, 264, 303, 311, 322
Gouin, Cdr Marcel E. A., 273
Grant, Lt(jg) Philip F., 219–220
Greenslade, LCdr John, 28
Griffin, Cdr John H., 231–232, 236-241, 261, 266, 300, 311, 314–316, 336–337
Guadalcanal Campaign, 49, 58, 82, 98, 145
Guadalcanal invasion, 193
Guadalcanal Island, Solomon Islands, 6, 8, 10, 18, 25, 44, 49–51, 53, 77, 84, 87–88, 92, 146

Haber, Lt(jg) Norman S., 312, 343, 349
Halsey, RAdm William F., Jr., 89–90, 154; VAdm, 91–93, 149–150, 156–157, 165, 180, 288, 345
Hamilton, Marine Gunner Henry B. (Tex), 79
Hanzawa, WO Yukio, 258
Hara, RAdm Chuichi, 197, 213, 226–227
Hardison, Capt Osborne B., 164 289, 304, 307, 319–321, 350
Harmon, MajGen Millard F., 85, 86, 92
Harris, Lt Leroy E. (Tex), 317–318
Harrison, RM3 Morse G. (Grant), 204
Henderson Field, Guadalcanal, 8–9, 12, 15, 17–18, 20–21, 50–52, 59–64, 66, 69, 71–72, 77, 80, 83, 87, 91, 93, 98, 102–103, 116, 156, 159, 179, 289
Hessel, Lt Edward W. (Red), 56, 240–

246, 261, 266, 282, 287
Hidaka, Lt Saneyasu, 192, 201, 209, 237
HIJMS *Akagi*, 112–114
HIJMS *Akigumo*, 379–380
HIJMS *Akizuki*, 103–105
HIJMS *Arashi*, 330
HIJMS *Asagiri*, 9
HIJMS *Atago*, 179
HIJMS *Chikuma*, 179, 197, 213, 226–230, 355
HIJMS *Haruna*, 61–62, 162, 331
HIJMS *Hiei*, 162, 197
HIJMS *Hiryu*, 113–114
HIJMS *Hiyo*, 75, 113, 148
HIJMS *Hosho*, 112–113
HIJMS *I-9*, 4–6
HIJMS *I-17*, 6
HIJMS *I-19*, 27, 41–43
HIJMS *I-21*, 296
HIJMS *I-26*, 10–12
HIJMS *I-123*, 6
HIJMS *Isokaze*, 177
HIJMS *Junyo*, 75, 102, 113, 148–149, 178–179, 298, 330–331, 356–358, 377, 380
HIJMS *Kaga*, 112–113
HIJMS *Kagi*, 114
HIJMS *Kirishima*, 162, 169, 197
HIJMS *Kongo*, 61–62
HIJMS *Makigumo*, 379-380
HIJMS *Nagara*, 197
HIJMS *Ryujo*, 16–17, 113, 149, 192
HIJMS *Shoho*, 113–114
HIJMS *Shokaku*, 25, 49, 70, 75, 113, 148, 150, 157, 178–179, 185, 188, 191–192, 194, 196, 216–217, 221–223, 226, 330, 357, 383–384
HIJMS *Soryu*, 113–114
HIJMS *Suzuya*, 197, 225–226
HIJMS *Taiyo*, 113
HIJMS *Teruzuki*, 223, 380
HIJMS *Tone*, 179, 189, 197, 213, 230
HIJMS *Yamato*, 357
HIJMS *Yudachi*, 9
HIJMS *Yura*, 103, 105–106, 146
HIJMS *Zuiho*, 25, 75, 113, 148, 163, 179, 185, 187–188, 192, 194–197, 216, 223, 355, 384
HIJMS *Zuikaku*, 25, 49, 70 75,, 113, 148, 150, 157, 166, 177-179, 185, 188, 192, 194, 196, 216, 323, 330–331, 355–356, 358, 380, 384
Hise, 2dLt Henry W., 8
Hoffman, Lt Glen E., 178, 184, 185
Holcomb, LtGen Thomas, 91–92
Holland, Lt(jg) Robert E., Jr., 245, 282, 314–317, 323
Holm, Lt(jg) Stanley R., 223, 343
Holmes, 1stLt Besby F. (Frank), 74–76
Holmgrin, AM2 Rexford B., 205
Holmshaw, LCdr Harry F., 269
Honmura, WO Masataka, 338
Hovind, Lt(jg) Ralph B., 218–222, 333
Hughes, Lt(jg) Richard Z., 310–311
Hume, Cdr John, 31–32, 35, 39
Hyakutake, LtGen Harukichi, 19, 50–51, 57–58, 85, 93

Ichiki, Col Kiyano, 17–18
Imajuku, Lt Shigeichiro, 212 314–316, 318, 322, 324
Imperial General Headquarters, 50–51, 94, 145
Imperial Japanese Army, 85
  2d (Sendai) Infantry Division, 50–51, 58, 94–95, 105
  4th Infantry Regiment, 94

16th Infantry Regiment, 94
17th Army, 52, 58, 85, 88, 93–94, 145–147, 149, 157–159, 161, 185
35th Infantry Brigade, 18, 21, 23–24, 50
38th (Nagoya) Infantry Division, 94
230th Infantry Regiment, 94
29th Infantry Regiment, 94
air force, 98–99
Ichiki Force (Ichiki *Butai*), 17
Imperial Japanese Navy, 50, 112, 146
Eighth Fleet, 105, 146, 147
Sixth Fleet, 147
Eleventh Air Fleet, 51
Advance Force, 147–149, 160-163, 178, 184, 197, 330–331
Advance Force Air Group, 147–148, 179, 197,330–331
Advance Force Main Body, 330
Advance Force Support Group, 147, 330
Advanced Expeditionary Force, 147
Base Air Force, 51, 53, 57, 69, 73, 76–80, 97, 99, 102–103, 146, 166
Carrier Division 1, 25, 75
Carrier Division 2, 75–76
carrier doctrine, 124–125
Combined Fleet, 16–17, 45, 49, 53, 75, 94–95, 145–150, 156-160, 185, 379, 384
Cruiser Division 8, 213, 227–228, 230
Guadalcanal Support Force, 147–148, 161, 175, 177, 179, 185, 379
Hiyo Air Group, 76-77, 148–149, 331
Junyo Air Group, 76–77, 102, 148–149, 330–331, 336–338, 340–345, 357–358, 360, 362, 364–366
Outer South Seas Force, 147, 160
pilot selection and training, 128–131
Shokaku Air Group, 192, 196, 217–218, 237, 239, 241, 247, 249, 252, 257–265, 268, 270, 281–284, 298–307, 310–312, 332-333, 343, 353, 355–358, 370
Striking Force, 147–148, 159–161, 163, 166, 178–179, 184–185, 191, 196–197, 212
Striking Force Carrier Group, 148–149, 158, 162, 200, 330, 355–357
Striking Force Vanguard Group, 148, 158, 162-163, 169, 177, 179, 185–188, 189, 191, 193, 196–197, 213, 216, 225–226, 289, 355, 379–380
Zuiho Air Group, 192, 201, 209, 213, 215–219, 235, 298, 308, 333, 355–357
Zuikaku Air Group, 169, 191–192, 196, 200, 212, 219, 237, 239, 241–247, 249, 252, 253–258, 260–266, 270, 282–284, 298, 314–323, 332, 333, 357–358, 360, 370
Irikiin, Lt Yoshiaki, 331, 357, 360, 362, 364, 366
Ironbottom Sound, 20–21, 44, 146
Irvine, Ens Charles B., 193–196
Ishida, PO1 Masashi, 258
Ishimaru, Lt Yutaka, 265–266, 332
Iverson, 1stLt Daniel, 8

♦

Jacksonville Naval Air Station, Florida, 127
Jennings, Lt(jg) Robert H., Jr., 215
Johnson, Lt(jg) Thomas C., 214–215, 230
Johnson, Ens William E., 187–188
Jones, Lt(jg) Enos L., 212

Kakuta, RAdm Kakuji, 75, 298 330–331, 357, 380
Kane, LCdr William R., 171, 236–237, 246, 262, 300–301, 314–315, 347
Kato, Lt(jg) Shunko, 340, 344, 358, 377
Kawaguchi, MajGen Kiyotake, 18
Kelber, Pfc Victor L., 253-254, 276, 362
Kernodle, Cdr Michael H., 28–29, 37–38, 40
Kiekhoefer, Lt(jg) Kenneth C., 243–244, 257–258, 287, 337
Kieta Airfield, Bougainville, 55
Kilmer, ARM2 Floyd D., 230
Kilpatrick, Lt Macgregor, 262, 264, 286
Kinashi, Cdr Takaichi, 27
King, Adm Ernest J., 81, 90
Kinkaid, RAdm Thomas C., 154,156, 157, 163, 165–166, 168-170, 176, 178-180, 183-185, 187, 235–236, 288–289, 299, 336, 345–346, 353, 364
Kirkpatrick, Lt(jg) Donald, Jr., 224
Kirkpatrick, Lt Raleigh C., 30, 35–36, 38–39
Kirn, LCdr Louis J. (Bullet Lou), 23
Knobel, S1 Edward, 254, 275, 362
Knuepfer, LCdr George, 28, 33, 39–40
Koli Point, Guadalcanal, 105
Komatsu, VAdm Teruhisa, 147
Kona, Ens Steve G., 266, 282–283, 286–287
Kondo, VAdm Nobutake, 147–148, 161, 163, 166, 167, 175, 179, 183, 185, 196, 330, 355, 357, 380
Kraker, Lt(jg) James A., 153, 339
Kukum, Guadalcanal, 74, 101
Kurita, VAdm Takeo, 330
Kusaka, RAdm Ryunosuke, 178
Kuykendall, EM1 Thomas S., 253, 275–276, 361

Lampshire, Lt(jg) Robert T., 163, 165
Landry, Lt(jg) Dupont P. (Paul), 243, 245, 257, 283
Lanvermeier, Pfc George E., 306, 319
Larsen, Lt Harold H. (Swede), 23, 69
Leder, Ens William H. (Hank), 316–317, 322
Lee, LCdr James R. (Bucky), 187–189, 194
Lee, RAdm Willis A., 58, 66, 150, 157
Leppla, Lt(jg) John A., 201, 205–208, 230
Lindsey, Lt Robin M., 172, 321, 336, 349-352
Lineweaver, ARM3 Wilson C., 343
Liska, ARM2 John, 190, 201
Livdahl, LCdr Orlin L., 152-153, 305–306
Long, Ens Merl P. (Phil), 315
Lunga Perimeter, Guadalcanal, 7–9, 15–18, 21, 24, 50, 61–63, 64, 66, 68, 80, 85, 95, 98–99, 101, 103, 105, 147, 149, 161, 180, 185
Lunga, Guadalcanal, 25, 79
Lunga Point, Guadalcanal, 19, 44, 59–60, 67, 84, 100–101

Lunga River, Guadalcanal 95
Lunga Roads, Guadalcanal 60
Lynch, Lt John J., 199, 226–228

Machinsky, Carp Joseph, 40
Marianas Turkey Shoot, 383
Marshall Islands Raid, 193
Maruyama, LtGen Masao, 94–96, 99
Mason, Capt Charles P. (Perry), 249, 258, 269, 271, 280, 366, 368, 370–371, 373, 376–378
Matanikau River, Guadalcanal, 50, 94
October offensive, 95–96, 105
Matthew, Lt(jg) Warren B., 162-163
McAteer, Lt(jg) Gerald H., 274
McBrayer, Lt(jg) John A., Jr., 25
McCain, RAdm John S., 82
McCampbell, Lt David, 39
McCarthy, WT1 Charles P., 292–293
McConnaughhay, Lt James W., 225
McDaniel, Lt George T., 328
McGraw, Lt(jg) Bruce A., 186–188, 289
McLean, ARM3 Samuel P., 333
Mead, Ens Albert E., 205,–206, 230, 380
Meredith, SM3 Dave, 295
Miami Naval Air Station, Florida, 130
Midway Battle, 10, 49, 59, 87–88, 128, 146, 148, 165, 178, 196, 232, 248
Mikawa, VAdm Gunichi, 105, 147
Miller, Lt Frank D. (Don), 171, 173
Miller, Lt(jg) Kenneth R., 188–189
Mitchell, MajGen Ralph J., 91–92
Miura, Lt Naohiko, 337–338, 341–342, 344
Miyajima, Lt Hisayoshi, 192, 258, 281
Moore, Lt Ben, Jr., 223
Moore, Capt Edward P. (Country), 184
Moran, Cdr Henry G., 277, 279-–280, 364, 373–374
Morgan, F3 Ralph C., 308–310
Mott, LCdr Elias B., II (Benny), 306, 320–321
Muccitelli, SM2 Albert G., 291–292
Murata, LCdr Shigeharu, 192, 200–201, 209, 213, 237, 239–241, 247, 249, 252, 257–259, 267–268
Murray, RAdm George D., 9–10, 13, 22, 49, 53–54, 58, 150, 154, 179–180, 236, 248, 271–272, 345–346, 360–361, 364, 378

Nadison, AM1 Stephen, Jr., 202–203
Nagumo, VAdm Chuichi, 147–148, 166–167, 179, 185, 191, 196, 298, 330, 336, 355
Naval Aviation Reserve Act of 1939, 127
Naval Disarmament Conference of 1922, 109, 111–113
Ndeni Island, Santa Crus Islands, 85–86
Nelson, ARM1 Thomas C., Jr., 202–203, 230, 381
New Caledonia, Island 66
New Georgia Island, 51
New Georgia Sound (The Slot), 52, 58–58, 66, 71
New Guinea, 20, 50, 159, 193
New Guinea Campaign, 58
New Hebrides Islands, 6, 52, 66, 157
Nimitz, Adm Chester W., 81–85, 87–90, 149–153, 156
Noone, Lt Robert J., 272
North Africa Campaign, 20, 88, 128
Norton, Lt Marvin D. (Doc), 171–174, 199, 205, 208, 289–290, 312–313

Noumea, New Caledonia, 13, 52, 82, 83, 87, 90, 91, 150
Noyes, RAdm Leigh, 13, 26–28, 37–39, 89

O'Connor, GySgt Eugene, 254
O'Neill, GM2 James ., 340
Ogden, Y2 Francois, 291, 294–295
Okumiya, Cdr Masatake, 149, 178–179
Omori, PO1 Shigetaka, 219
Oscar, Lt(jg) Robert E., 202–203, 225
Ota, PO1 Toshio, 79

Palau Islands, 18
Papua New Guinea, 19, 84, 95
Parker, Lt Edwin B., Jr. (Iceberg), 56, 198, 216, 224, 230
Patch, MajGen Alexander M., 83, 92
Patterson, 1stLt Robert, 68
Pearl Harbor Attack, 49, 222, 237, 241
Pearl Harbor Navy Yard, 151–152, 154
Pearl Harbor, Oahu, 44, 81–82, 88, 150, 153, 192
Pensacola Naval Air Station, Florida, 126–127, 129
Peterson, LCdr Wallis F., 377-–378
Philippine Sea Battle, 383–384
Phillips, ACRM Ralph, 223
Phillips, Lt Claude R., Jr., 242–243, 245, 282, 287
Pollock, Lt Albert D., Jr. (Dave), 265, 290–291, 296, 302, 314–317, 320, 323
Pollock, S2 Ross, 290–292, 294
Poulos, Lt(jg) George F., 210–212
Powell, AMM3 Thomas A., 203–204
Powell, Lt Ward F., 199, 226–227, 229–230
Presley, AM1 Sam Davis, 306
Pugh, ARM3 Jay B., 227

♦

Rabaul, New Britain, 7, 9, 15, 17–18, 20, 51, 55, 77, 79, 101–103, 147, 159
Ramsey, Capt DeWitt W., 11–12
Rapp, Lt(jg) Jerome A., Jr., 228-229, 351–352
Reding, Ens Willis B. (Chip), 205–207, 288, 322
Reed, Ens John M., 204
Reese, EM3 Thomas W., 278, 365, 367, 371, 374
Reiserer, Lt(jg) Russell L., 350
Rekata Bay, Santa Isabel, 56, 65, 71–72, 84
Rennell Island, 58, 158
Renner, Maj Joseph N., 68
Resen, FC3 Larry, 42–43
Rhodes, Ens Raleigh E. (Dusty), 205–207, 230, 380
Richey, Lt(jg) John F., 227
Riduka, CQM Frank, 326
Roberts, LCdr David G., 290, 295
Roberts, Lt(jg) William V., Jr., 214–215, 331–332, 335
Rodee, Cdr Walter F., 54–55, 199, 226, 351
Rogers, Lt(jg) C. A., 32
Roper, Lt Joseph C., 339
Rouse, Lt(jg) Wildon M., 79
Royal Air Force, 232
Royal Navy, 112
Ruehlow, Lt Stanley E., 316–317, 322
Runyan, ChMach Elmo, 30, 36, 39
Rusk, Lt(jg) Philip J., 10, 332
Russell Islands, 18, 51
Rynd, Lt Robert W., 240, 243–246, 264, 266, 287

Samoan Islands, 19, 24, 85, 86

San Cristobal Island, 7, 9, 70, 158
Sanchez, LCdr Henry G. (Mike), 198, 200–201, 213–216, 226–227, 235, 332, 335
Sanders, ACRM Irby A., 187
Santa Cruz Battle assessed, 383–384
Santa Cruz Islands, 25, 156, 159, 164, 183, 379
Sato, WO Shigeyuki, 262–263, 279, 297, 361
Savo Island Naval Battle, 7, 24, 59, 83, 150
Scott, RAdm Norman, 44, 58–59, 66
Seki, LCdr Mamoru, 196, 299–301, 305–306, 311
Semmes, Lt Benedict J., Jr., 37–38
Sesso, 1stLt Mario, 162–163, 165
Shea, LCdr John, 37
Sherman, Capt Forrest P., 26, 28–29, 31, 37–40
Shiga, Lt Yoshio, 331, 336–338, 342–343, 358, 377
Shigemi, WO Katsuma, 314, 322
Shimada, Lt(jg) Yozo, 253-255
Shingo, Lt Hideki, 196, 301, 311–312
Shinneman, ARM3 Charles E., 204
Shirane, Lt Ayao, 192, 242, 283, 333, 357
Shortland Islands, 8-9, 18, 52-53, 84, 147, 150
Shortland Islands Raid, 57
Simpler, LCdr Leroy C., 23, 71, 73–74, 79
Sims, LCdr Gelzer L., 316
Skinner, WT1 Lyle M., 255–256, 276, 363, 367–369, 374
Slot, The. *See* New Georgia Sound
Solomon Islands, 19, 50–51, 157
Solomon Islands Campaign, 52, 149
Sorenson, Lt(jg) Robert E., 215, 332
South Pacific Area (SoPac), 7, 15, 44, 53, 87, 90–91, 98, 149, 155, 157, 231–232, 288
  Aircraft South Pacific (AirSoPac), 58, 66, 83,158–159,161-163, 184, 210–211. *See also* Task Force 64
  Intelligence Section, 380
  South Pacific Force, 7, 15, 150
Souza, Ens Philip E., 214–215, 331–332, 335–336
Stebbins, Lt Edgar E., 332, 343–344
Stokely, ARM2 George D., 221, 230
Stormes, LCdr Max C., 313
Stout, 1stLt Robert F. (Tex), 99–101
Strong, Lt Stockton B. (Birney), 192–196
Sumiyoshi, MajGen Tadamasu, 95–96
Sutherland, Lt John F. (Jock), 228, 341
Sutherland, MajGen Richard K., 82
Suzuki, Lt(jg) Takeo, 259, 332
Swope, Lt(jg) Ivan L., 10–11, 54–55, 72, 263, 275, 361
Sword, ChElec David R., 363

Taivu Point, Guadalcanal, 9, 13, 18, 21
Taka, PO1 Asataro, 254
Takahashi, Lt Sadamu, 192, 237, 241, 244, 261, 357
Takata, Capt Toshitane, 178
Tallman, Lt(jg) Humphrey L., 229, 333, 351
Tanaka, Lt(jg) Ichiro, 357, 360, 369–370
Tanaka, RAdm Raizo, 8–9, 17–18, 52–53, 57, 84
Tannatt, RM3 R. C., 291–293
Tappan, Lt Ben, 263
Tassafaronga, Guadalcanal, 6--67, 77
Tatum, LCdr Laurice, 39
Taylor, Lt(jg) R. D., 31–32

Theobold, LCdr Robert A., 324–325, 327
Thomas, LCdr James A., 169–171
Thompson, Lt Macdonald (Tommy), 204, 208, 224
Tokyo Express, 44–45, 82
Tokyo Raid, 149–150, 248
Tongatabu Island, 12, 44, 151
Tonolei Harbor, Shortland Islands, 55–56, 159
Truk Atoll, 146, 9, 17–18, 52–53, 57, 71, 75, 84 ,146–147, 157, 355, 357, 380
Tsuda, Lt Toshio, 244, 252–253
Tsukahara, VAdm Nishizo, 57
Tulagi Harbor, 74, 100
Tulagi Island, 85, 99
Turner, RAdm Richmond Kelly, 24–25, 44, 50, 58, 86, 89, 91–92

United States Army, 20, 85
  25th Infantry Division, 89
  164th Infantry Regiment, 58, 60, 86–87, 96, 105
  Americal Infantry Division, 58, 83, 92
United States Army Air Forces, 82
  Fifth Air Force, 159
  11th Heavy Bombardment Group, 18, 63–64, 69, 77, 83, 104, 162, 169
  67th Fighter Squadron, 15, 60, 64, 103
United States Joint Chiefs of Staff, 85
United States Marine Corps, 20
  1st Marine Aircraft Wing, 68
  1st Marine Division, 14, 21, 50, 60, 62, 88, 93–95
  1st Parachute Battalion, 21
  1st Raider Battalion, 21
  2d Marine Division, 58, 92
  3d Defense Battalion, 101
  7th Marine Regiment, 85
  Marine Fighter Squadron 121 (VMF-121), 61, 65, 73, 76–78, 99, 101–102
  Marine Fighter Squadron 212 (VMF-212), 18, 69, 72, 74, 78–79, 100-102
  Marine Fighter Squadron 223 (VMF-223), 15
  Marine Fighter Squadron 224 (VMF-224), 9, 64
  Marine Observation Squadron 251 (VMO-251), 18, 79
  Marine Scout-Bomber Squadron 141 (VMSB-141), 62, 68, 98
  Marine Scout-Bomber Squadron 231 (VMSB-231), 9
  Marine Scout Bomber Squadron 232 (VMSB-232), 8, 15
United States Naval Academy, 126
United States Navy, 7, 20, 112,146
  advanced carrier training groups, 130
  Air Group 10, 88, 124, 218, 163–164, 166, 168–170, 174, 176, 180, 184–185, 193, 198, 200–202, 209, 224, 230, 285-286, 312, 321, 342, 346–347, 349, 351–353
  Bombing Squadron 6 (Bombing-6, VB-6), 65, 104
  Bombing Squadron 10 (Bombing-10, VB-10), 164, 168–169, 185, 186, 198, 227, 285, 289
  Bombing Squadron 8 (Bombing-8, VB-8), 53, 164, 198–199, 213, 216, 218–219, 221, 222–223, 226, 333, 343, 350

Bureau of Ships, 152
Carrier Air Group 10, *see* Air Group 10
Carrier defense doctrine, 231–235
carrier operations doctrine, 122–125
Carrier Reserve Air Group 9, 128
Carrier Reserve Air Group 10, 128, 130
Destroyer Division 5, 290
Destroyer Squadron 2, 274
Enterprise Air Group, 8, 23, 44, 52, 151, 153–154, 193, 227
Enterprise Flight 300, 8, 15, 23, 307
Fast Carrier Task Force, 383
Fighter Direction School, 232
Fighting Squadron 5 (Fighting-5, VF-5), 12, 23, 65, 69, 71, 73, 79
Fighting Squadron 6 (Fighting-6, VF-6), 23
Fighting Squadron 10 (Fighting-10, VF-10), 164, 166, 168, 171–172, 185–186, 198, 201, 205–208, 225, 230, 235–238, 241, 246, 261, 264–266, 281–283, 286, 288–289, 300, 302–303, 314–316, 318, 322, 342–343, 347–348, 351, 380
Fighting Squadron 71 (Fighting-71, VF-71), 25–26, 43, 72, 78–79, 101
Fighting Squadron 72 (Fighting-72, VF-72), 53, 56–57, 164, 166, 177, 186, 198–199, 213–217, 226–227, 229, 235, 237–238, 239–241, 244, 251, 258, 261, 263–265, 281-283, 287, 300, 310, 314, 316, 318, 322, 331–332, 335, 337–338, 341-342, 347, 351
Hornet Air Group, 22, 25, 45, 49, 53–55, 57, 71–72, 75 163–164, 166, 176, 179–180, 184–185, 199–201, 212–213, 215, 217, 225–226, 230, 254, 288, 332–333, 346–347, 349–351, 353, 365
Intelligence Division, 87
Naval Aviation Pilots (NAPs), 126, 128
Pacific Fleet, 59, 81, 149, 384
Pacific Fleet Intelligence Section, 88, 156–157
Patrol Squadron 11 (Patrol-11, VP-11), 177, 210
Patrol Squadron 24 (Patrol 24, VP-24), 163, 212, 312, 343, 349
Patrol Squadron 51 (Patrol-51, VP-51), 158, 177, 380
Patrol Squadron 91 (Patrol-91, VP-91), 158, 162, 178, 380
Saratoga Air Group, 12, 23, 44, 52
pilot selection and training, 126–128, 130-131
Scouting Squadron 3 (Scouting 3, VS-3), 12, 23
Scouting Squadron 5 (Scouting 5, VS-5), 193, 227
Scouting Squadron 8 (Scouting 8, VS-8), 54–55, 71–72, 164, 198, 213, 216, 218, 220–224, 263, 332–333, 343
Scouting Squadron 10 (Scouting 10, VS-10), 164, 168–169, 185, 187–189, 193, 198, 227, 282, 286, 343
Scouting Squadron 71(Scouting-71, VS-71), 26, 43, 52, 103
Scouting Squadron 72 (Scouting 72, VS-72), 6, 26, 43
Task Force 11, 3, 4
Task Force 16, 3, 6, 91, 150, 154,

157, 159, 236–237, 246, 258, 282–283, 285, 295, 299-300, 302, 305, 315–316, 318, 321–322, 324, 330, 332–333, 335–336, 343–346, 349, 353, 356, 365
Task Force 17, 9, 13, 41–42, 49, 54, 56–57, 150, 154, 159, 191, 235–237, 241, 245–246, 249, 251, 257, 264–265, 270, 281, 284, 288, 297–299, 314, 333, 336, 339, 345, 350, 360, 365, 378–379
Task Force 18, 3, 10, 13, 25
Task Force 61, 10, 12–13, 15, 22–24, 26–27, 49, 89–90 154–159, 163–166, 172, 176, 178, 180, 183–184, 186, 191, 200–201, 209, 231, 235, 237–239, 281, 283, 285, 289, 296, 301, 315, 331, 334, 341, 378, 380
Task Force 63, 161
Task Force 64, 150, 156–158, 165, 167. *See also* Aircraft South Pacific
Torpedo Squadron 6, (Torpedo-6, VT-6), 22, 55-56, 164, 198–199, 213, 215–217, 224–230, 332–333, 343, 351–352
Torpedo Squadron 7 (Torpedo-7, VT-7), 26
Torpedo Squadron 8, (Torpedo-8, VT-8), 12, 23, 63, 69
Torpedo Squadron 10 (Torpedo-10, VT-10), 164, 168, 171, 173, 198–199, 202–205, 208, 228–229, 289, 352, 380
United States Fleet, 83, 89, 110–111
War Plans Division, 89
Wasp Air Group, 3–5, 9, 25–26, 43, 52, 57
USS *Anderson*, 259, 375, 379
USS *Argonne*, 82, 91–92
USS *Ballard*, 162--163
USS *Barton*, 261
USS *California*, 235
USS *Colhoun*, 9
USS *Conyngham*, 312
USS *Curtiss*, 178, 211–212
USS *Cushing*, 311, 352
USS *Enterprise*, 3–4, 7, 10, 13, 15, 83, 88, 91, 110, 128, 150–153, 155–156, 159, 164–165, 168, 170–174, 180, 184–187, 192, 198–199, 210, 234–238, 246, 248, 261, 285–290, 299–300, 304–310, 312, 314, 318–321, 324, 333–338, 341, 344–347, 349–350, 352–353, 356, 358–359, 364
USS *Essex*, 111
USS *Farragut*, 10
USS *Gamble*, 6
USS *Grayson*, 3--5
USS *Gregory*, 21
USS *Hornet*, 9–11, 21–26, 41–44, 52–54, 56–58, 73–74, 91, 111, 159, 164, 176, 179, 186, 199–201, 234–235, 237, 239–241, 245–246, 248–253, 255–257, 259–280, 283–289, 297–299, 308, 314–315, 331–335, 345–346, 354, 359–380
USS *Juneau*, 251, 261, 265, 335, 347, 354, 365
USS *Langley*, 109–112
USS *Lansdowne*, 40–41
USS *Lexington*, 11, 110, 112, 114, 248, 274
USS *Little*, 21
USS *Long Island*, 111
USS *MacDonough*, 10–12, 44

USS *MacFarland*, 73–74
USS *Mahan*, 348
USS *Maury*, 305, 316, 318–319, 353
USS *Meredith*, 70, 75
USS *Minneapolis*, 12
USS *Monssen*, 5–6, 44
USS *Morris*, 261, 265, 273, 298, 373
USS *Mustin*, 42, 273–274, 361, 369, 372, 376–379
USS *North Carolina*, 10, 25, 42–44
USS *Northampton*, 54–55, 235–236, 239, 259–260, 270, 280, 286, 288, 297–299, 314, 336, 346, 354, 359–361, 366
USS *O'Brien*, 42, 44
USS *Patterson*, 5
USS *Pensacola*, 254, 260, 346, 364–365, 370, 378
USS *Phelps*, 12
USS *Porter*, 290, 292–296, 300, 313, 347, 352
USS *Portland*, 304, 321, 336
USS *Preston*, 313, 346, 351
USS *Ranger*, 110, 114
USS *Russell*, 258–260, 273–274, 297, 362, 365–366, 370, 373
USS *Sabine*, 155
USS *San Diego*, 251, 261
USS *San Juan*, 304–305, 340–341
USS *Saratoga*, 3, 7, 10–12, 22, 83, 110, 112, 151, 248, 384
USS *Seminole*, 100–101
USS *Shaw*, 294–295
USS *Smith*, 312, 320, 323–329, 338
USS *South Dakota*, 88, 258, 282, 288, 295, 299–301, 304–305, 311–312, 316, 319, 321, 326, 334–337, 340–342
USS *Trever*, 99–100
USS *Vireo*, 70
USS *Washington*, 24–25, 44, 58, 66, 150, 158
USS *Wasp*, 3–4, 7, 13, 21, 23–44, 49, 83, 111, 152, 378
USS *Yorktown*, 110, 113, 114, 248
USS *Zane*, 99–100

Vandegrift, MajGen Alexander A. (Archer), 62, 64, 83, 85–86, 91–94
Vanikoro Island, Santa Cruz Islands, 162
Vejtasa, Lt Stanley W. (Swede), 172, 241, 261, 315–318, 320, 322, 350
Vose, Lt James E. (Moe), 218–219, 221–222
Ward, Lt(jg) Leslie J., 189–191, 194, 286
Washimi, Lt Goro, 241, 252, 264, 270, 283
Welch, Lt Vivian W., 186–188, 193–194, 289
Welles, Lt(jg) George D., 352–353, 355–356
Wells, Lt Harold A., 293
Wells, Lt(jg) T. D., 28–30
White, Lt(jg) Kenneth B., 220
Wickendoll, Ens Maurice N., 236, 262, 281, 302–303
Widhelm, LCdr William J. (Gus), 54, 198, 55, 71, 200–201, 213, 216–226, 230, 381
Williams, Lt Dwight M. B. (Brad), 335–337
Williams, ARM3 Elgie, 195
Wood, Lt(jg) Albert H., 332
Wood, Lt(jg) H. William, 291, 293, 295
Wood, LCdr Hunter, Jr., 324, 326
Woods, Lt(jg) Thomas J., 343
Woodson, ARM2 Richard T., 224

Workman, LCdr J. T., 31
Wrenn, Ens George L., 243, 264–265, 282, 318, 338
Wright, RAdm Carleton H., 4
Wyllie, Lt(jg) Raymond G., 202, 225

Yamada, RAdm Sadiyoshi, 103
Yamada, Lt Shohei, 301–303, 310–311
Yamaguchi, Lt Masao, 330, 337, 339–340, 342–344
Yamamoto, Adm Isoroku, 16–17, 51, 94, 102, 145–148, 157–158, 175, 357; Capt, 129
Yamaoka, Capt Mineo, 179
Yoneda, Lt(jg) Nobuo, 261
Yusuhara, Lt Masayuki, 316–318, 320, 358

Zook,Ens Dott E. (Earl), 22; Lt(jg), 276–277, 280, 371, 375–376